THE FALTERING ECONOMY

John Bellamy Foster and Henryk Szlajfer, eds.

THE FALTERING ECONOMY
THE PROBLEM OF ACCUMULATION
UNDER MONOPOLY CAPITALISM

Monthly Review Press
New York

Library of Congress Cataloging in Publication Data
Main entry under title:
The Faltering economy.

Includes bibliographical references and index.
1. Capitalism—Addresses, essays, lectures.   2. Marxian
economics—Addresses, essays, lectures.   3. Keynesian
economics—Addresses, essays, lectures.   I. Foster, John
Bellamy.   II. Szlajfer, Henryk.
HB501.F26   1984   330.12′2   84-10804
ISBN 0-85345-603-8
ISBN 0-85345-604-6 (pbk.)

Monthly Review Press
155 West 23rd Street
New York, N.Y. 10011

Manufactured in the United States of America

10 9 8 7 6 5 4 3 2 1

CONTENTS

Editors' Introduction   7

PART I
Monopoly Theory and Marxian Economics   23

Paul M. Sweezy: *Monopoly Capital and the Theory of Value*   25
Paul M. Sweezy: *Competition and Monopoly*   27
Paul M. Sweezy: *Some Problems in the Theory of Capital Accumulation*   41
John Bellamy Foster: *Investment and Capitalist Maturity*   57

PART II
Income Distribution and Inflation   75

Michal Kalecki: *Class Struggle and the Distribution of National Income*   77
Maurice Dobb: *A Note on Distribution and the Price Mark-Up*   85
Howard Sherman: *Inflation, Unemployment, and the Contemporary Business Cycle*   91
Harry Magdoff: *A Note on Inflation*   118

PART III
Excess Capacity, Effective Demand, and Accumulation   125

Michal Kalecki: *The Mechanism of the Business Upswing*   127
Paolo Sylos-Labini: *The Problem of Effective Demand*   134
Michal Kalecki: *The Problem of Effective Demand with Tugan-Baranovski and Rosa Luxemburg*   151
Michal Kalecki: *The Marxian Equations of Reproduction and Modern Economics*   159
Josef Steindl: *On Maturity in Capitalist Economies*   167
Josef Steindl: *Stagnation Theory and Stagnation Policy*   179
John Bellamy Foster: *The Limits of U.S. Capitalism: Surplus Capacity and Capacity Surplus*   198

PART IV
Monopoly Profits and Economic Surplus   215

Jacob Morris: *Profit Rates and Capital Formation in American Monopoly Capitalism*   217

Paul M. Sweezy: *Marxian Value Theory and Crises*   236

Ron Stanfield: *A Revision of the Economic Surplus Concept*   251

Henryk Szlajfer: *Economic Surplus and Surplus Value Under Monopoly Capitalism*   262

PART V
Productive and Nonproductive Labor   295

Henryk Szlajfer: *Waste, Marxian Theory, and Monopoly Capital: Toward a New Synthesis*   297

PART VI
The State and Crisis   323

John Bellamy Foster: *Marxian Economics and the State*   325

EDITORS' INTRODUCTION

Is there a single pattern intrinsic to modern capital accumulation, which encompasses the Great Depression of the 1930s, the present-day imperiled economy, and the evolutionary path leading from one to the other? The answer, we think, is yes, and the essays in this collection have been brought together for the purpose of explaining why.

The last scientific revolution in economic thought occurred during the Great Depression itself, and is most frequently associated with the later work of John Maynard Keynes—by far the most influential and universally respected economist of the past half-century. Keynes' magnum opus, *The General Theory of Employment, Interest and Money,* published in 1936, was a devastating attack on the neoclassical economic illusion, known as "Say's Law" after the early nineteenth-century French political economist, that production, if forthcoming, creates its own demand. Keynes recognized that institutional factors, determining distribution, made it unlikely that effective demand, outside of government intervention in one form or another, would be sufficient to satisfy the enormous modern capacity to produce. He further contended that if an over-abundance of productive capacity in relation to final demand developed, this would bring down "the marginal efficiency of capital" (expected profits on new investment), investment would falter, and stagnation would result.

This prognosis reinforced the idea, of deep concern to the early radical Keynesians in the wake of the Great Depression, that the modern economy was weighed down, in the long run, by a powerful tendency toward stagnation. Few put the matter as succinctly as Keynes hmself, who wrote of "the gigantic powers of production" in an advanced capitalist economy. "Coupled with institutional factors which tend to encourage accumulation and retard the growth of consumption when incomes increase, this means that an unprecedented output has to be reached before a state of full employment can be approached."[1] And since Keynes also implied that the modern economy was gradually nearing a state of full maturity, in which the relative space for extensive growth would be increasingly circumscribed, the specter of stagnation became all the more haunting. The whole problem was to be commonly and euphemistically referred to as "the long-run Keynesian dilemma."

7

Alvin Hansen, the economist often credited with having brought Keynes to America, took the matter a bit further. Elaborating on Keynes' numerous hints with regard to industrial maturity, Hansen developed a notion of secular stagnation, or a trend of slow growth coupled with rising unemployment and idle productive capacity, as the gravitational tendency of advanced industrial economies. The short-run Keynesian theory had suggested that the possibilities for induced investment, or investment generated by the growth of income, were limited by the centralizing force of accumulation on income distribution. Productive capacity, reinforced by ever greater technological know-how, tended to grow at a pace which exceeded demand for consumption goods, while investment itself was self-limiting, deterred by plant and equipment produced in earlier rounds of capital formation. The emergence of monopolistic capital, it was sometimes contended, only served to make matters worse, since big business was inclined to introduce only those innovations which did not threaten existing capital values.

Hansen therefore argued, along lines partly mapped out by his then Harvard colleague Joseph Schumpeter, that long-term growth depended on the introduction of large "autonomous" innovations, detached somewhat from the normal flow of income and expenditures, which could launch investment into a self-reinforcing, and therefore cumulative, wave of expansion. But Hansen also believed that innovations of the kind and quality needed, in terms of their overall economic impact, were much harder to come by at present than they had been in the past. The closing of the frontier, the downturn in the rate of population growth, the gradual consolidation of a vast integrated national transportation network, and similar developments had cut into the possibilities for extensive growth, while intensive growth did not demand investment of adequate scope to compensate for the dynamic structural deficiency of consumption—sufficient, that is, to propel the economy forward into a new period of rapid growth.

Hansen's interpretation of stagnation in well-developed capitalist economies touched off a wide-ranging debate among economists in the United States, his main opponent being none other than Joseph Schumpeter himself. Labeling Hansen's views "the theory of vanishing investment opportunities," Schumpeter contended that massive outlets for extensive absorption of capital could still be found in the chemical, electrical, automobile, and aircraft industries.[2] If stagnation nonetheless seemed to persist, and Schumpeter argued that this was necessarily the case, it could be traced to the fact that new social, political, and intellectual currents, made inevitable by the course of previous capitalist development, interfered with the normal working-out of "the process of creative destruction," while the large corporations themselves lacked, as a consequence of rational corporate policy, some of the inner entrepreneurial dynamism that had brought them into being in the first place. Though Hansen's conclusions emphasized the need for greater government intervention to save capitalism, Schumpeter, from a more conservative standpoint, suggested that capitalism would not survive—if only because greater government intervention was the observable secular trend.

The debate over stagnation had taken place after the deep recession of 1937 ended all hopes that the U. S. economy would easily get back on the road to recovery. Unemployment, which had fallen off a bit, rose again to 19 percent in 1938. But the entire situation was soon radically transformed. The prolonged economic disaster, and with it the entire stagnation controversy, ended virtually overnight, swept away by the outbreak of World War II. With the stimulus of gigantic military contracts, U. S. capitalism literally took off, and during the next six years Gross National Product went up by more than two-thirds. For the moment, stagnation was a moot point, and economists turned their attention to the problem of inflation, caused, in this case, by an excess of aggregate demand.[3]

When some of the younger Keynesians, such as Alan Sweezy, Evsey Domar, Benjamin Higgins, Robert Gordon, Kenneth Kurihara, and Anatol Murad, resumed the lines of debate in the first decade of the cold war, the question no longer seemed to have the same historical force. A new capitalist order had emerged out of the ashes of the old. U. S. economic hegemony, the rebuilding of war-torn economies in Western Europe and Asia, a vast new wave of automobilization, unsatisfied consumer demand which had been deferred during the war, war-spurred technologies like the jet aircraft, a vast pumping up of the debt-credit structure, and the cold war itself, helped to guarantee a long period of more or less steady, if not overly dramatic, growth.[4]

To be sure, the new Keynesian growth theory developed by Roy Harrod in Great Britain and Evsey Domar in the United States stressed the underlying problem of stagnation.[5] But very few economists took this part of their analysis seriously in the climate of the times. It became the practice to assume that demand would somehow absorb all the savings produced in the system, guaranteeing an equilibrium which moved merrily along at the warranted or full-employment rate of growth. These were the halcyon days of Paul Samuelson's "neoclassical-Keynesian synthesis" in which Say's Law, or the pre-Keynesian notion of a tendency toward full employment equilibrium, was gradually resurrected, under the thin cover of what were presumed to be the infallible mechanics of "Keynesian" fiscal and monetary policy.

But it would be wrong to imply that the entire issue of stagnation was simply short-circuited by history and fobbed off by theoretical antics. The sad truth is that pure Keynesian economics was ill-equipped to answer the most important questions that it raised. Although recognizing the demand side limitations on economic growth, Keynes had struggled to put his vision across while breaking as little as possible with the neoclassical tradition.[6] The resulting concoction, though brilliant enough in its own way, was a profoundly contradictory doctrine. Put simply, Keynes retained two blind spots basic to the economics of modern liberal theory. He essentially ignored the main concern of the classical economists, from Adam Smith to Karl Marx, namely *the class composition of social output,* and the theory of accumulation which followed fast upon it. And the Keynesian product became further separated from reality through the unexamined assumption that free competition reigned supreme in both production and exchange. Mainstream economics, of course, still carries on in much the same vein, reaffirming with every new textbook its unworldly and apologetic character.

Keynesian theory was originally formulated in terms of broad-based aggregates on the demand side: consumption, investment, and government. It is not concerned with the way in which output is utilized, nor is it particularly concerned (except in the most general way) with the fact that output has to follow very definite channels determined by the class structure of income and demand. One type of spending is considered as good as another.[7] In contrast, business itself is neither so naive nor indifferent. Military spending, financed by huge government deficits, is regarded as the most acceptable way in which government can prop up the demand side of the economy. The economics profession first asserted (as a matter of faith and public relations) that there were other ways to prosperity and social well-being, and then proceeded to fall head over heels in an effort to comply with what business required.

To the extent that Keynesian economics did recognize that there was a problem associated with the class composition of output and demand, it suggested a redistribution of income and wealth from the rich to the poor. But only a very small minority of utopian reformists thought this possible (or desirable), on a sufficiently large scale, without a major social upheaval. Would-be radicals who remained Keynesian purists were thus caught in a fool's mate.

More damaging to the internal logic of the pure Keynesian argument was the implicit supposition that the individual giant firm did not really matter at the macroeconomic level. The classical theorists of competitive accumulation had largely neglected to develop a theory of the *level* (as opposed to the *class composition*) of output, since it was assumed, with some degree of plausibility, that competition would force firms to accumulate (utilize for the expansion of capital goods and wage goods) the vast portion of the economic surplus in their possession. If Say's Law was frequently broken, as Malthus and Marx alone among the great classical economists suggested, it was through a glut of commodities.[8] In the midst of the Great Depression, however, Keynes challenged the assumption of automatic accumulation, arguing that firms would not necessarily invest (or reinvest) the surplus generated by the previous round of growth, but might utilize the fund of investment-seeking savings in various spurious and unproductive ways. The implication was that the individual firm was not compelled to invest *by the force of competition alone,* and might actually blockade accumulation. Undoubtedly, this should have helped reinforce the view, already widespread at the time, that the nature of capitalist competition in the areas of price, output, and investment had been radically transformed with the rise of big business. But the tacit assumption of free competition remained an integral part of the pure Keynesian system (without which the analysis of the rate of interest and other factors would have fallen into disarray).

Fortunately, another more formidable theoretical tradition passed through "the Keynesian revolution" slightly ahead of Keynes himself, producing a higher synthesis which had none of the deficiencies of pure Keynesianism. The new synthesis, often known as "neo-Marxian" theory (but overlapping with post-Keynesianism of the Cambridge University type), developed straight out of the main body of Marxian (and, to a lesser extent, Ricardian) thought, taking account of changing historical conditions, but otherwise demonstrating a century of continuity in fundamental outlook.

The cutting edge of the new synthesis was the work of Michal Kalecki, Poland's greatest economist. To quote Joan Robinson, one of Keynes' younger colleagues, Kalecki had a "claim of priority of publication" over Keynes, with regard to the general theory of employment, which was "indisputable." In her usual point-blank style, Robinson goes on to state that "Kalecki had one great advantage over Keynes—he had never learned orthodox economics. . . . The only economics he had studied was Marx."[9] Building on both the Marxian reproduction schemes and the theory of monopoly capitalism, Kalecki pushed Marxian economics far beyond Keynes' mature theory, and succeeded in doing so unbeknownst to Keynes (in essays published in Poland) before *The General Theory* itself came off the press.[10]

It is not to be supposed that Kalecki developed his theory directly out of a dialogue with Marx's *Capital.* The context in which his vision grew is best conveyed if we recognize that he was very much influenced by the debate over the Marxian reproduction schemes that played a prominent part in socialist economic thought in the early twentieth century. Marx had divided all production into two departments, one producing capital goods (department 1) and one consumption goods (department 2). The entire demand for the first set of goods, at the aggregate level for a closed economy, came out of depreciation funds and capitalist profits. Consumption, which could be further divided into workers' consumption of wage goods and capitalist consumption of luxury goods, came out of both wages and profits, respectively. Following what he called the "eminent" example of Rosa Luxemburg, a leading early Marxist theorist and author of *The Accumulation of Capital* (written in 1913), Kalecki used the Marxian reproduction schemes to develop a theory of deficiency in effective demand, rooted in the underconsumption of the masses and the overaccumulation of capital.[11]

Although Luxemburg's early explanation of "the realization problem"—or the difficulty in converting commodity capital back into money capital (with a profit)—had contained some serious fallacies, Kalecki demonstrated that her instincts had been correct. Moreover, use of the Marxian reproduction schemes to develop a theory of effective demand and prospective output had an immediate consequence which carried the Kaleckian reasoning beyond the much vaguer Keynesian tradition. The entire reproduction framework for the former was based on an understanding of the interrelationship between the class composition of output and the corresponding class structure of final demand. Taken together, these two elements determined the level of capitalist output, with a given social technology. Rather than operating simply on the basis of undifferentiated aggregates, the theory immediately suggested the input-output matrix formed by the dialectical opposition of labor and capital.[12]

Given Kalecki's socialist background, we have every reason to believe that his famous concept of "the degree of monopoly," or the mark-up of gross profit margins over unit prime costs (cost-price), which is the other main component in his theory of accumulation, had its ultimate roots in the Marxian theory of concentration and centralization of capital. Here we must digress at some length to consider the question of monopoly capitalism, the underlying historical theme of this book.

A vast change took place in the history of capitalism during the final decades of the nineteenth century and the first decade and a half of the twentieth (the same period, significantly, in which neoclassical economists were refining their fundamental assumption of "perfect competition"). Up until this time industry had been composed of numerous small family enterprises. But with the hand over fist expansion of the giant multi-divisional corporation near the turn of the century the whole world economy underwent a massive transfiguration. Powerful business concerns were now capable of evading, to a considerable extent, the competitive discipline of the market, while serving as never before their own acquisitive ends. Stated simply, capitalism had evolved from its freely competitive to its monopoly stage.

By 1900 or thereabouts, the process of trust-building had reached such proportions that virtually everyone (with the notable exception of most certified economists, devoted as always to their finely chiseled mid-Victorian models) recognized that a revolutionary transformation, in the ways and means of doing business, was well underway. It has been estimated that "between a quarter and a third" of *all* U. S. capital stock in manufacturing underwent consolidation in mergers taking place between 1898 and 1902 alone. The mammoth merger of the period, the formation of U. S. Steel in 1901 under the financial guidance of the investment banking house of Morgan, fused 165 separate companies, to create a monopolistic corporation controlling about 60 percent of the total steel industry.[13] This was the first great wave of trustification, which had its ultimate basis in the overwhelming capacity of the very large industrial firm to outcompete small businesses in the same market (or production) sector—so much so that the nature of competition itself was rapidly transformed on a world scale, not only in the United States and Canada, but in Europe and Japan as well.

Quite naturally, the rise of big business was followed by an enormous outpouring of descriptive and popular protest literature. The first real theorist of the new era of monopoly capitalism was to be found in the character of Thorstein Veblen. Veblen was a rebel economist (and sociologist) of the left, deeply influenced by the work of Marx, but not himself a Marxist. In three iconoclastic works on North American capitalism, *The Theory of Business Enterprise* (1904), *The Vested Interests and the Common Man* (1920), and *Absentee Ownership and Business Enterprise in Recent Times: The Case of*

America (1923), Veblen developed many of the essential components and characteristic themes of the theory of monopoly capitalism: the decline of price competition; the tendency for monopolistic profit margins to widen at the expense of less powerful firms and workers; the systematic promotion of excess capacity and unemployment; problems of effective demand (underconsumption and underinvestment); and a secular trend toward stagnation in which business upturns could be traced to particularly fortuitous external events.

Aside from the anomaly of Veblen, the most important early theorists of monopoly capitalism all arose directly out of the Marxian tradition. This was to be expected. Marx alone among the classical economists perceived that accumulation was synonymous with a twofold process of concentration and centralization of capital. According to his own formulation, concentration of capital was the absolute growth of individual capitals as a normal accompaniment of the extension of social wealth as a whole. This was, in a sense, accumulation proper. A much more powerful process, however, was to be found in centralization, or the rapid relative growth of particular firms (and the absorption or liquidation of a much larger number of others). Numerous capitals were brought together into new combinations under unified ownership and control. This fusion of capitals was said to come about, in part, through economies of scale in the competition over costs, whereby "larger capitals beat the smaller." Moreover, the whole credit structure of capitalist society (in which Marx included so-called primary securities or share capital) speeded up the entire process of centralization. The system of credit begins "as the humble assistant of accumulation . . . but soon it becomes a new and terrible weapon in the battle of competition and is finally transformed into an enormous social mechanism for the centralization of capital." The importance of both centralization and the use of credit was summed up by Marx in one trenchant observation: "The world would still be without railways if it had had to wait until accumulation had got a few individual capitals far enough to be adequate for the construction of a railway. Centralization, however, accomplished this in a twinkling of an eye, by means of joint stock companies" (*Capital*, vol. 1, ch. 25, section 2).

Thus, Marx and Engels saw the growth of new and larger joint stock companies as a natural consequence of the annexation of smaller capitals by larger ones. And it is clear that their initial inclination was to see the new form of industry mainly as a harbinger of socialism to come. However, during the last few months before his death in 1895, Engels was working on a two-part supplement to Marx's *Capital*, examining controversial issues in Marxian value theory and the ongoing historical transformation of industrial finance. The first part was essentially completed but the second, which concerns us here, remained only in outline form. This outline, entitled "The Stock Exchange," starts with observations on the rise of the industrial securities market, ties this to the fact that "in no industrial country, least of all England, could the expansion of production keep up with accumulation, or the accumulation of the individual capitalist be completely utilized in the enlargement of his business," and sees this as the basis for the *founding* of giant capital and the acceleration of an outward movement toward world colonization.[14]

With the idea of concentration and centralization of capital at their disposal, and under the pressure of historical events, it is not surprising that Marxist theorists soon arrived at a theory of monopoly capitalism. The first Marxist to do so in a systematic way was Rudolf Hilferding in his *Finance Capital: A Study of the Latest Phase of Capitalist Development,* published in 1910; soon to be followed by Nikolai Bukharin's *Imperialism and World Economy,* written in 1915; and Lenin's *Imperialism, the Highest Stage of Capitalism,* written in 1916.[15] Hilferding described many of the institutional features of the new era of monopoly capitalism and imperialism, and Bukharin and Lenin extended this analysis to a fuller consideration of accumulation and conflict on a world scale. However, none of these early Marxist theorists tackled, in anything like a systematic manner, *the changes wrought on capitalism's law of motion within its advanced industrial core.*[16] To the extent that Hilferding wrote about crisis theory, he tended to lean in the direction of the early Russian Marxist Tugan-Baranovski, who believed that a smooth and crisis-free capitalism was possible in the age of trustification and the state. On the other hand, Lenin, who was in many ways the most sophisticated opponent of Tugan-Baranovski and Hilferding on this score, soon had other things on his mind. The theory of the monopoly stage of capitalism thus remained incomplete with regard to the most important problem of all: its laws of motion.

It was here that Michal Kalecki made important breakthroughs. Kalecki, it will be recalled, based his theory on Marx's reproduction schemes which specified the class composition of social output. To this Kalecki added a theory of the degree of monopoly, according to which profit margins were largely determined by a mark-up on cost price (or prime production costs) imposed by giant firms. Under these circumstances, the level of output itself became a function of the need of big business to carefully regulate both actual output and the growth of potential output (new productive capacity created by new investment) so as to maintain, wherever possible, monopolistic profit margins. Capital formation would proceed up to the point in which large amounts of plant and equipment were lying idle because of *implicit overproduction* of commodities, and this would in turn shut off, for the time being, further investment in productive capacity. With a downturn in the cycle, capital equipment (in both value and capacity terms) would be destroyed, and a new burst of investment would become possible.

This description of the capital adjustment mechanism, first worked out by Kalecki in the early years of the Great Depression before the publication of Keynes' *General Theory*, was a notable contribution to modern business cycle theory.[17] In Kalecki's hands, however, it was also the basis for a powerful critique of capitalism itself. The class composition of social output meant that prosperity for capital depended almost entirely on its own discretionary expenditures: formation of capital stock and consumption out of economic surplus. In a modern monopolistic economy, however, new investment was impeded by investment that had occurred in the past. "The tragedy of investment," wrote Kalecki, "is that it causes crisis because it is useful."[18] Growth therefore became increasingly dependent on the wasteful consumption of previously accumulated surplus.

The contradiction was clearly one of overaccumulation on the one hand, and underconsumption on the other. Unlike Keynesianism, this approach explained both the composition and the level of social output. And its analysis of the latter factor carried it far beyond traditional Marxian economics, which was still rooted in the conditions of the more competitive capitalism of the nineteenth century, when each individual capital had little choice but to invest and expand its output (if possible). A theory of the inner workings of monopoly capitalism had emerged.

Josef Steindl, an Austrian economist and Kalecki's colleague at the Oxford Institute of Statistics during World War II, carried Kalecki's theory a step further. In *Maturity and Stagnation in American Capitalism*, published in 1952, Steindl made explicit what had previously only been implicit in Kalecki's more laconic formulation. The utilization of productive capacity was said to be fundamental to the *planning* of monopolistic firms. This suggested that corporations were extremely sensitive to increases in unused capacity, which became the most important single factor determining profit expectations on new investment (also influenced by the existing ratio of profits and the debt-equity ratio). Confronted with a downward shift in final demand, corporations would not lower prices, as in a fully competitive system, but would instead cut back on output, capacity utilization, and new investment, maintaining, to whatever extent possible, prevailing profit margins. Analysis of the ways and means of monopoly capital therefore required an approach that focused increasingly on corporate overhead and unproductive consumption. Steindl's great contribution, which was systematically ignored by the economics profession, brought back the idea of secular stagnation; but this time it was rooted in the dynamics of monopolistic accumulation.

In 1957, Paul Baran, a Marxist economist at Stanford, published *The Political Economy of Growth.* This work is best known for its second part, generally recognized as an important addition to the understanding of imperialism as it affects the periphery of the capitalist world. But in the first part Baran worked out an avowedly Marxist theory of monopolistic accumulation within well-developed capitalism, based on the work of Marx, Hilferding, Lenin, Sweezy, Kalecki, and Steindl. Using the Kalecki-Steindl framework of widening profit margins, arising out of a mark-up on prime costs, and the resulting growth of excess capacity shutting off further investment, Baran developed an analysis of the economic surplus (linked to the Marxian concept of surplus value) which suggested that much of the potential accumulation fund of society appeared in the form of *waste* (or unutilized productive resources plus unproductive consumption and unproductive labor). In brief, the manner of monopolistic accumulation created a chronic and constantly compounded problem of realization. The standard way of getting around this in the United States, Baran argued, was through military spending and inflationary shots in the arm by government. This, he believed, would only complicate the underlying problem of stagnation, adding a further inflationary layer on top.

Similar views were advanced independently by Paolo Sylos-Labini in his book *Oligopoly and Technical Progress,* first published in Italian in 1956. Sylos-Labini, who had studied under Hansen at Harvard, presented a theory of deficiency in effective demand and secular stagnation, based on oversavings and underinvestment in the oligopolistic sector of the economy, which corresponded closely to the work of Kalecki, Steindl, Baran, and Sweezy.[19]

In 1966, *Monopoly Capital: An Essay on the American Social and Economic Order* by Paul Baran and Paul Sweezy appeared, two years after Baran's death. Using Marxian analysis to carry the Keynesian discoveries to their logical (but un-Keynesian) roots, it became a source of inspiration for elements of the renewed left of the 1960s.[20]

An eloquent testimony to the power and resilience of the Marxian vision, *Monopoly Capital* worked out, to a fuller extent, many of the theoretical positions of Baran's earlier study. And it formulated the impending crisis of U. S. capitalism in terms of a new "law": the tendency of the economic surplus, and its investment-seeking portion, to rise. Adding into the economic surplus all elements of economic waste (the channeling of the potential accumulation fund into areas other than the expansion of capital goods and wage goods), which would have been inconceivable under competitive capitalism, Baran and Sweezy conceptualized the problems of the existing economy in terms of a disjuncture between profit margins and profit rates, between potential economic surplus and actual, realized surplus, uncovering the cumulative contradictions of a developed monopoly capitalist order. Drawing on the earlier insights of Veblen, Hansen, and Schumpeter, they gave the thesis of secular stagnation, rooted in an understanding of monopoly capital, a more substantial foundation, emphasizing the importance of epoch-making innovations like the steam engine, the railroad, and the automobile, as the only real bases for rapid growth, and questioning the likelihood of innovations of this economic caliber in the immediate future. U. S. monopoly capitalism, Baran and Sweezy argued, depended all too heavily on military procurement and debt expansion. The contradictions of a prosperity erected on such foundations would soon bring the underlying stagnation to the fore in a more perilous form.

Baran and Sweezy had tried to construct a new, explicitly Marxian theory of accumulation, using the insights of Kalecki and others. But as Marxism and Marxian economics revived in the Western countries their analysis was increasingly characterized as un-Marxian by radical "purists," since the relation to Marxian value theory was not spelled out, in so many words, within *Monopoly Capital* itself (though Sweezy did so elsewhere);[21] and because their theory seemed to contradict some of Marx's own suppositions made a century earlier. Few understood that Baran and Sweezy were asking new questions about a transformed capitalist environment, making the theory of monopoly capitalism, as it applied directly to the advanced capitalist states, into much more than a mere catchphrase.

From the start, Baran and Sweezy had made it clear that their "essay-sketch" was far from being a "comprehensive study of monopoly capitalism" since it did not involve a thoroughgoing inquiry into the labor process itself. The better part of a decade later, Harry Braverman filled the gap with his important work, *Labor and Monopoly Capital: The Degradation of Work in the Twentieth Century*

(1974). Braverman showed the full impact of scientific management (or Taylorism), which emerged and developed along with the giant firm, on the cost-side of capitalist industry. It soon became clear that this was the real basis for the prodigious profitability of the giant corporation. Analyzing changes in the structure of industry and the working class, Braverman delved into the growth of new "middle layers" of unproductive workers, and the shift of employment to the marginal sectors (in terms of value production) of government, "service industries," and retail trade. Most important, he verified the fact that the general law of accumulation, as described by Marx, retained all of its validity at the level of direct production, as well as in the concentration and centralization of capital. It thus became evident that the qualitative changes wrought by the rise of monopoly capitalism were confined to the secondary, but nonetheless vital, area of the utilization of potential surplus product and its consequences for the productive employment of labor power.

By 1974-75 it was beginning to be generally perceived that stagnation had returned. This time, however, it came back in a different form. Unlike the years of the Great Depression, large and expanding amounts of unemployment and idle capacity were accompanied by a seemingly endless upward spiral of prices. Events thus confirmed what Paul Baran, almost alone within the economics profession, had suggested as a very real possibility of modern economic evolution, some twenty or so years before. The work of Harry Magdoff and Paul Sweezy, writing in *Monthly Review,* carried on along similar lines, as they continued to describe the perils of accelerated debt on top of an underlying base of slow growth.

In his most recent writings, Sweezy has returned to the question of secular stagnation. His focus has been the established, but all too easily forgotten, fact that every accumulation boom has its basis in an expansion of output in the capital goods industries (department 1) which exceeds the pace of the corresponding augmentation of the consumption goods sector (department 2). Building on this theme, Sweezy has insisted that the semi-autonomous character of department 1, necessary for accelerated growth, is weakening in the face of industrial maturity (the historical phase in which the underlying means of rapid and prolonged expansion in both departments is firmly established). Thus the historical path of accumulation leads to a situation—during the mature monopoly stage when department 1 has been intensively built up—in which "a sustainable growth rate of Department I comes to depend essentially on its being geared to Department II." Put simply, during a business upswing the monopoly capitalist system very rapidly reaches the point of "unsustainable disproportionality" between the two departments, and stagnation, or a normal trend-rate of slow growth, reasserts itself.[22]

In "Why Stagnation?," first delivered as a lecture at Harvard in March 1982 and published the following June in *Monthly Review,* Sweezy resurrected the Hansen-Schumpeter debate on secular stagnation, suggesting that it is high time that "the search for an answer" to the problem of enduring stagnation be taken up again. The present introduction, and the essays which follow, are intended to contribute to this task. Each part provides a sketch of a different aspect of the constellation of monopoly capitalism, and a short preface to each part is provided to set the overall context for the contributions contained therein.

We would like to dedicate this book to the memory of Patricia Foster, and to the living example of Emma Maria Chmielewska-Szlajfer.

Notes

1. J. M. Keynes, "The United States and the Keynes Plan," in *Collected Writings,* vol. XXII (London: Macmillan, 1978), p. 149.
2. Joseph A. Schumpeter, *Capitalism, Socialism and Democracy* (New York: Harper & Row, 1950), pp. 117-20.
3. See Alvin H. Hansen, *Full Recovery or Stagnation?* (New York: W. W. Norton, 1938), pp. 267-318, and *Fiscal Policy and Business Cycles* (New York: W. W. Norton, 1941), pp. 313-65; Joseph A. Schumpeter, *Business Cycles: A Theoretical, Historical and Statistical Analysis of the Capitalist Process,* vol. II (New York: McGraw Hill, 1939), pp. 1011-50, and *Capitalism, Socialism and Democracy,* pp. 111-21; Paul M. Sweezy, "Why Stagnation?," *Monthly Review* 34, no. 2 (June 1982): 1-10.
4. Benjamin Higgins, in particular, made several significant attempts to revitalize the stagnation thesis in the late 1940s and early 1950s. See, for example, "The Theory of Increasing Underemployment," *The Economic Journal* 60 (June 1950): 255-74, and "The Concept of Secular Stagnation," *The American Economic Review* 40 (1950): 160-66.
5. See especially Evsey D. Domar, *Essays in the Theory of Economic Growth* (New York: Oxford University Press, 1957), pp. 83-128; also R. F. Harrod, *The Trade Cycle: An Essay* (Oxford: Oxford University Press, 1936).
6. As Keynes himself put it, using the term "classical" for what is now usually labeled "neoclassical," "our criticism of the accepted classical theory of economics has consisted not so much in finding logical flaws in its analysis as in pointing out that its tacit assumptions are seldom or never satisfied, with the result that it cannot solve the economic problems of the actual world. But if our central controls succeed in estab-

lishing an aggregate volume of output corresponding to full employment as nearly as is practicable, the classical theory comes into its own again from this point onwards." Keynes, *The General Theory of Employment, Interest and Money*, in *Collected Writings*, vol. VII, p. 378.

7. Joan Robinson, who represented the left wing of Keynesian theory, would probably have accepted this as a critique of current orthodoxy, but not as a defect inherent to Keynesianism itself.

8. On classical and Keynesian theories of output see Roy Green, "Money, Output and Inflation in Classical Economics," *Contributions to Political Economy* 1, no. 1 (1982): 59-85.

9. Joan Robinson, *Contributions to Modern Economics* (Oxford: Basil Blackwell, 1978), pp. 55-56.

10. The essays appeared in print in Warsaw in 1933, in a book entitled *Proba teorii koniunktury (Essays on Business Cycle Theory)*. The first considerably abridged version of this book appeared as a separate article entitled "A Macrodynamic Theory of Business Cycles," *Econometrica* 3, no. 3 (1935).

11. Dr. Jerzy Osiatynski, editor of the first full Polish edition of Kalecki's works, states that Kalecki's model "originated in the maincurrent of the Marxian economic tradition, through a synthesis of elements of Tugan-Baranovski's and Rosa Luxemburg's theories, the use of further elaborations of Tugan-Baranovski's theory introduced by Aftalion, Bouniatian and other representatives of the theory of overinvestment, and the application of Tinbergen's analytical apparatus and mathematical tools." See Michal Kalecki, *Dziela (Works)*, vol. I (Warszawa: PWE, 1979), p. 449. For more background information on Kalecki and his works see G. R. Feiwel, *The Intellectual Capital of Michal Kalecki* (Knoxville: University of Tennessee Press, 1975), and *Oxford Bulletin of Economics and Statistics* 39, no. 1 (1977). (Special issue: Michal Kalecki Memorial Lectures.)

12. See Michal Kalecki, *Essays in the Theory of Economic Fluctuations* (New York: Russell and Russell, 1939); also "The Marxian Equations of Reproduction and Modern Economics," and "The Problem of Effective Demand with Tugan-Baranovski and Rosa Luxemburg," both reprinted in this volume.

13. Richard Edwards, *Contested Terrain: The Transformation of the Workplace in the Twentieth Century* (New York: Basic Books, 1979), pp. 44, 226-27.

14. Frederick Engels, *On Marx's Capital* (Moscow: Foreign Languages Publishing House, 1956), pp. 118-20.

15. The original title of Lenin's pamphlet when published in 1917 was *Imperialism, the Newest Stage of Capitalism*. Stressing this fact, Witold Kula, a Polish historian, wrote: "The methodological differences between these formulations are fundamental. The determination 'the newest stage' refers to the past. . . . Whereas the determination 'the highest stage' says something more, also about the future; that in the future there will be no 'higher stage' than this one." Witold Kula, *Problemy i metody historii gospodarczej (Problems and Methods of Economic History)* (Warszawa: PWN, 1963), p. 178.

16. Paul A. Baran and Paul M. Sweezy, *Monopoly Capital* (New York: Monthly Review Press, 1966), p. 5.

17. The idea, so clearly enunciated by Kalecki, of a nonlinear investment function precluding both full and zero employment, due to "dynamic switches" in investment behavior, was also to be found, to some extent, in the work of Keynes, and became a major research problem in the early Keynesian era. For a concise explanation, see Kenneth K. Kurihara, *Introduction to Keynesian Dynamics* (New York: Columbia University Press, 1956), pp. 122-28.

18. *Essays in the Theory of Economic Fluctuations*, p. 149. See also Michal Kalecki, *Theory of Economic Dynamics* (New York: Augustus M. Kelley, 1969), and two articles reprinted in this volume: "The Mechanism of the Business Upswing," and "Class Struggle and Distribution of National Income."

19. Chapter 10 of this work, "The Problem of Effective Demand," is reprinted in this volume. *Oligopoly and Technical Progress* is also noteworthy for Sylos-Labini's effective defense of the concept of "degree of monopoly" against the attacks of Kaldor and others.

20. The years 1965 and 1966 might be thought of as a time when Marxian economics took up the challenge raised by Keynes with a fervor, not equaled in any time before or since. Aside from *Monopoly Capital,* these years saw the publication of Kalecki's *Theory of Economic Dynamics,* 2nd ed. (1965); Sydney Coontz' much neglected *Productive Labor and Effective Demand* (London: Routledge and Kegan Paul, 1965); and Joseph Gillman's *Prosperity in Crisis* (New York: Marzani and Munsell, 1965), which extended to a critique of Keynesianism the analysis begun in his earlier book, *The Falling Rate of Profit* (New York: Cameron Associates, 1958). On Coontz' work see John Bellamy Foster, "Marxian Economics and the State," reprinted in this volume. For discussions of Gillman's early contributions see Jacob Morris, "Profit Rates and Capital Formation in American Monopoly Capitalism," and Henryk Szlajfer, "Economic Surplus and Surplus Value Under Monopoly Capitalism," both in this volume.

21. See the selections by Paul Sweezy in this volume.

22. Paul M. Sweezy, *Four Lectures on Marxism* (New York: Monthly Review Press, 1981), pp. 26-45. See also Harry Magdoff and Paul M. Sweezy, "Listen Keynesians!," *Monthly Review* 8, no. 34 (January 1983): 1-11.

Part I

MONOPOLY THEORY AND MARXIAN ECONOMICS

The essays in Part I are concerned with the general theory of accumulation under monopoly capitalism. The first three contributions by Paul M. Sweezy attempt to clarify certain aspects of the relationship between the theory advanced in *Monopoly Capital* by Paul A. Baran and Paul M. Sweezy and that of *Capital* by Karl Marx, emphasizing historical changes in the underlying pattern of accumulation that have taken place in the century since Marx's death. The last contribution by John Bellamy Foster seeks to place the analysis of monopoly capital within the larger historical stagnation thesis, providing at the same time a critique of supply-side economics.

Paul M. Sweezy

MONOPOLY CAPITAL AND THE THEORY OF VALUE

It gives me a great deal of satisfaction that Paul Baran's and my book on monopoly capitalism has been made available to Greek readers and has been so well received by them that a second printing is now called for. The special relation which has existed between the United States and Greece in the period since the end of World War II makes it particularly important that the Greek people should understand the socioeconomic structure and the political functioning of the world's most developed and powerful capitalist country. It is my hope, which I am sure would have been shared by Paul Baran had he lived, that this book, so different in its focus and emphasis from the vast majority of studies of the U. S. economy and society, will help them to attain that understanding.

Monopoly Capital first appeared in 1966 and has since been translated into a number of languages, and has been the subject of dozens of reviews by economists and other social scientists, both bourgeois and Marxist. Judging from these reviews and from criticisms appearing in many books and articles, I am sorry to have to say that there has been a great deal of misunderstanding of what Baran and I said or intended to say. This is not the place to attempt to review and correct these misunderstandings, but I would like to take the opportunity to clarify our position on one point.

Many of our Marxist critics have stated, as though it were a self-evident fact, that Baran and Sweezy reject the Marxist theory of value (hence also, by implication, the theory of surplus value). This is not so. At no time in our long period of association and collaboration did it ever even occur to us to reject the Marxist theory of value. Our procedure in *Monopoly Capital* was to take the labor theory of value for granted and go on from there. I can now see that this was an error. We should have begun our analysis with an exposition of the theory of value as it is presented in volume 1 of *Capital*. We should then have proceeded to show that in capitalist

---

This preface to the second printing of the Greek translation of *Monopoly Capital*, prepared by the Athens publisher Gutenberg, first appeared in the January 1974 issue of *Monthly Review*.

reality, values as determined by socially necessary labor time are subject to two main kinds of modification: first, values are transformed into prices of production, as Marx recognized in volume 3; and second, values (or prices of production) are transformed into monopoly prices in the monopoly stage of capitalism, a subject which Marx barely mentioned, for the obvious reason that all of *Capital* was written well before the onset of the monopoly capitalist period. At no time did Baran and I explicitly or implicitly reject the theories of value and surplus value but sought only to analyze the modifications which become necessary as the result of the concentration and centralization of capital. If we had pursued this course, I believe many misunderstandings could have been avoided. This is not to argue, of course, that our analysis of the modifications made necessary by monopoly is necessarily complete or even correct. That is for the critics to judge. But I insist that they cannot form a useful or valid judgment unless they first have a clear understanding of what we are trying to do. To the extent that lack of such understanding is the fault of the authors, I am truly sorry and offer sincere if belated apologies.

Paul M. Sweezy

COMPETITION AND MONOPOLY

In his *Principles of Political Economy*, John Stuart Mill summed up the classical view of competition as follows:

> Political economists . . . are apt to express themselves as if they thought that competition actually does, in all cases, whatever it can be shown to be the tendency of competititon to do. This is partly intelligible, if we consider that only through the principle of competition has political economy any pretension to the character of a science. So far as rents, profits, wages, prices, are determined by competition, laws may be assigned for them. Assume competition to be their exclusive regulator, and principles of broad generality and scientific precision may be laid down, according to which they will be regulated. The political economist justly deems this his proper business: and as an abstract or hypothetical science, politicial economy cannot be required to do, and indeed cannot do, anything more.[1]

Competition, in other words, does not determine the *content* of the laws of economics, but it does provide the pressures which constrain economic subjects (capitalists, workers, landlords, consumers, etc.) to act in ways that conform to these laws. Marx's view was basically the same, though he expressed it differently. The following passages from the *Grundrisse* are representative of his comments on competition:

> Competition generally, this essential locomotive force of the bourgeois economy, does not establish its laws, but is rather their executor. Unlimited competition is therefore not the presupposition for the truth of the economic laws, but rather the consequence—the form of appearance in which their necessity realizes itself. . . . Competition therefore does not *explain* these laws; rather, it lets them be *seen*, but does not produce them. (p. 552)
>
> Competition executes the inner laws of capital; makes them into compulsory laws toward the individual capital, but it does not invent them. It realizes them. (p. 752)
>
> *Free competition* is the relation of capital to itself as another capital, i.e., the real conduct of capital as capital. The inner laws of capital— which appear merely as tendencies in the preliminary historic stages

Reprinted from Paul M. Sweezy, *Four Lectures on Marxism* (New York: Monthly Review Press, 1981), pp. 55–70.

of its development—are for the first time posited as laws; production founded on capital for the first time posits itself in the form adequate to it only insofar as, and to the extent that, free competition develops, for it is the free development of the mode of production founded on capital; the free development of its conditions and of itself as the process which constantly reproduces these conditions. . . . Free competition is the real development of capital. By its means what corresponds to the nature of capital is posited as external necessity for the individual capital; what corresponds to the concept of capital is posited as external necessity for the mode of production founded on capital. The reciprocal compulsion which the capitals within it practice upon one another, on labor, etc. (the competition among workers is only another form of the competition among capitals), is the *free,* at the same time the *real,* development of wealth as capital. So much is this the case that the most profound economic thinkers, such as e.g., Ricardo, *presuppose* the absolute predominance of free competition in order to be able to study and to formulate the adequate laws of capital—which appear at the same time as the vital tendencies governing over it. But free competition is the adequate form of the productive process of capital. The further it is developed, the purer the forms in which its motion appears.[2]

Like the classics before him, Marx thus assigned to competition a very important, indeed an indispensable, role, that of enforcer of the laws of capitalism. But, again like the classics, what interested him were the laws themselves and not the means of their realization. He took for granted that competition would develop along with capitalism and that the laws which competition enforces would become closer and closer approximations to reality. Given this perspective, there was no need for lengthy disquisitions on competition, and in fact Marx's comments on the subject were mostly incidental to discussion of other topics and often more concerned with earlier writers' misconceptions about the role of competition than with analyzing its workings.[3]

In this connection it is necessary to keep in mind not only that Marx's focus was on the laws of capitalism rather than on the means of their realization but also that his concern was with the system's "laws of motion," as he explicitly stated in the Preface to the first edition of volume 1 of *Capital.* For him competition could not be "perfect" or "pure," nor could it end in equilibrium situations lending themselves to analysis as to their uniqueness, stability, etc. Fantasies of this kind were imported into economics only much later by those more interested in concealing than revealing the real role of the economy in shaping the history and destiny of bourgeois society. Neither Marx nor the classics had any interest in playing such intellectual games. For them, and for Marx most of all, competition was an elemental force, somewhat comparable to the force of gravity, which keeps the parts of the system in place and interacting with each other in intelligible ways.

Marx of course recognized that in practice the freedom of competition met with many obstacles and blockages, but he considered these to be leftovers from precapitalist social formations which were in the process of disappearing with the development and spread of capitalist relations. He did not discuss the possibility that such barriers to competition might arise from the operation of the laws of capitalism itself. And yet his analysis of the concentration and centralization of capital and of the role of the credit system in making possible the creation of much larger units of capital than could be assembled by individual capitalists, obviously implied ongoing changes in the conditions of competition.

In the middle years of the nineteenth century, when Marx was gathering his material and writing the three volumes of *Capital,* the typical English industry, exemplified most clearly in the production of textiles, comprised hundreds of establishments each too small to influence the overall supply-and-demand situation and each striving with might and main to make a greater profit (or avoid a loss) through reducing its costs of production. "The battle of competition," Marx wrote, "is fought by cheapening of commodities. The cheapness of commodities depends, *ceteris paribus,* on the productiveness of labor, and this again on the scale of production. Therefore the larger capitals beat the smaller" (*Capital,* vol. 1, ch. 25, section 2). Further, the credit system, which begins as a "modest helper of accumulation," soon "becomes a new and formidable weapon in the competitive struggle, and finally it transforms itself into an immense social mechanism for the centralization of capitals" (ibid.).

A consequence and bearer of these changes was the "formation of stock companes" (i.e., corporations) to which Marx devoted several pages in volume 3, chapter 27, commenting on phenomena (like the separation of ownership and control) which bourgeois economics was to take into account only much later. The conclusions to which the analysis pointed are summed up in the following paragraph:

> This is the abolition of the capitalist mode of production within capitalist production itself, a self-destructive contradiction, which represents on its face a mere phase of transition to a new form of production. It manifests its contradictory nature by its effects. It establishes a monopoly in certain spheres and thereby challenges the interference of the state. It reproduces a new aristocracy of finance, a new sort of parasites in the shape of promoters, speculators, and merely nominal directors; a whole system of swindling and cheating

by means of corporate juggling, stock jobbing, and stock speculation. It is private production without the control of private property.

In preparing this material for press two decades later, Engels added a long editor's insert, beginning, "Since Marx wrote the above, new forms of industrial enterprises have developed which represent the second and third degree of stock companies," and leading to the conclusion that "the long cherished freedom of competition has reached the end of its tether and is compelled to announce its own palpable bankruptcy." These new forms of enterprise were the cartel and what we know today as the holding company, that is, a corporation which owns the shares of other corporations and in this way brings them under its control. As an example of the latter he cited the then recently formed United Alkali Trust, "which has brought the entire alkali production of the British into the hands of one single business firm. . . . In this way competition in this line, which forms the basis of the entire chemical industry, has been replaced in England by monopoly, and the future expropriation of this line by the whole of society, the nation, has been well prepared."

As this last statement and similar remarks by Marx suggest, Marx and Engels did not see these changes as foreshadowing a new phase of capitalism but, in the words of Marx quoted above, as a "phase of transition to a new form of production," which they doubtless thought would soon come to occupy the center of the historical stage.

In the light of all this, it certainly cannot be said that Marx was unaware of the changing conditions of competition arising from the capital accumulation process itself. If nevertheless he did not inquire into the possible implications of these changes for capitalism's "laws of motion," there are at least two explanations which readily come to mind. One is that at the time of writing *Capital* (the early 1860s) these changes were still only beginning to appear and very little empirical material was available on which to base an analysis. And the second is that he saw the changes as basically symptoms of an impending transition from capitalism to a new form of production. Now, more than a century later, we know that he was too optimistic (as most revolutionaries are likely to be). Not that the beginnings of such a transition were all that far in the future; it was only that they first made their appearance not in the historical heartlands of capitalism but in the less capitalistically developed periphery of the global system. But even before this started to happen, the concentration and centralization of capital proceeded at an accelerating pace in the metropolitan centers of Western Europe, North America, and soon Japan.

With industry after industry falling under the domination of a few giant corporations, it could not but become clear to economists and other interested observers that the conditions of competition which had characterized the earlier stage of capitalism had been radically altered. Bourgeois economists began to deal with the new situation in a descriptive way even before the turn of the century, and an extensive popular literature of exposure and protest developed. In the United States, Thorstein Veblen, who was much influenced by Marx but could not be called a Marxist, was the first social scientist to treat the subject theoretically (in his *Theory of Business Enterprise*, 1904); and the Austrian Rudolf Hilferding was the first to do so from an avowedly Marxist point of view (*Das Finanzkapital*, 1910). A few years later Lenin, who was much influenced by Hilferding's work, produced his *Imperialism, the Highest Stage of Capitalism* (written in 1916); and since then it has become a widely, if not universally, accepted tenet of Marxist theory that by the end of the nineteenth century the concentration and centralization of capital had proceeded to the point of transforming capitalism from its competitive stage, on which Marx had focused attention, to a new stage variously referred to as finance capitalism, imperialism, or monopoly capitalism.

The term monopoly recurs with great frequency throughout this literature, but almost never is it used to imply the exclusion or absence of competition. In this respect, the explanation offered by Veblen would almost certainly have been approved by practically all the other writers referred to and by those who have continued to work in this tradition in later years. All producers, he said, are guided by the principle which, in the language of the railroads, is known as "charging what the traffic will bear." And he continued:

> Where a given enterprise has a strict monopoly of the supply of a given article or of a given class of services, this principle applies in the unqualified form in which it has been understood by those who discuss railway charges. But where the monopoly is less strict, where there are competitors, there the competition that has to be met is one of the factors to be taken account of in determining what the traffic will bear; competition may even become the most serious factor in the case if the enterprise in question has little or none of the character of a monopoly. But it is very doubtful if there are any successful business ventures within the range of modern industries from which the monopoly element is wholly absent.* They are, at any rate, few and not of great magnitude. And the endeavor of all such enterprises that look to a permanent continuance of their business is to establish as much of a monopoly as may be.[4]

What is at issue in the transition from competitive to monopoly capitalism, therefore, is not at all the *elimination* of competition but rather a change in the *forms* and *methods* of competition. In the earlier period when each individual firm supplied only a small share of the market, the main weapons of competition were lowering costs and improving quality: by such means the firm could hope to survive and increase its profits. The competition was not perceived as coming from particular rival firms which were also small and might enter or depart from the industry without noticeably affecting the market as a whole. Rather the competition was perceived as coming from all the other firms in the industry. In order to stay in business and grow, one had to do better than the average of all the other firms, for it was the latter that determined the value (or price of production) of the commodities being produced. Firms with costs above average would be squeezed out, those with costs below average would prosper. None could influence the market as a whole, either in terms of the commodities in demand or in terms of the prices at which they could be sold; all had to accept these as the givens of the situation.

As concentration and centralization proceeded, however, this situation changed. The number of firms in industry after industry (though of course not in all) declined to the point where each one supplied a considerable share of the market. The smaller the number of firms ("oligopolists" in the terminology of neoclassical economics), the greater the possibility for each one to differentiate itself from the others in significant ways and thus to add new dimensions to the competitive struggle. The key problem for a firm was to acquire a special position in a part of the market—through such methods as brand names, advertising and other forms of aggressive salesmanship, reciprocal favors to large buyers, etc.—and then to fight to fortify and extend its share. In this situation a firm conceived its competition as coming no longer from the industry as a whole but rather from one or perhaps two or three firms nearest to it in the market. Competition, in other words, became much more visible and open and often much fiercer than it had previously been. In the early stages of this emerging mode of competition, there was a strong tendency for firms to try to improve their market position through price-cutting. Experience, however, gradually taught the lesson that this was a self-defeating strategy. Price-cutting could be as easily used to defend as to extend market share, with the only result being lower prices and profits for all contenders. In the closing decades of the nineteenth century price-cutting of this kind was very widespread and certainly played an important part in bringing prices sharply down from the peak reached during the Civil War and its aftermath boom to a much lower level by the end of the century. With 1873 = 100, the wholesale price index fell to 53 in 1898 to the accompaniment of a steady stream of bankruptcies and loud complaints and cries of alarm from the business community which experienced the period as one of almost unrelieved hard times.[5]

It was then that U. S. businessmen learned the self-defeating nature of price-cutting as a competitive weapon and started the process of banning it through a complex network of laws (corporate and regulatory), institutions (e.g., trade associations), and conventions (e.g., price leadership) from normal business practice.[6] In this respect the years around the turn of the century marked a watershed in the development of U. S. capitalism: the nineteenth century which, except for the Civil War period, was a century of falling prices, gave way to the twentieth which, again with an exception for the Great Depression, has been equally notable for its rising prices.

The question we now have to ask is whether the transformation of competition brought about by concentration and centralization of capital negates the role assigned to competition by the classics and Marx, that is, as the realizer and enforcer of the laws of capitalism. The answer is definitely not, and in one very important respect it is even true that this role is enhanced and strengthened. This is in the realm of relations between capital and labor. In the classical/ Marxian scheme of things, competition forces capitalists to produce at the lowest possible cost, which of course is the other side of the coin of maximizing profits. This means that they will buy labor power as cheaply as possible and, having bought it, will squeeze out of it the maximum attainable amount of production. This is a necessary, though not necessarily sufficient, condition for the validity of all the laws of value, surplus value, and profit. And the mechanism which produces it operates after, as well as before, the transition to monopoly capitalism. Capitalists are still forced by competitive pressures to produce at lowest possible costs. A weighty tome by Michael Porter, a Harvard Business School professor, explains why. There are, according to the author, five competitive forces which "continually work to drive down the rate of return on invested capital toward the competitive floor rate of return, or the return that would be earned by the economist's 'perfectly competitive' industry."[7] And in "coping with the five competitive forces, there are three potentially successful generic strategic approaches to outperforming other firms in an industry: (1) overall cost leadership, (2) differentiation, (3) focus." Of these the first is by far the most important. In Porter's words:

> Having a low-cost position yields the firm above-average returns in its industry despite the presence of strong competitive forces. Its cost position gives the firm a defense against rivalry from competitors, because its lower costs mean that it can still earn returns after its competitiors have competed away their profits through rivalry. A low-

cost position defends the firm against powerful buyers because buyers can exert power to drive down prices to the level of the next-most-efficient competitor. Low cost provides a defense against powerful suppliers by providing more flexibility to cope with input cost increases. The factors that lead to a low-cost position usually also provide substantial entry barriers in terms of scale economies or cost advantages. Finally, a low-cost position usually places the firm in a favorable position vis-à-vis substitutes relative to its competitors in the industry. Thus a low-cost position protects the firm against all five competitive forces because bargaining can only continue to erode profits until those of the next-most-efficient competitor are eliminated, and because the less efficient competitors will suffer first in the face of competitive pressures.[8]

There can thus be no doubt that survival and growth are as crucially dependent on minimizing costs as they were in the earlier stage of capitalism. But we can go further and say that in its ability to squeeze the most out of labor power, the giant corporation of today has greatly surpassed its small-scale ancestor. Here we can do no better than to quote the leading authority on the subject, Harry Braverman:

> The crucial developments in the processes of production date from precisely the same period as monopoly capitalism. Scientific management and the whole "movement" for the organization of production on its modern basis have their beginnings in the last two decades of the last century. And the scientific-technical revolution, based on the systematic use of science for the more rapid transformation of labor power into capital, also begins . . . at the same time. In describing these two facets of the activity of capital, we have therefore been describing two of the prime aspects of monopoly capital. Both chronologically and functionally, they are part of the new stage of capitalist development, and they grow out of monopoly capitalism and make it possible.[9]

Marx considered that the "determining element" in all class societies—that which defines their fundamental nature—is "the specific economic form in which unpaid surplus labor is pumped out of the direct producers" (*Capital*, vol. 3, ch. 47, section 2). Under capitalism this specific form is the capital/wage-labor relationship. The transformation of competitive into monopoly capitalism not only does not negate this relationship, it refines and perfects it. With respect to certain secondary characteristics of the system, most notably the distribution and forms of utilization of the surplus value, however, the transformation does bring about important changes, and this is why a specific theory of monopoly capitalism is necessary.

The altered forms of competition which prevail in monopoly

capitalism create not the tendency toward a system-wide average rate of profit which Marx analyzed in part II of the third volume of *Capital* but rather a hierarchy of profit rates, highest in the industries which approach most closely to a monopoly status and lowest in those in which small-scale competitive enterprise continues to predominate. Since surplus value is distributed through the mechanism of profit rates, and since there is a rough correlation between the height of the profit rate and the number and size of firms in a given industry, it follows that there is a strong tendency, given a continuing process of concentration and centralization, for more and more surplus value to be sucked up from the smaller scale and more competitive sectors to the larger scale and more monopolistic ones. But since the amount of surplus value available for accumulation is always greater in proportion to the size and profitability of the unit of capital to which it accrues, it follows that the same total amount of surplus value will tend to support a more rapid rate of accumulation the more monopolistic the overall structure of the eonomy is.

There are important implications of this for the actual unfolding of the accumulation process which cannot be analyzed here. But I do want to call attention to several points which have not been mentioned and which would require further exploration in a fuller treatment of competition and monopoly.

First, one should be careful not to freeze monopoly capitalist theory into the kind of rigid static molds which are the hallmark of neoclassical economics. When we say that the average rate of profit is superseded by a hierarchy of profit rates, there is no implication that the industries (or firms) at various levels of the hierarchy must always be the same. There is constant movement within the hierarchy in response to both internal and external factors. At the time of writing (early 1981), a particularly dramatic example is the reversal of the positions of the U. S. oil and automobile industries. A few years ago the automobile industry was on top by a wide margin, with oil at a considerably lower rung on the ladder. The sharp and increasing rise in the price of oil since 1973, together with sluggish adaptation to new conditions by the auto giants, has propelled oil to the top and plummeted autos to the bottom. Estimates appearing in the business press put the profits of the oil industry, dominated by a dozen or so huge corporations, at 30 to 40 percent of total nonfinancial corporate profits—clearly an unprecedented situation—while the three auto giants have been reporting the largest losses in U. S. corporate history. This relationship obviously will not last: oil will come down and autos will go up. But there is no guarantee that their relative positions will be restored to what they were before. Similar, if less dramatic, examples could be drawn from the experience of many other industries. To which should be added that with the trend of recent years toward conglomeration, the relationship between firms and industries becomes increasingly blurred: most of the big oil companies are into petrochemicals and other forms of energy, and many are moving into mining; U. S. Steel, the biggest steel producer, is diversifying into chemicals, coal, oil, and gas; Armco, the fifth largest steel producer, already gets more than half its profits from energy-related operations, especially oil-field equipment; and so on and so on. Since profits accrue to firms rather than to industries, the meaning of ranking industries by profitability becomes increasingly problematic. At the same time, however, the general proposition that the distribution of surplus value is increasingly skewed in favor of the larger units of capital is less and less open to question. And this is the heart of the matter as far as the relation between monopoly and accumulation is concerned.

Second, it is of more than passing interest to note that while Marx made no attempt to analyze the effect on the accumulation process of changing forms of competition, there is an intriguing passage very near the end of the third volume of *Capital* (in a chapter entitled "The Semblance of Competition") which suggests the direction his thinking might have taken if he had lived two or three decades longer:

> [I]f the equalization of the surplus value into average profit meets with obstacles in the various spheres of production in the shape of artificial or natural monopolies, particularly of monopoly in land, so that a monopoly price would be possible, which would rise above the price of production and above the value of the commodities affected by such a monopoly, still the limits imposed by the value of commodities would not be abolished thereby. The monopoly price of certain commodities would merely transfer a portion of the profit of the other producers of commodities to the commodities with a monopoly price. A local disturbance in the distribution of the surplus value among the various spheres of production would take place indirectly, but they would leave the boundaries of the surplus value itself unaltered. If a commodity with a monopoly price should enter into the necessary consumption of the laborer, it would increase the wages and thereby reduce the surplus value, if the laborer would receive the value of his labor power the same as before. But such a commodity might also depress wages below the value of labor power, of course only to the extent that wages would be higher than the physical minimum of subsistence. In this case the monopoly price would be paid by a deduction from the real wages (that is, from the quantity of use values received by the laborer for the same quantity of

labor [power]) and from the profit of other capitalists. The limits within which the monopoly price would affect the normal regulation of the prices of commodities would be accurately fixed and could be closely calculated.

While Marx has in mind in this passage only a "local disturbance in the distribution of surplus value," clearly the reasoning can be extended to encompass a more generalized spread of monopoly, that is, of industries able to charge prices above price of production or value, whichever is higher, and a continuing process of concentration and centralization. In addition to a redistribution of surplus value from more competitive to less competitive sectors, there could take place an increase in total surplus value at the expense of real wages (implying a rise in the rate of surplus value) if workers are unable to protect themselves against monopoly prices for wage goods. To this it might be objected that monopoly prices cannot raise the rate of surplus value except through depressing wages below the value of labor power, and that this would be essentially an unstable and temporary effect. This objection, however, fails to see monopolization as a process which must be viewed historically and as an ongoing part of the accumulation process. While at any particular time the value of labor power can be treated as a given, over a period of time it tends to rise (because of increasing costs of producing labor power and workers' struggles to improve their standard of living). In this context growing monopolization must be seen not as depressing wages below the value of labor power but as slowing down the rise in the value of labor power. To this extent it favors capital against labor by raising the rate of surplus value above what it would otherwise have been. It thus appears that two of the central ideas of the modern theory of monopoly capitalism— that the transformation of competition brought about by concentration and centralization of capital both raises the rate of surplus value and skews the distribution of surplus value in favor of the larger units of capital—are logical developments of a line of thought which Marx clearly adumbrated in the third volume of *Capital*.

The same cannot be said, however, of the other central thesis of monopoly-capitalist theory, namely that the changing size and composition of surplus value are accompanied by changes in the utilization of surplus value, exemplified especially by the enormous growth, both absolute and relative, of selling costs in the last hundred years or so. In discussing the costs of circulation, Marx clearly established that these are deductions from the surplus value going to productive enterprises, and he thought of them as falling within the realm of merchant capital. Since there was thus a conflict of interest between industrial and merchant capital, and since the former was growing more powerful all the time, he thought that the tendency in the course of capitalist development was for the relative importance of the costs of circulation to decline. This was true enough in the period of competitive capitalism. But with the decline of price competition, other forms of gaining market share came to the fore, and these were heavily focused on the realm of salesmanship (product differentiation, branding, advertising, packaging, and the like). Some of these activities add use value to the buyer, but by far the larger proportion are concerned with salability pure and simple and are therefore, for the most part, to be treated as additions to the cost of circulation. Both the labor and the capital devoted to these purposes are unproductive (they consume but do not produce surplus value) and therefore, from a social point of view, are to be accounted as sheer waste.

In the further course of development of monopoly capitalism, additional changes in the pattern of utilization of surplus value—notably those related to imperialism, militarism, and efforts by the state to counteract blockages in the accumulation process—emerged and grew steadily more important. In the second generation of Marxist theorists, these questions were placed at the center of inquiry by Hilferding, Rosa Luxemburg, and Lenin; and they have of course continued to preoccupy Marxists ever since. But in closing this brief discussion of competition and monopoly from a Marxist point of view, it is fitting that we should recognize that the first theorist to achieve a comprehensive vision of monopoly capitalism and its long-run consequences was an American, Thorstein Veblen. As early as 1904 Veblen delivered the following diagnosis which rings truer today than it did three-quarters of a century ago:

A disproportionate growth of parasitic industries, such as most advertising and much of the other efforts that go into competitive selling, as well as warlike expenditure and other industries directed to turning out goods for conspicuously wasteful consumption, would lower the effective vitality of the community to such an extent as to jeopardize its chances of advance or even its life. The limits which the circumstances of life impose in this respect are of a selective character, in the last resort. A persistent excess of parasitic and wasteful efforts over productive industry must bring on a decline. But owing to the very high productive efficiency of the modern mechanical industry, the margin available for wasteful occupations and wasteful expenditures is very great. The requirements of the aggregate livelihood are so far short of the possible output of goods by modern methods as to leave a very wide margin for waste and parasitic income. So that instances of such a decline, due to industrial exhaustion, drawn from the history of any earlier phase of economic life, carry no well defined lesson as to what a modern industrial community may allow itself in this respect.[10]

One may legitimately wonder, as we enter the last two decades of the twentieth century, whether this safety margin is not now at long last in grave danger of being used up. This is the question which lies at the heart of the crisis of our time.

Notes

1. John Stuart Mill, *Principles of Political Economy* (Toronto: University of Toronto Press, 1965), ch. 4, section 1.
2. Karl Marx, *Grundrisse*, Martin Nicolaus, trans. (London: Penguin, 1973), pp. 650-51.
3. Volume 1 of the *Marx-Lexikon zur Politischen Okonomie*, compiled under the direction of Samezo Kuruma of the Ohara Institute for Social Research of Hosei University, Tokyo, is devoted entirely to *Konkurrenz* (Competition). It contains, apart from prefaces, appendices, and the like, 359 pages, of which half are Japanese translation, in other words, about 180 pages taken from a wide variety of Marx's original texts. There are 176 separate passages, averaging just over a page apiece. And much of the space is taken up with providing the context of the remarks on competition rather than bearing directly on the subject. The *Marx-Lexicon,* of which eleven volumes had been published up to the end of 1979, is an invaluable source book and reference work.
4. Thorstein Veblen, *The Theory of Business Enterprise* (1904; New Brunswick, N.J.: Transaction Books, 1978), p. 54. The asterisk refers to a note which reads as follows: "'Monopoly' is here used in that looser sense which it has colloquially, not in the strict sense of an exclusive control of the supply, as employed, e.g., by Mr. Ely. . . . This usage is the more excusable since Mr. Ely finds that 'monopoly' in the strict sense of the definition practically does not occur in fact."
5. It should be noted, however, that in terms of physical output, as distinct from prices and profits, the period was one of fairly rapid growth. Gross Domestic Product increased about threefold from 1870 to 1900, which compares favorably with any other three-decade interval for which estimates are available. See *Historical Statistics of the United States from Colonial Times to 1957* (Washington, D. C.: U. S. Department of Commerce, 1961), pp. 140-41.
6. The classic study of this whole process is Arthur R. Burns, *The Decline of Competition: A Study of the Evolution of American Industry* (1936; reprinted Westport, Conn.: Greenwood Press, 1974), an influential work in the late 1930s but one that has been almost totally ignored since the Second World War, a fact reflecting the ideological swing to the right

of all the academic social sciences which was initiated by the cold war and strengthened by McCarthyism. (Arthur R. Burns is not to be confused with Arthur F. Burns, the erstwhile chairman of the Federal Reserve Board.) It should be added that the banning of price competition has not been, and indeed could not be, complete. There are conjunctures in which an aggressively managed company with ample financial banking finds it worthwhile to deliberately incur losses in order to increase its market share, confident of its ability to raise prices and recoup when the dust of battle has settled. Still more important is the case of new industries (like electronics in the last two decades) in which the whole question of which of many small firms will survive and grow has yet to be decided. Here we have to do with a shakedown process which in effect repeats the experience through which many older industries had to pass many years earlier. These are exceptions which should not be allowed to obscure the truth of the dictum enunciated by the editors of *Business Week* when they wrote (June 15, 1957) that the price system "works only one way—up."

7. Michael E. Porter, *Competitive Strategy* (New York: The Free Press, 1980), p. 5.
8. Ibid, pp. 35-36.
9. Harry Braverman, *Labor and Monopoly Capital* (New York: Monthly Review Press, 1974), p. 252. See also Richard Edwards, *Contested Terrain: The Transformation of the Workplace in the Twentieth Century* (New York: Basic Books, 1979).
10. Veblen, *Theory of Business Enterprise,* pp. 64-65.

Paul M. Sweezy

SOME PROBLEMS IN THE THEORY OF CAPITAL ACCUMULATION

A recent article by Mario Cogoy contains an interpretation of Marx's theory of capital accumulation which appears to be shared, with variations, by a growing number of Marxist economists.[1] This is a complicated and difficult problem which I have no intention of trying to treat exhaustively in a brief essay. But there are a number of basic points of view expressed or implied in this literature which seem to me erroneous, potentially seriously misleading, and hence in need of explicit criticism.

First, however, since the work of the late Paul Baran and myself (especially but not exclusively our joint book *Monopoly Capital*) is a favorite target of the authors referred to, I must clear up a misunderstanding which seems to be common to all of them. This is that Baran and Sweezy, like Joan Robinson and other left-Keynesians, reject Marx's theory of value. I can assure them that this is simply not so. At no time in our long period of close association and collaboration did it ever occur to Baran and me to call into question, let alone reject, the labor theory of value as elaborated by Marx and as we understood it. In this connection let me quote two points emphasized by Cogoy (p. 398) as being opposed to neo-Marxism, a category in which he includes Baran and Sweezy:

> (a) The theory of value is an instrument for the analysis of accumulation and total social reproduction. It is not a theory of relative prices; the academic critiques directed at the theory of value (and in particular that which considers that the monopolistic structure of the market has abolished the conditions for the validity of the theory of value) rest on a fundamental incomprehension of Marxist theory: they attribute the central role to empirical exchange relations (prices), while for Marx it is the social relations of production (wage labor–capital) which are the true objects of the theory of value.
>
> (b) Not only is the theory of value not modified by state intervention into the economy and by the development of waste, but rather the function of the state and the growth of the unproductive sector

---

This essay originally appeared in *Sozialismus, Geschicte und Wissenschaft: Festschrift für Eduard März* (Vienna: Europaverlag, 1973).

flow from the dialectic of value and of the laws of capital accumulation.

Cogoy will perhaps be surprised to learn that I entirely agree with both these points, and I commend him for stating them so clearly and concisely. At the same time, I would hope that he will agree with me that the theory of value in its most abstract expression, that is, as elaborated in volume 1 of *Capital*, is not the final form of the "instrument" he is talking about. There are two issues involved here: (1) the dropping of the assumption that all industries have the same organic composition of capital; and (2) the introduction of monopolistic market structures. Let us consider them in turn.

(1) In reality of course the organic composition of capital varies widely from one industry to another. Once this is taken into account, as Marx showed in part II of volume 3, we move from values to prices of production. Bourgeois economists from Böhm-Bawerk on have seen in this a contradiction and an abandonment of the Marxian value theory. This view is absolutely incorrect. Prices of production are not what Cogoy calls "empirical exchange relations" but *modified values:* without the theory of value there could be no theory of prices of production. The question then arises as to whether the passage from values (volume 1) to prices of production (volume 3) brings with it significant changes in the accumulation process. And the answer is definitely that it does not.[2] It follows that in discussing capitalism's overall laws of motion one is fully justified in ignoring prices of production and operating directly with the theory of value and accumulation as developed in volume 1.

(2) Matters are different when it comes to taking account of monopoly. Marx himself did not take this step in any systematic way, in spite of the fact that in his dynamic theory (in this respect totally different from orthodox neoclassical theory) competition of capitals is virtually identical with the concentration and centralization of capitals. The period of monopoly capitalism was just beginning at the time of his death, and it is not surprising that he produced no theory of the transformation of values (or prices of production) into monopoly prices. However, there is one very striking passage near the end of volume 3 which permits us to see that he was fully aware of the problem and to surmise some of the ways he would have handled it. In the chapter "The Semblance of Competition," he wrote that

> if the equalization of the surplus value into average profit meets with obstacles in the various spheres of production in the shape of artificial or natural monopolies, particularly of monopoly in land, so that a

monopoly price would be possible, which would rise above the price of production and above the values of the commodities affected by such a monopoly, still the limits imposed by the value of commodities would not be abolished thereby. The monopoly price of certain commodities would merely transfer a portion of the profit of the other producers of commodities to the commodities with a monopoly price. A local disturbance in the distribution of the surplus value among the various spheres of production would take place indirectly, but they would leave the boundaries of the surplus value itself unaltered. If a commodity with a monopoly price should enter into the consumption of the laborer, it would increase the wages and thereby reduce the surplus value if the laborer would receive the value of his labor power the same as before. But such a commodity might also depress wages below the value of labor power, of course only to the extent that wages would be higher than the physical minimum of subsistence. In this case the monopoly price would be paid by a deduction from the real wages (that is, from the quantity of use values received by the laborer for the same quantity of labor) and from the profit of other capitalists.[3]

Here Marx treats monopoly price not as a mere "empirical exchange relation" but as a modification of value and/or price of production which in no sense transcends "the limits imposed by the value of commodities." But this does *not* mean what many of today's younger Marxist economists seem to assume, that the presence or absence of monopoly makes no difference to the accumulation process. I believe it can be shown that in this crucially important respect, the modification of values brought about by the introduction of monopoly is quite different from the modification of values brought about by the introduction of unequal organic compositions of capital.

Marx does not analyze the effects of monopoly on the accumulation process, but the above passage provides valuable guides. Monopoly does not change the total *amount* of value produced— except indirectly to the extent that it affects the total volume of employment—but it does bring about a *redistribution* of value. Marx indicates that this can take two forms: first, a transfer of surplus value from competitive to monopolistic capitals; and second, a transfer of value from wages to surplus value. If we are talking about an isolated instance of monopoly, as Marx seems to be doing in the quoted passage, these effects would obviously be of negligible importance in relation to the economy as a whole. In this case it is not only justified but necessary to abstract from monopoly in the analysis of the accumulation process, which of course is what Marx does. But as soon as monopoly seizes hold of quantitatively significant sectors of the economy, this is obviously no longer so.

Then, following Marx's line of reasoning, we would have to say that the total of surplus value increases relative to the total of wages (this is also equivalent to an overall rise in the rate of surplus value), and that more of this larger total of surplus value is concentrated in fewer hands. Both of these changes would obviously tend to raise the rate of accumulation.

If we leave the matter there, however, we would be guilty of treating the problem in a static, and hence completely un-Marxian, way. We know that a fundamental aspect of the accumulation process is the concentration and centralization of capital which, at a certain stage, brings about the transformation of competitive capitalism into monopoly capitalism. But concentration and centralization do not cease at this point: both theory and historical experience teach that they form an integral and inseparable part of the whole accumulation process from beginning to end. What we have to deal with, therefore, is not simply an economy which contains *elements* of monopoly but an economy which is becoming *increasingly more monopolized.* And this creates powerful tendencies, which are not present in competitive capitalism, for the rates of surplus value and accumulation to rise (the latter not only because of the rising rate of surplus value but also because of the concentration of surplus value in larger and larger units).[4] These tendencies of course operate along with other tendencies of a social and technological character, and there is no a priori way to say which one or which combination will predominate. But I for one have no hesitation in saying that to refuse to take account of these "monopolistic" tendencies and the forces which generate them can only have the effect of paralyzing Marxian theory at a time when what is most needed is further to strengthen and develop it to cope with situations and problems which Marx did not and could not analyze a hundred years ago.

Let me now turn to another aspect of the literature typified by the works of Cogoy and Yaffe cited above, that is, a tendency toward what I consider to be the fetishization of the falling tendency of the rate of profit. Cogoy, for example, speaks approvingly (p. 398) of "a tendency of accumulation which rests on *(s'appuie sur)* the tendential fall of the rate of profit," a formulation which obviously transforms a deduction from the theory of accumulation into its foundation. And while the other authors in question may not be quite so specific, they nevertheless all treat the falling tendency of the rate of profit as the pivot around which the whole Marxian theory of accumulation and crises revolves. This subject deserves much fuller treatment than can be accorded to it in a brief essay: I will try only to indicate some of the main points which need elaboration.

Basically there are two issues here. The first has to do with the logic and interpretation of the theory of the falling tendency of the rate of profit as such. The second concerns its role in the overall theory of accumulation.

If we denote the rate of profit (the ratio of surplus value to total capital) by p, the rate of surplus value (the ratio of surplus value to variable capital) by s', and the organic composition of capital (the ratio of constant to variable capital) by o, then we have

$$p = \frac{s}{c + v}, s' = \frac{s}{v}, \text{ and } o = \frac{c}{v}.$$

Dividing the numerator and denominator in the expression for the rate of profit by v, we get

$$p = \frac{\dfrac{s}{v}}{\dfrac{c + v}{v}} = \frac{\dfrac{s}{v}}{\dfrac{c + v}{v}} = \frac{\dfrac{s}{v}}{\dfrac{c}{v} + 1} = \frac{s'}{o + 1}$$

from which it follows that the rate of profit varies directly with the rate of surplus value and inversely with the organic composition of capital.

The theory of the falling tendency of the rate of profit is given formal expression by Marx in part III of volume 3 of *Capital*, but the essential elements are worked out much more fully and satisfactorily in part IV ("Production of Relative Surplus Value") and part VII ("The Accumulation of Capital") of volume 1. The kernel of the argument is that capitalists in pursuing their unchanging goal of increasing the amount and rate of surplus value progressively mechanize the processes of production. The consequence is twofold: the amount of machinery per worker increases, and each worker operating machines processes more raw and auxiliary materials than a worker using more primitive methods. Both effects contribute to increasing the amount of constant capital relative to the amount of variable capital, that is, to raising the organic composition of capital. At the same time, of course, the productivity of the worker is increased, which means that he now reproduces the value of his labor power in less time and therefore has more time left over to work for the capitalist, which is only another way of saying that the rate of surplus value rises. The law of the falling tendency of the rate of profit asserts that in the long run there is a strong and persistent tendency for the rise in the organic composition of capital to outweigh the rise in the rate of surplus value in their opposite effects on the rate of profit, hence for the rate of profit to fall.

Why did Marx feel so sure that the organic composition of capital must rise relatively faster than the rate of surplus value? For my part, I have no doubt that the reason is that this is precisely what happened during the period of the industrial revolution beginning in the eighteenth century and still continuing at the time in the 1850s and 1860s when he was working on *Capital*.[5] The transition from *manu*facture to *machino*facture manifestly represented a quantum leap forward in the relative importance in industry of constant capital (or dead labor) compared to variable capital (or living labor). The rate of surplus value of course also increased sharply—this indeed is what the introduction of machinery was all about—but it was obvious to Marx, who was an extremely close student of all aspects of capitalist reality, that the relative increase in the organic composition had been the dominant trend in the preceding century. It was only natural, therefore, for him to assume that this would continue to be the case in the future.

What has to be emphasized, in contrast to the views of the present-day Marxist economists with whom we are here concerned, is that while it was perfectly natural for Marx to make this assumption—indeed, given what he knew, what other assumption could he possibly have made?—it was not something which was logically dictated by his theory of accumulation. From the point of view of the capitalist there is obviously no inherent virtue in increasing the organic composition of capital: he does it only because that is the way to increase the rate of surplus value. But if he can see ways to increase the rate of surplus value while at the same time economizing on constant capital, he will of course be delighted to avail himself of them. And whether or not this is possible depends not at all on the "concept of capital" (as Yaffe seems to believe) but on the direction and potentialities of technological change.[6] And in this respect the situation of an already *mechanized* economy is significantly different from that of the *mechanizing* economy of Marx's day. The problem for the capitalist is no longer so much that of substituting machines for hand labor but rather of substituting more productive machines and processes for less productive machines and processes all along the line.[7] And there is no a priori reason whatever for supposing that this must involve an increase (or a decrease either for that matter) in the organic composition of capital.

The only way this question can be decided is through the empirical study of capitalist practice, much as this view may offend those like Yaffe who wish to deduce everything from "pure" theory. And in this respect there are available by now numerous studies which demonstrate beyond a reasonable doubt that while the organic composition of capital rose in accordance with Marx's assumption through the nineteenth and into the twentieth century, for the last half-century the tendency has been in the other direction. Most of these studies have been carried out by bourgeois researchers using non-Marxian concepts and categories, with a consequent problem of translating their findings into the language of Marxism. But at least one, that of Joseph Gillman, is the work of a Marxist economist, and its findings are unequivocal: the organic composition of capital in the United States rose up to 1919, leveled off in the 1920s, and thereafter declined (except for the early 1930s when the trend was temporarily obliterated by the unprecedented severity of the Great Depression).[8] Gillman's statistical procedures have been justifiably criticized, but so far as I am aware no one has suggested that his basic findings would have been different had all the criticisms been fully met.

It is no part of my intention in these brief notes to suggest that from now on the organic composition of capital in the advanced capitalist countries can only fall, still less to undertake a comprehensive critique of Marx's law of the falling tendency of the rate of profit. But I do want to contend, emphatically, that underlying the entire argument of Cogoy, Yaffe, and others who think like them is an absurdly untenable notion, that is, that the capital accumulation process necessarily implies a runaway organic composition of capital, increasing without assignable limit and much more rapidly than the rate of surplus value.[9] Whatever else may be said about Gillman's statistics, they are surely accurate enough in indicating orders of magnitude to demolish this notion as totally unfounded. They show that in the United States during the three decades 1923-1952 the organic composition (c/v) fell from 4.2 to 3.6 (by 14 percent), while the rate of surplus value (s/v) rose from 121 to 132 (by 9 percent). Not only are these results contrary to the expectations of the falling tendency law; even more important from our present point of view, these ratios move within quite narrow limits and so cannot possibly sustain the grand generalizations which our authors wish to rest upon them.

In this connection—and here we come to the second point noted above for subsequent analysis—it is necessary to understand the argument which is being deduced from the theory of the falling tendency of the rate of profit in this recent literature. A comparison with the classics and Marx may be helpful.

The classical theory of the falling rate of profit rested on two supposed natural laws, the law of diminishing returns and the Malthusian population law. With wages relatively fixed at or near the subsistence minimum and with population expanding under the stimulus of capital accumulation, it is necessary to have recourse to progressively inferior land. The consequence is that more and more of the surplus product (over and above that which goes to the laborers) must be paid out by the capitalists to the landlords. Rent rises and the rate of profit falls, eventually to the point where total profit also begins to decline. At some point in this process the rate of profit falls so low that the incentive to further accumulation is extinguished. This was the nightmare which haunted the classical economists who, no less than Marx, regarded capitalism as quintessentially a process of capital accumulation. To be sure, John Stuart Mill tried to soften the blow by picturing the "stationary state" which would emerge when capital accumulation stopped as a rather more attractive condition than the frantically expanding capitalism of Victorian England, but in taking this tack Mill really only revealed his incipient apostasism from the ranks of loyal bourgeois ideologists. For them there was no doubt that the end of accumulation would be effectively the end of capitalism, and this is why classical political economy earned for itself the name of the "dismal science."

It is clear that Marx was fascinated by this aspect of the thought of the classical political economists. He wrote:

> Those economists who, like Ricardo, regard the capitalist mode of production as absolute, feel nevertheless that this mode of production creates its own limits, and therefore they attribute this limit not to production but to nature (in their theory of rent). But the main point in their horror over the falling rate of profit is the feeling that capitalist production meets in the development of productive forces a barrier which has nothing to do with the production of wealth as such; and this peculiar barrier testifies to the finiteness and the historical, merely transitory character of capitalist production. It demonstrates that this is not an absolute mode for the production of wealth, but rather comes in conflict with the further development of wealth at a certain stage.[10]

And again:

> The rate of profit is the compelling power of capitalist production, and only such things are produced as yield a profit. Hence the fright of the English economists over the decline of the rate of profit. That the bare possibility of such a thing should worry Ricardo shows his profound understanding of the conditions of capitalist production. The reproach moved against him, that he has an eye only to the development of the productive forces regardless of "human beings,"

regardless of the sacrifices in human beings and capital *values* incurred, strikes precisely at his strong point. The development of the productive forces of social labor is the historical task and privilege of capital. It is precisely in this way that it unconsciously creates the material requirements of a higher mode of production. What worries Ricardo is the fact that the rate of profit, the stimulating principle of capitalist production, should be endangered by the development of production itself. And the quantitative proportion means everything here. There is indeed something deeper than this hidden at this point, which he vaguely feels. It is here demonstrated in a purely economic way, that is, from a bourgeois point of view, within the confines of capitalist understanding, from the standpoint of capitalist production itself, that it has a barrier, that it is relative, that it is not an absolute but only a historical mode of production corresponding to a definite and limited epoch in the development of the material conditions of production.[11]

Much of Marx's discussion of the falling tendency of the rate of profit is in a similar vein. He regarded it as a significant and striking contradiction of capitalism that the increase in the productive power of labor should express itself in a manner tending to obstruct the unfettered development of the system. But he did not formulate a specific theory of crisis, let alone capitalist breakdown, on this basis; and he was careful to make the point that he was not *predicting* an actual fall in the rate of profit but was dealing only with a *tendency* which, like other tendencies, was opposed by various counteracting causes. For Marx, the falling tendency of the rate of profit was a manifestation of only one of capitalism's many contradictions, and I see no reason to believe that he would have considered the system to be any more viable had he foreseen that the future direction of technological change would mitigate or even eliminate this particular contradiction in the form which it assumed in the period of the transition from manufacture to modern industry.

Matters are different in the case of the theorists with whom we are here dealing. For them, the falling tendency of the rate of profit is the central contradiction of the accumulation process. Problems of realization and underconsumption (and/or overproduction) are *derived* from the theory of the falling tendency of the rate of profit and have no independent existence. The following passage from Cogoy's article is representative of the position held by all these authors:

If the increase in the organic composition is not counterbalanced by an increase [in the rate] of exploitation, the rate of profit will have a tendency to fall. If exploitation does not increase, it is no longer possible to produce a sufficient quantity of surplus value for the continued expansion of capital *(pour la mise en valeur du capital)*, and the conditions cease to be fulfilled which alone permit, in a regime of capitalism, production for consumption.

As Mattick demonstrates, Marx was not an underconsumption theorist, because the overproduction of goods and the decline of consumption are manifestations of the contradiction of capitalism rather than its causes. For Marx, in effect, the result of the process described above is certainly also a fall of consumption, but this effect is produced by a path different from that described by [Joan] Robinson. The starting point of the depression process is not, for Marx, on the side of consumption but on the side of the expansion *(valorisation)* of capital which cannot take place because of the tendential fall in the rate of profit.[12]

It would seem to follow from this line of reasoning that any questioning of the general and universal validity of the falling tendency of the rate of profit for all capitalist societies in all stages of their development is tantamount to saying that capitalism's contradictions are only relative and under certain conditions may even disappear. Since the authors in question obviously do not want to be forced into this position, they are obliged to assert the validity of the law of the falling tendency of the rate of profit in the most absolute way possible. And in the course of doing so they have recourse to some rather strange arguments. I quote Cogoy again:

> The formula for the rate of profit . . . shows that the fall in the rate of profit can be checked by raising [the rate of] exploitation or by maintaining the same organic composition. In other words, capitalist development can take place on condition that it seizes all opportunities to brake the fall in the rate of profit. Empirical data purporting to prove the maintenance of the rate of exploitation or of the organic composition therefore do not prove either the truth or the falsity of this law. They are rather the provisional result of the effort put forward by the system to maintain its variables in a constant relation or to make them vary according to precise proportions with a view to avoiding the fall in the rate of profit. Marx does not consider these variables as data which should be the starting point of the analysis, but rather as the resultants of the social forces which underlie them and which it is the task of analysis to reveal. In this sense the central task of modern Marxist political economy is to analyze how, up to a point, the social system of production provisionally organizes itself with a view to maintaining certain variables at the required level in conditions of rapid technological development with strong capital intensity. . . .
>
> The Marxist law of accumulation and of the tendential fall of the rate of profit . . . does not express empirically verifiable relations from which the analysis can begin. The fall of the rate of profit, seen as a tendency of the system to depart from the narrow path of growth can never manifest itself empirically except in crises. It is the negative rule

of capitalism; it represents the shoals to be avoided if capital is to be able to continue to be accumulated without shocks.[13]

It will be seen that Cogoy sets up a straw man by introducing the notion of the rate of exploitation and the organic composition as "empirically verifiable relations from which the analysis can begin." Those of us who question the universal (for capitalism) validity of the law of the falling tendency of the rate of profit obviously entertain no such ridiculous idea. Moreover, I imagine that most if not all of us would agree that these variables "are the resultants of the social forces which underlie them and which it is the task of analysis to reveal." But Cogoy should ask himself what these social forces are before assuming, as he evidently feels entitled to do, that they naturally and normally operate in such a way as to produce a falling rate of profit, for it is precisely this assumption which we maintain cannot be justified.

What, then, are these forces? They are many and interrelated in complicated ways: here we can do no more than mention the most important. First, there are the forces (including, according to Marx, historical and moral elements) which determine the value of labor power. Second, there are science and technology which govern the productivity of labor and the composition of capital. And third, there is the class struggle which controls the length of the working day and the intensity of labor, and which is also of course a codeterminant of the value of labor power. Marx studied all these forces, historically and empirically, on the basis of the data available to him more than a hundred years ago. He reached certain conclusions which he formulated as capitalism's "laws of motion," including the law of the falling tendency of the rate of profit and its counteracting causes.

The question I would like to put to Cogoy and the others who think like him is this: Do you maintain that these laws were established once and for all by Marx, that they are invariant to changes in the forces which underlie them, and that there is therefore no reason for us to follow Marx's example in studying capitalist reality and drawing our own conclusions from our studies?

If the answer is yes, if these theorists really believe that Marx said the last word on capitalism's laws of motion, then I for one can only say that I cannot take them seriously. Their Marxism has degenerated into a sterile orthodoxy which cannot help us to understand and deal with the problems of capitalism in the last third of the twentieth century.

On the other hand, if one rejects the notion that all of Marx's laws are as valid now as they were in his time, and if one concludes

on the basis of the data available to us today that the law of the
falling tendency of the rate of profit is no longer operative, then
one must conclude that an analysis of accumulation which, in
Cogoy's expression, "rests on the tendential fall of the rate of
profit" is doomed from the outset to futility. And it follows of
course that one must pursue a different course in seeking to unravel the contradictions of the accumulation process. How this can
be done was indicated very clearly by Marx himself in the same part
of volume 3 which is devoted to the falling tendency of the rate of
profit. Here is the relevant passage:

> The conditions of direct exploitation and those of the realization of
> surplus value are not identical. They are separated logically as well as
> by time and space. The first are only limited by the productive power
> of society, the last by the proportional relations of the various lines of
> production and by the consuming power of society. This last-named
> power is not determined either by the absolute productive power or
> by the absolute consuming power, but by the consuming power based
> on antagonistic conditions of distribution, which reduces the con-
> sumption of the great mass of the population to a variable minimum
> within more or less narrow limits. The consuming power is further-
> more restricted by the tendency to accumulate, the greed for an ex-
> pansion of capital and a production of surplus value on an enlarged
> scale. This is a law of capitalist production imposed by incessant revo-
> lutions in the methods of production themselves, the resulting depre-
> ciation of existing capital, the general competitive struggle, and the
> necessity of improving the product and expanding the scale of pro-
> duction for the sake of self-preservation and on penalty of failure.
> The market must therefore be continually extended so that its inter-
> relations and the conditions regulating them assume more and more
> the form of a natural law independent of the producers and become
> ever more uncontrollable. This internal contradiction seeks to bal-
> ance itself by an expansion of the outlying fields of production. But to
> the extent that the productive power develops, it finds itself at vari-
> ance with the narrow basis on which the condition of consumption
> rests. On this self-contradictory basis it is no contradiction at all that
> there should be an excess of capital simultaneously with an excess of
> population. For while a combination of these two would increase the
> mass of the produced surplus value, it would at the same time inten-
> sify the contradiction between the conditions under which this sur-
> plus value is produced and those under which it is realized.[14]

Some people have called the kind of theory toward which this
passage points "underconsumption." The designation is perhaps
unfortunate since it singles out for emphasis one strand of a complex whole. A better description might be to call it a theory which
centers on the contradiction between the capacity to produce and
the capacity to consume of a society organized on capitalist lines.

This contradiction—but not the falling tendency of the rate of profit—is in fact already implicit in the concept of capital as self-expanding value. Capitalism's utopia in a sense is a situation in which workers live on air, allowing their entire product to take the form of surplus value; and in which capitalists accumulate all their surplus value. This would represent the maximum conceivable rate of expansion of capital. But, alas, it would also represent the total abolition of value as such, since the aggregate of commodities produced, not entering into human consumption, would lack use value without which there can be no value.[15] The ultimate contradiction of capitalism is that it strives with might and main to reach this utopia, acting in the process as though use value were only an obstacle to its success; but the closer it seems to approach, the more imperatively does use value assert its character as the alter ego of the very value which is the object of the frantic efforts at expansion.[16]

This contradiction between the power of production and the power of consumption, between self-expanding value and contracting use value, vents itself in crises and stagnation which capitalism seeks to overcome not through producing what the workers need to live decent lives (that would be to negate its own nature), but by creating irrational and inhuman modes of consumption more in keeping with the spirit of capital.

I believe that it is along these lines that a fruitful analysis of the accumulation process must proceed. It will be noted that the central contradiction between the power to produce and the power to consume grows in severity with the increasing productivity of labor and the rising rate and volume of surplus value which characterize advanced capitalist societies. It is in this context that the monopolistic tendencies discussed above—acting to raise both the rate of surplus value and the rate of accumulation—take on their greatest significance. It is only under conditions of fully developed monopoly capitalism that lagging consuming power threatens to plunge society into a profound and permanent stagnation and hence gives rise to the most monstrous and destructive forms of forced consumption.

Notes

1. Mario Cogoy, "Les Théories Néo-Marxistes, Marx et l'Accumulation du Capital," *Les Temps Moderne* (September-October 1972): 396-427. Another recent example is David S. Yaffe, "The Marxian Theory of Crisis, Capital and the State," *Bulletin of the Conference of Socialist*

Economists (Winter 1972): 5-58. Both Cogoy and Yaffe pay tribute to the work of Paul Mattick, who perhaps deserves to be called the dean of this school of thought.

2. For a demonstration of this, see my *Theory of Capitalist Development* (first published in 1942; reprinted New York: Monthly Review Press, 1968), pp. 125-30. Only if there were a systematic tendency for the organic compositions of capital to develop differently in different sectors of the economy (means of production, wage goods, luxury goods) would it be possible to argue that the accumulation process in an economy of prices of production would differ significantly from that in an economy of values. I know of no suggestion, let alone proof, that there is any such systematic tendency for the organic composition to differ in different sectors. Unfortunately, some Marxist economists have never understood what is involved in the transformation of values into prices of production and have continued to treat it as a real process with important consequences for the functioning of the system. See, e.g., James F. Becker, "On the Monopoly Theory of Monopoly Capitalism," *Science & Society* (Winter 1971); and Michael A. Lebowitz, "The Increasing Cost of Circulation and the Marxian Competitive Model," *Science & Society* (Fall 1972).

3. *Capital*, vol. 3 (New York: International Publishers, 1976), pp. 1003-4.

4. It might be objected that monopoly prices cannot raise the rate of surplus value except through depressing wages below the value of labor power, and that this would be an essentially unstable and temporary effect. This objection, however, fails to view monopolization as a process which must be considered historically and as an integral part of the accumulation process as a whole. While at any particular time the value of labor power can be treated as a given, over a period of time it tends to rise. (There are several reasons for this, the most important of which are increasing costs of production of labor power and the workers' struggle to improve their standard of living.) In this context growing monopolization must be seen not as depressing the value of labor power but as impeding the rise in the value of labor power. To this extent it favors capital against labor by raising the rate of surplus value above what it otherwise would have been.

5. On Marx's relation to the industrial revolution, see "Karl Marx and the Industrial Revolution," in Paul M. Sweezy, *Modern Capitalism and Other Essays* (New York: Monthly Review Press, 1972), pp. 127-46.

6. On Yaffe, note the following statement: "What we have tried to show from an examination of the concept of capital is the necessity of . . . replacing on an increasing scale living labor by objectified (dead) labor. It follows from this that both the *technical composition of capital* and the *organic composition of capital* must increase in the process of capitalist production." (Yaffe, "The Marxian Theory of Crisis," p. 19.) There is not the slightest justification for this view. Nothing follows from the concept of capital except that capital is self-expanding value. This is the beginning of any serious analysis of capitalism, but no deductions or conclusions can be drawn from it without the introduction of

further assumptions which are either dreamed up out of nowhere (in the manner of present-day neoclassical economics) or are historically and empirically based, as in the case of Marxism. Yaffe and others who pride themselves on their Marxian orthodoxy are simply accepting and attributing universal validity to assumptions derived from nineteenth-century reality. That this is the way to stultify rather than develop Marxism as a social science seems to have escaped them altogether.

7. Marx was of course aware of this and if he had lived to complete volume 3 it is quite conceivable that he would have incorporated it into his analysis of the tendency of the rate of profit. See, for example, the following passage from volume 1 (which, it must be remembered, was completed after the texts which make up volume 3): "A part of the functioning constant capital consists of instruments of labor such as machinery, etc., which are not consumed, and therefore not reproduced or replaced by new ones of the same kind until after long periods of time. . . . If the productiveness of labor has, during the using up of these instruments of labor, increased (and it develops continually with the uninterrupted advance of science and technology), cheaper machines, tools, apparatus, etc., replace the old. The old capital is reproduced in a more productive form. . . . Like the increased exploitation of natural wealth by the mere increase in the tension of labor power, science and technology give capital a power of expansion independent of the given magnitude of the capital actually functioning. They react at the same time on that part of the original capital which has entered upon its stage of renewal. This, in passing into its new shape, incorporates gratis the social advance made while its old shape was being used up" (volume 1, pp. 663-64).

8. Joseph M. Gillman, *The Falling Rate of Profit* (New York: Cameron Associates, 1958). See especially the chart on p. 57 and the fold-out statistical table facing p. 61.

9. Yaffe, for example, attempts to support this notion in "The Marxian Theory of Crisis," pp. 24-26.

10. *Capital*, vol. 3, p. 283.

11. Ibid., pp. 304-5.

12. Cogoy, "Les Théories Néo-Marxistes," p. 406. There is a problem of translating into English such expressions as *mise en valeur* and *valorisation*. I assume that they are used as equivalents of Marx's *Verwertung* which is generally best rendered as "expansion of value" or in some cases "self-expansion of value."

13. Ibid., pp. 407-8.

14. *Capital*, vol. 3, pp. 286-87. Cf. also the powerful passage a few pages later which begins: "*The real barrier of capitalist production is capital itself.* It is the fact that capital and its self-expansion appear as the starting and closing point, as the motive and aim of production, that production is merely production for *capital*, and not vice versa, the means of production mere means for an ever-expanding system of the life process for the benefit of the *society* of producers" (p. 293).

15. To quote the opening paragraph of the *Critique of Political Economy:* "At first sight the wealth of society under the capitalist system presents itself as an immense accumulation of commodities, its unit being a single commodity. But every commodity has a twofold aspect, that of *use value* and *exchange value.*"

16. It is important to understand the radical difference between this theory and the shortage-of-effective-demand theory of the left-Keynesians. Cogoy correctly cites Joan Robinson as an exponent of the latter theory, quoting her ("Les Théories Néo-Marxistes," p. 403n) as follows: "The maldistribution of income restricts consumption, and so increases the rate of investment required to maintain prosperity, while at the same time it narrows the field of profitable investment, by restricting the demand for the consumption goods which capital can produce." (The quotation is from *An Essay on Marxian Economics,* 2nd ed. [London: Macmillan, 1966], p. 71.) The crux of the matter here is what the Keynesians consider to be maldistribution of income, clearly implying that matters can be put right by a suitable *re*distribution of income and thus opening the way for all sorts of reformist illusions. Apart from matters of formulation, this places the Keynesians squarely in the tradition of such liberal and social democratic reformers as Hobson in England and Conrad Schmidt in Germany. Marxism, on the other hand, has no place at all for the concept of maldistribution of income: the root of the problem lies in the very nature of capital as self-expanding value, and this cannot be changed except through the overthrow of the system and the establishment of entirely new relations of production.

John Bellamy Foster

Investment and Capitalist Maturity

Strange as it may seem, the concrete problem of the level of output (or employment) has not been a central concern of orthodox economic theory during most of its history. I think it is safe to say that prior to the Great Depression of the 1930s this omission was as much a product of limited historical vision as of any deliberate attempt at ideological mystification. But when we turn to the ongoing attack on full employment policy instigated by contemporary supply-side theory, what Marx called "the bad conscience and evil intent of the apologetic" immediately comes to the fore.[1]

In the nineteenth-century world of free competition and early industrialization, an all-around overaccumulation of capital, in the sense of a superabundance of potential surplus product available for new capital formation, appeared all but inconceivable. The unbridled competition that emerged with the advent of industrial capitalism meant that, in order simply to survive, the typical family firm had to utilize nearly all of the social surplus at its disposal to accumulate new capital stock. And the immense task of building means of production from scratch, during the industrial revolution, ensured that investment opportunities were not lacking in themselves. Hence, according to the usual Victorian "vision of capitalism," to quote Harry Magdoff and Paul Sweezy,

> . . . there was no need for a special theory of the demand side of the investment process. The presence of what was for all practical purposes an unlimited demand for additional means of production could be taken for granted. The determination of the actual rate of accumulation was therefore shifted entirely to the supply side of the equation.[2]

The formal expression of this unbalanced emphasis on supply was to be found in the dictum—known as "Say's Law,"—that supply creates its own demand. David Ricardo, the greatest of the liberal classical political economists, presented the matter in the following terms:

> No man produces, but with a view to consume or sell, and he never sells, but with an intention to purchase some other commodity which

may be immediately useful to him, or which may contribute to future production. By producing then, he necessarily becomes the consumer of his own goods, or the purchaser and consumer of the goods of some other person.[3]

On this basis, it was confidently asserted that a general crisis of overproduction was impossible, except as a temporary reflection of wage, price, and monetary imbalances, as long as the market was given free rein.

John Stuart Mill, the heir to the Ricardian legacy in England, and the foremost authority in mainstream political economy for a generation or more, provided a straightforward explanation of what was really at stake in the acceptance or rejection of Say's Law:

> The point is fundamental; any difference of opinion on it involves radically different conceptions of political economy, especially in its practical aspect. On the one view, we have only to consider how a sufficient production may be combined with the best possible distribution; but on the other there is a third thing to be considered—how a market can be created for produce, or how production can be limited to the capabilities of the market.[4]

Mill himself naturally stuck to the first of these views and therefore had no need to consider "the third thing" mentioned here— the problem of effective demand. Moreover, he provided what was to become (and still is) the standard liberal argument supposedly reconciling Say's Law with the actual existence of periodic crises. Commercial crises, he declared, were the result of "a glut of commodities" in relation to money, or "an undersupply of money," resulting from "excess speculation" and "a sudden recoil from prices extravagantly high." A contraction in the supply of credit was therefore the proximate cause of any slump, and simply mirrored a general decline of public confidence, the restoration of which would come about naturally as wages and prices fell. "It is a great error," Mill wrote, "to suppose . . . that a commercial crisis is the effect of a general excess of production."[5]

Criticism of Say's purported law (or "the metaphysical equilibrium of purchases and sales") "belongs," as Marx pointed out, "to the sphere of logic and not of economics."[6] The idea that products exchange for products, and that supply therefore always calls forth its own demand, is true only for a simple commodity economy in which there is no separation of purchase and sale for the individual producer, with use value, not exchange value, as the sole object of production. It is no accident that all of the early formulations of Say's Law (including the argument of Ricardo quoted above) were based upon examples taken from a world consisting entirely of self-employed proprietors, producing their own goods and exchanging them directly on the market for the necessary means of sustaining themselves and carrying on their trade. The situation thus conceived, in the minds of political economists, was little more than a highly developed barter economy, since money served only as a means of exchange, and not also as a device (store of value) through which the original allocation of capital for means of production, on the one hand, and the end realization of commodity values in final sales, on the other, were divided into entirely distinct acts, separated by both time and space. Under a developed capitalist system (or generalized commodity production), Marx pointed out, commodities are not (as in simple commodity production) produced directly by proprietors and then immediately exchanged (if all goes well) for the money necessary to purchase other use values (commodities) of equal worth (C–M–C); instead money capital is used to purchase the labor power and material capital required for the creation (over time) of added value in the form of new commodities, destined to be eventually exchanged for still more money capital, with a surplus above the original cost-price (M–C–M'). The presence of money (which does not automatically find its way into the spending stream), the clear separation of purchase and sale (for each individual capitalist), the necessity of realizing the full value of commodities (including the surplus portion), and the fact that enhanced exchange value is the prime motivation for production, all pose the *possibility* of a general interruption in the process of capitalist reproduction. It was an infantile exercise, Marx argued, to postulate a law for a developed capitalist economy on the logically inadmissible grounds of relations of production and exchange largely confined to precapitalist societies.[7]

In a word, Say's Law was devised by simply abstracting from the developed money form (and exchange value basis) of a capitalist economy. The way was then open to reconcile the "law" with the actual reality of recurrent crises by reintroducing money as the sole cause of the latter. This is what J. S. Mill and others proceeded to do. While Marx was arguing that the presence of money made a temporary breakdown in the reproduction process *possible* (the real causes lying in production itself), liberal economists claimed that crises were a sign of monetary imbalances, and not a reflection of actual overproduction in the so-called real economy, which was thought impossible. The error (as Marx explained and Keynes later rediscovered) lay in viewing money as a "neutral" phenomenon.[8]

To establish the formal possibility of a break in the accumulation process is obviously only the first step in dealing with the overall problem of economic disruptions. The inevitability of cyclical crises under capitalism arises out of the class composition of social output. This is most clearly revealed, in my judgment, in the case of "underconsumption" (or the tendency toward overexploitation intrinsic to capitalism, which, when accompanied by underinvestment, manifests itself as a crisis of overaccumulation). According to Marx,

> the ultimate reason for all real crises remains the poverty and restricted consumption of the masses as opposed to the drive of capitalist production to develop the productive forces as though only the absolute consuming power of society constituted their limit.[9]

Why "the ultimate reason"? The answer implicit in the above statement, I think, is that this is simply the other side of the ultimate rationale of capitalist production. The realization of value (and surplus value) through the sale of commodities is, as Marx wrote at another point,

> . . . restricted by the tendency to accumulate, the drive to expand capital and produce surplus value on an extended scale. This is the law for capitalist production, imposed by incessant revolutions in the methods of production themselves, by the depreciation of existing capital always bound up with them, by the general competitive struggle and the need to improve production and expand its scale merely as a means of self-preservation and under penalty of ruin. . . . But the more productiveness develops, the more it finds itself at variance with the narrow basis on which the conditions of consumption rest.[10]

Crises can arise for capital in any number of ways, including underexploitation (or underaccumulation) at the level of production; but the last cause, in a logical sense, must mirror capitalism's own necessity, its drive to increase the productivity of labor power, and to appropriate the resulting social surplus, at an unlimited pace—as if the level of consumption imposed no constraint whatsoever on the ability to realize the full value of potential output.

To be sure, the underconsumption of the masses, even where the disparity between wages and potential surplus product is very great, does not inherently pose an immediate obstacle to capitalist reproduction. A simplified model of the class composition of social output (as envisioned in Marx's reproduction schemes) should serve to clarify what is, in truth, a very complicated problem.

Let us assume, for the moment, that the wages of workers are spent entirely on consumption and that the entire social accumulation fund in the hands of capital (the sum of depreciation reserves and surplus product) is automatically invested in new capital stock.

This is consistent with the "ideal" concept of capitalism (in which Say's Law "applies"), since all capital would be fully employed.[11]

It should be readily apparent that a situation of this sort could only persist for any length of time where historical conditions were extraordinarily favorable for capital formation. Any continual plowing back of profits into new investment would mean that means of production (department 1 in the Marxian reproduction schemes, the demand for which comes entirely out of gross profits) would expand very much faster than articles of consumption (or department 2, the demand for which according to our simplifying assumptions is derived entirely from wages). Investment, in other words, would grow far more rapidly than consumption. This, in fact, is an extreme example of the basic pattern of every accumulation boom. But it is a self-annihilating process. Sooner or later (depending on historical conditions determining the degree to which the investment process is self-sustaining) the means of production are built up to such a prodigious extent that a social disproportionality develops between the capacity to produce and the corresponding capacity to consume. A crisis of overaccumulation (underconsumption, overproduction, and underinvestment) then occurs.

This broad path of development, it must be understood, is inherent in the class composition of social output, which is the basis of all capital accumulation. The demand for capital goods is equal to reinvested gross profits, while the demand for wage goods (the great bulk of the consumption goods sector) equals total wages. Rapid accumulation requires a much faster rate of growth in the former than in the latter, but this eventually generates inordinate productive capacity in relation to effective demand, as the gap between the capacity to produce and the capacity to consume widens—although once again it is necessary to stress that the degree to which this contradiction actually surfaces depends on the relative autonomy of investment from final consumption characteristic of any particular phase of capitalist development.

The historical record, I think, tells us that throughout the nineteenth century, overaccumulation in this sense, while surfacing in periodic crises of overproduction, was clearly of secondary importance. As already indicated, this can be traced to two transitory historical circumstances: the process of initial industrialization, involving the building of means of production virtually from scratch, and the prevalence, at the same time, of atomistic competition. Given these conditions, capital formation, or the savings-and-investment process, was not hindered for long periods of time by a lack of demand. Both outlets for investment and a powerful incentive to invest ("as a means of self-preservation and under penalty of ruin," as Marx put it in the statement quoted above) could be pretty much assumed as the normal condition of things.[12] Individual capitals, moreover, had so little control over the process that a crisis, when it occurred, usually took the form of a general glut of commodities and bankruptcies across the board, rather than the carefully managed curtailments of output, employment, and investment that we have come to expect today.

It is not surprising, therefore, that nineteenth- (and early twentieth-) century economists generally assumed that the availability of savings (the social accumulation fund) determined investment, and hence the pace of capital accumulation as a whole. Nor does it give us much occasion for surprise that establishment economists tried to give this a rigid, formal expression in Say's Law, doing violence to both logic and history in the process. A theory of the level of output as such was not considered necessary; and it fit well with the broad theoretical orientation and apologetic purpose of economic orthodoxy to discount altogether the issue of effective demand—the "third thing" mentioned by John Stuart Mill.

In the eighth and final edition of his *Principles of Economics,* which appeared in 1920, Alfred Marshall argued for Say's Law on the basis of Mill's earlier discussion, tracing crises to lack of confidence and want of credit (following a period of overconfidence and over-proliferation of credit).[13] In his book *Unemployment* (written in 1913), A. C. Pigou advanced the notion that the full employment guarantee, implicit in Say's Law, was virtually assured as long as wage rates were "perfectly plastic."[14] A further prop provided for Say's dictum, or "the law of the preservation of purchasing power," at the turn of the century (by Pigou and others) was the idea that the rate of interest, as long as it corresponded to the so-called natural rate, which was supposed to equilibrate supply and demand for savings, assured that all available savings would be channeled into new investment. Such was the general state of mainstream economics with regard to the question of output, at the time of the 1929 crash (and for some time afterward).

The Great Depression represented a new situation but it took professional economists some seven or eight years to even begin to appreciate the fact. What drove the matter home was the downturn of 1937-38, the sharpest cyclical decline in U. S. history up to that time, with unemployment rising in a matter of a few months from its 1937 Depression low of 14.3 percent to 19.0 percent in 1938. This was a severe contradiction occurring while the economy was already seriously depressed. It was labeled "the recession of 1937," and it was something new under the sun. Prior to this economists had taken it for granted that the economy, once it resumed its upward course (as it did in 1933), would gradually rise to the point of full recovery. The main concern in the 1930s was that things seemed to be happening very slowly. But in 1937 the economy turned down again when it was still far short of recovery. There seemed to be no accounting for this from the traditional standpoint of automatic investment (not to mention Say's Law in the strict sense), since savings have been clearly rising. And money capital was available to potential investors at nominal rates.[15]

It was in this context that John Maynard Keynes' magnum opus, *The General Theory of Employment, Interest and Money* (1936), began to have considerable influence (the initial reviews had been quite negative), though "the New Economics"—as applied Keynesianism was sometimes called—did not really take hold (in the United States at least) until after the intervention of World War II. *The General Theory* was a massive attack on Say's Law by one of the most respected economists of the day. In its essentials, it recognized that the gap (equal to intended savings) between consumption and full employment income was not automatically filled, on the demand side, by new investment. Despite the best wishes of neoclassical economists, the rate of interest did not automatically equilibrate intended investment with intended savings.[16] A contraction in over-all income, due to oversavings (ex ante) and underinvestment, would invariably bring total savings (ex post) back into conformity with actual investment, but under conditions of "unemployment equilibrium," hitherto deemed impossible (by mainstream theory). Not only was full employment not inevitable, but it might, Keynes suggested, remain beyond reach indefinitely, without the aid of government spending.

The refutation of Say's Law, in the strict sense, was only the first step in raising the larger historical question of capitalist evolution. In addition to the realization that it was not acceptable to ignore the demand side of the investment process, it also became evident that the appropriate inference with respect to causality was the complete opposite of the traditional view. Investment generated savings, rather than the other way around. The problem of capital formation (or investment in new productive capacity) had to be dealt with directly. Herein lay the real theoretical significance of the Keynesian revolution.

During the stagnation debate of the late 1930s, the larger historical issue of investment, in this sense, was at the forefront of economic discussion. Alvin Hansen, often credited with having brought the economics of Keynes to the United States, followed the lead of Keynes himself in attributing investment shortfalls to the gradual emergence of capitalist "maturity." With the United States in mind, Hansen pointed to such factors as the closing of the frontier; the downward drift in the rate of population growth; the gradual consolidation of the vast national transportation network; and the growing tendency for business to implement capital-saving innovations. All of this seemed to suggest that much of the force of "autonomous" (non-income-induced) investment outlets had been spent.

Hansen's notion of secular stagnation, though largely undeveloped, represented a bold departure from the orthodox outlook. However, economists, accustomed to viewing capital scarcity as an inherent trait of the capitalist system (and of all economic systems, for that matter), found Hansen's ideas, in this respect, unconvincing. The most penetrating criticism came from Joseph Schumpeter, Hansen's colleague at Harvard, who endeavored to counter Hansen's theory with an alternative interpretation of long-run stagnation, stressing the growth of an antibusiness climate, long cycles in the introduction of major innovations, and a gradual weakening of industrial entrepreneurship.[17]

What emerged most clearly from this debate, I think, was the extent to which rapid growth—particularly in a more developed capitalist environment—depended on the appearance of "epoch-making innovations" (like the steam engine, railroad, and automobile), and new frontiers for investment in general that did not stem from the "pure logic" of the capitalist economy itself, but were bound up instead with the fact that capitalism was, by its very nature, a changing order.[18]

Although Hansen no doubt overemphasized the degree to which powerful autonomous investment stimuli were a more or less permanent missing ingredient of the modern economy, he was, I am convinced, on very solid ground in his basic understanding of the dilemma of maturity. Here it is useful to quote from an article that he wrote on the subject shortly after the Korean war:

> In the early nineteenth century nearly all gross investment had to be financed out of current *net* saving. On the one side the capital stock was scarce and the marginal efficiency of capital [expected profits on new investment] was high. On the other side the main source of capital was current *net* saving. Under these circumstances the rate of growth of capital accumulation was limited, not by demand, but by the amount of current net saving that could be pumped out of the community. Such a society tended to draft, to the full, all its productive resources. Such a society was able to "generate its own steam." There was no problem of inadequate effective demand. . . .

Eventually, however, the society acquired a vast accumulated stock of capital. The society was no longer capital poor. The marginal efficiency of capital tended to decline. The bulk of gross investment was fed from depreciation funds. Net savings were no longer the primary source of investment funds. Net savings thus found investment outlets less readily available than in the early periods when net savings were practically the sole source of investment funds.[19]

It is this situation that makes investment, or the demand side of the accumulation process, such a critical problem for advanced capitalist economies. Understood in Marxian terms, the issue of maturity appears historically, as Paul Sweezy has written, "when Department I [producing means of production] is sufficiently built up to supply all the needs of replacing worn-out means of production, and, in addition, to provide the inputs for an ample expansion of Department II [producing articles of consumption]. . . ."[20] Beginning early in the twentieth century, it was no longer as easy, as it had been during the "maturing capitalism" of the nineteenth century, for department 1 to advance, for extended periods of time, at a faster rate than department 2, with the former largely feeding itself through the insatiable demand for new investment characteristic of the early phases of industrialization. The Great Depression of the 1930s, I believe, can be best understood as a crisis of overaccumulation, reflecting this historical transformation in the marginal efficiency of investment, as the economic order evolved from conditions of capital scarcity to those of capital abundance.[21]

The tendency toward secular stagnation in modern capitalism, however, is much more deeply rooted in the system than even these general observations on an economic "climacteric," separating the youthful days of capitalism from its middle age, would suggest. Also involved is a transformation in the underlying conditions of competition. The question of economic maturity is inextricably bound up with the rise of monopoly capitalism at the turn of the century.

Considering its overriding importance, the transition from competitive to monopoly capitalism, or the rise of big business, is one of the more neglected aspects of contemporary historical analysis. Marxist theorists have been disinclined to look closely at the concrete history of this metamorphosis due to the power and accuracy of Marx's own vision, which emphasized the twofold process of concentration and centralization of production, the former representing the growth in scale of individual enterprises, the latter the bringing together of individual capitals already formed into "a huge mass in a single hand."[22] The more specific issue of the key institutional forms of this takeover can be telescoped, I believe, into the following points: (1) emergence of a market for industrial securities and a more elaborate financial environment; (2) growth of giant, multidivisional firms with both national and international spheres of influence; (3) introduction of scientific management of the labor process; (4) demise of internecine competition; (5) accelerated export of money capital; (6) intensification of militarism and imperialism; and (7) expansion of state activity—having the effect of (a) enabling the monopolistic victors in the industrial shakedown process to consolidate their gains through the development of a "regulatory" system, (b) backing-up and extending the imperial aspirations of large corporate interests, (c) defending concentrated capital against the onslaught of industrial unionism, and (d) eventually serving as a bulwark for the threatened macroeconomy. With the consolidation of monopoly capitalism, secular inflation and a widening underemployment gap emerged as built-in structural contradictions of the system.

The main variable in the new equation, forming the historical precondition for the whole dilemma of maturity, and lying beneath the surface of the new order of monopoly capitalism, was the highly successful battle of the employers and an army of industrial engineers to put the management of the labor process on a scientific footing, in other words, the implementation of Taylorism. In the words of Harry Braverman, "the crucial developments in the processes of production [associated with Taylorism, and accompanying the scientific-technical revolution] date precisely from the same period as monopoly capitalism."[23] It was this, more than anything else, that made the rise of monopoly capital possible and inevitable.

Alfred Chandler, the Pulitzer Prize-winning business historian, tells us that Andrew Carnegie, the captain of industry behind the formation of U. S. Steel, was concerned "almost wholly with prime costs" (i.e., chiefly with labor and raw material costs at the point of production). "He and his associates appear to have paid almost no attention to overhead and depreciation."[24] Keeping this in mind, the following quote (also from Chandler) is instructive:

> Technological and organizational innovation paid off. Carnegie's prices were lower and his profits higher than any other producer in the industry. . . . In 1878 Carnegie's rail mill recorded a profit of $401,000 or 31 percent on equity. It rose in the next two years to $2.0 million. As the business grew, so did its profits. At the end of the 1890s Carnegie's larger and more diversified enterprise had profits of $20 million. For the year 1900 they stood at $40 million. By becoming a pioneer in the methods of mass production in steel, Carnegie

quickly accumulated, as John D. Rockefeller had done in petroleum, one of the largest fortunes the world had ever seen.[25]

The rise of the giant firm and scientific management were thus inseparably linked. The growth in firm size made the implementation of industrial engineering cost efficient, becoming the main source of the "economies of scale" of big business.[26] The prodigious profitability of this form of industrial organization enormously accelerated the transition from freely competitive capitalism to the new regime of monopolistic competition.[27]

Once the effects of monopoly capital on the overall economy are taken into account, it becomes readily apparent that there are "behavioral" disincentives with respect to capital formation built into the modern economy, quite apart from the adequacy of investment outlets in themselves.

In the early 1930s, the Polish economist Michal Kalecki constructed a model of capital accumulation, utilizing both the Marxian conception of the class composition of social output, and the radical analysis of monopoly capitalism that anticipated all of the essential features of the Keynesian theory of output.[28] Based on the implications of Kalecki's analysis, Josef Steindl made a major effort to examine the secular trend of the U. S. economy, in *Maturity and Stagnation in American Capitalism* (1952). In 1966 *Monopoly Capital* by Paul Baran and Paul Sweezy appeared, constituting both a more popular version of the Kalecki-Steindl analysis, and an attempt to incorporate it within the larger historical "problematic," utilizing insights from Marx, Veblen, Hansen, and Schumpeter.

These works emphasized the fact that monopoly capital constantly strives to control the expansion of productive capacity and the implementation of new innovations. In the face of a deficiency in effective demand, monopolistic corporations generally cut back on output, employment, and investment, rather than reducing prices (and hence profit margins), as would be the case in a freely competitive system. But demand deficiencies become increasingly serious without an increasing rate of investment by monopoly capital itself, since the potential surplus product available to the giant corporations continues to rise relative to the total income of society. Under these circumstances, unemployment and unproductive (or unreproductive) employment can be expected to rise. The savings potential of society increasingly leaves its "statistical trace" in economic waste, including actual unemployment and excess capacity.[29] By maintaining high profit margins (and excessive rates of surplus value) monopoly capital tends to induce a widening underemployment gap, holding down the rate of growth and the proportion of potential surplus product realized.

Such is the underlying tendency of the modern economy, which can be offset, to some extent, by the appearance of major capital absorbing innovations or massive injections of government spending (for the most part, inflationary in character). It was the latter, during the years of U. S. imperial hegemony, that constituted the decisive factor staving off stagnation. Virtually alone in the 1950s, Paul Baran argued that applied Keynesianism, or the doctrine of spending, would eventually produce an enormous inflationary overhang, on top of an economy with a deep structure of stagnation, leading to even greater contradictions for the system as a whole. And so it occurred, with the sudden onset of stagflation in the early 1970s.[30]

Many economists on the left, together with the vast majority of liberal theorists, now argue that the present economic crisis can be traced—at least as far as the triggering factors are concerned—to a slowdown in productivity growth and a rising wage share in national income.[31] I do not think the data upon which these conclusions are based are particularly meaningful in themselves. On the misuse of productivity measurements, five points should be noted. (1) Long-run comparisons of average productivity for the entire economy are invariably distorted by changes in the composition of production. (2) The statistics on productivity are clearly of dubious value with respect to the greater number of workers in the economy. How does one measure the productivity of construction workers, transport employees, teachers, medical workers, clerical staff, sales clerks, advertising and marketing personnel, and so on? In all of these cases the conditions governing output per hour of work vary enormously, and mere expansion of "productivity," in the strict economic sense, could be interpreted as meaning any number of things (therefore signifying very little). (3) Available data provide no legitimate basis for distinguishing between the productivity of socially necessary productive workers, on the one hand, and socially unproductive (or unreproductive) workers, on the other. (4) Use of money-value based productivity indexes by the Bureau of Labor Statistics masks (and often falsifies) movements in physical output per human hour. (5) An alteration in the amplitude of "average productivity," to the extent that it indicates anything, mainly reflects shifts in the level of output (or employment). Thus the rate of productivity growth in the crucial manufacturing sector, according to existing statistics, did not slow down until after the level of production and capacity utilization began its secular decline in 1969.[32] Ironically, it might, therefore, be argued that the single most important factor behind the "decline" in the rate of increase in manufacturing productivity (as conventionally measured), insofar as this simply mirrored the drop in overall output, was the devastating defeat imposed on the U. S. imperial state by the Vietnamese peasantry.[33]

The statistical basis for contending that there is an increasing share of wages in national income is perhaps even more absurd. At best, this can only be argued for the Vietnam war period (1965-73), though this too remains doubtful.[34] Still, even if this was so, it would make more sense to attribute this situation to the war economy itself than to "slack workers" and underexploitation. In addition, it has long been recognized by national income analysts that the aggregate wage and profit shares in national accounts tells us nothing about the underlying profit margins at the point of production, since the former reflect (among other things) the utilization of capital, the composition of the workforce, and the level of output.[35] The fallacy of post hoc reasoning is well known.

If we look at the productivity and wage share issues historically the root dilemma stands out. Since the consolidation of monopoly capitalism early in the twentieth century, the main challenge of the advanced capitalist order has been to absorb a vast productive potential. In a very real sense, it can be argued that what is needed is less, not more, productivity. This is a paradox, not of analysis, but of the capitalist system itself.

Where the wage share is concerned, we need only note that it makes more sense *historically* to attribute the long-run stability (and any short-term increase) in the wage share in national income to a rising, rather than a falling, rate of exploitation. As Paul Baran wrote:

> A constant, and indeed a rising, share of labor in national income can coexist with rising surplus simply because the increment of surplus assumes the form of an increment of *waste*. And since the "production" of waste involves labor, the share of labor may well grow if the share of waste in national output is increasing. Treating productive and unproductive labor indiscriminately as *labor* and equating profits with surplus obviously obscure this very simple proposition.[36]

The proliferation of waste is the chief means by which monopoly capital compensates for deficiencies in effective demand. But this tends to overload the system. A rising rate of exploitation and the resulting "underconsumption of the masses"—to the extent that this is accompanied by (and partly engenders) underinvestment—leads to overconsumption (the wasting away of potential surplus product) by capital, and thus to a failure of net realized profit ratios to live up to the promise of gross profit margins. It is no wonder then that corporations, in search of "a killing," increasingly resort to the realm of pure financial speculation, leaving production far behind.[37]

The liberal supply-side theory that now dominates state policy, of course, goes much further than merely tracing the problem to such false demons as low productivity and high wages. It amounts to nothing less than the ghostly resurrection of the practical implications (if not always the strict theoretical formulation) of Say's Law. Once again it is the prevailing wisdom that savings automatically generate new investment, provided only that business has access to sufficient capital and confidence in the future course of events. But capital, we are told, is in short supply and business is frightened off, due to an overly obstreperous labor force and the "crowding out" of the private sector by the state. The solution: redistribution of income from the poor to the rich, a reduction in state assistance to the needy, an open assault on organized labor and national minorities, and a mammoth upsurge in military expenditure to finance a renewed policy of manifest imperialism. Up until the time of the Great Depression, adherence to Say's Law was tragic; today it is a farce.

Notes

1. Karl Marx, *Capital,* vol. 1 (New York: International Publishers, 1967), p. 15 (author's preface).
2. Harry Magdoff and Paul M. Sweezy, "Listen, Keynesians!" *Monthly Review* 8, no. 34 (January 1983): 2.
3. David Ricardo, *On the Principles of Political Economy and Taxation* (Cambridge: Cambridge University Press, 1951), p. 290.
4. John Stuart Mill, *Principles of Political Economy* (New York: Longmans, Green, 1904), p. 340.
5. Ibid. Also Alvin H. Hansen, *A Guide to Keynes* (New York: McGraw-Hill, 1953), pp. 11-20.
6. Karl Marx, *A Contribution to the Critique of Political Economy* (Moscow: Progress Publishers, 1970), p. 96.
7. Karl Marx, *Theories of Surplus Value,* vol. 2 (Moscow: Progress Publishers, 1968), pp. 492-517.
8. It is noteworthy that Keynes used the Marxian formula for the circuit of productive capital (M–C–M'), and made explicit reference to the "realization" problem, in his lectures on "the monetary theory of production" (which became "the general theory") during the early 1930s. See Dudley Dillard, "A Monetary Theory of Production: Keynes and

the Institutionalists," *Journal of Economic Issues* 14, no. 2 (June 1980): 257, 272.

9. *Capital*, vol. 3, ch. 30.

10. Ibid., ch. 15, section 1.

11. Although this would conform to full employment by ideal capitalist standards (full capacity utilization), a substantial reserve army would still remain. In fact, certain social liberal economists have gone so far as to label the level of unemployment that would exist under these conditions "Marxian unemployment." See Adrian Wood, *A Theory of Profits* (Cambridge: Cambridge University Press, 1975), pp. 124–28.

12. See Paul M. Sweezy, *Four Lectures on Marxism* (New York: Monthly Review Press, 1981), pp. 37-38; Magdoff and Sweezy, "Listen, Keynesians!"; and Francois Crouzet, "Capital Formation in Great Britain during the Industrial Revolution," in Crouzet, ed., *Capital Formation in the Industrial Revolution* (London: Methuen, 1972), pp. 162-220.

13. Alfred Marshall, *Principles of Economics* (London: Macmillan, 1949), pp. 591–92.

14. A.C. Pigou, *Unemployment* (London: Williams and Norgate, no date, preface signed 1913), pp. 75-93.

15. Magdoff and Sweezy, "Listen, Keynesians!" p. 5.

16. Keynes attacked the traditional interest-rate theory by demonstrating that interest was determined by supply and demand for means of payment (based on liquidity preference, and the speculative demand for money in general), rather than simply reflecting supply and demand for "capital" (savings/investment) as previously thought. This was basically consistent with the views of Marx and Veblen. See Michal Kalecki, "Some Remarks on Keynes' Theory," *Australian Economic Papers* 21, no. 39 (December 1982): 250; Dudley Dillard, "A Monetary Theory of Production"; and Ken Woodward, "Finance Capital: A Review," *Social Concept* 1, no. 1 (May 1983): 55-70

17. For more complete discussions of this debate see Paul M. Sweezy, "Why Stagnation?" *Monthly Review* 34, no. 2 (June 1982): 1-10; William E. Stoneman, *A History of the Economic Analysis of the Great Depression in America* (New York: Garland Publishing, 1979); and John Bellamy Foster, "Understanding the Significance of the Great Depression," *Studies in Political Economy*, no. 11 (Summer 1983): 177-96.

18. See Paul A. Baran and Paul M. Sweezy, *Monopoly Capital* (New York: Monthly Review Press, 1966), pp. 219-22, 238-39.

19. Alvin H. Hansen, "Growth or Stagnation in the American Economy," *Review of Economics and Statistics*, November 1954, pp. 411-12.

20. Sweezy, *Four Lectures on Marxism*.

21. See Harold G. Vatter, "The Atrophy of Net Investment and Some Consequences for the U.S. Mixed Economy," *Journal of Economic Issues* 16, no. 1 (March 1982): 237-53; Harry Magdoff and Paul M. Sweezy, "Supply-Side Theory and Capital Investment," *Monthly Review* 34, no. 11 (April 1983): 1-9; and Michael A. Bernstein, *Long-Term Economic Growth and the Problem of Recovery in American Manufacturing: A Study of*

the Great Depression in the United States, Ph.D. diss., Yale University, 1982.

22. Marx, *Capital,* vol. 1, ch. 25, section 2.

23. Harry Braverman, *Labor and Monopoly Capital* (New York: Monthly Review Press, 1974).

24. Alfred Chandler, *The Visible Hand* (Cambridge, MA: Harvard University Press, 1977), p. 268. See also Richard B. DuBoff and Edward S. Herman, "Alfred Chandler's New Business History: A Review," *Politics and Society* 10, no. 1 (1980).

25. Ibid., p. 269.

26. See Richard Edwards, *Contested Terrain: The Transformation of the Workplace in the Twentieth Century* (New York: Basic Books, 1979), pp. 48-49.

27. It is reasonable to argue, as David Noble does in his *America by Design* (New York: Oxford University Press, 1979), pp. 260-62, that the rise of big business preceded the modern movement for managerial control, and was mainly motivated by a desire to limit competition. But it was the introduction of the new managerial techniques, as Noble also notes, that made the consolidation of concentrated capitalism possible.

28. See especially Michal Kalecki, *Essays in the Theory of Economic Fluctuations* (New York: Russell and Russell, 1939).

29. Baran and Sweezy, *Monopoly Capital,* p. 218.

30. Paul A. Baran, *The Longer View* (New York: Monthly Review Press, 1969), pp. 115-38; *The Political Economy of Growth* (New York: Monthly Review Press, 1957), pp. 120-29; Paul M. Sweezy, "Baran and the Danger of Inflation," *Monthly Review* 26, no. 7 (December 1974): 11-14; and John Bellamy Foster, "Marxian Economics and the State," *Science & Society* 45, no. 3 (Fall 1982): 257-83.

31. See, for example, Samuel Bowles, "The Post-Keynesian Capital-Labor Stalemate," *Socialist Review* 12, no. 5 (September-October 1982): 45-72; Samuel Bowles, David M. Gordon, and Thomas E. Weisskopf, *Beyond the Waste Land* (New York: Anchor Press, 1983); and Arthur M. Okun and George L. Perry, "Notes and Numbers on the Profits Squeeze," *Brookings Papers on Economic Activity,* no. 3 (1970): 466-73.

32. *Monthly Labor Review,* various issues; *Economic Report of the President, 1983,* p. 213.

33. See Harry Magdoff, "The Purpose and Method of Measuring Productivity," *Journal of the American Statistical Association* 34, no. 206 (June 1939): 309-18; "The Economist's New Clothes," *The Nation,* March 27, 1982, pp. 359-61; and "A Statistical Fiction," *The Nation,* July 10-17, 1982, pp. 47-48; Harry Magdoff and Paul M. Sweezy, *The Deepening Crisis of U.S. Capitalism* (New York: Monthly Review Press, 1981), pp. 115-26, 169-77; Baran, *The Political Economy of Growth,* p. xxin; Solomon Fabricant, *Basic Facts on Productivity Change* (New York: National Bureau of Economic Research, 1959), pp. 10-22; Victor Perlo, "The False Claim of Declining Productivity and Its Political Use," *Science & Society* 46, no. 3 (Fall 1982): 284-327; and Joan Robinson, *Essays in the Theory of Employment* (London: Macmillan, 1937), pp. 82-101.

34. Bowles, Gordon, and Weisskopf, *Beyond the Waste Land,* pp. 49 and 422.

35. See W. S. Woytinsky et al., *Employment and Wages in the United States* (New York: The Twentieth Century Fund, 1953), pp. 40-5, 63-81. I am grateful to Gabriel Kolko for referring me to Woytinsky's work.

36. Baran, *The Political Economy of Growth*, p. xxi.

37. See Hyman P. Minsky, *Can "It" Happen Again?* (Armonk, N.Y.: M. E. Sharpe, 1982), especially pp. 14-58; Harry Magdoff and Paul M. Sweezy, "Production and Finance," *Monthly Review* 35, no. 1 (May 1983): 1-13, "Unemployment: The Failure of Private Enterprise," *Monthly Review* 35, no. 2 (June 1983): 8-9; Jacob Morris, "Underconsumption and the General Crisis: Gillman's Theory," *Science & Society* 47, no. 3 (Fall 1983): 323-29; and Henryk Szlajfer, "Economic Surplus and Surplus Value: An Attempt at Comparison," *Review of Radical Political Economics* 15, no. 1 (Spring 1983): 107-30.

Part II

INCOME DISTRIBUTION
AND INFLATION

The essays in Part II are concerned with class struggle and income distribution in advanced capitalism. In his last major discussion of his general theory of income distribution and capitalist dynamics, Michal Kalecki demonstrates that an increase in money wages in a monopolistically competitive economy would tend to raise employment in the system as a whole, due to its effect on the degree of monopoly and aggregate consumption. The following selection by Maurice Dobb considers some difficult theoretical questions posed by Marx's wage theory when considered in a modern capitalist context, with particular emphasis on Kalecki's contribution. Howard Sherman's essay discusses class struggle, effective demand, inflation, and income distribution in a cyclical context, offering a critique of contemporary profit-squeeze theories. Harry Magdoff, in the last selection, provides a long historical perspective on the problem of inflation and its structural basis within the system.

Michal Kalecki

CLASS STRUGGLE AND THE
DISTRIBUTION OF NATIONAL INCOME

Until fairly recently it was generally accepted that if wages are raised profits decline *pro tanto*. Even though in the analysis of other phenomena Say's Law was not adhered to, at least not strictly, in this case the preservation of purchasing power was not put to doubt. And the analysis of increase or reduction in wage rates dealt with the physical consequences of this absolute shift from profits to wages or vice versa. In the case of the rise in wage rates, the reconstruction of capital equipment in line with the higher spending on wage goods and lower outlays on investment and capitalists' consumption was emphasized, as well as the tendency to higher unemployment as a result of substitution of capital for labor that has become more expensive.

Although even today quite a number of economists would argue in this fashion the fallacy of this approach is fairly widely recognized, even though it may be countered by various economists in a somewhat different way. My counterargument runs as follows. I assume in it a closed economic system and a proportional rise in all wage rates.

1. Suppose that in a short period of time the annual wage bill increased as a result of raising wage rates by ΔW. We may assume realistically that workers spend all their incomes and that they spend them immediately. As contrasted with this, it may be assumed that the volume of investment and capitalists' consumption is determined by decisions taken prior to the short period considered and are not affected by the wage rise during that period.

If we now subdivide the economy into three departments, producing investment goods (department 1), consumption goods for capitalists (department 2), and wage goods (department 3)— including into each of them the respective intermediate products— it follows that employment in the first two departments is not affected by the rise in wages. Thus denoting the wage bills in these

First published in *Kyklos* 24, (1971): 1–9. Reprinted in Michal Kalecki, *Selected Essays on the Dynamics of the Capitalist Economy, 1933–1970* (Cambridge: Cambridge University Press, 1971), pp. 156–64.

departments measured in "old" wage rates by W_1 and W_2 and the fraction by which wages are raised by α we obtain for the increment of the aggregate wages in departments 1 and 2 $\alpha(W_1 + W_2)$. The profits in these two departments decline *pro tanto* (provided prices of their products have not risen which in any case is assumed in the argument based on "preservation of purchasing power").

The position in department 3, however, is quite different because of immediate spending of the additional proceeds of the workers due to the wage rise. In particular the increment of the wage bill of departments 1 and 2, equal to $\alpha(W_1 + W_2)$, must unavoidably cause profits of the department 3 to rise *pro tanto.* Indeed, the profits of this department consist of the proceeds out of the sale of the wage goods which are not consumed by the workers employed in that department to the workers of departments 1 and 2. Thus the increment in the wage bill of these departments, $\alpha(W_1 + W_2)$, means an equal rise in profits of department 3. This may occur either through the rise in output in that department or through the rise of the prices of its products.

As a result the total profits remain unaltered, the loss of the departments 1 and 2 by $\alpha(W_1 + W_2)$ being counterbalanced by an equal gain of the department 3. It follows that no absolute shift from profits to wages occurs and the argument based on Say's Law would thus prove fallacious—at least with regard to the short period considered.

The last qualification is essential. For it may be argued that the decline in the volume of investment and capitalists' consumption as a result of the wage rise, although not immediate, would still come about with delay, say, in the next short period. And this would be true if capitalists at least *decided* to cut their investment and consumption immediately after having agreed to raise wages. But even this is unlikely: for their decisions are based on current experience; and this according to the above will show that no loss in total profits occurs in the short period following the wage rise and thus it will give no reason for a cut in investment and capitalists' consumption in the next period. If a decision for such a cut is not taken right away on the basis of the bare fact of the wage rise, it will not be taken at all. And as a result profits will not shrink in the next period either. The argument on the shift from profits to wages as a result of a wage rise based on Say's Law is thus fallacious even if we consider all the ramifications of this event.

The same applies obviously to a wage cut: no increase in profits will occur either in the short period following it or subsequently.

2. So far we assumed that prices of investment goods and consumption goods for capitalists remain unchanged when wages in-

crease, which was in line with the theory of shift from profits to wages to the extent of the wage rise. (The preceding section amounted in a sense to the *reductio ad absurdum* of this theory.) In fact, however, this is unlikely to be the case: rather, these prices will rise under the impact of the wage increase—perhaps not in the short period directly following the wage rise but subsequently. But to discuss this question as well as other repercussions of the wage rise—or of the wage cut—we want to know more about price formation in the system considered.

We shall first abstract from all semimonopolistic and monopolistic factors, in other words, we shall assume so-called perfect competition. Let me add immediately that this is a most unrealistic assumption not only for the present phase of capitalism but even for the so-called competitive capitalist economy of past centuries: surely this competition was always in general very imperfect. Perfect competition, when its actual status of a handy model is forgotten, becomes a dangerous myth.

As follows from the argument in the preceding section, the volume of capitalists' investment and consumption is maintained in the short period following the wage rise and consequently thereafter. On the assumption of perfect competition and of supply curves sloping upward at some point, the rise in wage rates must cause a proportional rise in prices at given levels of respective outputs— perhaps not in the first short period but subsequently. As a result profits in departments 1 and 2 will rise in the same proportion as wages, that is, $1 + \alpha$ times.

Now it is easy to prove that the volume of production and consumption of wage goods also remains unchanged. Indeed, in such a case profits in department 3 as in the other two departments increase in the proportion of the wage rise, or $1 + \alpha$ times; now, as mentioned in section 1, the profits in department 3 are equal to the proceeds out of sales of the wage goods to the workers of departments 1 and 2 and therefore must increase in the same proportion as wages in these departments, or $1 + \alpha$ times. If the volume of production and consumption of wage goods increased or declined, such could not be the case.

Thus with perfect competition the volume of production in all three departments remains unchanged while its value increases in each of them $1 + \alpha$ times. In this proportion thus the total wage bill increases and the total profits, that is, the distribution of national income, remain unaltered.

Consequently, having shown the fallacy of the theory based on Say's Law which maintained that wage movements have a direct and full impact upon the distribution of national income, we now

arrive at the opposite extreme, that they have no influence whatever upon this distribution. But this conclusion is based on the
untenable assumption of perfect competition. In fact only by dropping it and penetrating the world of imperfect competition and
oligopolies are we able to arrive at any reasonable conclusion on the
impact of bargaining for wages on the distribution of income.[1]

3. In fact a major part of the economy may be plausibly represented by a model very different from perfect competition. Each
firm in an industry arrives at the price of its product p by "marking
up" its direct cost u consisting of average costs of wages *plus* raw
materials in order to cover overheads and achieve profits. But this
mark-up is dependent on "competition," that is, on relation of the
ensuing price p to the weighted average price of this product $\bar{p}$ for
the industry as a whole. Or:

$$\frac{p - u}{u} = f\left(\frac{\bar{p}}{p}\right) \tag{1}$$

where f is an increasing function: the lower p is in relation to $\bar{p}$, the
higher the mark-up will be fixed. From formula (1) we obtain:

$$p = u\left[1 + f\left(\frac{\bar{p}}{p}\right)\right] \tag{2}$$

It should be noted that the function f may be different for various firms of an industry. They will reflect semimonopolistic influences referred to above, resulting from imperfect competition
or oligopoly. The more intensive are these factors, the higher $f(\bar{p}/p)$
corresponding to a given relation $\bar{p}/p$. Prices p will be in general
different for various firms because of the differences in direct costs
u and because of those in the functions f.

The price system is determined. Indeed with s firms in an industry there will be $s + 1$ price values to be determined, in other
words, $p_1, p_2, \ldots p_s, \bar{p}$, and as many equations: s equations of the
type (2) and one determining $\bar{p}$ in terms of $p_1, p_2, \ldots p_s$.

If all direct costs u, with given functions f, increased $1 + \alpha$ times,
so do all prices $p_1, p_2, \ldots p_s$. Indeed, this solution satisfies the
equations (2) because u by assumption increases $1 + \alpha$ times and
$\bar{p}/p$ remains unaltered.

If, however, the direct cost u_k increases only for one firm (again
with given functions f), it is easy to see that p_k increases in a lesser
proportion because $\bar{p}$ will then not rise in the same proportion as u_k.

4. Since prices p for a product are in general not equal, the
above applies strictly to imperfect competition or differential oligopoly but not to nondifferential oligopoly or monopoly. However,
in fact, apart from basic raw materials produced frequently in con-

ditions approaching perfect competition, most of the products *have* differential price. (Let us not forget that absolutely identical products with the same transport costs but different periods of delivery may have different prices.)

It seems therefore a fairly good approximation to an actual economy if we assume it consisting of the model described above and the sector of basic raw materials conforming in their price formation to that of perfect competition.

Let us now imagine that in a closed system of this type wage rates in all industries increase in the same proportion, $1 + \alpha$ times. It follows easily that all prices will also increase $1 + \alpha$ times *provided that functions f in industries to which they are relevant are unchanged.* It follows that if these conditions were fulfilled we should arrive at the same conclusion as for perfectly competitive economy in section 2—that a general increase in money wages in a closed economy does not change the distribution of national income. The same would apply to the case of the decrease in money wages. However, we shall argue that the functions f do depend on the trade-union activity.

5. High mark-ups in existence will encourage strong trade unions to bargain for higher wages since they know that firms can "afford" to pay them. If their demands are granted but the functions f are not changed, prices also increase. This would lead to a new round of demands for higher wages and the process would go on with price levels rising. But surely an industry will not like such a process making its products more and more expensive and thus less competitive with products of other industries.[2] To sum up, trade-union power restrains the mark-ups, in other words, it causes the values $f(\bar{p}/p)$ to be lower than would be the case otherwise.

Now, this power manifests itself in the scale of wage rises demanded and achieved. If an increase in bargaining capacity is demonstrated by spectacular achievements, there is a downward shift in functions $f(\bar{p}/p)$ and the mark-ups' decline. A redistribution of national income from profits to wages will take place then. But this redistribution is much smaller than that which would obtain if prices were stable. The rise in wages is to a great extent "shifted to consumers." And "normal" wage increases will usually leave the functions f unaffected while otherwise mark-ups may tend to get higher because of the rise in productivity of labor.

6. Let us imagine that a spectacular wage rise depresses somewhat the mark-ups so that a redistribution of national income from profits to wages occurs. Now from section 1 it follows that profits in department 3 will increase in the same proportion as wage rates. But, as there is a redistribution of income from profits to wages as a

result of the reduction of mark-ups there, the wage bill in department 3 increases more than wage rates, in other words, there is a rise in employment and output there. In consequence output and employment will be unaltered in departments 1 and 2 while they will rise in department 3. Or the volume of investment and capitalists' consumption will not change, but workers' consumption will increase. Such an expansion of total output and employment will be feasible because in fact our model of semimonopolistic price-fixing, as developed in section 3, presupposes the existence of excess capacities.

As to the (money) value of the wage bill it will clearly increase in a higher proportion than the wage rates. However, total profits will increase *less* than the wage rates: indeed, profits in department 3 increase proportionately to the wage rates, employment in departments 1 and 2 being unaltered, but profits in the latter two departments increase less than the wage rates as a result of the decline of mark-ups there.[3]

If the trade union power declined the process described above would be reversed. Employment and output in departments 1 and 2 would remain unchanged, but in department 3 they would decline. Or the volume of investment and capitalists' consumption would remain unchanged and the consumption of workers would fall. The total output and employment would thus decline. The value of the wage bill would fall more than the wage rates while the value of profits would decline less than the wage rates.[4]

Since the decline in the mark-ups tends to increase aggregate output, this would cause a rise in prices of basic raw materials, subject to conditions of perfect competition, in relation to wages. As a result the increase in output and employment would be somewhat restrained. In the same fashion this factor would somehow restrain the fall in output and employment caused by the rise of the mark-ups.

It follows from the above that a wage rise showing an increase in the trade-union power leads—contrary to the precepts of classical economics—to an increase in employment. And conversely, a fall in wages showing a weakening in their bargaining power leads to a decline in employment. The weakness of trade unions in a depression manifested in permitting wage cuts contributes to deepening of unemployment rather than to relieving it.

7. It follows from the above that the class struggle as reflected in trade-union bargaining may affect the distribution of national income but in a much more sophisticated fashion than expressed by the crude doctrine: when wages are raised, profits fall *pro tanto*. This doctrine proves to be entirely wrong. Such shifts that occur are: (a) connected with widespread imperfect competition and

oligopoly in the capitalist system; and (b) contained in fairly narrow limits. However, the day-by-day bargaining process is an important codeterminant of the distribution of national income.

It should be noted that it is possible to devise other forms of class struggle than wage bargaining, which would affect the distribution of national income in a more direct way. For instance, actions may be undertaken for keeping down the cost of living. The latter might be achieved by price controls which, however, may prove difficult to administer. But there exists an alternative: subsidizing of prices of wage goods which is financed by direct taxation of profits. Such an operation, by the way, will not affect aggregate net profits: the argument is the same as used in section 1 in the case of a wage increase. The same is true of the effect of price controls. And, if such measures cannot be carried out by political parties associated with trade unions in the parliament, the power of the trade unions may be used to mobilize supporting strike movements. The classical day-by-day bargaining for wages is not the only way of influencing the distribution of national income to the advantage of the workers.

8. The redistribution of income from profits to wages, as described in the last two sections, is feasible only if excess capacity is in existence. Otherwise it is impossible to increase wages in relation to prices of wage goods because prices are determined by demand, and functions f become defunct. We return then to the position described in section 2 where the wage rise could not affect a redistribution of income.

Price control of wage goods will lead under the circumstances to scarcities of goods and haphazard distribution. Also subsidizing prices of wage goods (financed by direct taxation of profits) can reduce prices only in the longer run by stimulating investment in wage-good industries.

It should be noted, however, that even contemporary capitalism, where deep depressions are avoided as a result of government intervention, is in general still fairly remote from such a state of full utilization of resources. This is best shown by the fact that prices of finished goods *are* fixed on a cost basis rather than determined by demand.

Notes

1. We abstracted here from the influence of the increase in the price level upon the rate of interest by assuming tacitly that the supply of money by the banks is elastic. Otherwise the higher demand for money would

have increased the rate of interest which would affect adversely invest-ment and consequently profits. Such effect seems unlikely to be of any greater importance, especially because the changes in the bank rate are reflected on a much reduced scale in the long-term rate of interest.
2. Despite the fact that for the sake of simplicity we assumed that all wage rates are raised simultaneously in the same proportion, we consider realistically that bargaining is proceeding by industries.
3. This, however, is subject to the following qualification. As a result of the increase of total output there will be an increase in prices of basic raw materials, *inter alia* those used alike by department 1 or 2 and department 3. This, although not very likely, may offset the influence of the decline in mark-ups in departments 1 and 2 upon the distribution of income between profits and wages. In any case, however, total profits will rise in a lower proportion than total wage bill.
4. Subject to a qualification analogous to that stated in the preceding foot-note.

Maurice Dobb

A NOTE ON DISTRIBUTION AND THE PRICE MARK-UP

Some may deem it sufficient to say simply that a postulate as to the
level of real wages (or alternatively the ratio of surplus to wages) is
introduced "from outside" as a sociological datum (dependent,
e.g., on the state of class relations existing at a given time and
place). Others, however, may feel some impatience with this, even
to the point of regarding it as question-begging, and may sense a
need to "close the model" by introducing some more explicit explanation of the forces that determine the division of the total product
between profit (or property-income) and wages. While it may have
been legitimate at an early stage of capitalism to accept that wages
were governed competitively by something akin to Marx's "value of
labor power," and surplus accordingly treated as a residual, does
not such an approach (which certainly had the merit of including
labor power, and hence wages, within the circle of value-relations)
lose its relevance as soon as capitalism develops beyond its earlier
competitive stage? Does it not lose both relevance and plausibility
in a stage of monopoly capitalism, with monopolistic (or oligopolistic) firms endowed with the power to pass on a wage rise into
prices and to enforce something like a minimum profit margin or
surplus ratio? Some might feel inclined to maintain that in such
circumstances real wages are determined as the residual rather
than profits.

A complaint of this kind would seem to have inspired a recent
statement by Dr. Nuti about "the relation between the real wage
rate and the profit rate uncovered by Sraffa and before him by the
Russian economist Dmitriev." This, he observes, "provides scope
for the concept of class struggle in the determination of relative
shares." But he goes on to say: "unfortunately, however, there is no
simple way of closing his system, *i.e.* of determining which point of
the wage-profit relation is actually reached and how in any economy"; and this for two reasons. First, "the real wage-rate cannot be

taken as exogenously determined as in the classical thought, fixed at a subsistence level in conditions of elastic labour supply." Secondly, "it cannot be determined *directly* by the class struggle . . . because after Keynes we have to recognize that wage bargaining determines *money* wages, while the real wage rate is determined by the behaviour of the price level."[1] This latter is a cogent objection, and, in conjunction with the former, might incline one to think that under modern capitalism, with its high degree of concentration and monopoly, one may well need to look, in explaining distribution, toward factors that set a minimum to profit, rather than as formerly a minimum to wages. Otherwises (it may well be asked) do not critics of the orthodox theory of distribution place themselves in as vulnerable a position as those they criticize and seek to dethrone?

We have seen that Kalecki provided an explanation of distribution of this very type, and with the situation of modern capitalism evidently in mind. According to this the share of profits in (gross) output was determined by the degree of monopoly, which gave the firm or *entrepreneur* the *power* to exact a mark-up on prime cost by price-raising.[2] Whatever the level of money-wages, the ratio of prices to it (and hence the real wage and profit margin) will be dependent upon the price-raising power with which firms are endowed—something that varies in inverse relation to the amount of effective competition. By such means, it would seem, capitalism has acquired the power to negate the growing influence of trade unionism over money-wages, and the ability to tolerate conditions in which the industrial reserve army can no longer play its former "stabilizing" role.

There are some formal difficulties about this theory as to how the degree of monopoly is to be appropriately defined. Kalecki himself interpreted this in terms of the inelasticity of the demand curve (and hence the ratio of average demand-price to marginal revenue and to marginal and average cost). But how is this to be transferred from the level of a particular product to the macroscopic level of the economy as a whole? And what real content does the notion have if the transfer can be satisfactorily achieved?[3] A more substantial difficulty is that by implication the mark-up would be zero under conditions of perfect competition. If surplus value is *solely* the creation of monopoly, its emergence under the "normal" competitive conditions envisaged by the classical economists and by Marx would seem to be denied. This objection would not be a serious one if the theory were clearly labeled as one appropriate to monopoly capitalism per se; an alternative explanation of surplus value being admittedly appropriate to an earlier, competitive stage of the system, in conditions of a reserve of labor and elastic labor supply.[4]

Alternatively, and with a somewhat different emphasis, one might say that, while the classical Marxian explanation for the emergence of surplus value continues to apply to modern capitalism, as to its earlier stage, the influence of monopoly enters in as an additive element in the stage of monopoly capitalism—an influence reminiscent of forms of exploitation characteristic of precapitalist stages òf development.

An analogous difficulty applies to the post-Keynesian theory, according to which the share of profit in national income is dependent on the growth rate of the economy together with the saving (or alternatively spending) propensity of capitalists. The implication of this would seem to be that in static conditions with zero capital accumulation (Marx's "simple reproduction") profits could be zero. This, however, could only be the case if capitalists persistently refused not only to invest but also to spend their (potential) incomes: surplus value would then fail to accrue simply because it could not be "realized," even though conditions favorable to its "creation" were in existence. Since there must necessarily be an equality between aggregate capitalist spending (including investment) and the total output less what is sold to wage earners, it follows that total *realized* surplus must vary with the size of capitalist expenditure (including investment). This equality condition, however, could only become a sufficient theory of profit if, say, investment were singled out as the independent variable: then it would appear to follow that amount of profit or surplus is *consequent* on investment, and determined by the size of the latter. But while this might well be a plausible view in a planned socialist economy, where growth, and hence investment, is postulated as a key policy element in the plan, it is plainly inappropriate to an unplanned atomistic market economy. In the latter investment as much as individual capitalist spending is a variable that has to be explained in terms of the total situation, and is affected by expectations of future capitalist income, which is in turn related to what has come to be regarded as "normal" income on the basis of past income experience. The equality condition in question, accordingly, cannot be treated as a *substitute* for a theory of profit and distribution in socioeconomic terms (explaining, e.g., the *rate* of surplus value, or profit-wage ratio, which is otherwise left unexplained).

Yet another plausible hypothesis is that a minimum rate of profit is somehow fixed by some kind of quasi-political or institutional decision mechanism. This is a plausible interpretation, perhaps, of a tentative hint given by Mr. Sraffa when he suggests that in his system the rate of profit, rather than the real wage, could be postulated as the independent variable: the former is "susceptible of being determined from outside the system of production, in particular by the level of the money rates of interest."[5] The latter would presumably be fixed, in the main, by the central bank, whether acting on its own initiative or as an instrument of governmental monetary policy. If one is inclined to view state policy as an instrument or reflection of class interest, or of powerful pressure groups within the ruling class, one will tend to regard monetary policy as a way of enforcing (more or less consciously),[6] on behalf of capital owners as a whole, such a profit share in the proceeds of production as existing circumstances permit. True, they may at times decide to *lower* interest rates in pursuit of "cheap money policy," as in time of war or of economic depression, or under the influence of international economic relations.[7] (At times of excess capacity, for example, it may well be in the collective interest of profit receivers to lower interest and profit rates if thereby investment expenditure and hence capacity-working can be augmented.) But the very fact that the idea of a "normal" long-term rate is so stubbornly long-lived, apparently, even in disturbed times, lends support to the notion that the conventional upshot of banking policy is to set a substantial minimum to the profit share.[8]

Finally, before leaving such questions, mention should no doubt be made of a difficulty that some feel about postulating real wages as an independent variable if this is done (as by Marx) in value terms (i.e., of labor) or in terms of Sraffa's Standard Commodity. In the former case objection is made that wage goods are not, in fact, bought by workers at their values but at their prices of production;[9] in the latter case it is objected that the actual consumption of workers will probably not consist of the standard commodity but of a quite different assortment of goods. In either case substantial content is lost from the postulate. This difficulty, however, would seem to be more apparent than real provided one is willing to accept the notion of a given standard of living as consisting of a variety of assortments of wage goods that are considered as equivalent by a typical worker's household, and to interpret "a given level of real wages" in this sense. Then a definition in terms of one member of an equivalent set (whether in terms of labor necessary to produce it or of standard commodity) will retain its meaning when translated into another member of the same set of equivalents.

One can only conclude, at the time of writing, that such alternative explanations of distribution in our twentieth-century world are *sub judice* in current economic discussion, and that discussion (or even elaboration) of them has proceeded insufficiently far as yet to make final judgment possible, still less to speak of a *consensus*. Unsatisfactory this may be as a concluding note; nonetheless it would appear unavoidable. At least it may be an indication that political economy is not a closed text and that it remains open to the creative molding of controversy with which its past is so richly endowed. Indeed, this is probably more true today than it was half a century ago when Keynes could write of "the general principles of thought which economists now apply to economic problems" as though these were an agreed corpus of theory.[10]

Notes

1. D. M. Nuti, "Vulgar Economy in the Theory of Income Distribution," *Science & Society* 35, no. 1 (Spring 1971): 32 (being a paper presented at the first Conference of Socialist Economists in London in January 1970).
2. If one could imagine all firms vertically integrated so as to include the production of all nonlabor inputs, this would be equivalent to a mark-up on wage cost. Insofar as firms also possess a degree of monopoly in the labor market as buyers, they are able to exert a downward pressure on money wages: to this extent the markup is now wholly accounted for by price-raising.
3. Kalecki suggested that this could simply be done by taking a weighted average of the gross margins established in the several industries (by the inelasticity of their various demand curves and by the state of oligopoly in them), "using as weights the respective value of sales." *Studies in Economic Dynamics* (London, 1943) p. 11. A difficulty here is that when oligopoly is introduced, one has to deal with what has been called an "imagined demand curve."
4. Kalecki's own answer to this kind of objection was that "perfect competition" constitutes "a most unrealistic assumption not only for the present phase of capitalism but even for the so called competitive capitalist economy of past centuries: surely this competition was always very imperfect. Perfect competition when its actual status as a handy model is forgotten becomes a dangerous myth." *Selected Essays on the Dynamics of the Capitalist Economy* (Cambridge: Cambridge University Press, 1971), p. 158.
5. Piero Sraffa, *Production of Commodities by Means of Commodities* (Cambridge: Cambridge University Press, 1963), p. 33.
6. To some extent, perhaps, *un*consciously and influenced by what has become traditional.
7. For example, excessive accumulation of reserves of gold or of foreign currencies.
8. As does also the apparent constancy of the share of profit in total

income, on which Kalecki especially laid stress in expounding his monopoly theory.

9. Cf. Arghiri Emmanuel, *Unequal Exchange,* trans. from the French by Brian Pearce (New York: Monthly Review Press, 1972), App. v, esp. pp. 397, 407.

10. In his Editor's Introduction to the early works in the Cambridge Economic Handbook Series—although he was to add that "even on matters of principle there is not yet complete unanimity of opinion."

Howard Sherman

INFLATION, UNEMPLOYMENT, AND THE CONTEMPORARY BUSINESS CYCLE

This article attempts a brief survey of recent Marxist debates on capitalist economic crises. First, the three most widely known Marxist explanations are discussed. In each case, it is emphasized that there are no long-run downturns or final automatic collapses of capitalism. Thus all theories of long-run crises are incorrect, even though each of these three approaches does help to understand actual, short-run business cycles. Second, the article attempts to synthesize these insights into one consistent theory of the business cycle. This theory explains why crises are caused *both* by demand and by cost factors, so cycles of boom and bust are unavoidable. Third, this article analyzes the American economy in its present stage. In this new stage, unemployment persists both in recoveries and in "prosperity" periods. The new stage also has a high level of inflation, not only in expansion periods, as is usual, but even in periods of contraction. Fourth, this new period of capitalism is explained in terms of the historical emergence of new structural features: (1) extraordinary new levels of monopoly power, especially conglomerates, (2) far greater government economic activity, and (3) the decline of American economic power abroad. Finally, some implications for socialist political action are spelled out.

Underconsumption

Virtually all capitalist economies experience cycles, with periods of very heavy unemployment alternating with periods of much less unemployment. Some Marxists also talk about secular or long-run

Reprinted from *Socialist Review* 9, no. 2 (#44, March April 1979): 75–102. The author wishes to thank for very useful comments Mason Gaffney, Michael Sherman, Tom Weisskopf, and several anonymous editors of *Socialist Review*, though none of these has responsibility for statements or conclusions.

crises. This is confusing and incorrect if it means a long-run down-turn in output and employment. There are periods of expansion as well as depression, and each peak is usually higher than the preceding one. Capitalism does not permanently collapse by itself, but must be defeated by political organization.

Some Marxists have talked about secular crises of "underconsumption." They argue that workers are exploited, and that the rate of exploitation rises over time. Yet most goods must be bought by consumers and most consumers are workers. A higher rate of exploitation means that wages are falling as a proportion of national income. Therefore, consumption must also drop as a proportion of national income. As a result, there is a continually deepening crisis of underconsumption.

A modern liberal underconsumptionist, Warren Gramm, puts it this way: "It is held that the demonstrable phenomenon of chronic excess productive capacity under monopoly capitalism is caused fundamentally by insufficiency of consumer demand. This stems, in turn, from excessive inequality in the distribution of income."[1] In the similar—but very sophisticated and insightful—underconsumptionist approach of Baran and Sweezy, capitalist production has a permanent downward trend.[2] Production rises at times only because of (1) temporary increases in the wage share (e.g., with increases in union strength), (2) increases in military spending, or (3) major new inventions. (Liberals and trade-union economists generally like a reformist version of the underconsumption view in which the complete remedy seems to be an increase in wages.)

The underconsumptionist tradition does have some basis in Marx. Sometimes Marx emphasized the limited demand resulting from the exploitation of workers. "The ultimate cause of all real crises always remains the poverty and restricted consumption of the masses."[3] Expansions are brought to an end by the limits imposed by class structure:

> The epochs in which capitalist production exerts all its forces are always periods of overproduction, because the forces of production can never be utilized beyond the point at which surplus value can be not only produced but also realized; but the sale of commodities, the realization of the commodity capital and hence also of surplus value, is limited not only by the consumption requirements of society in general, but by the consumption requirements of a society in which the great majority are poor and must always remain poor.[4]

In Marx's day, however, there were already a number of naïve "underconsumption" theories, which he attacked and which differ from his own formulation. First, even in the short run, it is naïve to say that the problem is falling wages. On the contrary, it was true in Marx's day (and is still true today) that the *real wage rises* throughout the expansion. Marx's point is that *profits rise faster than wages,* so the share of labor falls in most of the usual expansion period.

Second, it is naive to say that the problem is that workers are exploited, so they can *never* buy back the product they produce. Some of the product *is* bought by capitalists for their own consumption or for investment; the real problem is why capitalist demand sometimes fills the gap and sometimes does not. This naïve view, which emphasizes that workers can never buy back their product, often leads to theories of permanent crisis or permanent stagnation. Theories of permanent crisis sound very revolutionary, but they fly in the face of the fact that capitalism does continue to grow, though with periodic depressions. Moreover, they imply that socialists can sit back and watch capitalism collapse by itself, which puts a brake on political activity. We will see later, however, that a short-run underconsumptionist theory of cycles does make some useful points about limited consumer demand, based on exploitation of workers.

Rising Wage Costs

A second type of Marxist secular crisis theory is exactly the opposite. It postulates a long-run *falling* rate of exploitation, caused by stronger trade unions and workers' political activity (e.g., rising welfare payments).[5] The falling rate of exploitation means a falling rate of profit, which causes a deepening long-run crisis. Besides being contrary to fact, this theory also cannot explain short-run downturns, nor can it explain any upturn in output and employment. (It might be called a long-run "wage-push" theory.)

Many conservative theorists also attribute cyclical contractions primarily to rising wages which "squeeze profits." Their solution is to hold down costs, particularly wage costs. Those who emphasize the rising costs of labor claim that more employment can only come by cutting wages. A recent textbook says, "The general solution to involuntary unemployment is a reduction in real wages until the amount of labor demanded equals the amount supplied."[6] (The Nixon administration followed this advice by combining strict controls on wages with loose controls on prices.)

The notion of solving unemployment by cutting wages conveniently ignores the fact that lowering wages means less demand for consumer goods, which makes it harder for capitalists to realize their profits. Both Marx and Keynes emphasized this. Nevertheless, some leftists join conservatives in blaming every crisis on low profits caused by high wages. Thus Ray Boddy and Jim Crotty, citing the *Wall Street Journal,* say, "Knowledgeable observers of the labor scene have pointed directly to an increasingly obstreperous labor force as an influence on the decline in productivity during the expansion."[7] Like the conservatives, they argue that high employment levels lead to a militant labor force that forces higher wages and lower productivity, thus causing a crisis by squeezing profits.

It is true that capitalists must produce profits by forcing workers to create a surplus above costs. Boddy and Crotty do not seem to realize, however, that capitalists must also realize their profits by sales in the market, which require high consumer demand and high wages. Profits cannot be squeezed from only one side at a time; they are squeezed from both sides. The capitalist's dilemma is to want both lower wage costs *and* higher consumer demand.

Marx acknowledged that, in some extraordinary cases, capitalist investment could be so rapid as to cause a shortage of labor. This shortage leads to high wages, cutting into the rate of profit, and causing a crisis. "If the quantity of unpaid labor supplied by the working class, and accumulated by the capitalist class, increases so rapidly that its conversion into capital requires an *extraordinary* addition to paid labor, then wages rise, and all other circumstances remaining equal, the unpaid labor diminishes in proportion."[8] He goes on to say that this fall in the rate of profits leads to a depression, which causes wages to fall again.

Note, however, that Marx calls this an extraordinary rise in wages. He also says that such cases have occurred only in exceptional periods, such as the American railway boom of the nineteenth century. Marx emphasized that in most periods of capitalist expansion, there is a *rising* rate of exploitation, that is, profits are rising faster than wages. Marx makes the point very clear: "The falling tendency of the rate of profit is accompanied by a rising tendency of the rate of surplus value, that is, the rate of exploitation. Nothing is more absurd, for this reason, than to explain a fall in the rate of profit by a rise in the rate of wages, although there may be exceptional cases when this may apply."[9] It appears to be Marx's view—and it is the reality—that in the *usual* case wages rise more slowly than profits during most of the expansion of capitalism. Nevertheless, the notion of a declining profit share at some crucial moments in the cycle *does* lead to some useful insights that will be utilized in a later section.

Table 1
Profit Rate on Stockholders' Equity Capital, 1933-75
(All U.S. Manufacturing Corporations)

Cycle	Average profit rate	Events
1933-38	3.8%	Great Depression
1938-45	16.2	World War II
1945-49	17.8	Recovery from war
1949-54	24.3	Korean war
1954-58	21.0	Continuing cold war
1958-61	17.3	Lessening cold war
1961-70	19.3	Vietnam war
1970-75	19.5	Vietnam war, wage-price controls

Sources: 1933 to 1949, annual data from U.S. Internal Revenue Service, *Statistics of Income, Corporate Income Tax Returns* (Washington, D.C.: GPO, 1935-51); 1949 to 1975, quarterly data from U.S. Federal Trade Commission and Securities and Exchange Commission, *Quarterly Financial Report of Manufacturing Corporations* (Washington, D.C.: GPO, 1st quarter 1949 to 4th quarter 1975).

Rising Costs of Material Capital

A third type of secular crisis theory is the "rising costs of material capital" (or "rising organic composition of capital") theory.[10] This theory claims that the ratio of material or physical capital (Marx's "constant capital") to human labor (Marx's "variable capital") is always being increased by the march of technology. But only human labor creates profit. Therefore, the rate of profit tends to drop, producing a long-run capitalist crisis.

Marx did discuss the reasons why there was a *long-run* trend toward a falling rate of profit in the early nineteenth century. He speculatedthat part of the problem might be a growing amount of capitalist spending on capital goods per worker. Many Marxists have tried to turn this view of long-run trends into a theory of cyclical crises. But there are three problems with this approach.

First, there is no evidence of any trend toward a present-day falling rate of profit. Table 1 shows the facts cycle by cycle. The average rate of profit is measured over each whole cycle to eliminate the effects of short-run excesses of supply or demand. *There is no trend.* The rate of profit was lowest in the Great Depression of the 1930s, rises in every war period, and usually declines when the war is over.

One could argue about exact definitions of the rate of profit (such as including rent and interest to approximate Marx's "surplus value"), but a test of all kinds of alternative definitions reveals that they make little difference as to the long-run pattern.[11] There is no long-run trend, but the rate of profit does rise rapidly in every cyclical expansion and falls rapidly in every cyclical contraction.

The second problem is that there is no good factual evidence that the ratio of physical capital to labor has been rising; rather, the pattern is a mixed up-and-down movement. Moreover, there is no theoretical reason to expect a constantly rising ratio of physical capital to labor. Sometimes, new capital replaces a larger amount of old capital (such as smaller but better computers replacing older ones). Sometimes, the value of new capital in labor terms is cheaper than the old (as when better technology allows television sets to be produced in fewer labor hours). A huge literature has discussed the nature of technological change under capitalism. This complex debate, however, need not be discussed here because these long-run trends are *not* relevant to short-run cycle changes—though some trends may change the structural background of cycles, as discussed below.

The third problem is that *no* long-run trend can explain the rapid rise of the profit rate in a few months in each recovery. Nor can any long-run trend explain the rapid decline of the profit rate in a few months at the onset of each crisis. When Marx turned to explain the falling profit rate in a short-run crisis, he did *not* refer to his theoretical explanation of possible long-run trends. Instead, one of the factors he examined was the short-run changes in *prices* of capital goods, affected by temporary excesses of supply or demand.

Marx found that one side of the profit squeeze was the rising cost of capital goods, including plant, equipment, and raw materials. The rising cost of capital goods is a normal occurrence as capitalists accelerate their demand in an expansion:

> The same phenomenon (and this as a rule precedes crises) can occur if the production of surplus capital takes place at a very rapid rate, and its retransformation into productive capital so increases the demand for all the elements of the latter that real production cannot keep pace, and consequently there is a rise in the prices of all the commodities which enter into the formation of capital.[12]

Not only does Marx point to the rising cost of capital goods in an expansion, he also shows how a fall in the price of capital goods is a very necessary part of the adjustment process of capitalism in the depression. Marx describes this process of price-cost adjustment very colorfully:

> The principal work of destruction would show its more dire effects in a slaughtering of the values of capitals. . . . One portion of the com-

modities on the market can complete the process of circulation and reproduction only by an immense contraction of its prices, which means a depreciation of the capital represented by it. In the same way the elements of fixed capital are more or less depreciated. . . . The depreciation of the elements of constant capital itself would be another factor tending to raise the average rate of profit. . . . And in this way the cycle would be run once more. . . . The same vicious cycle would be described once more under expanded conditions of production, in an expanded market, and with increased productive forces.[13]

Once again, there is *no* long-run trend towards a declining rate of profit due to rising costs of material capital. Rather these costs rise and fall relative to prices over the cycle as one crucial element of cyclical crises.

Production and Realization of Profits

The three types of Marxist short-run cycle theory can be synthesized into one more general theory by examining how each of these factors affects the rate of profit. All capitalist profits come out of *surplus* value, which is that amount of value produced by workers *over and above* that value *necessary* to pay their wages. Profits must, therefore, first be produced by workers in the form of surplus value. If, however, the capitalist cannot sell the product in the market at a price equal to its long-run value, then he or she cannot realize the surplus value embodied in the product. Thus, the capitalist still may make no profit or a low rate of profit even though he or she has exploited the worker. As Marx puts it:

The creation of . . . surplus value is the object of the direct process of production. . . . But this production of surplus value is but the first act of the capitalist process of production. . . . Now comes the second act of the process. The entire mass of commodities . . . must be sold. If this is not done, or only partly accomplished . . . the laborer has been none the less exploited, but his exploitation does not realize as much for the capitalist. . . . The realization of surplus value . . . is not determined . . . by the absolute consuming power, but by the consuming power based on antagonistic conditions of distribution, which reduces the consumption of the great mass of the population to a variable minimum within more or less narrow limits.[14]

Profits, therefore, may be and are squeezed from two directions at the peak of expansion: (1) by rising costs of production, which may prevent creation of surplus value, and (2) by limited demand, which may prevent realization of surplus value. Some Marxist—and some non-Marxist—theories emphasize *only* the capitalist's problems in producing surplus value. These include theories of rising wage costs, as well as theories of rising material capital costs (and financial capital costs).[15] Other Marxist (and some non-Marxist) theories emphasize *only* the capitalist's problems in selling the product or realizing surplus value. These are called theories of overproduction or underconsumption.[16]

Why is profit so crucial in the causation of economic crises? Because profitability determines whether capitalists continue to produce, expand their production through new investment, or cut back their production. Capitalist investment is affected by profits in two ways. First, the total amount of profit realized determines the total funds available for new investment. Second, the expected rate of profit on investment is the prime motive for making any investment at all. Therefore, most cycle theories are devoted to explaining *why* the rate of profit declines at the peak of expansion and *why* the rate of profit rises again from the trough of depression.

Tom Weisskopf has very cleverly explained how all three Marxist cycle theories can be shown to postulate various effects on the rate of profit.[17] By definition, he says, let the rate of profit equal:

$$\frac{\text{Profit}}{\text{Capital}} = \frac{\text{Profit}}{\text{Output}} \times \frac{\text{Output}}{\text{Potential Output}} \times \frac{\text{Potential Output}}{\text{Capital}}$$

Thus the rate of profit is a function of (1) the ratio of profit to output, (2) the ratio of actual output to potential output, and (3) the ratio of potential output to capital. The rising-wage-cost theory will be reflected in element number one (profit/output). The underconsumptionist theory will be reflected in element number two (actual output demanded/potential output). The rising-material-capital-costs theory will be reflected in element number three (potential output/capital).

On this basis, we can say that all three theories may have some elements of truth. Each may identify a source of the decline (or rise) in the rate of profit in each cycle. We may measure to some degree the importance of each of the three theories.

Profits and Wages over the Cycle

For simplicity, all income is divided into *profits* (including rent and interest payments) and *wages* (including salaries and fringe benefits). So the percentage of income going to profits plus the percentage of income going to wages equals 100 percent, or:

$$\frac{\text{Profits}}{\text{Income}} \ + \ \frac{\text{Wages}}{\text{Income}} = 1.00$$

Thus, if the wage share is known, so is the profit share.

Both the underconsumptionists and the rising-wage-cost theorists focus on the distribution of income between profits and wages, so it is necessary to chart their behavior over the cycle. For this purpose, the business cycle may be divided into nine stages. Stage one is the initial trough at the lowest point of the depression. *Stage five is the peak of expansion.* Stage nine is the final trough at the low point of the next contraction. Stages two, three, and four divide the expansion into three equally long pieces; stages six, seven, and eight divide the contraction similarly. The average of the variable over the whole cycle is set equal to 100.0

Within this framework, the labor share (wage/income) may be shown as in Table 2. Total *real* national income (*real* means dollars of constant purchasing power) rises from stage one to stage five (peak) and falls from stage five to stage nine of each cycle. Total real wages also rise from stage one to five and fall from stage five to

Table 2
Wages and Income over the Cycle

Stages	Trough	Expansion			Peak	Contraction			Trough
	1	2	3	4	5	6	7	8	9
Cycle of 1970-75									
Real national income	91	94	99	105	106	104	103	100	98
Total real wages	92	94	98	104	105	105	105	102	101
Ratio of wages to income	101	100	99	98	99	101	102	102	103
Average of Four Cycles from 1949 to 1970									
Ratio of wages to income	100	98	99	101	102	103	103	103	103

Source: U.S. Department of Commerce, Economic Analysis Bureau, *Business Conditions Digest,* October 1977 and November 1977.

nine of most cycles. *But* the ratio of wages to income changes over the cycle *in a systematic way.* The changes don't seem dramatic, but every percentage point repesents billions of dollars.

Table 2 shows that the wage share (ratio of wages to national income) falls in the early expansion and rises in the late expansion of each cycle—and also usually rises in the contraction. The lowest point is reached in stage two in the average of the four cycles from 1949 to 1970. The lowest point in the 1970-75 cycle was in stage four. The 1970-75 cycle *appears* to support the underconsumptionists in that the wage/income ratio falls for almost all of the expansion. The four cycles of the 1950s and 1960s *appear* more favorable to the thesis that the wage share increases before the cycle peak (while the profit share declines).

Which of these cycles is "typical"? That is a silly question. All capitalist cycles are different, though they all have things in common. The 1949-54 cycle includes the Korean war. The 1961-70 cycle is dominated by the Vietnam war. But the 1970-75 cycle still includes some of the Vietnam war as well as Nixon's wage and price controls. All four of the cycles of the 1950s and 1960s are extraordinarily mild in intensity of rise and fall. The 1970-75 cycle is much stronger and is more like the cycles of the 1920s and 1930s. The available evidence (which is incomplete) indicates that the ratio of wages to income also declined for all or most of the expansion period in those more severe cycles.

A more general formulation—which may be based on Weisskopf's rate-of-profit equation—must account for cycles in which the ratio of wages to income stops falling at various points in the expansion. Let us first be clear exactly why the wage/income ratio falls in every early expansion, but also why it may tend to rise again in late expansion near or at the cycle peak.

Why do wages rise so slowly in expansions, particularly in the first half of expansion? In the recovery phase of the cycle, there are still large numbers of unemployed willing to take new jobs at low pay. The bargaining power of unions in the early phases of business expansion is also relatively weak, partly because of the existence of the reserve of unemployed workers, but also because of general attitudes. The public is sympathetic to workers resisting wage cuts, but less sympathetic to fights for wage increases. Even workers are more easily aroused to resist wage cuts than they are enthusiastic to strike for wage increases.

In early expansion, however, the big profit increases come primarily from increased productivity. Expansion, particularly the initial recovery, is a period of rising demand, better utilization of factories (plus investment in new machinery), and better utilization of workers. Finally, increased demand for goods causes prices to rise during expansion. It takes workers a while, however, to realize that these price increases are holding down their real wages (this is called the money illusion). Thus wage increases lag behind output increases in the first half of the expansion, and sometimes in the whole expansion.

Why does the wage/income ratio often begin to rise before the peak of expansion? By the peak of expansion, there is much less unemployment. This gives unions greater bargaining power. Worker militancy also increases as workers become fully aware that productivity increases are raising profits, while price increases are slowing the increase of real wages. Moreover, lack of demand may reduce the utilization of workers though not yet producing firings. For these reasons, real wages usually rise faster than total income near the peak of expansion.

Why do real wages fall relatively slowly in contraction? During the recession, workers strongly resist wage cuts, while productivity usually falls because workers are not fully utilized (that is, are partially idle) as demand declines. Capitalists do not immediately fire unutilized workers because they expect another upturn in demand at any moment. Thus the ratio of wage income to profit income falls in most of the expansion (but often rises before the peak), while it rises in most of the contraction.

One point should be stressed in this explanation. Some wage-push theorists talk as if the profit share falls at or before the peak *because* wage rates are accelerating upward. *That is incorrect.* In the expansion periods of all five cycles from 1949 to 1975, real hourly wage rates rose fastest in early recovery, then rose less and less as the cycle peak was approached. In the 1970-75 cycle, the real hourly wage rose per quarter at 0.7 percent from stage one to two; 0.5 from stage two to three; 0.4 from stage three to four; and -0.2 from stage four to five. Similarly, in the average of all four cycles from 1949 to 1970, the real hourly wage rose 0.7 (stage one to two), 0.6 (stage two to three), 0.6 (stage three to four), and 0.5 (stage four to five).[18]

Since wages were rising more slowly, why did the wage/output ratio start to rise near the cycle peak? The answer is that product per worker hour (which may be called *labor productivity*) at first rises more rapidly than real wages, then rises more slowly than real wages as the peak of expansion is neared. Product per hour of work—by all workers, black and white, female and male—rose in the 1970-75 cycle by 0.8 percent per quarter (from stage one to two), 0.6 percent (stage two to three), 0.6 percent (stage three to four), and -0.3 percent (stage four to five). So just before the peak the ratio of wages to income (or output) *rose,* even though the real wage per hour fell, because the output per worker fell even more. Similarly, in the average of the four cycles from 1949 to 1970 the output per hour of work rose by 0.8 percent (stage one to two), 0.5 percent (stage two to three), 0.4 percent (stage three to four), and was constant at 0.0 percent from stage four to five.[19] Once again, near the peak real hourly wages were rising very slowly, but the ratio or wages to income (or output) still rose because labor productivity was constant.

Labor productivity is affected by three main factors: technology, the class struggle, and the degree of utilization of labor in capitalist enterprise. The first factor, technology, is dominant in the long run, but may be mostly ignored in any short period. This is clear because technology is always improving the productivity of labor, yet labor productivity actually is constant or falling at the peak of expansion, *and falls in much of the contraction period.* In the class struggle (the second factor) capitalists are always trying to speed up workers, while workers are always trying to resist speed-up. It is true, as Boddy and Crotty assert, that workers are better able to resist speed-up at the peak of expansion. It does not seem likely, however, that workers could actually lower product per labor hour (and certainly could not do so in a contraction).

Contrary to the Boddy and Crotty view, most of the decline in labor productivity appears to be due to the nonutilization of some employed workers in capitalist enterprises at the peak of expansion (and in the contraction). Near the peak of expansion, there are many industries in which potential output is already greater than demand. Therefore, many employed workers are not fully utilized. As a result, measured labor productivity may decline even before the peak.

At the beginning of the recession, labor productivity may decline rapidly. Actual output declines rapidly as demand declines. At first, however, capitalists believe the decline is only temporary, so they hold on to many workers, especially skilled workers. Thus, "productivity" per labor hour appears to decline because the employment decline lags behind the output decline. This is one reason for the rapid decline in the rate of profit in the recession or depression.

In summary, the ratio of profit to income rises rapidly at the beginning of the expansion (mostly because of the rise in labor productivity as labor is again fully utilized). The ratio of profit to income, however, remains constant or falls toward the peak of expansion (mostly because of constant or declining labor productivity). This is *one* factor affecting total profits and the rate of profit on capital—and hence the amount of investment.

Limitations on Output Demanded

Under capitalism the actual output produced is dependent on the effective demand in money terms—which is a function of class relations. The potential output depends directly on the growth of the forces of production—labor, capital, natural resources, and technology. The second factor which Weisskopf shows determining the rate of capitalist profit is the ratio of actual output demanded to potential output. (This is Marx's problem of the realization of potential profit.)

To understand the reality of present-day problems of profit realization, we may begin by looking at actual limitations on consumer demand. In every expansion, national income rises faster than consumer demand, so the ratio of consumption to income declines. For example, in the expansion of November 1970 to November 1973, the average ratio of consumption to income fell by 24 percent.[20] Similarly, in every contraction, consumption declines more slowly than national income, so the average ratio of consumption to income rises. For example, in the contraction of November 1973 to March 1975, the average ratio of consumption to income rose by 15 percent.

Why does the ratio of consumption to income fall in expansions and rise in contractions? Keynesians attribute it to innate psychological propensities of all people to save more out of rising income and to save less out of falling income. Marx, on the other hand, traced these changes back to the capitalist relations of production, in which (1) workers have mostly low incomes and capitalists high incomes, and (2) workers' wages lag behind capitalist profits in every expansion.

The consumer behavior of affluent capitalists and lower-income workers differs. As capitalist income rises in an expansion, capitalists do consume a smaller and smaller proportion of it. This is partly because they still consider their earlier consumption level satisfactory, and partly because the profit outlook has improved, so they wish to save a large part of their income for investment.

Workers, on the other hand, continue to spend almost their whole income on consumption. Since their standard of living was below normal at the bottom of the depression, they use most of their increased income to pay off debts and buy necessities. Their ratio of consumption to income remains over .95 even at the peak of the cycle.

Since capitalists have a much lower ratio of consumption to income than workers, the distribution of income between workers and capitalists is very important in determining the national average ratio of consumption to income. Even if there were no changes in psychological propensities to consume in either class, a shift in income distribution could explain a change in the average ratio of consumption to income. The declining average rate in an expansion may be explained by a shift of income from workers (with high ratios of consumption) to capitalists (with low—and falling—ratios of consumption). The rising ratio of consumption to income in a depression could be explained by an income shift back from capitalists to workers.

As we saw earlier, there *is* an income shift from workers to capitalists in the first half of expansion. Therefore, in this period, the ratio of consumption to income declines. In the expansion of 1970-73, the wage/income ratio declined all the way to stage four. Therefore, in that cycle the consumption/income ratio declined all the way to stage five (since there is a time lag of one stage). This means that limited demand would cause actual output to drop below potential output, thereby lowering the rate of profit. In the 1970-73 expansion, the rate of profit did reach its peak in stage four. Finally, investment in that cycle reached its peak in stage five and then declined (again, there is a time lag of one stage).

Wage-push theorists such as Boddy and Crotty correctly point out that in the four preceding cycles (1949 to 1970) the income shift from workers to capitalists only occurred in early expansion (from stage one to stage two). In the rest of the expansion, income shifted back a bit from capitalists to workers. They conclude that the falling profit share lowered the rate of profit, which reduced investment. They are wrong, however, to concentrate on the income shift at the peak of expansion. The harm was done much earlier, at the beginning of expansion, when the wage share was falling and the profit share rising. As a result of this income shift to a class with lower consumption ratios, the consumption/income ratio fell in these four cycles in early expansion (from stage one to stage three). The weakening consumer demand caused the utilization of capacity (actual to potential output) to stop rising in stage three, and then *fall* in late expansion and in the contraction.

Because of the decline in the ratio of consumer demand to income and its unfavorable effect on actual output demanded, the rate of profit also peaked in stage three, then fell. Finally, because the rate of profit peaked so early, net investment reached its peak in stage three, then declined. This decline in investment eventually led to the overall economic decline.

It is true that in late expansion—*after* the rate of profit and investment were already falling significantly—the wage share rose (because productivity was falling as workers were still employed, but not fully utilized). This late rise in the wage share did cause the consumption/income ratio to rise again in late expansion. This positive factor in consumer demand, however, came much too late to stop the recession. In the recession, total wages and total consumption fell, even though the wage share and the consumption income ratio were rising. Finally, these improving ratios did cause the process to reverse itself, and a recovery began.

Rising Costs of Constant Capital

The third factor affecting the rate of profit—in Weisskopf's formulation—is the ratio of potential output to capital. This factor may be divided into real, physical terms (output/capital) and price terms (price of output/price of capital), the result being the product of the two. The long-run ratio of output to capital is, of course, determined by technology. In the short run, however, the output/ capital ratio fell in every one of the five expansions and rose in every one of the five contractions since 1949. Presumably, this is *not* the effect of technology, but results from raw material shortages, bottlenecks, and entrance into the market of thousands of inefficient firms in the last part of the expansion. At any rate, this is another negative influence on the overall profit rate in the late expansion.

The ratio of the price of output to the price of capital also has some systematic impact on the rate of profit. There is some dispute, but most of the facts point toward a negative impact on profit rates in the late expansion, and a positive effect in the contraction. In a careful study of costs and prices, Frederick Mills collected data for many cycles—from the 1890s to the 1930s—on prices of consumer goods, prices of plant and equipment, and prices of raw materials.[21] Mills found that in the average expansion period consumer-goods prices rose very slowly. He found, however, that prices of plant and equipment rose sharply and raw materials prices rose even faster. Similarly, in the average depression consumer-goods prices fell, but plant and equipment prices fell much more—and raw-materials prices fell even further. Because of rapid shifts in demand and slow changes in supply, prices of all capital goods (and especially raw materials) rose more rapidly in expansions and fell more rapidly in contractions than did prices of consumer goods.

In recent business cycles, some changes have occurred, since costs seldom decline in recessions. In the most recent cycle (1970-75), however, nonwage costs (mainly materials) still rose more rapidly than other prices in expansion, and fell more (or rose less) in recession. In the expansion from November 1970 to November 1973, the price of finished goods rose considerably (by thirteen percentage points), but the price of raw materials rose an extraordinary amount (by fifty percentage points) in the same period.[22] Thus, *the rising costs of raw materials did contribute to the profit squeeze in the expansion in 1973.*

In the contraction from November 1973 to March 1975, the price of finished goods actually *rose* (by eighteen points). The price of raw materials, however, reached a peak in the stage just after the cycle peak (stage six), then *declined* for the rest of the contraction. Thus the movements of raw-materials prices actually helped American profit margins in most of the contraction because they fell in most of the period.

Since producers of raw materials are also capitalists, why should a relative rise in their prices harm the overall capitalist outlook for profits? Most raw materials used in the United States are imported from abroad. Hence a relative rise in raw-materials prices will raise the profit rates of some foreign capitalists, but will definitely lower the internal rate of profit in the United States. (This conclusion may be modified to the extent that raw materials are controlled by American-based multinational corporations.)

At any rate, the ratio of output prices to raw-materials prices did decline in most previous expansions and rise in most previous contractions. This includes the 1920s and 1930s in Mills' study, cited above. It also includes, in my study of present government data, the same pattern for the cycles of 1949-54 and 1970-75. On the other hand, my research confirms Boddy and Crotty's finding that this pattern is *not* observed in several other recent cycles. From 1954 to 1970, there is simply a long-run secular *rise* in the ratio of output prices to raw-materials prices (due to the overwhelming power of the imperialist countries, and other factors). So this factor tended to hold profit rates up in the three cycles from 1954 to 1970.

The Two-Horned Dilemma

Capitalists are caught at the crucial point in each expansion between two problems. Problems of profit creation are caused by rising costs of raw materials, lower output/capital ratio, and lower output/labor ratio. The other problem is profit realization, caused by limited demand or "underconsumption," due to limited wages. It is impossible to solve both parts of the dilemma at the same time under capitalism. At the crucial point in expansion, *both* the limited consumer demand *and* the rising cost per unit act together to squeeze profits and choke off economic circulation. At the trough of the depression, the end of decline in consumer demand *and* the falling costs per unit increase profits and stimulate economic activity.

The theory that contraction is caused by both limited demand (underconsumption) *and* high costs (overinvestment) shows that cycles are unavoidable under capitalism. Some liberals believe they could prevent contractions by giving higher wages to increase demand, but that ignores the cost problem. Some conservatives would prevent contractions by lowering wages and interest rates, but that ignores the demand problem.

Traditional Capitalist Government Policy

Most economists now agree that cycles of boom and bust are inherent in unregulated capitalism. Liberals have fallen back to a second line of defense: depressions can be prevented by monetary and fiscal policies of the government (in the ways suggested by John M. Keynes).

The traditional Keynesian policies against unemployment, including lower taxes, higher government spending (mainly military), and easier credit have been discussed by me at great length elsewhere.[23] Suffice it to say that they don't work very well because of (1) administrative barriers to accurate timing and action, (2) political barriers to constructive spending, (3) political barriers to sufficient tax reductions for the working class, and (4) the fact that the increase of inflation is much, much greater than the reduction of unemployment. Many major establishment economists, including Paul Samuelson, simply admit that ending inflation and getting full employment at the same time is one little thing not yet solved by establishment economists: "Experts do not yet know . . . an incomes policy that will permit us to have *simultaneously* . . . full employment and price stability."[24] Yet this is the major, specific problem of the decade!

Inflation and Wage-Price Controls

The Keynesian explanation boils down to the idea that inflation results when aggregate demand is greater than the aggregate supply provided by a fully employed labor force. The aggregate monetary or effective demand includes not just coins and paper money and demand deposits, but all the forms of credit in the economy—in short, demand includes anything that allows an individual or business or government to purchase goods and services now, whether they pay now or later. This means that demand may be expanded to some extent by banks and financial institutions and/or by government manipulation of the financial system. This Keynesian manipulation of inflation by excess aggregate demand, including credit, is adequate to explain most of the inflation of past American history up through the 1940s. In the 1950s, however, traces of a new kind of inflation emerged that were confusing in Keynesian terms. Moreover, the inflation of the late 1960s and early 1970s was definitely a new variety that the usual Keynesian model has not been able to explain. The present inflation *continues even in contraction periods* with deficient demand and mass unemployment.

How have prices behaved in recent decades? Prices fell rapidly during the Great Depression of 1929-33. Then, with the recovery of demand, there was a price rise until 1937. The recession of 1938 caused a price drop, which was followed by the slow rise of prices during World War II. This rise would have been much more rapid except that price controls held down inflationary pressures. Immediately following World War II, however, the vast demand for consumer and investment goods burst the dam and flooded the market with purchasing power, resulting in the rapid price rises of 1946-48. A recession lowered prices in 1949, then the Korean war caused a second major round of inflation in 1950-51. Another recession kept prices steady at the end of the Korean war, after which they rose steadily until 1960. Prices remained fairly stable in the early 1960s but rose sharply from 1965 to 1971 because of the Vietnam war.

The surprising point is that the price index rose rather than declined in the recessions of 1958, 1969, and 1974; and prices remained approximately stable in the recessions of 1954 and 1961. During all these recessions the prices of industries with monopolistic power actually rose in the face of declining aggregate demand.

Such evidence forces us to distinguish the inflations of the late 1950s, 1969, and 1974 from the ordinary *demand-pull inflation*, which is caused by the upward pull of aggregate demand. Now, instead, prices apparently are pushed upward by individual firms and industries; this *cost-push inflation* occurs when prices are pushed upward by either higher profit margins or higher wage costs. Many conservative economists argue that monopoly or oligopoly power of firms is *not* responsible for spiraling prices. On the contrary,

Table 3
Competitive and Monopoly Prices
(Changes in Price Indexes from
Cyclical Peak to Trough, i.e., in Contractions)

Dates of cycle peaks and troughs	Changes in competitive prices	Changes in monopoly prices
Nov. 1948-Oct. 1949	−7.8%	−1.9%
July 1953-Aug. 1954	−1.5	+1.9
July 1957-Apr. 1958	−0.3	+0.5
May 1960-Feb. 1961	−4.0	+0.1
Nov. 1969-Nov. 1970	−3.0	+5.9
Nov. 1973-March 1975	+1.8	+27.0

Sources: Price changes for 1948-49 and 1957-58 from Robert Lanzilotti, *Hearings before the Joint Economic Committee of the U.S. Congress: Employment, Growth and Price Levels* (Washington, D.C.: GPO, 1959), p. 2238. Price changes for 1949-70 from John Blair, "Market Power and Inflation," *Journal of Economic Issues*, June 1974. Price changes for 1960-61 and 1973-75 calculated by author from U.S. Department of Labor, *Wholesale Prices and Price Index* (Washington, D.C., GPO, April 1961 and August 1975).

conservatives argue that the bargaining power of labor unions pushes wages upward and that prices only follow wages. The opposite view, held by most radicals, is that prices are pushed up by monopolies to make higher profits, that wages mostly lag behind profits, and that wage increases are merely bemoaned as an excuse for higher prices.

In the Great Depression from 1929 to 1932, prices in the competitive sector fell 60 percent, but prices in the monopoly sector fell only 10 percent.[25] In the depression of 1937-38 competitive prices fell again by 27 percent, while monopoly prices fell only 3 percent! Monopoly prices are clearly very resistant to the decline of demand in depressions. The stability (or increase) of monopoly prices is achieved at the expense of large price declines for small and competitive businesses, lower purchasing power for consumers, and high unemployment of workers.

Data for more recent contractions show similar patterns, becoming only more dramatic in the latest depression. The competitive sector is defined in Table 3 as all those industries where concentration of sales by eight firms is under 50 percent. The monopoly sector is defined as all those industries where concentration of sales by eight firms is over 50 percent.

Table 3 reveals that the pattern for the 1948 recession was the same as in the 1929 and 1937 depressions. In all three cases, monopoly prices declined a little, while competitive prices declined enormously. In the 1954 and 1958 recessions, we see the first indications of the new stagflation behavior (that is, inflation *plus* unemployment). Competitive prices decline as usual, though by a small amount. But monopoly prices actually rose in the recessions, though again by a small amount. The new situation is very clear in the 1969-70 recession, in which competitive prices decline by a significant amount, while monopoly prices reveal a considerable rise. A finer division indicates still stronger price declines in the more competitive industries. Whereas prices in all industries under 50 percent concentration fell 3.0 percent, prices in industries under 25 percent concentration fell by 6.1 percent.

Price data on the 1973-75 depression indicate that monopoly prices rose in the depression by an astounding percentage. This very large price increase throughout the now-dominant monopoly sector caused even competitive prices to show a slight rise in a depression for the first time on record. This undoubtedly caused great disruption in the competitive sector, decreased production, increased bankruptcies, and increased unemployment.

President Nixon "solved" the inflation by wage and price controls. As a result of very loose price controls and very strong wage controls, wages were held down while prices rose, so the real wage fell by 4 percent in the year 1973. One way Nixon achieved these results was by appointing a probusiness Pay Board to make wage decisions. The big unions first joined it, hoping to salvage some crumbs, then withdrew when they found they were to be allowed nothing.

While real wages were declining, profit rates were actually climbing under the wage-price controls. Profit rates on investor's equity (before taxes) in all of manufacturing were "only" 16.5 percent in 1971, but rose to 18.4 percent in 1972, then rose to 21.6 percent in 1973; then rose to 23.4 percent in 1974, in the first year of the depression. A strange depression!

Finally, in the first quarter of 1975, the profit rate fell to 15.0 percent (not seasonally adjusted). When this fall in the profit rate occurred, Congress and President Ford took immediate action to stimulate the economy by lower taxes, and the profit rate jumped back up to 19.2 percent in the second quarter of 1975.

One must conclude that wage-price controls under a capitalist government lead to additional corruption and inefficiency, as well as a shift in income distribution away from wages and toward profits. The meaning of the political business cycle is also clarified. At the peak of expansion, when workers are pushing for higher wages, the government talks about inflation; and it uses restrictive monetary or fiscal or direct controls to lower wages and even promote a little unemployment. At the bottom of the depression, the government is moved by corporate pleas to stimulate the economy. The capitalist system would generate boom and bust cycles without government interference, but the government does reinforce them and may often serve as the catalyst setting off the downswing as well as the upswing (at such times as the economy was ripe for a change in direction anyway).

Stages in American Capitalism

There are no long-run economic declines in capitalist economies, *but* there certainly are many other long-term trends. These trends are usually very slow, quantitative changes, not easily visible. After many years, however, such trends result in basic historical changes; socialists can make horrible political mistakes if they shape their tactics to a bygone stage, rather than the contemporary reality.

In the early United States, from 1776 till the 1890s, the economy consisted to a very large degree of small businesses, small farmers, and craftspeople (except for slavery in the South). In the first half of that period, American business cycles closely followed British cycles with a slight time lag, showing the dominance of British imperialism. The American economy was also characterized by a completely unregulated banking system, so each production crisis led to a monetary and credit panic, producing some very large downturns (as in the 1870s).

In the 1890s and early 1900s, a wave of mergers created giant corporations, such as U. S. Steel, in most industries. These were "horizontal" mergers, meaning the elimination of direct competitors. This stage of monopoly power, as the predominant structural feature of the U. S. economy, was strengthened by a new wave of mergers in the 1920s—mostly "vertical" mergers stretching monopoly control back to raw materials and forward to retail outlets. Finally, there was another enormous wave of business mergers in the 1960s. These were mostly "conglomerate" mergers of completely unrelated firms, creating new giant corporations dominant in several industries at once.

This monopoly structure was one of the reasons (but not the only reason) for very bad depressions in the 1890s and 1930s. In the face of falling demand, monopoly firms try to maintain high prices by drastically reducing supply (and therefore increasing unemployment). The vast increase of monopoly power in the 1960s, therefore, is one of the reasons for the new phenomena of the 1970s: (1) *unemployment* that is very high in recessions, but remains high even in so-called recovery or "prosperity" periods, and (2) *inflation* that is very high in war periods, but remains high in peaceful expansions and even in some recessions! This entirely new situation of combined stagnant production and unemployment with inflation has been labeled "stagflation." Whatever it is called, it was the major economic problem of the 1970s, and is powerful enough to shake up the political scene and create new possibilities.

Increased monopoly, however, is not the only structural change in American capitalism. As late as 1929 the government played only a tiny direct role in the economy, though the police and army have always protected private property at home and imperialist investments abroad. Beginning with the New Deal, however, the American government has become far more active and has given a political dimension to the business cycle. By the 1970s, the state, local, and federal governments have come to comprise over 30 percent of all demand for goods and services in the United States. The largest single demand remains for military items and payment of military personnel, but nonmilitary government purchases are also huge. Add to this that taxation is also over 30 percent of all income and we can see that the new structure of American capitalism is defined by monopoly in the private sector, and hugely expanded government spending and taxation.

As outlined above, government activity has contributed mightily to stagflation, though it was not the initiating cause. When the government stimulates the economy in a recession, it prevents prices from dropping. In every recession through 1948, prices did drop. Since then the American economy has entered a new stage, based on government support plus monopoly control of prices, in which inflation continues even in the midst of depression. Moreover, toward the peak of expansion the private economy tends toward vast optimism and full employment. In recent cycles, however, government—especially the Federal Reserve—has used monetary and fiscal measures to hold down wages and deflate the economy. Therefore, unemployment remains remarkably high at the peak of expansion. This second structural change—enormous government interference in the macroeconomy—has thus resulted in a new stage of continuing high unemployment combined with high inflation, though there are still large cyclical swings.

The third and last major structural change has been in the international arena. Ever since the 1890s U. S. corporations have been expanding their overseas investments. Today, international conglomerates, mostly based in the United States, control most of the production and investment of the capitalist world. Nevertheless, the position of U. S. international trade and currency, after rising to remarkable heights, has now declined considerably.

After the devastation of World War II, the United States alone produced over two-thirds of all capitalist production for a lengthy time. United States currency was the only acceptable international medium of exchange, as "good as gold." Every bit of saving during the war—both in the United States and some other countries—now appeared in the form of demand. But American corporations had no competitors, and were the sole producers of many items. The destruction of war thus led to a long boom period for the United States, whose affluence trickled down to other capitalist countries. Since they had to rebuild from scratch, Japan and Germany did particularly well in the installation of new technology. This boom for the United States, Western Europe, and Japan continued from 1945 to 1970. There were continued cycles and recessions in this era, but they were very mild. Moreover, the boom was further fed by the military spending of the Korean and Vietnam wars.

All this has changed. While United States investment and trade is still the largest in the capitalist world, it is now severely challenged by competition from Japan and Western Europe. The United States, for the first time in this century, runs up huge trade deficits. The value of the dollar sinks versus West European and Japanese currencies. The lack of demand for American goods hurts American employment. The fact that Americans must pay more for foreign goods increases American inflation.

The current high rates of unemployment and inflation are caused by three structural changes: (1) increased concentration, (2) increased government, and (3) increased international competition. These three trends are not likely to change, so high unemployment and inflation are likely to remain in the near future.

Political Implications

When both unemployment and inflation exist together, there is *no* conceivable set of government fiscal and monetary policies that will cure them both. If the government stimulates the economy to lessen unemployment, it will increase inflation. If the government holds back economic demand to reduce inflation, it will increase unemployment. This means that there are no simple and easy reforms available anymore. Far more drastic steps are necessary to combat these twin evils. Moreover, while unemployment usually hurts only the lowest-income strata of the working class, inflation hurts everyone on a fixed wage or salary or pension—which is over 90 percent of Americans.

What can be done to create more employment and reduce inflation within the limits of capitalism? The main direction of left-liberals, such as John Kenneth Galbraith, is a two-pronged program. One part is the stimulation of employment by increasing demand. Government spending must be increased directly (by such measures as health-care spending). Private spending must be increased by reducing taxes. Tax reduction will be more effective to the extent that taxes are reduced most for the poor, because the poor have a very high ratio of consumption spending to income.

The other part of Galbraith's program is directed against inflation. If the economy is stimulated to achieve full employment, then only direct price controls will stop inflation. It is certainly possible for very strictly enforced price controls to prevent inflation. The AFL-CIO has followed this reasoning, and has endorsed complete mandatory price controls. Galbraith recognizes that the main offenders are the monopoly corporations. Therefore, the most effective way to enforce controls would be to put them only on the prices of these corporations. If their prices are strictly controlled, then small business and labor unions would "voluntarily" comply by force of competition.

Such a program—higher government spending coupled with price controls on the giant corporations—could be supported enthusiastically, not only by the labor movement, but also by socialists. Our support, however, should be qualified because (1) this program could only be achieved by a new, left-coalition government, and (2) even this program would not solve unemployment and inflation in a permanent way.

The program could only be instituted by a left government because it is resisted at present not only by Republicans, but by most of the Democrats in Congress and in the White House. President Carter was elected on the basis of a strong promise to end unemployment. He broke that promise—just as he broke promises on national health care and reduction of military spending. Instead, Carter cut every kind of constructive government spending, with an increase only in military spending. Carter and Congress raised individual taxes by a small cut in income taxes combined with a larger rise in social security taxes (only corporations had a net tax reduction).

On the inflation side, Carter followed Nixon in appointing an antilabor Wage-Price Control Board. Carter and his board promulgated regulations that include clear "voluntary" controls on wages, which the board is making every effort to enforce. The voluntary controls on prices, however, were ambiguous and very permissive, lacking serious attempts to enforce them. The Carter program generated more unemployment (as was tacitly admitted by most establishment economists), but did not significantly lower the rate of price inflation (because of ineffective controls). Only a massive campaign and a change in government could possibly have brought an effective program.

Even if an effective program of government spending and strict controls on monopoly prices were instituted by a left-liberal administration, this would be a stopgap. To the extent that massive redistribution to the working class and poor is implied—by government spending, progressive tax shifts, and strict controls on monopoly prices—there will be resistance and big problems in enforcement. Corporations might well go on strike by reducing investment, thereby reducing employment. To enforce price controls would require a large bureaucracy, open to various sorts of corruption. If strictly enforced, price controls would distort economic decision-making by preventing expansion in areas of low return (even if socially desirable) and by promoting other areas (even if socially undesirable). Eventually, therefore, price controls would necessitate rationing of both consumer and producer goods. To do all this while retaining private property would combine the worst of both capitalism and bureaucratic central planning.

Thus while supporting a left-liberal program of government spending and price controls as a temporary measure, socialists must emphasize the longer-run necessity for social ownership of the giant monopoly corporations. Only this step can finally end the agonies of unemployment and inflation. In the next year or so, a major recession is likely; in the context of widespread popular antagonism to "big government," a left-liberal program that seems to amount only to the expansion of government power will encounter very serious obstacles. The problem for socialists is to support the positive aspects of this program, while making clear that a permanent elimination of capitalist inflation and unemployment would require much more radical steps, steps that could only be undertaken by a democratic socialist government based on massive social movements. Thus even though a socialist government lies far in the future, the vision of a democratic, pluralistic socialism is an important part of an immediate programmatic effort by the left.

Notes

1. Warren Gramm, "Credit Saturation, Secular Redistribution, and Long-Run Stability," *Journal of Economic Issues* (June 1978): 311.
2. See Paul Baran and Paul Sweezy, *Monopoly Capital* (New York: Monthly Review Press, 1966).
3. Karl Marx, *Capital*, vol. 3 (New York: International Publishers, 1967), p. 568.
4. Ibid., vol. 2, p. 363*n*.
5. See, for example, Andrew Glyn and Bob Sutcliffe, *British Capitalism, Workers, and the Profit Squeeze* (Baltimore: Penguin, 1972).
6. Richard Leftwich and Ansel Sharp, *Economics of Social Issues* (Homewood, Ill.: Irwin, 1974), p. 249.
7. Raford Boddy and James Crotty, "Class Conflict and Macro-Policy," *Review of Radical Political Economies* 7 (Spring 1975): 8.
8. Marx, *Capital*, vol. 1, p. 620. Italics added.
9. Marx, *Capital*, vol. 3, p. 281.
10. See, for example, Anwar Shaikh, "An Introduction to the History of Crisis Theories," in Union for Radical Political Economics, *U.S. Capitalism in Crisis* (New York: distributed by Monthly Review Press, 1978), pp. 219-40.
11. See Howard Sherman, *Profits in the United States* (Ithaca: Cornell University Press, 1968), ch. 1.
12. Karl Marx, *Theories of Surplus Value* (New York: International Publishers, 1952), p. 371.
13. Marx, *Capital*, vol. 3, pp. 297-99.
14. Ibid., p. 286.
15. See Boddy and Crotty, "Class Conflict"; also see non-Marxist theories in Gottfried Haberler, *Prosperity and Depression* (Cambridge, MA: Harvard University Press, 1960), ch. 3.
16. The history of Marxist underconsumption theory is given in Paul Sweezy, *The Theory of Capitalist Development* (New York: Monthly Review Press, 1942); the history of non-Marxist underconsumption theory is given in Haberler, *Prosperity and Depression*, ch. 5.
17. Thomas Weisskopf, "Marxist Perspectives on Cyclical Crisis," in Union for Radical Political Economics, *U.S. Capitalism*, pp. 241-60.
18. U.S. Department of Commerce, Economic Analysis Bureau, *Business Conditions Digest*, May 1977, October 1977, and November 1977.
19. Ibid.
20. Derived from U.S. Department of Commerce, *Survey of Current Business*, July 1973 and August 1975.
21. Frederick Mills, *Price-Quantity Interactions in Business Cycles* (New York: National Bureau of Economic Research, 1946), pp. 132-33.
22. All data in this and the following paragraph are from U.S. Bureau of Labor Statistics, *Monthly Labor Review*, January 1971 and August 1975.
23. See Howard Sherman, *Stagflation, a Radical Theory of Unemployment and Inflation* (New York: Harper & Row, 1976), ch. 9. Also see E. K. Hunt

and Howard Sherman, *Economics: An Introduction to Traditional and Radical Views,* 3d ed. (New York: Harper & Row, 1968), chs. 20, 29.
24. Paul Samuelson, *Economics,* 9th ed. (New York: McGraw-Hill, 1973), p. 823.
25. See Gardiner Means, "Inflation and Unemployment," in John Blair, ed., *The Roots of Inflation* (New York: Franklin, 1975), pp. 1-15.

Harry Magdoff

A NOTE ON INFLATION

Inflation is a possibility in any society that uses money as a medium of exchange, but it is an inescapable and distinguishing feature of capitalism—and most especially in its monopoly stage. From their beginnings, and throughout their long history, capitalist countries have at times been plagued and at other times stimulated by bursts of inflation. In essence, these recurring waves are both symptom and cause of the instability inherent in the anarchic production system of capitalism. It is true that especially severe inflationary episodes have resulted from currency mismanagement by governments and banks. And even more severe currency depreciations have been caused by armaments races, wars, and the aftermath of wars. But the distortions created by these special progenitors of inflation—currency manipulation and wars—are themselves either products of, or means adopted to cope with, the unremitting instability of capitalism.

Whatever the immediate causes of inflation may be—and without taking into account the inflation-induced contradictions which are resolved by economic depressions—rapid price rises produce two important results for a capitalist society. First, they act as a stimulus to investment. This is especially the case when price advances are persistent and do not spiral too quickly. Under such circumstances, speculative fever is rife, the urge to accumulate inventory is strong, and the environment is favorable for new risk-taking by entrepreneurs. Second, inflation serves to redistribute income in favor of some sectors of the population and to the disadvantage of others. Typically, it is an instrument for the protection and expansion of surplus value, that is, the share of the national product appropriated by the capitalists. The propensity to start and feed the flames of an inflationary spiral grows naturally out of a society that is guided by the profit motive. Since it is the duty and destiny of each capitalist enterprise to increase its profits, every

This is the text of a reply by Harry Magdoff to a request for a brief statement on inflation from the editors of the Mexican journal *Problemas del Desarrollo: Revista Latinoamericana de Economía*. It originally appeared in the December 1973 issue of *Monthly Review*.

practical device for this purpose is seized upon, whether it takes the form of reducing costs of production or raising the price of the finished product. The capitalist is hence always on the lookout for ways to raise his prices. the price-raising path to higher profits is, however, restricted when competition among capitalists is widespread. On the other hand, the inflationary tendency begins to take over as the force of competition diminishes.

The relevance of inflation in capitalism is best understood against the background of historical changes in the structure of this socioeconomic order. Infant capitalism was rooted in rampant inflation, the latter spurred by the commercial revolution, the looting of the treasures of colonial acquisitions, and the flood of cheap gold and silver obtained with forced labor from the mines of Latin America. Although long upward waves of prices were followed by prolonged deflations (tied up with alternating periods of prosperity and stagnation and often associated with the successes and failures of colonial exploitation), the dominant and most influential trend during the centuries of evolution of merchant capitalism was inflation.

Quite the opposite is the case as capitalism moved from the commercial to the industrial phase. Declining commodity prices not only became a characteristic phenomenon, but were in fact elements contributing to economic success, instead of, as in the past, accompaniments of stagnation. Reductions in production costs achieved in the age of machinery were reflected in long-run price declines, under the impetus of competition. When there were many relatively small firms in each industry, among which collusion was difficult or impossible, businessmen were forced to fight each other by cutting prices, where cost savings permitted. The common method of increasing profits was to capture the markets of competitors by underselling them. Even under these conditions, wars and cyclical booms created waves of inflation, but these were overtaken eventually by relatively long periods of declining prices, made possible and necessary by technical advance and competition.

This type of price behavior changed dramatically when concentration and centralization of capital reached the point where direct and indirect collusion and control of markets by relatively few giant firms in each industry became the rule. With the appearance of monopoly capitalism, a secular trend of inflation set in. Cyclical depressions at times produced a downward adjustment of prices. In addition, war-induced hyperinflations often led to major price corrections. But the innate tendency of capitalism toward inflation became dominant as soon as monopolistic-type control spread throughout the industrial system.

Table 1
U.S. Wholesale Price Index
(1823 = 100)

1823	100
1848	75
1873	139
1898	74

Source: Hearings before the Joint Economic Committee on Employment, Growth, and Price Levels, Part 2 (Washington, D.C.: GPO, 1959), pp. 395–96.

The contrasting behavior of prices in the stages of competitive and monopoly capitalism can be observed in the following two tables, which summarize the major trends in U. S. wholesale prices during the past 150 years. First let us look at the earliest 75 years of this time span, from 1823 to 1898, a period that covers the inception and maturation of competitive capitalism in the United States.

As can be seen, the net wholesale price change in the United States between 1823 to 1898 was downward. In the interim there was a wild cyclical price swing due to the huge volume of paper currency issued by the U. S. government to finance the Civil War. This war-induced inflation was followed by a long period of deflation, with wholesale prices getting back to pre-Civil War levels in the 1880s. Thus, the height of the wholesale price index shown above for 1873 still reflects the impact of the induced inflation associated with the Civil War and its aftermath. Given the eventual return of conservative monetary practices, the downward price pressure of competitive capitalism reasserted itself. By 1898, when monopoly capitalism was already blossoming and affecting price practices, the wholesale price index was roughly the same as that of fifty years earlier. Now note how very different the experience of the past seventy-five years has been.

These data suggest that the present inflationary process is not at all a new phenomenon. While the rates of price increase have recently been accelerating and while this acceleration may be an omen of an approaching new hyperinflation, it is nevertheless important to recognize the consistency of the secular inflationary trend over the past three-quarters of a century. The year-to-year changes over this long period have been far from regular: each big war contributed to the hyperinflation of some currencies in the advanced capitalist nations; in addition, the Great Depression of the 1930s lowered price levels throughout the capitalist world. But despite erratic and cyclical year-to-year movements, the inflationary trend always reasserted itself; at the end of each twenty-five-year interval summarized in Table 2, the price level reached a new high.

Usually when one finds such a persistent trend in economic behavior, it is the result of more than one simple cause. Here too the contributing factors are many. But what is significant is that the multifaceted and mutually reinforcing promoters of inflation are all related in varying degrees to the nature and structure of monopoly capitalism. The following are some of these:

(1) The new imperialism of this stage of capitalism stimulates the growth of armaments and the spread of wars.

(2) The tendency, however reluctant, on the part of powerful sectors of the capitalist class to grant wage concessions to sections of the working class in the hope of getting popular support for imperialist wars and policies.

(3) The widespread use of protective tariffs and other trade barriers as weapons of commercial warfare.

(4) The greater integration of the world capitalist system, resulting in the spread of inflation from one country to another.

(5) The growth of large-scale banking and credit expansion as financial instruments for the spread of giant corporations. With this comes the larger use of credit and the pumping up of the money supply.[1]

(6) With the possibility of controlling large segments of the market, the giant corporations compete for market shares by manipulating consumers through advertising, other means of sales promotion, and fostering consumer credit—leading to higher costs and higher prices in times of prosperity and to resistance to price declines in depressions.

(7) The tendency to economic stagnation characteristic of monopoly capitalism induces greater economic activity by the state. This takes various forms, including money manipulations and gov-

Table 2
U.S. Wholesale Price Index
(1898 = 100)

1898	100
1923	208
1948	331
1973 (first 8 months)	530

Sources: 1898 to 1948: same as Table 1; 1948 to 1973: *Economic Indicator* (Washington, D.C.: GPO, various monthly issues). The price indexes were spliced and converted to an 1898 base.

ernment spending designed to create a favorable (i.e., inflationary) environment for business.

While all these factors have in one way or another played a role in furthering the inflation of the post-World War II period, it appears that the last item (point 7) has been the most important contributor to present ills. The manipulators of government finance suffer from the illusion that they can regulate the economy to obtain an even and moderate pace of price increases. But the truth is that such "fine-tuning" is not feasible amidst the contradictory economic pressures and the very distortions that inflation induces. The experience of recent decades supplies ample evidence that the inflationary techniques used to stimulate the economy artificially neither resolve the contradictions of monopoly capitalism nor basically reverse the underlying tendency to stagnation. In fact, the very methods used to moderate business slumps and create jobs help engender new distortions and imbalances, which in turn call for ever more inflationary measures and make the entire economy addicted to these stimulants.

Disturbances in the international monetary system have been adding still another dimension to the problem. Built into the Bretton Woods system was the contradiction between its goals of stabilizing foreign exchange rates and maintaining the imperialist system. The burdens of financing imperialist control, by war and other means, eventually nullified the exchange rate stability. The breakdown of the Bretton Woods system, coming on top of the huge pile-up of U. S. dollars abroad, fostered enormous and rapid shifts of currencies among the leading capitalist powers. Such shifts, and the defensive measures taken to counter their effects (notably, support of unusually high interest rates concurrently with accelerated inflation), have played havoc with prevailing fantasies about the possibility of keeping inflation within reasonable limits.

As the inflation-induced distortions became more evident and appeared to be getting out of control, the ruling circles in the advanced capitalist nations have been turning to the problem of moderating instead of generating inflation. But the hard fact is that in a capitalist society the correction of a long stretch of inflation, and especially one that threatens to become hyperinflation, can only take the form of economic depression. Short of such a radical readjustment, temporary alleviating measures are merely means of shifting the burdens of inflation from one class or stratum to others. In a bourgeois society, this obviously means protecting business profits at the expense of the working class. The extent to which the ruling class can accomplish this depends on the vigor with which the workers pursue the class struggle. In the final analysis, however, the only defense the working class has against the alternative evils of inflation and depression is the abolition of the capitalist social system.

Notes

1. For an explanation of the expanding credit system and its role, see Thorstein Veblen, *Absentee Ownership* (New York: Huebsch, 1923), ch. 12.

Part III

EXCESS CAPACITY, EFFECTIVE DEMAND, AND ACCUMULATION

The essays in Part III focus on the problem of insufficiency of effective demand—the nemesis of mature capitalist economies. The initial essay by Michal Kalecki was published in Polish in 1935 (one year before the appearance of Keynes' *General Theory*), and is one of a series of now-classic studies in which he anticipated all of the essentials of the Keynesian revolution. The following contribution by Paolo Sylos-Labini, from his book *Oligopoly and Technical Progress,* examines the connection between the problem of effective demand and the growth of the modern firm. The next two essays, also by Michal Kalecki, discuss the importance of the work of Rosa Luxemburg and Mikhail Tugan-Baranovski, and the centrality of Marx's reproduction schemes, for any analysis of long-run instability in advanced capitalist economies. The following two selections by Josef Steindl are attempts to elaborate upon and update his work in *Maturity and Stagnation in American Capitalism,* accounting directly for the course of capitalist development during the entire post-Second World War period, and criticizing the recent trend of promoting stagnation as economic policy. The last contribution by John Bellamy Foster delves into the question of unused productive capacity and investment shortfalls in the U. S. economy during the past half century.

Michal Kalecki

THE MECHANISM OF THE BUSINESS UPSWING

1. Mass unemployment seems to be the most obvious symptom of depression. Is this unemployment due to the shortage of capital equipment, in other words, to inadequate accumulation of fixed capital in relation to the increase of population? Certainly not. The position is rather the reverse. During the depression the existing capital equipment is utilized to a small degree: the idle capital equipment is the counterpart of the unemployed labor force. To what should be attributed the fact that the owner of unutilized equipment who encounters a lasting supply of idle labor does not embark upon production? Any single entrepreneur would certainly answer that this would be an unprofitable proposition: the prices at which he could sell would not even cover his current costs, that is, the outlay on raw materials, labor, taxes, etc. Thus a reduction of wages is being recommended as a way to overcome the depression. Now, one of the main features of the capitalist system is the fact that what is to the advantage of a single entrepreneur does not necessarily benefit all entrepreneurs as a class. If one entrepreneur reduces wages he is able *ceteris paribus* to expand production; but once all entrepreneurs do the same thing the result will be entirely different.

Let us assume that wages have been in fact generally reduced, and likewise taxes as a counterpart of cuts in civil servants' salaries. Now the entrepreneurs owing to the "improved" price-wage relation utilize their equipment to capacity and in consequence unemployment vanishes. Has depression been thus overcome? By no means, as the goods produced have still to be sold. Now, production has risen considerably and as a result of an increase in the price-wage relation the part of production equivalent to profits (including depreciation) of the capitalists (entrepreneurs and rentiers) has grown even more. A precondition for an equilibrium at this new higher level is that this part of production which is not

First published (in English) in *Studies in the Theory of Business Cycles 1933–1939* (Oxford: Basil Blackwell, 1966). Originally published in Polish in 1935.

consumed by workers or by civil servants should be acquired by capitalists for their increased profits; in other words, the capitalists must spend immediately all their additional profits on consumption or investment. It is, however, most unlikely that this should in fact happen. In general, capitalists' consumption changes but little in the course of the business cycle. It is true that increased profitability stimulates investment but this stimulus will not work right away since the entrepreneurs will temporize until they are convinced that the higher profitability is going to last. Therefore the immediate effect of increased profits will be an accumulation of money reserves in the hands of entrepreneurs and in the banks. Then, however, the goods which are the equivalent of the increased profits will remain unsold. The accumulating stocks will sound the alarm for a new price reduction of goods which do not find any outlet. Thus the effect of the cost reduction will be canceled. On balance only a price reduction will have occured, offsetting the advantage of the cost reduction to the entrepreneurs since unemployment going hand in hand with underutilization of equipment will reappear.

In fact wage reduction does not, as a rule, result even in the temporary increase in production described above. Indeed, not only investment but even utilization of existing equipment will not respond immediately to an improvement in profitability. For immediately after the reduction of wages and before the entrepreneurs manage to increase production within the existing capital equipment a fall in prices makes its appearance. As the entrepreneurs do not at once make use of the means taken away from the workers for buying consumption or investment goods, the revenue of industry is reduced *pro tanto*. What the entrepreneurs gain on wage reductions is soon dissipated through price declines. All this could be noticed in all countries during the world depression in the period 1931-32, when the wave of wage reductions brought about a rapid fall in prices rather than an increase in production.

2. The doctrine of wage cuts as the way out of depression is sometimes supplemented by a remedy against the price fall. The creation of cartels is recommended to stop the "cutthroat competition." Let us assume that in all industries cartels have been formed, that wages have been duly reduced, but that the diminished demand of the workers could not have any repercussions on prices since they are maintained by cartels at a stable level. Will the "improved" price-wage relation be of any help in overcoming the depression? Now, it is rather unlikely that cartels would invest profits derived by wage reductions more promptly than the entrepreneurs under conditions of "free competition." The opposite is rather the

case. Thus in a totally cartelized system, just as under "free competition," the proceeds of industry will diminish as much as their costs, and as prices remain unchanged the sales of goods will drop in the same proportion as the proceeds have shrunk. Thus while wage reductions do not cause any increase in production in the case of a competitive economy, in a fully cartelized system they lead, as a result of rigidity of prices, to a shrinkage of production and a rise in unemployment.

In a "mixed" system, consisting of a cartelized and a competitive sector, the result of wage cuts will be something intermediate: a fall of production will ensue but it will be weaker than in a fully cartelized system.

3. It follows from the above argument that a reduction of wages does not constitute a way out of depression, because the gains are not used immediately by the capitalists for purchase of investment goods. Now we shall try to prove that the opposite is the case: the increase in investment per se unaccompanied by a wage reduction causes a rise in output.

Let us assume that as a result of some important invention there is an increase in investment associated with its spreading. Now, is it possible for the capitalists to step up their investment, even though their profits have not increased (there was no reduction in wages) nor have they curtailed their consumption ad hoc (this, indeed, is most unlikely). The financing of additional investment is effected by the so-called creation of purchasing power. The demand for bank credits increases and these are granted by the banks. The means used by the entrepreneurs for construction of new establishments reach the industries of investment goods. This additional demand makes for setting to work idle equipment and unemployed labor. The increased employment is a source of additional demand for consumer goods and thus results in turn in higher employment in the respective industries. Finally, the additional investment outlay finds its way directly and through the workers' spending into the pockets of capitalists (we assume that workers do not save). The additional profits flow back as deposits to the banks. Bank credits increase by the amount additionally invested and deposits by the amount of additional profits. The entrepreneurs who engage in additional investment are "propelling" into the pockets of other capitalists profits which are equal to their investment, and they are becoming indebted to these capitalists to the same extent via banks.

In the preceding sections we were faced with the problem of whether the profits resulting from the reduction of costs are invested. In the case presently considered, the profits, to put it paradoxically, are invested even before they come into being. Profits that are not invested cannot be retained because they are annihilated by the ensuing fall in production and prices. The creation of the purchasing power for financing additional investment increases the output from the low level reached in the depression and thus creates profits equal to this investment.

It should be pointed out that the increase in output will result in an increased demand for money in circulation, and thus will call for a rise in credits of the central bank. Should the bank respond to it by raising the rate of interest to a level at which total investment would decline by the amount equal to the additional investment caused by the new invention, no increase in investment would ensue and the economic situation would not improve. Therefore the precondition for the upswing is that the rate of interest should not increase too much in response to an increased demand for cash.

What will happen, however, when the new invention has been spread and the original source of the business upswing has dried up and thus the stimulus for investment vanishes? Is the downswing unavoidable then? No, because in the meantime the increased profitability prevailing in the economy as a whole will have resulted in a rise in investment. It is this investment caused by higher profitability which will step in when the effect of the new invention will have petered out.

4. We described in the preceding section a business upswing resulting from the investment stimulated by an important invention, which to some extent is a matter of chance. Without such an external stimulus, would the depression last forever? Is it not inherent in the depression to breed forces that put an end to it by causing an increase in investment?

Let us assume that the economy became stabilized at the bottom of the depression at a very low level of economic activity; that investment in particular has shrunk to such a degree that it does not cover the necessary replacement of the aging capital equipment. Let us suppose that this equipment consists of 2,000 establishments and that every year 100 of them get out of use, but only 60 establishments are constructed. Thus the capital equipment shrinks every year by 40 establishments. However, it is this destruction of equipment that after a rather prolonged period initiates a business upswing. For owing to the shrinkage of capital equipment the same demand is met by a declining number of existing establishments which as a result improve their degree of utilization. Once the profitability of the existing capital equipment has thus increased, the level of investment will increase as well. The finance for it will be provided—as was described in the preceding section—

by creation of additional purchasing power. This will result in an increase of the output of investment goods and of employment in the respective branches of industry. Moreover, the rise in demand on the part of the newly employed workers for consumption goods will cause fuller employment in the consumer-goods industries. This general increase in production brings about a further rise in profitability, followed by a new expansion of investment activity, a new creation of purchasing power, and so on.

This is, indeed, a cumulative process causing a steady upswing. However, once investment starts to exceed the level of necessary replacement of fixed capital—that is, once more establishments are constructed per year than the 100 establishments which are scrapped—then the factors hampering the upswing make their appearance. Just as during the depression the shrinkage of capital equipment was the inception of the upswing, so now the expansion of this equipment finally brings the boom to a stop and starts the downswing.

The process of collapse of the boom is the reverse of that starting the upswing from the bottom of depression. Let us assume that at the top of the boom investment is stabilized at the level of 140 establishments and, as 100 establishments are scrapped per annum, the capital equipment is expanding by 40 establishments per annum. Now the demand will be met by an increasing number of establishments and as a result the degree of utilization of each of them will diminish. The resulting lower profitability will be followed by a decline in investment. And just as the increase in investment at the bottom of depression meant the start of the upswing of production and of a decline in unemployment, a fall in production and an increase in unemployment will ensue here. And this downward movement will gather momentum as in the period of the upswing the upward tendencies were cumulative in character.

It is not, of course, the purpose of this essay to present a complete theory of business fluctuations. An attempt is made to give a general idea of the mechanism of a "natural" upswing, and in particular to clarify one of its aspects. It now becomes apparent that investment has a favorable effect upon the economic situation only at the time when it is executed and provides an outlet for additional purchasing power. On the other hand, the productive character of investment contributes to the slackening of the upswing and finally brings it to an end. For it is the expansion of capital equipment that in the light of the above analysis causes the collapse of the boom. We face here one of the most remarkable paradoxes of the capitalist system: the expansion of the capital equipment, that is, the increase in the national wealth, contains the seed of a depression in the course of which the additional wealth proves to be only potential in character. For a considerable part of capital equipment is idle then and becomes useful only in the next upswing.

This statement sheds some light on the problem of government anti-slump intervention by means of public investment, with which we shall deal now.

5. After we have studied the mechanism of the business cycle let us turn again to the case where the upswing is started by a new invention which stimulates some entrepreneurs to embark upon "extra investment." By making use for this purpose of additional purchasing power, they set in motion the mechanism of the upswing. This case is very close to that of government anti-slump intervention. In order to pass from the former to the latter it suffices to substitute, for the entrepreneurs induced to invest by the new invention, the government taking up investment which is financed likewise by means of additional purchasing power in order to break the deadlock of the slump.

Let us assume that the government issues treasury bills and sells them to the banks. The government spends the money—for example, on construction of railways. As in the cases described above, employment in investment-goods industries increases and subsequently, as a result of the higher purchasing power of the workers, in consumption-goods industries as well. The amounts spent by the government flow as profits directly or through spending of the workers into the pockets of capitalists, and return to the banks as their deposits. On the side of bank assets, the government debt accrues in the form of discounted bills; on the side of liabilities there is an increase in deposits equal to the additional profits. Thus the government gets indebted via banks to the private capitalists by an amount equal to the value of the investment effected. It will be seen that a complete analogy exists between the case now being considered and that of an upswing resulting from a new invention. And in both instances increased profitability of the industry as a whole will stimulate investment and thus enhance the upswing which as a result will continue even if the government gradually reduces its investment activity. Thus an upswing started by a new invention continues after its impact has spent itself.

It should be emphasized that the pattern of public investment taken up is not essential for the effect of government intervention; what matters is that investment should be financed by additional purchasing power. The creation of purchasing power for the sake of financing the budget deficit, whatever its reason, renders a similar effect. The divergence consists only in that the additional purchasing power flows initially into different industries. Let us assume, for instance, that the amount derived from discounting treasury bills is used for the payment of doles. In this case the direct effect of government intervention will be felt in consumer-goods industries. Only after some time, when their increased profitability will induce them to invest, will prosperity be shared by investment-goods industries as well. This increased investment activity financed by creation of purchasing power will enhance the upswing, so that the latter will continue even after the budget deficits have vanished—owing to the increase in tax revenues resulting from the rise in incomes and sales.

Thus after some time private investment "takes over" from public investment: the "artificial" prosperity is replaced by a "natural" one which, by the way, sooner or later will come to a stop as a result of expansion of capital equipment.

It must be added that the precondition of successful government intervention—and of the natural upswing as well—is the possibility of meeting the increased demand for credits by the banking system without increasing the rate of interest too much. Should the rate of interest increase to such an extent that private investment is curtailed by exactly the amount of government borrowing, then obviously no purchasing power would be created, but only a shift in its structure would take place.

Paolo Sylos-Labini

THE PROBLEM OF EFFECTIVE DEMAND

In an economy with little concentration, where the entry of new firms is relatively easy and the market form is, therefore, largely competitive, no entrepreneur controls enough output to have to worry about total demand. Each firm's investment decisions are based on price, which the entrepreneur cannot alter, and on cost, which he can modify only to the extent that he manages to change the technical coefficients through better production methods. (He cannot influence factor prices.) A firm will invest on two conditions: it must have some funds of its own, since it cannot finance its investment entirely on credit, and it must be able to produce, or to expand production, at costs which are lower than price in order to earn at least what is considered a normal profit. If production expands because of a great deal of new investment and prices eventually fall, there is nothing the individual firm can do about it. The less efficient firms, which produce at the highest cost, go bankrupt and disappear from the market. (In competition, exit is as "easy" as entry.) In a competitive economy a prolonged price depression is therefore perfectly compatible with growth of national product in real terms.[1] This was, indeed, a familiar development over long stretches of the past century.[2] In our century's highly concentrated economies this can no longer happen. Prices may fall, of course, and they do for a relatively long time, but then output necessarily also falls or stagnates, as happened, for instance, in the 1930s. Today many and important markets are dominated by large firms, which do—and must—think in terms of their own market's total demand. It is not enough that these firms should have disposable funds from their own and other sources, or that they should be able to produce at costs lower than the price at any given moment. Just because they are large and because changes in their output necessarily have an influence on prices, these firms invest and expand production only when they believe they can count on growing money demand and thus on expanding sales at constant

or only slightly reduced prices, which would assure them of growing total profits.

Demand and Market Form

The investments of competitive firms are basically limited by
disposable funds, those of oligopolistic and monopolistic firms by
demand. Although the simple formulas expressing the equilibrium
position of competitive, monopolistic, and oligopolistic firms are no
more than a first approximation, they do at least show that under
monopoly and oligopoly, but not under competition, demand enters directly into the equilibrium conditions of the firm.[3]

Here we are reminded of two of Ricardo's fundamental proposi-
tions. The first is that under competition the individual firm's accumulation is limited only by the level of profit, which depends on
the level of prices and costs, especially wages; and profit supplies
both the motive and the funds for accumulation. The second is that
the equilibrium price under competition depends on cost and
under monopoly on supply and demand; this is true of competition
also, but only "for a limited period."[4] Demand may, of course,
indirectly influence the investment decisions of competitive firms.
Growing demand (in cyclical recovery and boom) creates favorable
conditions for the entry of new firms and, more important, causes
prices and, hence, profits and investable funds to rise. As a result,
the basic limit to the investment of competitive firms becomes less
restrictive.

The small firms which do business alongside the large ones in
relatively highly concentrated oligopolistic branches are, in certain
respects, in much the same position as competitive firms. Their
investment decisions, too, are governed by disposable funds and by
the relation between cost and a price which they cannot influence,
and they can also be indirectly affected by demand insofar as it may
cause profits and investable funds to grow. However, unlike competitive firms, the small firms in a concentrated market are, in
addition, subject to the influence of the large firms' policy. If the
size of the market grows and the large firms merely intend to keep
their market share, the field of action of the small firms broadens
and they can expand in proportion with the market, without fear
of reprisals.

We see that in a highly concentrated economy effective demand
becomes the principal regulatory element of employment.
Moreover, not only the volume of demand but also its composition

is apt to create difficulties for the growth of investment and employment. A highly concentrated economy is, in practice, also a highly industrialized one. In such an economy, personal incomes are high and a large proportion of consumer expenditure is directed to products other than subsistence goods. As a consequence, states Alfred E. Kahn,

> . . . demand becomes unreliable, requires stimulation, may fluctuate within wide limits. And much of demand becomes postponable, because it is for consumer durables, replacements for which can be postponed, and because it is for instruments of production, demand for which, especially in a private enterprise economy (where investment depends on uncertainties, incentives, vagaries of psychology, innovation), may fluctuate widely.[5]

The Problem of Excessive Saving

Because the investment decisions of large firms are decisively influenced by demand, it may happen that disposable funds exceed the requirements of self-financing. Since profit taxes constitute an external datum for the firm, and since dividends have to be paid whether business is good or bad, varying but little in the short run, disposable funds are a residual.[6]

These funds may be invested to raise the firm's own productive capacity; but if the firm decides not to plow back all its disposable funds because it cannot see sufficient demand ahead to guarantee a profitable market for increased output, these funds may, at least in part, be otherwise employed. They may be deposited with banks or invested in other firms. But they may also be kept as a cash reserve or used for the repayment of debts; they may be used merely to extend the firm's financial control over other companies, for example, by mergers; or they may find their way into some sort of speculative stock-market transaction. All these uses may be advantageous or profitable for the firm, but they are not investment in the proper sense of the word: they do not increase productive capacity anywhere in the economy. Nor do they cause effective demand to grow; on the contrary, in some cases they may reduce it.

Thus we are faced with a problem of savings, in terms which recall Keynes'; but the problem arises not from "psychological motives" but from the objective conditions which govern the managerial decisions of large firms and which are, in the last analysis, connected with the broad question of outlets in highly concentrated markets.[7]

Keynes' psychological motives may seem to be relevant for personal saving, but this statement needs very important qualifications. First of all, in recent years numerous investigations concerning personal saving have shown that both the marginal and the average propensity to save are conditioned not so much by purely subjective motives deriving from some abstract concept of immutable "human nature" as by objective and measurable economic and social factors, such as the highest income previously earned, the saver's position in the income distribution of a group, or changes over time in the stream of personal income. These factors are, of course, anything but constant and immutable. Second, we have to remember that personal saving nowadays accounts for only a small part of total saving and falls far short of corporate and public saving.[8] Finally, personal saving tends to become institutionalized through the diffusion of insurance and pension schemes, all of which tend to straighten out the income stream over time. In these circumstances, personal savings are administered in much the same way as corporate and public savings.

However, having said all this about the "motives" of saving, we can accept Keynes' conclusion that personal saving depends principally on the level of income and is not sensitive to changes in the rate of interest. A fall in the rate of interest does not necessarily mean a reduction in the supply of personal savings and a corresponding increase in consumption.

Apart from corporate and personal saving, there is, of course, public saving effected by governmental and public authorities, mainly by means of taxation. Quantitatively, this is by far the largest category today. We shall have more to say about this later. Neglecting government saving for the moment, we note the existence of a Keynesian savings problem: the formation and variations of corporate and personal savings are independent of variations in the rate of interest, and they may tend to exceed investment, which in its turn depends more and more on variations in demand.

Investment, Effective Demand, and Credit Policy

Concentration in the banking sector, which has been even more rapid than industrial concentration, has greatly increased the central bank's power to control the entire banking system.[9] In turn, this has enhanced the government's power to control the whole body of monetary and credit policy through the central bank, and, having this power, governments have been compelled to exercise it

in times of crisis and depression. Government became "the monetary authority."[10]

The implications of these developments on the effectiveness of
monetary and credit policy were amply examined on many occasions during the first half of this century. These studies, most of
which took their inspiration from Wicksell's monetary analysis, had
a practical purpose: to find ways and means of shortening cyclical
downswing and depression and to reduce the amplitude of fluctuations. Two oft-discussed questions were whether the greater power
of control over money and credit was matched by a corresponding
ability to influence the volume of investment, and whether the most
suitable instrument for this purpose was the bank rate. It seemed
obvious that the answer to both questions was in the affirmative,
and the authors of most of these studies did, in fact, arrive at this
conclusion. But they could do so only because they assumed explicitly or, more often, implicitly the existence of perfect competition not only on commodity but also on credit markets. In a
competitive commodity market, as we have seen above, the firm
decides to expand production, and hence to invest, in the light of
prices (which it cannot influence), costs, and disposable funds. If
the credit market is a perfect market, demand for loans is
homogeneous and its variations depend solely on the rate of interest. On the assumption that perfect competition prevails in all markets, it is therefore legitimate to maintain that the demand for
loanable funds and their supply are governed solely by the level of
the rate of interest. But if we admit that in reality conditions are
generally very far from perfect competition, the whole discussion
has to be reopened.

Keynes—repeating, with slight modifications, a neoclassical
proposition—says that investment continues up to the point where
the marginal efficiency of capital (the expected profit rate) equals
the rate of interest. This is true only in conditions of competition.
Under monopoly, a reduction in the rate of interest may have no
influence whatever on investment decisions. Under concentrated
oligopoly, the large firms are financed largely by their own funds,
and the level of the rate of interest has little bearing on their investment decisions.

Changes in the rate of interest may have an effect on the investments of small firms operating either in a not highly concentrated
branch or alongside large firms in a highly concentrated one; this is
particularly true of such industries as building, where interest is an
important cost element. These changes may also have an effect on
the composition of investment, insofar as they modify the cost of
keeping inventories, independently of the conditions of the market

in which the firm operates. Finally, interest changes may have an effect on credits to consumers. But in prevalently oligopolistic industries the effect of interest changes on the volume of investment, and thereby on production, cannot be more than slight; demand is the dominating factor.[11]

These observations on the relationship between rate of interest and investment correspond to now generally accepted conclusions.[12]

The imperfections of the credit market are seen in the varying degrees of difficulty which firms, at a given interest rate, experience in obtaining bank credits—to the point, sometimes, of being unable to obtain any credit at all. In these circumstances, the level of the rate of interest is not the only relevant factor on the credit market; the banks' willingness to lend or, in other words, the degree to which the banking system's credit policy is liberal or restrictive acquires importance. This is again a problem which concerns primarily the small firms, whose self-financing potential for expansion is limited.

Thus, both variations in the rate of interest and the restrictive or liberal nature of banking policy affect mainly small firms. Since large firms carry far and away the greatest weight in modern industry and small firms are most often directly or indirectly subordinated to the large firms' policies, we are led to conclude that, on the whole, credit policy has little influence on the volume of investment. In any event, it is well to remember that countercyclical credit restrictions principally affect small firms—either indirectly, through higher interest rates, or directly, through a reduction in the credits granted.

Spontaneous Expansion of Demand

We have said that in a predominantly oligopolistic or monopolistic economy all investments can increase, including those which raise the demand for labor, if demand expands at a sufficiently high rate. In the presence of the latter condition, unemployment can gradually be absorbed. But how can demand expand? In particular, how can it expand spontaneously, that is, without government intervention?

Many economists have pointed to population growth as one of the main causes generating an expansion of demand. But the connection is not immediate. Unless the new labor force finds its place in the productive apparatus and so earns additional incomes, population growth generates an increase not in demand but in poverty.

In the first place, demand can expand when productivity increases, so that incomes (profits and wages) rise and, with them, demand. However, the entire income increment is not consumed; part of it is saved. Therefore, although an expansion in the demand for consumer goods makes it possible to expand production, it is not enough to keep employment stable. The difficulty may be attenuated to some extent by a relatively greater increase of wages than of profits because wage earners have a lower propensity to save than profit earners. It is true, as will be seen when we examine the concrete example of the U.S. economy, that an expansion in the demand for consumer goods (and especially services) through higher productivity does contribute to the development of the system; but it is not, and cannot be, sufficient in itself to prevent an increase in unemployment.

Demand can grow, in the second place, when new firms are created or existing firms expand. This leads directly to an increase in the demand for capital goods and indirectly, through the multiplier, to an increase in consumer demand.

Third, demand can expand as a result of the introduction of major innovations. In the nature of things, innovations of this kind are largely unpredictable and so are their effects. It may well happen that monopolistic or oligopolistic firms introduce such innovations without the inducement of an already rising demand. In this case total demand may spontaneously expand to the extent necessary to keep employment stable. However, as we have seen, not even major innovations can be introduced by the large firms without some sort of reference to the size of the potential market—which means considering both the size of the market for goods similar to the new ones to be produced as the result of the innovation and the size the market must be to make the innovation profitable. Investment occasioned by these innovations is, therefore, not nearly so "autonomous" as many seem to think. At certain times, when technological progress is particularly marked, investment called forth by major innovations does help to generate a spontaneous expansion of demand sufficient to offset the labor-repelling forces and to raise employment. But we must at once add the qualification that in a highly concentrated economy occasions of this kind are more subject to limiting factors and, therefore, tend to become rarer than they are in a less concentrated economy.

The facts are that, in the presence of technical progress, employment can remain stable or rise only if there is an expansion not merely in consumption but also in investment. As oligopolistic and monopolistic formations continue to spread, such an increase in investment comes more and more to depend on expanding demand. It is a vicious circle, which can be epitomized in the following points.

(1) In a highly concentrated economy, there is a bias in favor of labor-saving investment.

(2) In oligopolistic and monopolistic industries, investment that increases the demand for labor depends on a rise in effective demand; this is not so where competition prevails. The inducement to such investment, which could derive from a widespread reduction of prices, and especially of factor prices, works within narrow limits because the competitive mechanism works within narrow limits.

(3) Wage increases do not solve the problem; at best, they mitigate it. Looking at the problem in static terms, a wage reduction might seem advisable, in line with Wicksell's view. But such a reduction would only aggravate the dynamic problem: the problem of unemployment due to a *continuous* process of mechanization, in which labor is displaced even by the new machines bought out of depreciation funds to replace those gradually wearing out.

(4) Unless demand expands rapidly enough, oligopolistic or monopolistic profits may yield more disposable funds than are required for self-financing, and these may be kept in liquid form or employed "unproductively"; in these circumstances, a part of personal savings may also be hoarded.

In summary, in a highly concentrated economy the forces generating unemployment tend to be stronger than those absorbing it. There seems to be no *spontaneous* mechanism tending, even in an intermittent (cyclical) manner, to equalize the two sets of forces. The situation looks rather like Keynes' unemployment equilibrium, but in this case the unemployment is not static but dynamic.

Keynes has offered various prescriptions for breaking out of the vicious circle: a reduction in the rate of interest; a redistributive tax policy apt to increase the propensity to consume; a policy of massive public expenditure, productive and unproductive; and the "social control of investment." A reduction in the rate of interest is now generally recognized to have little effect. Progressive taxation of higher personal incomes and corporate profits may be helpful, though of course only up to a "critical point" beyond which it defeats its own purpose and, naturally, only if the government spends the money which would otherwise have been hoarded or employed in such a manner as not to raise demand. A redistributive tax policy may attenuate, though not solve, the problem, just as trade-union action may be effective up to a point through pushing up wages relatively more than profits.

Public expenditure seems to hold out the best promise for

mitigating the effective-demand problem. At any rate, this is true in a closed economy; in an open economy, foreign demand, or exports, must also be considered. In reality, of course, all economies are "open"; the question is how important exports are in relation to Gross National Product. If exports account for a large proportion of Gross National Product, as they do, say, in Great Britain and West Germany, the expansion or contraction of exports may assume considerable relevance for the problem under discussion; if they are relatively small, as in the United States, export changes have little effect, and the nub of the question remains public expenditure.

Profits, Investment, and Growth

In the preceding essay I recalled Ricardo's well-known proposition, according to which the individual firm's "accumulation" under competition is limited only by the level of profit; and profit supplies both the motive and the funds for accumulation. The same applies to small firms which do business alongside the large ones in relatively highly concentrated oligopolistic industries. In general, the small firm's investment decisions are influenced mainly by the level of profits and the supply of bank credits, since their total profits and hence their self-financing potential are limited, even if the rate of retained profits is kept near unity. Small firms produce as much as possible, whatever the behavior of the total demand for their products, since each of them produces too small a fraction of total output to influence the price.

I also observed that the situation is different for large firms; for them, bank credits are of secondary importance, whereas their decisions to invest—in real assets—are influenced mainly by demand. I pointed out that funds available from current profits may exceed the requirements of self-financing, if those firms do not expect sufficient demand to guarantee a profitable market for increased output. If this is the case, profits can be directed into other channels. But if this demand is expected, and the cost-price relationships are such as to allow a rate of profit not less than the desired one, expenditure for real investment may even exceed the funds deriving from current profits. In other words, expected profits are the incentive for real investment, whereas current profits are the main source of its financing. Both current and ex-

---

This section was written as a postscript to the preceding essay and included in the 1969 edition of *Oligopoly and Technical Progress.*

pected profits, then, are among the determinants of investment decisions in the case of large firms also, provided that demand is increasing fast enough.

The book on managerial capitalism and other essays by Robin Marris have opened an important discussion on these problems. I should like to make a few remarks on the (short-run) relations between profits, investment, and growth, which, although on a line notably different from Marris', have been stimulated by his work.[13]

Profits and Investments

We have to distinguish between real investment (plant, machinery, buildings, and inventories) and financial or portfolio investment (trade and consumer credit, currency and bank deposits, stocks and bonds, credits to subsidiaries and associated corporations). The former generates an increase in productive capacity, whereas the latter fulfills different functions: it enhances the "security" of the firm—that is, its ability to overcome unfavorable situations—and it increases its earning capacity beyond that depending on physical production. The firm aims at financing real investment as much as possible from its current gross profits, since this investment entails greater costs and risks if externally financed. This is evident in the case of debt; but the issue of new stock also involves greater costs and risks than self-financing, owing to the imperfections of the stock market, to the costs of intermediaries, and to the risk of takeover. To finance real investment, then, the firm resorts to external sources only after having exhausted the internal ones.

For a large firm, the primary determinant of decisions to invest in real assets is given by the expected demand in the markets in which it operates. This demand depends upon the behavior of aggregate demand in the economy as a whole and upon the—costly—efforts which the firm itself makes, or can make, to raise the volume of sales: advertising campaigns and product diversification. Hence there are exogenous and endogenous demand variations. The efforts made by a single firm to raise the volume of sales may have the effect of enlarging the size of the market of the firm to the detriment of the market of other firms; but it may also have, in the aggregate, the net effect of raising the community's propensity to consume. On the other hand, exogenous demand variations have their origin not solely in the dynamics of the firms as a whole but also in foreign demand and in measures of public administrations (including those of the central bank and of the government).[14] Moreover, the sales efforts will be more successful the more rapid the expansion of aggregate demand. Therefore, in analyzing the behavior of an individual firm, the size of the market of goods produced by the firm is to be considered as a function of the sales efforts *and* of total demand. But since we focus our attention on the variables which are relevant in the aggregate, here we consider demand as an external datum and its variations as exogenously determined. (This is the main reason why our line of reasoning departs from that of Marris, who, being mainly interested in who maximizes what, focuses his attention on the single firm in isolation.)

As I said, the real investment of corporations is determined principally by the expected rate of profit and the expected demand:

$$I^r = f\left(\frac{P*}{K}, D*\right) \tag{1}$$

where $P*$ is the expected total profit, K the value of the net capital stock, and $D*$ the expected demand.[15]

More precisely, we have to consider not only the expected demand but also existing capacity (= fixed assets), which we assume to be measured by the value of net capital, K:

$$I^r = \varphi\left(\frac{P*}{K}, D*, K\right) \tag{2}$$

or, better,

$$I^r = \phi\left(\frac{P*}{K}, U*\right) \tag{3}$$

where $U*$ is the expected degree of capacity utilization, or the ratio between expected real output, and the maximum potential output of existing capacity. (Changes in this ratio embody the substance of the most recent version of the acceleration principle, the "capital stock adjustment principle.")

Financing Real Investment

Once the above factors have determined the amount of real investment, how does the firm finance it?

I consider gross real investment (that is, including depreciation) and current gross profits after taxes *(P)* and I neglect changes in the value of inventories.

Net self-financing can be determined as follows. The firm uses a certain share of profits, r, for increasing its reserves in some proportion to the expansion of real investment. Then, a certain minimum amount of dividends has to be paid out of current profits, or, if these are insufficient, out of reserves. Dividend distributions may be expressed as the product of minimum share yield, δ, times the total value of the equity, which, for simplicity, we will assume to be equal to the value of the capital stock, K.

Self-financing can, therefore, be expressed by the equation

$$A = P - rP - \delta K$$

or

$$A = (1 - r)P - \delta K. \tag{4}$$

This relation presupposes that $(1 - r)P > \delta K$. If the second term becomes higher than the first one, and, in any case, if gross profits become very low, the firm is compelled to draw on previously accumulated reserves to pay the minimum dividends and even to provide capital consumption allowances.

In a relatively short period, barring the case of serious depression, r, δ, and K are comparatively constant, so that the amount of self-financing available for real investment will be proportional to profits and the proportion will be fairly stable.

Writing

$$1 - r = \alpha,$$

we have

$$A = \alpha P - \delta K, \tag{5}$$

where in a relatively short period, α and δK are approximately constant.[16]

Provided the expected rate of profit is high enough, we have seen that investment depends on the rate of expansion of aggregate demand.

If A exceeds these investment requirements, the firm may distribute above-normal dividends, or may increase its portfolio investment, or use the surplus funds in other nonproductive activities.

If A falls short of those requirements, the firm has to resort to external finance, and the more so the greater the expected increase in demand. In so doing, however, the firm cannot increase its equity or its debt beyond certain limits. Some of the limits are mainly internal (for example, unwillingness to meet the increasing risk of take-over, unwillingness to increase its long-term debt in relation to its net capital and to expected gross profits). Other limits are mainly external (for example, the "supply of money" and of short-term credits, which depend on the policy of the central bank and the difficulty of floating stocks or bonds on the Stock Exchange). Apart from special circumstances, however, these limits are not important for large corporations, although, strictly speaking, this applies only to the external limits, which are important for the small firms. In any case, here we neglect both the external and the internal limits.

In conclusion, the resort to external sources to finance real investment is a residual quantity ($E^r = I^r - A$) which is generally positive, but can be zero if self-financing covers all the requirements of real investment and can be negative if a part of internal sources is devoted to portfolio investment or other uses.

Financing Portfolio Investment

The requirements of real investment having been met, the resort to external sources of finance is determined by the decisions concerning portfolio investment. The factors governing these decisions are much more complex and less easily expressed by simple relations. I shall limit myself to classifying the "motives" for purely financial investments—with some analogies with the motives put forward by Keynes to explain the liquidity preference function—and to adding a few brief comments.

The main motives for portfolio investment seem to be five: (1) transaction motives (trade and consumer credit); (2) precautionary motives (liquid assets); (3) speculative motives (stocks and bonds bought for earning purposes); (4) "saving" for financing future real investment (liquid assets, stocks and bonds); (5) "group strategy" (credits toward subsidiaries and associated corporations). My comments are that, given these motives, the main factors affecting the decisions to invest in financial assets are the following:

(a) the behavior of aggregate demand: when demand is expected to fall and current profits exceed the needs of financing real investment, liquid or quasi-liquid assets (such as demand deposits and currency) will rise, whereas trade and consumer credit will probably also go up when demand is expected to rise;

(b) the policy of the central bank, which governs total liquidity and the short-term rate of interest;

(c) the return expected on stocks and bonds, which depends on (a), (b), and other specific factors.

Profits, Growth, and Effective Demand

With the help of a few drastic simplifications, it is easy enough to relate the rate of growth of the firm to the rate of profit. The simplifying assumptions are: (1) constant degree of utilization of capacity, which means that, for some reason, demand expands continuously over time at the appropriate rate; (2) marginal and average capital/output ratios equal and constant over time; (3) constant prices and costs. On the basis of these assumptions we have

$$I^r/p\Delta X = K/pX \text{ or } I^r/K = \Delta X/X \qquad (6)$$

where p is price, ΔX the increment to output, X the current level of output, and K the value of the capital stock.

If the firm finances real investment without drawing on outside sources of finance, equation (5) becomes

$$A = I^r = \alpha P - \delta K.$$

By dividing both terms by K we get

$$I^r/K = \alpha P/K - \delta \quad \text{or, since} \quad I^r/K = \Delta X/X,$$

$$\Delta X/X = \alpha P/K - \delta. \qquad (7)$$

This relation, which says that the rate of growth of output is proportional to the rate of profit minus a constant term, is similar to that already derived, in different contexts, by Kaldor and Joan Robinson with reference to the economy as a whole.

The above-mentioned assumptions, by which this relation may be formally justified and which are either explicit or implicit in "golden age" growth models, imply such drastic simplification as to leave little interpretative value to the models which use them. In an economy with widespread oligopoly, the growth of investment and income is governed precisely by demand variations. The hypothesis that demand will grow at the appropriate rate assumes away precisely the most tricky problem in the growth of modern economies. Oddly enough, some of the most distinguished followers of Keynes, who seem to accept his teachings in the static context, in fact reject them in the transition to dynamic analysis.

An Overall View of Investment Decisions

If we combine the previous analysis, concerning the relations between profits and investment, with the analysis worked out in the first three sections of the preceding essay, we may take an overall view of what determines investment, with special reference to industry.

(a) The investment decisions of *large firms* are influenced by changes in effective demand or, more precisely, by changes in the ratio between effective demand and capacity and by variations in the rate of profit; variations in credit policy (supply of bank credit) have a limited relevance.

(b) The investment decisions of *small firms* are governed mainly by variations in the profit rate and in credit policy, while demand has only an indirect influence.

If, therefore, we want to "explain" the course of investment in a large firm or in a branch of industry dominated by large firms, we need consider only two of the explanatory variables: effective demand in relation to plant capacity (an index of the degree of capacity utilization will do very well) and the rate of profit. The first of these variables may be expected to explain more than the second. If, on the other hand, we want to "explain" investment in small firms or in branches of industry where small firms are prevalent, we should consider instead the profit rate and the supply of bank credit (measured, say, by an index of liquidity variation); the degree of capacity utilization will probably explain very little. If, finally, we want to "explain" the variation of aggregate investment, we need to consider all three variables.

Innovations have a bearing on both the major investment determinants. They influence the profit rate via cost reductions in the case of existing goods, and they influence demand in the case of goods not previously produced. In this second case, demand for the new goods entails a contraction of demand for existing goods or, in an expanding economy, a slowdown in the expansion of demand for existing goods. The introduction of new goods may, however, raise the community's propensity to consume or may prevent it falling. When this happens, the new demand depresses neither the absolute level nor the rate of expansion of demand for existing goods. In any event, innovations that can be financed from depreciation funds do not raise total demand. In its turn, demand determines what type of innovations will actually be put into effect.

Notes

1. However, national product in money terms (which is an expression of total money demand) and total money investment may fall if the decline in prices is faster than the increase in the volume of output.
2. Especially in the 1820s and 1830s, 1870s, 1880s, and part of the 1890s.

Some economists, like Schumpeter, maintain that prices had a basic falling trend right through the century.

3. I have in mind the formulas $p = m$ (for competition), $p - (p/\eta) = m$ (for monopoly), and $p = v + qv$ or, if direct cost equals marginal cost, $p = m + qm$ (for oligopoly), where q depends jointly on the elasticity of demand, the absolute size of the market, the state of technology, and possibly on initial selling expenditure.

4. In chapter 30 of his *Principles,* Ricardo refutes Say and Lauderdale, who maintain that price depends on supply and demand in all cases, by adducing the example of a cost reduction in the production of an agricultural commodity on the assumption of unchanged demand: the cost reduction is sufficient to lead to a price reduction. On rereading this chapter of the *Principles,* it seems almost incomprehensible how Ricardo should so often have been reproached for neglecting demand as an element which, together with cost, determines "value." Marshall's defense (*Principles of Economics,* Appendix I) of Ricardo against Jevons does more to obscure the question than to clarify it.

5. These observations were addressed to me in 1955 by Alfred Kahn in a letter commenting upon my thesis, then barely embryonic, regarding the relation between monopoly, oligopoly, and effective demand. Professor Kahn made it clear that he regarded the idea expressed by his observations as an alternative explanation. More precisely, he thought that if the problem of effective demand had recently become serious enough to worry everybody, this was not so much because of the process of concentration and oligopolistic formations, but rather because of the high level of average personal incomes. But it would seem that the two aspects, size and composition of demand, are complementary rather than mutually exclusive.

   To Professor Kahn, too, I would like to acknowledge a debt of gratitude for many long and stimulating discussions, in writing and personal conversations.

6. This argument was fully developed by J. R. Meyer and E. Kuh in *The Investment Decision: An Empirical Study* (Cambridge, MA: Harvard University Press, 1957), and was first briefly mentioned by L. Tarshis in "The Flow of Business Funds, Consumption and Investment," in K. K. Kurihura, ed., *Post-Keynesian Economics* (New Brunswick: Rutgers University Press, 1954).

7. In the case of corporate saving, as in the case of public saving, the irrelevance of "psychological motives" is immediately obvious, as G. Haberler has rightly pointed out (*Prosperity and Depression* [Cambridge, MA: Harvard University Press, 1964], p. 228).

8. Tarshis shows that in recent years United States corporate saving was roughly two to three times as much as personal saving, and public saving was about twice as much again as corporate saving.

9. See M. Fanno, *Lezioni di economia e di scienza bancaria* (Padua, 1937).

10. See A. Breglia, *L'economia dal punto di vista monetario,* 3rd ed. (Rome, 1951), esp. pp. 259-60, 327–30.

11. If, in a highly concentrated market, the fall in the rate of interest is sharp and enduring enough to reduce the cost of inventories for all

firms, even though in different degrees, it leads to a general cost reduction, which in its turn tends to cause price reductions and so to stimulate demand. The increased demand may stimulate investment. In oligopoly, then, any effect which a fall in the rate of interest may have on investment is indirect. If it takes place at all, it takes place by way of an expansion of demand. If demand fails to expand when prices fall, investment does not expand.

12. See P. Wilson and P. W. S. Andrews, eds., *Oxford Studies in the Price Mechanism* (Oxford: Oxford University Press, 1959), ch. 1, "The Rate of Interest" (essays by R. S. Sayers, H. D. Henderson, J. E. Meade, P. W. S. Andrews, and A. J. Brown).

13. See Robin Marris, *The Economic Theory of "Managerial Capitalism"* (New York: The Free Press, 1964), and "Incomes Policy and the Rate of Profit in Industry," *Transactions of the Manchester Statistical Society 1964-65 Session.* I am grateful to Robin Marris, Michele Salvati, Rainer Masera, Lucio Izzo, and Enrico Zaghini for their critical comments, which led me to revise the original text of this postscript. Needless to say, these economists do not necessarily share the views here expounded.

14. The main forces governing the variations of total demand are discussed in the previous section.

15. Contrary to a common assumption, profits and demand—actual or expected—do not necessarily vary in the same direction, since cost variations may intervene.

16. In the United States, during the period 1954-67 the amount of self-financing as a function of P in industrial corporations closely fitted a linear regression function with a slope, α, of 0.757 (for the data see *Economic Report of the President,* submitted to Congress, January 1968, p. 290). In Italy, during the period 1958-64, the corresponding value of α is 0.754. The data refer to 200 industrial corporations covering about 26 percent of employment in manufacturing industry and were derived from legal budgets, after appropriate corrections, by a painstaking empirical enquiry, organized by F. M. Pacces and conducted by G. Zanetti and E. Filippi, *Finanza e sviluppo della grande industria in Italia* (Milan, 1966). Although the values of the coefficient α are practically the same in both countries, the amount of real investment financed internally is very different in the two countries and in the two periods considered: over 90 percent in the United States and less than 50 percent in Italy. This may depend partly on the fact that, in spite of the corrections, the Italian data underestimate the true amount of self-financing; partly on the higher rate of increase of demand and hence of real investments in Italy; and partly on lower profit margins (owing to the more acute external competition) in Italy.

Michal Kalecki

THE PROBLEM OF EFFECTIVE DEMAND WITH TUGAN-BARANOVSKI AND ROSA LUXEMBURG

In the discussions about the market for the national product in terms of the Marxian schemes of reproduction, the positions taken by Mikhail Tugan-Baranovski and Rosa Luxemburg are on the two opposite poles. Tugan-Baranovski denies altogether that the problem of markets may constitute an obstacle to the development of capitalism which thus depends entirely on the increase in productive capacity. Rosa Luxemburg on the contrary considers expanded reproduction in a closed capitalist system impossible, attributing all its development to the possibility of selling its wares in the markets external to it, that is, in the noncapitalist sector of the world economy.

It is most interesting that both authors commit important errors in their arguments and that nevertheless their theories give a correct picture of some essentials of capitalist economy. Tugan-Baranovski rightly stresses the "antagonistic character" of the capitalist regime, as a result of which the production of consumer goods is not its final aim and the demand for them is not the motive force of its development. Similarly, although Rosa Luxemburg's theory that the development of capitalism depends solely on the "external markets" is not correct, they are still an important part in its dynamics.

The two theories find something like a point of intersection in present-day—especially U. S.—capitalism where a decisive role is played by a market created by the government for armament production.

The theory of Tugan-Baranovski is in fact very simple: the author maintains that with "appropriate proportions" of use made of national product the problem of effective demand does not arise.

First published in Polish, in *Ekonomista* 2 (1967): 241–49, Warsaw. Reprinted in Michal Kalecki, *Selected Essays on the Dynamics of the Capitalist Economy, 1933–1970* (Cambridge: Cambridge University Press, 1971), pp. 146–55.

This argument, illustrated numerically by means of Marxian schemes of reproduction, is in fact tantamount to the statement that at any level of consumption of workers and capitalists the national product may be sold provided investment is sufficiently large. These are the "proportions" between consumption and investment, which must be established in order that the total production should be purchased. A distortion of this proportion leads to crises in the course of which the deviation from it is being corrected. Thus the fundamental idea of Tugan rests on an error that what *may* happen is actually happening, because he does not show at all why capitalists in the long run are to invest to the extent which is necessary to contribute to full utilization of productive equipment.

Tugan stresses the point that his theory will be right even in the most adverse conditions of actual curtailment of consumption of the workers and stability of that of capitalists. Obviously on paper even this may be offset by a sufficiently high level of investment. The author, by the way, does not anticipate the criticism that capitalists may be unwilling to use the surplus value by investing so much. He rather answers a critic of a different type who would consider absurd investment the purpose of which is production of investment goods rather than that of consumer goods. After having "fixed" his critic in this way Tugan gives a perfectly sensible answer.

The capitalist system is not a "harmonious" regime, whose purpose is the satisfaction of the needs of its citizens but an "antagonistic" regime which is to secure profits for capitalists. As a result there is nothing absurd in basing the development of the system on expansion of a production of "coal and steel" which serves to develop the production of these commodities. The production of "coal and steel" is as justified as production of bread if it is profitable. Consumption is the final aim and proof of a "harmonious" but not of an "antagonistic" regime.

It is this part of the argument of Tugan-Baranovski that I consider his lasting contribution to the analysis of the functioning of capitalism in its various phases. It is worth noticing that the theory of Tugan is, despite his "optimism," deeply anticapitalistic: it is just the absurdity of capitalism that makes its development immune to the problem of finding markets for its products.

Let us go back, however, to our critique of the theory of Tugan-Baranovski (which is equivalent to the statement of Rosa Luxemburg on the subject of this theory). Tugan considers the *possible* use of the national product created by full utilization of the productive forces as the actual fact—in any case if we disregard the business cycles. The following problem arises here: the approach is certainly faulty, from which however it does not follow that Tugan's theory is wrong, but merely completely unfounded. Perhaps after all the problem of the markets does not really constitute an obstacle to expanded reproduction of a capitalist economy. In order to give a complete answer to this query it is necessary to construct a theory of investment decisions such that it would cover all the aspects of dynamics of capitalist economy and not only those relevant to the business cycle. This is not the place however, to develop such a theory which I always considered to be the central problem of the political economy of capitalism. Here I shall try to show that expanded reproduction—even in conditions much more favorable than were on purpose assumed by Tugan-Baranovski—is by no means obvious and that it requires a certain supporting factor, for instance, dependent on innovations (and thus not necessarily Rosa Luxemburg's "external markets").

Imagine the process of accumulation of capital, say 4 percent per annum. Let us assume that at the start the capital equipment and labor are fully utilized. Let the depreciation amount to 3 percent per annum so that gross investment is equal to 7 percent of capital. Let us also assume a constant share of gross profits (including depreciation) in the Gross National Product, and constant proportions in the distribution of gross profits between gross accumulation and capitalists' consumption. Thus gross accumulation bears a constant relation to the national income. The process of accumulation consists in the expansion of productive equipment at 4 percent per annum due to investment, and since gross accumulation bears a constant relation (7 percent) to capital, gross accumulation also expands 4 percent per annum. Given the constant share of gross accumulation in national income, income would also grow at the 4 percent per annum rate. Thus full utilization of equipment continues and the problem of effective demand does not seem to arise.

All right, but why should capitalists continue to invest at a level of 7 percent of capital? Simply because the process has been going for some time, this investment has been "justified" and the capitalists do not anticipate any difficulties in selling their products with reproduction expanding 4 percent per annum, and therefore they do not hesitate to continue their game.

Let us, however, consider a case when—for instance, as a result of a change in the social structure of the capitalist class—capitalists are prepared to invest only 6 percent of the capital per annum (without changing the relative share of their consumption in gross profits). The problem of effective demand then immediately makes its appearance. The ratio of investment to the stock of capital falls by one-seventh, that is, by about 14 percent. There arises thus the problem of overproduction: because of the constancy of relation between accumulated and consumed part of profits the latter will also fall by 14 percent in relation to capital; through reduction of employment in investment-goods industries and in industries producing consumption goods for capitalists there will be also a reduction of demand for wage goods and reduction of employment in those industries—until working class income also falls by 14 percent in relation to capital so that the proportion between profits and wages be maintained as assumed. This general situation of overproduction affects in turn adversely the investment decisions of capitalists. Now they are not willing to invest even 6 percent of capital, contributing thus to further deterioration of the situation.

Yes, somebody may say, this is a typical crisis which will be followed by a period of prosperity and these fluctuations will just occur around the process of expanded reproduction described initially. There is, however, nothing to substantiate this argument. After a breakdown of the moving equilibrium no trace of the 4 or 3 percent annual long-run increase was left in the economy. The economy may as well settle to a state of simple reproduction with cyclical fluctuations around it.

We have moved one step forward: we have shown that the development of capitalism which does not encounter the problem of effective demand, even if it is possible, is unstable. However, a process of an unstable equilibrium ceases to exist if it is not supported by some stabilizing force. In relation to our problem it may be said that an expanded reproduction will take place if there exist factors that simply do not permit the system to remain in the state of simple reproduction (or stationary state): the initial state of simple reproduction leads to a level of gross investment exceeding depreciation.

Such a factor may be first and foremost the influence of technological innovations, discovery of new sources of raw materials and the like which opens before the capitalists new perspectives. The technical progress appears in this approach not merely as depreciating old plants, which leads to their replacement by new ones; it is also a stimulus for investment over and above that level resulting from the fact that capitalists investing "today" think to have an advantage over those having invested "yesterday" because of technical novelties that have reached them.

The above should not be construed in the sense that such a possibility of expanded reproduction—without "external markets"—is tantamount to the elimination of influence of inadequate effective demand. Indeed the rate of expanded reproduction resulting from this factor is by no means necessarily adequate to secure the full utilization of equipment or even to keep the degree of this utilization at a constant level. Innovations break the impasse of a simple reproduction only to some extent and they do not warrant the utilization of resources in the sense of Tugan-Baranovski.

From the last two sections it follows in any case: (a) as a result of the problem of effective demand, expanded reproduction is not a natural and obvious state of the capitalist system; (b) nevertheless such reproduction is not necessarily a result of "external markets." Thus although these sections are meant primarily as a criticism of the theory of Tugan-Baranovski they constitute at the same time a starting point for a discussion of views of Rosa Luxemburg with which we shall deal subsequently.

Rosa Luxemburg considers expanded reproduction in the long run without existence of "external markets" to be not only far from obvious but outright impossible. It should be noticed that she argues this point as naïvely as does Tugan-Baranovski showing the irrelevance of the problem of effective demand for the development of capitalism. In her consideration of the making of investment decisions by capitalists she somehow implies that they are being taken by the capitalist class as a whole. And this class is frustrated by the knowledge that there is no final market for the surplus of goods corresponding to accumulation: so why invest?

Now capitalists do many things as a class but they certainly do not invest as a class. And if that *were* the case they might do it just in the way prescribed by Tugan-Baranovski. But despite this error in her argument, it is valuable in being imbued by the spirit of scepticism with regard to the market for the surplus of goods corresponding to the accumulation. Even though following a different line of thought, we also have come to the conclusion that expanded reproduction is by no means a "natural" phenomenon, and we tried to find the source of expanded reproduction—which is, though, by no means equivalent to permanent full utilization of equipment—in certain aspects of technical progress.

Rosa Luxemburg, as we mentioned time and again above, sees the possibility of finding the market for surplus goods merely *outside* the world capitalist system. She does not mean here underdeveloped countries only but also the noncapitalist sectors of developed economies, for example, peasant agriculture. Only the "exports" from the capitalist system are the mainspring of development. Hence her pessimistic view of the future of capitalism: by undermining the noncapitalist production and gradually pervading all the world, capitalism eliminates at the same time the possibility of its further development.

To the quantitative overestimate of the role of "external markets" Rosa Luxemburg contributes a fundamental mistake which she perpetrates in the analysis of the impact of these markets on development of capitalism. She considers—in any case in the main current of her argument—that the market for the surplus is created to the extent of *total* exports to the noncapitalist sector and not only to the extent of the *excess* of exports over imports.

It is easy to show, however, that this approach of Rosa Luxemburg's is erroneous: the imported goods absorb purchasing power just like those produced at home, and thus to the extent that exports are offset by imports they do not contribute to the expansion of the markets for national product. Or, to approach it from a different angle, imports, like wages, are costs, and the part of disposal of profits is, alongside capitalists' consumption and investment, solely the export surplus. And in order that this should be possible, export of capital is necessary. Only to the extent to which the capitalist system lends to the noncapitalist world (or the latter sells its assets) is it possible to place abroad the surplus of goods unsold at home. Only in this way do "the external markets" solve the contradictions of the world capitalist system.

Obviously the net "external markets" as well played their role in development of capitalism, but a much more modest one than would have been the case if *all* the exports to the noncapitalist world really contributed to the absorption of surpluses corresponding to accumulation.

One of the most interesting elements of the theory of Rosa Luxemburg is taken into consideration in her "external markets," alongside those mentioned above, also the market created by government purchases and in particular armament orders. She consistently makes, by the way, the mistake of treating the *whole* of government expenditure, for instance on armaments, without paying due consideration to its financing, as absorbing the surplus.

If, however, this expenditure is covered by taxes burdening the working class they have no effect upon the absorption of national product because the new "armaments markets" are offset by an equal curtailment of workers' consumption.

If armaments are financed by the issue of government securities, then the surplus of goods is sold by capitalists in exchange for the money obtained in turn by the government through sale of their bills and bonds to the financial capitalists. The capitalists—taken as a whole—thus grant the government a credit with which to buy their surplus goods. Also here capital is being "exported" to the "foreign market" created by the government (this operation may be transacted through the banking system)—the government sells bills to the latter using the amounts obtained to purchase armaments, while in the banking system there is an equal increase in deposits representing the accumulation corresponding to the armament production. As a result the capitalists grant to the government credits through the medium of the banking system.

Finally even when the armament expenditure of the government is covered by the tax on profits it also constitutes a way of absorbing to this extent accumulation but in a different way from the case of financing this expenditure by internal credits. Imagine that profits accumulated by capitalists as a whole as a result of armament orders are taken away by taxation rather than in exchange for government securities.

The profits do not increase then as a result of new armament orders but the surplus is nevertheless absorbed by its expropriation by the government. The difference from the case considered previously consists in the fact that while there the capitalists granted credits to the government, they pay taxes in the case presently considered.

Thus Rosa Luxemburg rightly saw in the armament orders an "external market" which can absorb a part of accumulation—but she should have excluded from this type of "external markets" the case where armaments are financed by taxation of the workers.

It should still be added that Rosa Luxemburg does not treat the "external markets" created by the government as a problem of first-rate importance. Thus while predicting the general crisis of capitalism caused by the exhaustion of noncapitalist markets, she does not anticipate the possibility of counteracting the crisis by the "external market" of government purchases.

It follows from the above what was said at the outset of this essay, that theories both of Tugan-Baranovski and Rosa Luxemburg find in a sense their confirmation in contemporary, in particular American, capitalism. While perpetrating grave mistakes in their arguments the authors show a striking perspicacity in the evaluation of certain basic elements of late-stage capitalism.

The "external markets" in the broad sense of Rosa Luxemburg in the form of armament orders and ancillary expenditure—insofar as they are financed by loans and taxation of capitalists—play today a leading role in the functioning of modern capitalism.

It is true that Rosa Luxemburg did not anticipate the enormous role of this type of "external market" in the absorption of accumulation. But one way or another she maintained that capitalism is saved by "external markets." In her time it was no doubt exaggerated but it has proven right today.

As for Tugan-Baranovski, contemporary capitalism indeed put into focus his view of the paradoxical and absurd character of "antagonistic systems" whose main task is not catering to human needs. In his vision of future capitalism, machines were to produce machines for production of machines. But making the high level of employment and workers' consumption dependent on production of the means of destruction is even more absurd.

Both, despite slips in their arguments, contributed to the understanding of the queer and perverse world in which we are living.

Michal Kalecki

THE MARXIAN EQUATIONS OF REPRODUCTION AND MODERN ECONOMICS

1. Before we start dealing with the proper subject of this paper we shall modify somewhat the Marxian division of economy into departments in order to simplify our argument and in order to focus on the basic problem of the reproduction schemes.

First, instead of including producer goods in department 1, we will assume that this department covers the total value of gross investment inclusive of the respective raw materials. Thus it represents the integrated production of all final nonconsumer products. (We disregard in our argument as does Marx—when he deals with reproduction schemes—both foreign trade and government revenue and expenditure.)

Second, we treat consumer goods likewise, that is, we include in the department which covers their output the production of respective raw materials from top to bottom. Moreover, fully in the Marxian spirit, we distinguish the following two departments: department 2 producing consumer goods for capitalists and department 3 producing wage goods.

We obtain thus the following *tableau économique* of the national income where P_1, P_2, P_3 are gross profits (before deduction of depreciation) in the respective departments, W_1, W_2, W_3—the respective wages; P and W aggregate profits and wages, and finally I—gross investment, C_k—capitalists' consumption, C_w—workers' consumption, and Y—gross national income (before deduction of depreciation).

First published in *Social Science Information* 7, no. 6 (December 1968): 73–79. This article was presented as a background paper for the Symposium on the Influence of Karl Marx on contemporary scientific thought, Paris, May 8-10, 1968, organized under the auspices or Unesco by the International Social Science Council and the International Council for Philosophy and Humanistic Studies.

1	2	3	
P_1 W_1	P_2 W_2	P_3 W_3	P W
I	C_k	C_w	Y

2. We will assume, as Marx does, that the workers do not save. Moreover, we shall disregard the problem of possible piling up of stocks of unsold goods as only a passing phenomenon. It is then easy to arrive at the fundamental Marxian "equation of exchange" between departments 1 and 2 on the one hand and department 3 on the other.

Profits in the latter, P_3, are materialized in the wage goods which are left to the capitalists of that department after payment of wages W_3 which absorb an equal amount of wage goods. Thus the wage goods of the value P_3 are sold to the workers of departments 1 and 2, that is:

$$P_3 = W_1 + W_2 \tag{1}$$

Marx considers this equation in the context of expanded reproduction proceeding at a given constant rate r. It is easy to see, however, that the equation holds good under *all* circumstances as long as there is no piling up of stocks of unsold goods, as mentioned above.

Considered in this general context equation (1) leads to a proposition that—given the distribution of income between profits and wages in the three departments—investment I and consumption of capitalists C_k determine profits and the national income. Indeed, let us add $P_1 + P_2$ to both sides of equation (1). We obtain:

$$P_1 + P_2 + P_3 = P_1 + W_1 + P_2 + W_2$$

Hence:

$$P = I + C_k \tag{2}$$

Moreover, if we denote $\dfrac{W_1}{I}, \dfrac{W_2}{C_k}, \dfrac{W_3}{C_w}$ by w_1, w_2, w_3 respectively, we obtain from equation (1):

$$(1 - w_3)C_w = w_1 I + w_2 C_k$$

Consequently, we have for the consumption of wage goods:

$$C_w = \frac{w_1 I + w_2 C_k}{1 - w_3} \tag{3}$$

and for the national income:

$$Y = I + C_k + C_w = I + C_k + \frac{w_1 I + w_2 C_k}{1 - w_3} \qquad (4)$$

Thus the national income (or product) Y which can be sold and the profits P which can be realized are determined in all circumstances (and not only in a state of uniformly expanding reproduction) by the level of investment I and consumption of capitalists C_k (given the distribution of income between wages and profits). A question may be raised as to why equations (2) and (4) must be interpreted in this way and not the other way around, in other words, that investment and consumption of capitalists are determined by profits and national income. The answer to this rather crucial query is as follows.

Investment and capitalists' consumption in the short period considered are the outcome of decisions taken in the past and thus should be considered as given. With regard to investment, this follows directly from the time lag dependent on the period of construction. But changes in capitalists' consumption also follow those in profits with some delay. Now, sales and profits in a given period cannot be a direct outcome of past decisions: the capitalists can decide how much they will invest and consume next year but they cannot decide how much they shall sell and profit. The independent variables in a given period are investment and capitalists' consumption. It is these magnitudes that through the equations (2) and (4) determine the levels of national income and profits which can be realized.

3. The decisions of capitalists with regard to their investment and consumption are made in "real" rather than in money terms, that is I and C_k should be calculated in stable prices. If w_1, w_2, w_3 are constant and money wage rates in all three departments change in the same proportion, the same is true in this case of prices of the produce of these departments. Moreover, as is easy to see, equations (2) and (3) will also hold in "real" terms. Any increase in "real" investment or capitalists' consumption results under these circumstances in an increase in output of department 3, C_w to provide for a surplus of this department P_3 sufficient to meet the demand generated by the higher wage bills in departments 1 and 2, that is, $W_2 + W_3$.

However, such repercussions of an increase in I or C_k are obviously possible only if there exist unused capacities in department 3.

Imagine that such is not the case. Then C_w is fixed in real terms, that is, is equal to a constant B. In this case the increase in money value of $W_1 + W_2$ will cause a rise in prices rather than in production of wage goods. The result will be that the "real" value of W_1, W_2, and W_3 will be reduced as compared with the levels which would be achieved if unused capacities existed in department 3. Consequently $w_1 = \dfrac{W_1}{I}$, $w_2 = \dfrac{W_2}{C_k}$, $w_3 = \dfrac{W_3}{C_w} = \dfrac{W_3}{B}$, where all magnitudes involved are to be now interpreted in "real" terms, will decline in the proportion reciprocal to the increase in the prices of wage goods. Equation (3) can now be written in the form:

$$\frac{w_1 I + w_2 C_k}{I - w_3} = B$$

When I and/or C_k increase, w_1, w_2 *and* w_3 decline in such a proportion as to render the left hand side of the equation equal to B.[1]*

Sections 2 and 3 represent in fact the gist of the modern theory of effective demand. As will be seen, this theory may be derived in full from the Marxian equation (1) representing the exchange between departments 1 and 2 on the one hand and department 3 on the other, if this equation is considered in the general context rather than in that of uniformly expanding reproduction.

4. Let us now turn to the significance of the equations (2) and (4) just in the latter context, that is, in the process of a uniform accumulation of capital. Let us denote the "real" stock of capital by K, the rate of net accumulation by r, and the rate of depreciation by δ. In this case we may write the "equation of accumulation," recalling that I is investment *gross* of depreciation, in the form:

$$I = (r + \delta) K \qquad (5)$$

Since we are considering the long-run progress of growth, let us postulate that capitalists' consumption C_k is proportional to profits P. Since according to formula (2) the latter are equal to $I + C_k$ it follows that C_k bears a constant relationship to I. We thus have:

$$C_k = m I$$

In consequence we may write equation (4) in the form:

$$Y = (1 + m)I + \frac{I(w_1 + m w_2)}{1 - w_3} = I\left(1 + m + \frac{w_1 + m w_2}{1 - w_3}\right) \qquad (6)$$

---

*Editors' Note: an erratum discovered by Dr. Jerzy Osiatynski, in the editing of the Polish edition of Kalecki's works, has been corrected here.

and substituting in it for I its value from equation (5) we obtain:

$$Y = K(r + \delta)\left(1 + m + \frac{w_1 + mw_2}{1 - w_3}\right) \qquad (7)$$

The national income Y thus bears a constant relationship to the stock of capital K (provided that w_1, w_2, w_3 do not change).[2] With a given relationship of productive capacity to the stock of capital the degree of utilization of equipment is constant. Thus if capital equipment is satisfactorily utilized in the initial position, this state of affairs is maintained in the course of expanded reproduction and the problem of effective demand does not arise.

It is this approach that is inherent in many contemporary theories of economic growth. In particular if we differentiate the equation (7) we obtain:

$$\frac{dY}{dK} = \frac{Y}{K} = r\frac{Y}{rK}$$

Now, with a constant satisfactory utilization of equipment, $\frac{dK}{dY}$ is the so-called capital-output ratio which we denote by R. Moreover, rK is the *net* investment and thus $\frac{rK}{Y}$ is the relative share of accumulation in the national income which we shall denote by a. We thus have:

$$\frac{1}{R} = \frac{r}{a}$$

or:

$$r = \frac{a}{R}$$

which is the basic formula of the Harrod-Domar theory (in which, however, the coefficient a represents the "propensity to save of the population" rather than the ratio of net accumulation out of profits to the national income which depends on its distribution between capitalists and workers).

In fact many of the contemporary theories of growth are simply variations on the theme of Marxian schemes of expanded reproduction which are represented in this paper by equations:

$$W_1 + W_2 = P_3 \qquad (1)$$

and

$$I = (r + \delta) K \qquad (5)$$

5. The repercussions of changes in investment and capitalists' consumption described in section 2 do not raise, I believe, any major misgivings. In contrast to this, the moving equilibrium described in section 3 depends on the very far-reaching assumption that capitalists are willing to engage in investment which increases their capital at a constant rate r per annum. What happens, however, if having become more cautious (perhaps under the influence of a change in the social structure of their class) they decide to reduce investment from $(r + \delta) K$ to $(r' + \delta) K$ where $r' < r$?

It follows directly from formula (7) that $\dfrac{Y}{K}$ and thus the degree of utilization of equipment declines in the proportion $\dfrac{r' + \delta}{r + \delta}$ as a result of the decline of effective demand. It is clear that in this situation the "cautious" capitalists will not be any more agreeable to a lower rate of accumulation r' but will reduce it further to $r'' < r'$, and this will in turn affect correspondingly the degree of utilization of equipment.

Some economists tend to consider this phenomenon as a downswing phase of the business cycle which takes place around the initial path of growth. However, such a proposition is not well founded: there is no reason why having left the initial unstable path, investment must fluctuate around it rather than around the depreciation level δK. Or to put it in Marxian terms: why cannot a capitalist system, once it has deviated downward from the path of expanded reproduction, find itself in a position of a long-run simple reproduction?

In fact we are absolutely in the dark concerning what will actually happen in such a situation as long as we have not solved the problem of determinants of investment decisions. Marx did not develop such a theory but nor has this been accomplished in modern economics. Some attempts have been made in the development of the theory of cyclical fluctuations. However, the problems of the determination of investment decisions involving the elements associated with the long-run trend are much more difficult than in the case of the "pure business cycle" (that is, in a system which in the long run is subject to simple reproduction). I myself tried to do something along these lines but I consider my work in this field to be definitely of a pioneer nature.[3] One thing, however, is clear to me: the long-run growth of the national income involving satisfactory utilization of equipment in a capitalist economy is far from obvious.

6. That Marx was deeply conscious of the impact of effective demand upon the dynamics of the capitalist system follows clearly

from this passage of the third volume of the *Capital*: "The conditions of direct exploitation and those of the realization of surplus
value are not identical. They are separated not only by time and
space but logically as well. The former are limited merely by the
productive capacity of the society, the latter by the proportions of
various branches of production and by consumer power of the
society."

However, he did not systematically scrutinise the process described by his reproduction schemes from the point of view of the
contradictions inherent in capitalism as a result of the problem of
effective demand.

It is one of his most prominent followers, Rosa Luxemburg, who
expressed very definite and even extreme views on the subject: she
rejected altogether the possibility of long-run expanded reproduction if no "external markets" are in existence. By "external markets" she understood those outside the world capitalist system
consisting not only of underdeveloped countries but also of the
noncapitalist sectors of developed capitalist economies, for instance, peasant agriculture as well as government purchases.

Her argument suffers from the fact that she considers investment decisions as being made by the capitalist class as a whole and
this class is frustrated by the knowledge that finally there is no
market for the economic surplus. However, her scepticism as to the
possibility of long-run expanded reproduction is valuable because
the self-propelled growth of capitalist economy cannot, indeed, be
taken for granted. If this economy expands at all without the assistance of "external markets," this, to my mind, is due to certain
aspects of technical progress which, however, do not necessarily
assure a satisfactory long-run utilization of equipment.

Nor should the significance of "external markets" in the development of capitalism be disregarded. In particular, in present-
day capitalism the "external markets" in the form of government
expenditure, especially on armaments, play an important role in
the functioning of capitalist economies. This expenditure, to the
extent that it is financed by loans, or even by taxation of capitalists,
contributes to the solution of the problem of effective demand
because its effect is not offset by the decline in investment and
consumption. (The latter would be the case if this expenditure
were financed by indirect or direct taxation of workers.) Thus today the "external markets" in this particular form are of even
greater significance for expanded reproduction than at the time
when Rosa Luxemburg propounded her theory.

The high degree of utilization of resources resulting in fact from
these government-made "external markets" has a paradoxical impact upon Western economic theory. It creates an atmosphere fa-

vorable to the construction of models for the growth of "laissez-faire" capitalist economies unperturbed by the long-run problem of effective demand.

Notes

1. In a socialist economy prices of consumer goods are *always* fixed relative to wages in such a way as to secure a full utilization of the productive capacity B, that is, the equation $\dfrac{w_1 I}{1 - w_3} = B$ is permanently fulfilled (C_k obviously equals 0 in this case).
2. If the productive capacities of all three departments expand at the same rate the shortage of wage goods discussed in the preceding section will not come into the picture.
3. See Michal Kalecki, "Trend in the Business Cycle," *Economic Journal*, June 1968.

Josef Steindl

ON MATURITY IN CAPITALIST ECONOMIES

What Has Become of Maturity?

In this paper I want to deal briefly with a few questions which readers of my *Maturity and Stagnation in American Capitalism* (Oxford 1952) have been inclined to ask. They refer to:

(1) the contrast in the U. S. and West European employment situation between the period before and since World War II;

(2) the weakening of the incentive to invest in advanced stages of capitalism; and,

(3) the role of innovations in the secular trend movement.

From Keynes to Haavelmo

I shall argue, in relation to the first of the above points, that increased public spending has played a major role, both in the United States and in Western Europe. There has not been more deficit spending since the war, it is true, even rather less than before. However, the increase in public spending financed out of taxation tended to raise output and employment. Following Haavelmo, we use a simple model to demonstrate this.[1] Let consumption be a linear function of income, and assume that the taxation does not alter the distribution of incomes. In the absence of taxation national income will be

$$Y_0 = aY_0 + B + I$$

$$Y_0 = \frac{B + I}{1 - a}$$

where I is investment, a is the marginal propensity to consume, and $aY_0 + B$ is consumption. Assume now that a proportion λ of in-

First published in *Problems of Economic Dynamics and Planning: Essays in Honour of Michal Kalecki* (Oxford: Pergamon Press, 1966), pp. 423–32.

come is taxed away and spent by the government. In addition the government incurs a deficit of the amount d. We have then for the new income Y

$$Y = aY(1 - \lambda) + B + I + \lambda Y + d$$

where $\lambda Y + d$ is the government's spending on goods and services. From this we find

$$Y = \frac{Y_0}{1 - \lambda} + \frac{d}{(1 - \lambda)(1 - a)} = \frac{Y_0}{1 - \lambda}\left(1 + \frac{\delta}{1 - a}\right) \qquad \left(\delta = \frac{d}{Y_0}\right).$$

If the deficit spending is zero the original income Y_0 is raised by a multiplier $\dfrac{1}{1 - \lambda}$ determined by the rate of taxation (we might call it the "tax multiplier"). This result is based on the assumption that the government's spending does not directly affect the consumers' real income, or rather, what they think their real income is (unlike the case of free medical service, for example, which directly affects consumers' real income). In the United States the additional government spending was on arms, in Western Europe, mainly on public investment and arms. The above assumption therefore broadly holds. Another important assumption is that the taxation is "neutral" with regard to income distribution. The additional postwar taxation in the United States and Europe was hardly regressive; in so far as it was progressive the effect on employment was greater than appears from the above simple model.

We shall now use the following figures to make it plausible that public spending was in fact a major factor in the achievement of high levels of employment after the war.

Using the U. S. data to evaluate the algebraic formula given above we find, assuming, rather arbitrarily, a multiplier of 1.5

	U.S. (in percent of national income)	
	Government purchases of goods and services	Government deficit spending
average 1929 to 1937	16.4	2.6
average 1951 to 1961	24.3	0.4

	U.K. (in percent of gross national product at factor cost)	
	Public authorities current expenditure plus public investment	Deficit in public accounts
1938	18.8	4.2
average 1951-1958	27.2	0.8

$$Y\ (\text{prewar}) = \frac{Y_0}{1 - 0.138}\left(1 + \frac{0.031}{1 - a}\right) = 1.21\ Y_0$$

$$Y\ (\text{postwar}) = \frac{Y_0}{1 - 0.239}\left(1 + \frac{0.005}{1 - a}\right) = 1.32\ Y_0$$

The net effect of public spending and taxation appears to have increased the national income by a factor of 1.32/1.21, in other words, by about 9 percent above the level it would have reached without the additional taxation.

If employment is taken to be proportionate to the spending, then, with a full-time equivalent labor force of about 62 million (including self-employed) in the period concerned, the 9 percent additional spending corresponds to 5½ million employees. A prima facie case seems to be made out in favor of the assumption that public spending has played a major role in the reduction of unemployment.

We have, however, to consider also the secondary effect of the public spending. It increases the demand for the goods and services produced by the private sector, but, unlike private investment, it does not increase the productive capacity. Now this is flagrantly untrue in Western Europe where much of the public spending goes into investment in certain key industries (especially the production of energy); however, it remains true that the capacity of *private* industry is not increased. Therefore, the utilization of capacity in the private sector is increased as a consequence of an increased public spending-*cum*-taxation. (In fact, the investment in public utilities, by obviating bottlenecks, in many cases only ensures that the stimulating effect of the demand on the private sector leads to a smooth growth.) The effect of the increased utilization is a rise in private investment to a level permanently higher than it would have been without the public spending.

As the figures given earlier on show, the increase in public spending is important also in the case of Great Britain. The same could be shown for Sweden and Holland, and probably for France, if the prewar data were not so inadequate in the case of this country.

Thus the prewar technique of deficit spending has been replaced since the war by the technique of increased public spending financed by taxation, but this has been practiced on a much greater scale, and with correspondingly greater effect on employment. A full analysis would have to take account, of course, of the possible redistributive effects of the postwar taxation, and of the effects of the tax relief accorded to business in various forms as an incentive to invest.

The Role of Consumer Credit

We start from a consideration of the special character of durable consumer goods. The studies of consumer behavior have often treated spending on new durables in the same way as spending on nondurables, and related both to the current income. It would seem more logical to relate the depreciation of durables, or the stock of them, to the current income of the consumer. The standard of life, which is thought to depend on the income, is shown in equilibrium by the current spending on nondurables and by the stock of durables owned. When the income changes from a lower level to a higher one, however, the stock of durables will change only after a certain time, because the consumer has to save up until he can buy all the durables appropriate to his new higher standard of life (we exclude consumer credit for the time being). We can imagine that, with a jump in income, the "depreciation" of a fictitious durable product is started, and at the end of the depreciation period this durable is actually bought (being afterwards depreciated in the same way, if the owner's standard of life remains unchanged). Thus, there will be a lag between income and consumption of durables corresponding to the lifetime of the durable product. (In a less abstract model the lag will be shorter, because people often reduce current consumption of nondurables in order to reduce the time of waiting for the purchase of a new durable product.)

It seems very plausible that this lag is the reason for a phenomenon described by Modigliani and Duesenberry, namely the discrepancy between short-term and long-term propensity to consume. If we take ten-year moving averages of income and consumption, then these figures will reflect the average spending on durables over a ten-year period, corresponding more or less to the "depreciation" notion used above: the long-term data will be a "true" propensity to consume in the sense that they take account of the spending on durables. In a regression of *annual* data of income and consumption, however, a different pattern will appear: the rise in incomes over a few years' boom will not be fully reflected in consumption in the same period, because much of the spending on durables can only materialize at a later date owing to the lag explained above. In a deep slump, on the other hand, the spending will never be fully adapted to the current income, because some spending on durables will take place out of savings made in more prosperous years. Thus the short-term propensity to consume will be lower than the "true" propensity to consume; part of what appears as saving in the short run is in fact only saving for durable goods.

It is evident that the introduction and wide acceptance of consumer credit will very much reduce the lag between income and consumption of durables. (The lag will probably not disappear entirely, even if nobody is excluded from or refuses the credit facilities, because the permanence of an increase in income may be doubted by the consumer until the increase has persisted for some time.) If the preceding explanations are correct, the reduced lag must lead to a closing of the gap between long-term and short-term propensity to consume: the short-term propensity to consume will increase as a consequence of the habit of buying durables on credit and it will tend to approach the long-term propensity to consume. A cursory examination of the time series of consumption and disposable income in the United States (in real terms per head of population) does seem to confirm this expectation: we get a marginal propensity to consume of 0.78 for 1929–40, and of 0.91 for 1950–59.[2]

The introduction of consumers' credit on a very large scale has, in fact, been a characteristic feature of the U. S. postwar economy. What are the consequences of such a reduction in the spending lag on the dynamics of the system?

Intuitively it is obvious that a considerable lag in spending on durables must act somewhat as a stabilizer. The additional money earned in the boom is in part withheld and is spent later, presumably largely in the course of the following slump, and this may help to bring about the turning point of the slump.[3] If, in consequence of the prevalent use of consumer credit, the lag in spending on durables is reduced to a small interval, so that any increase in income has its full consequence on the demand for durables almost immediately, then the effect on the cycle is *undamping*. The sequence income–consumption–income . . . (representing a *positive* feedback) will proceed more quickly to higher and higher (or lower and lower) levels. The countereffect (*negative* feedback) which appears once the new equipment has become ready to produce is correspondingly greater (in view of the greater investment during the construction period). Intuition tells us that the effect of the shortened lag in spending will be to undamp the cycle and to shorten it. The amplitude of the cycle will probably in practice not be much affected; it depends to a large extent on the magnitude of the random shocks which are essential for keeping the cycle going.[4]

Another effect is not so obvious: the undamping will affect the secular growth of the economy by increasing the long-term rate of growth. This can best be explained by reference to Professor Kalecki's model of the trend and cycle.[5] The movement of *net* investment i around the trend value is governed by the equation

$$i_{t+\theta} = ni_t + \mu\frac{di_{t-\omega}}{dt} \tag{1}$$

while the movement of the trend values themselves is governed by

$$y_t + \theta = ny_t + m\dot{y}_{t-\omega} + [(1 - n)\beta + \gamma]K_t \tag{2}$$

this equation referring to the trend value of *gross* investment. K_t is the stock of capital.

It will be seen that the parameters n and μ which occur in the equation of the cycle, are met also in the equation of the trend (m is, in fact, a sum of μ and some other term). The close connection between the two phenomena of trend and cycle could perhaps be shown as follows: the term K_t, the capital stock, which occurs in the trend equation, depends obviously on the investment; we can determine it, if a uniform lifetime τ is given, as the integral of gross investment over a past period τ. This integral $\int_{t-\tau}^{t} y_{t'}, d_{t'}$, can be replaced, making use of the intermediate value theorem, by the approximation $\tau y_{t-\sigma}$ where σ is a value intermediate between 0 and τ. If we introduce this expression $\tau y_{t-\sigma}$ instead of K_t into (2), we have a homogenous equation in gross investment; now we may add to this the equation (1) for the oscillations around the trend, and the equation so constituted will govern at the same time the cycle and the trend. It will yield an exponential solution, due to the term in $y_{t-\sigma}$, which represents the impact of innovations, and an oscillation due to the action of the other two terms. The term in $\dot{y}_{t-\omega}$ is a destabilizer, and the greater its coefficient m, the smaller the damping of the oscillation. The term in y_t embodies the action of the negative feedback, which is due to the depressing effect of the growing capital stock on the rate of profit and to the incomplete reinvestment of internal savings.

Both trend and oscillation are determined by the same set of data. It can be shown that the parameter m, which acts as a destabilizer in the oscillation (the greater m, the smaller the damping), will at the same time promote the long-term growth. This is apparent from Professor Kalecki's analysis of the exponential solution: it follows from it that if an exponential trend is obtained at all (that is, as long as m is not too large) the rate of growth will be the greater, the smaller $\theta - m$ (that is, the greater m), given the other parameters.[6] Thus, the parameter which undamps the cycle at the same time stimulates secular growth.

Now the decrease of the lag in spending on durables, if it were introduced explicitly into this system, would play the same role as the increase of the coefficient m. The essence is in both cases the strengthening of a positive feedback, which leads at the same time to antidamping in the cycle and to a larger growth rate in the long run.

It is possible that changes in lags have played an important role apart from consumption. The tax relief accorded to businessmen on condition of investment of their profits has, in certain European countries at least, sped up the process of investment of internal savings: the lag between earning and investment of profits which in the above equation is denoted by θ has become shorter. Since this is the lag with which the "negative feedback" operates, it is plausible that its reduction has tended to shorten the cycle. At the same time, the reduction of θ must have stimulated the secular growth, as the above quoted analysis of Professor Kalecki shows: the smaller $\theta - m$, the larger the real exponential solution of the equation.

In countries with an endemic price increase there is, of course, still another reason for a shortening of θ. On the other hand, difficulties on the supply side, for example in construction, or delays in deliveries of capital goods, may work in the opposite direction. It is, nevertheless, a fair guess that the factors making for a reduction of θ in the postwar era have dominated.

Safety versus Investment

My original explanation of maturity rests on the idea that the economy can move upwards only if some capital is knocked out of existence, and that this happens by competition; once only a few oligopolists remain in an industry, however, competition to the point of the knife involves too much loss. Since "knocking out" of capitals does not take place, there is a tendency to low utilization of capacity and a fear of excess capacity dominates the investment decisions of business.

In elaborating the theory I have made use of some arguments which cannot stand up to the stress of time. I have argued that the oligopolists have some difficulty in moving into other sectors of the economy which are not yet oligopolized, and where they could consequently expand, knocking out some of the existing capital without too much competitive effort. The movement into a different branch requires know-how and this takes time; there is therefore a delay in investment which is tantamount to a disincentive to investment. But the big oligopolists in the United States nowadays are so organized as to spread their tentacles into a host of the most diverse lines of business. Since they have their finger in every pie, it is quite possible to argue that the impediments against moving into another branch do not exist for them any more. This situation, which has arisen only in the postwar era, involves no doubt a much easier flow of capital from the point of inception (earning) to the investment.

Whatever the possibilities of movement of funds between industries, the fact remains that the competitive sector of the economy, which offers better prospects for investment than the oligopolistic sector, has been *greatly reduced* in proportion to the whole economy. This alone is sufficient to account for a weakening of the incentive to invest.

There exists, however, another reason for the weakening of the incentive to invest in advanced capitalism which is supplementary to my original explanation. The reason is that large concerns prefer to barter the chances of great profit for greater safety, and the policies designed to meet this aim involve in most cases less investment than would otherwise have been decided. Therefore, the larger the concerns become, and the greater the relative weight of large concerns in the economy, the smaller is the incentive to invest. The oligopolistic market situation is partly an incidental consequence of size, partly a symptom of the safety-mindedness of big business.

The striving for safety is, of course, common to all business. It is patent, however, that most of the roads to safety are blocked to small business. The small man has to indebt himself heavily, or he will in many cases not be able to run his business at all. He cannot afford to keep reserves and he has to put his one egg willy-nilly into one and the same basket. The bigger the business becomes, the more opportunities open up for a leisurely decision whether to choose a high mathematical expectation of profit associated with great risk, or a lower one with greater safety.

The safety preference of large concerns is an assumption which we do not make just for the purpose of explaining a weakening of the incentive to invest in mature capitalism, but which is forced on us by data which hardly admit of another interpretation. It is undeniable, on the one hand, that big firms have the advantages of large-scale economies, and can therefore earn a higher profit rate than small firms. It should be expected, therefore, that firms grow more quickly the greater they are. Such data as we have on the correlation of growth rate and size of firms suggest that it is rather uncertain, sometimes positive, sometimes negative, but always very small.[7] There is no strong evidence that large firms grow more quickly and earn higher profit rates than small firms. On the other hand, there is pretty good evidence that the mortality rate of firms decreases with the size; big firms manage to be safer. Linking the two strands of evidence together we should say that the larger firm uses the greater opportunities open to it due to larger scale economies to increase its safety rather than its profits. This involves reducing the relative indebtedness (or even holding bonds), and therefore investing less than could be done at a fixed proportion of debt to own capital. A smaller proportion of debt involves a reduction of the mathematical expectation of profit rate, and a reduction of the variance of the profit rate.[8] It is, therefore, an ideal way of bartering away profit for security.

Not all the methods of buying safety involve a smaller investment, but it is clear that the whole investment policy is affected by the relative value put on safety. The security preference may lead to the elimination of risky investment projects, and it may also lead to a greater lag in spending on investment, if the aim of collecting more experience about a new process, or whatever, is coming to weigh more strongly than the aim of getting in first and reaping the profits.

Technically speaking, what happens in maturing capitalism (the United States in the period from 1890 to 1939) is therefore this: the share of large concerns in the market and in the total internal saving grows. For the large concerns the effect of a given internal saving on investment is smaller than for the medium and small business, and possibly also the time lag of spending on investment is bigger. With the growing share of the big concerns the investment effect of a given internal saving in the total economy will therefore decline.

The Role of Innovations and the Generation of the Trend

In denying the active role of innovations in the investment process I have formerly taken up an extreme position which I have no wish to uphold. I was reacting against the view that maturity had arisen from a drying up of the flow of innovations—why it should have done so, nobody had explained, and the fact of drying up itself seemed not very well documented (except to the extent that the concepts of innovation and investment were quietly merged, which made the result obvious). I have been wrong, however, to disregard the economic function of innovations in capitalism which, as Professor Kalecki's work has made clear, is to make a more than temporary enlargement of the capital stock profitable. The capitalist system as represented by Kalecki's model of the pure business cycle is subject to a badly working servo-mechanism (or rather, a controller) which in the absence of innovations (and certain other influences, like outside savings) keeps the capital stock constant. It does so, because it happens to work in this way, not because anybody designed it. Whenever the capital stock grows, and a boom develops, a negative feedback operates so as to push the investment back. This is due to the depressing effect which a growth of the capital stock has on the rate of profit. This feedback, which operates with a not inconsiderable lag (up to one year), produces an oscillation around a stable position where net saving is zero and the capital stock is constant. Innovations make it possible to break through this closed circle and set an upward path for the capital stock; the controller henceforth pins the system down to oscillations around this path. The function of innovations is to offer the prospect of additional profits which make it possible to enlarge the capital. In Kalecki's formulation: an innovation is *analogous* to an increase in profit, and a steady stream of innovations is *comparable* in its effects on investment to a steady rate of increase in profits.[9]

One might wish to go a little further and ask: is it not actually the belief of the innovator-investor that he will get the additional profit, and if so, must we not exclude that his belief is consistently disappointed, or else the innovations would lose their fascination for the investor? There is room for comment here and I offer the following interpretation of the effect of innovations.

A steady stream of innovations means that a given proportion of the existing capital stock is knocked out every year owing to technical obsolescence (it does not pay to work it any more, because the current costs are not covered, owing to the competition of new processes or products). An equal amount of investment in proportion to the capital stock then becomes possible every year without the negative feedback operating against it. This investment (which will embody the innovations) causes an additional stream of profits which makes it possible to actually enlarge the capital stock by some further investment without depressing the rate of profit.

The way in which Kalecki introduces the innovations into the last version of his model (1954) makes it actually an *endogenous* theory of the trend. The effect of innovations (represented by the term γ

K_t in (2)) depends on the size of the capital stock, which evidently depends on gross investment over a certain long period in the past. The innovations are, therefore, an influence of gross investment with a certain relatively long lag. I suggest this could also be interpreted as follows: innovations arise in a stochastic process of learning, the knowledge being embodied in the capital stock, and new innovations are thrown up in proportion to the capital stock with a given intensity γ.[10] The innovations would then represent random positive shocks proportionate to the capital stock.

Kalecki, in his model of 1954, has in fact brought about the synthesis of cycle and trend in the form of an endogenous theory which I desired but failed to achieve in my book. I think that this synthesis is essential for the analysis of economic development. It permits us to analyze the effects which certain parameters of the trade cycle, as for example, saving propensities or lags, have on the secular development. Naturally a closer understanding of the dynamic process of learning which throws up the innovations remains desirable.

I should like briefly to mention a modification or variant which could be made of Kalecki's model. The negative feedback which operates in this model acts via the rate of profit. One could imagine it to act, in an analogous way, via the degree of utilization. This requires only that the investment is made to depend not on the rate of profit on existing capital, but on the degree of utilization of capacity. The boom, in this version, will break because of the accumulation of new capacity which will depress the degree of utilization. In this version the business cycle represents a controller which tends to keep capacity constant by a feedback operating via utilization. This view is, in fact, implicit in the theory contained in *Maturity and Stagnation*. It might seem that the problem of the trend—the question of how the economy breaks out of the closed circle and sets on an upward path—takes a different form in this version: required is a steady stream of *additional demand* of a type which will not set the negative feedback operating. Innovations will again fulfill the requirement, in so far as they destroy existing capacity. But will not also a steadily increasing stream of export surpluses, government deficits, or public expenditure financed by taxation do the trick?

Historically the stimulants to growth have been very strong at times and it is not entirely perverse to look for a systematic brake. It may be found in the assumption that the share of profits in the national income is elastic in the long run and influenced by utilization, so that it tends to adapt itself to some extent to the rate of growth. This theory has been extensively discussed and motivated in my book. This kind of damping effect acting in the secular development might explain how the secular evolution has most of the time avoided running headlong into inflation.

An alternative explanation, which I did not mention, suits the postwar conditions, at any rate, much better: if they cannot get labor, entrepreneurs are driven to use their investment funds for automation rather than for creating additional employment capacity. This adaptiveness of investment explains why full employment in Western Europe has been maintained for many years now without hyperinflation.

Notes

1. "Multiplier Effects of a Balanced Budget," *Econometrica*, 1945.
2. The regression equations are:
   consumption per head (prewar) = $0.78y + 190$
   consumption per head (postwar) = $0.91y + 26$
   (where y is real income in $ of 1954 per head).
   The "basic consumption" (consumption at zero income) has declined to a small amount, so that the pattern more nearly approximates to the proportionality of consumption and income which is supposed to hold in the long run.
3. The spending is not necessarily on durables. The money saved for this purpose may be spent on necessities in the slump.
4. Michal Kalecki, *Theory of Economic Dynamics* (London: Allen & Unwin 1954), p. 129.
5. Ibid., Part 6, p. 146.
6. Ibid., pp. 152–55.
7. I give some of these data and elaborate on the above argument in my book *Random Processes and the Growth of Firms: A Study of the Pareto Law* (Monticello, N.Y.: Lubrecht and Cramer, 1965).
8. Cf. "On Risk," *Oxford Economic Papers* (Oxford: Oxford University Press, 1943).
9. Ibid., p. 158 (my italics).
10. T. Haavelmo, *A Study in the Theory of Economic Evolution* (Amsterdam, 1954); Kenneth Arrow, "Economic Implications of Learning by Doing," *Review of Economic Studies*, June 1962.

Josef Steindl

STAGNATION THEORY AND STAGNATION POLICY

Following the traditions of Kalecki and Keynes, we are led to believe that a high long-term rate of growth is necessary to establish an adequate use of capacity and full employment, because somehow our economy is rather inflexibly adjusted to such high long-term rates of growth. In this line is Harrod's theory, as well as my own *Maturity and Stagnation*.[1] Both explain the secular depression of the prewar decade in these terms: the economy is unable to adjust to low growth rates because its savings propensity is adapted to a high one.

From this point of view it is not, in principle, difficult to understand how the prewar conditions of underuse of resources were avoided after the last war; a very high long-term rate of growth imposed by certain favorable exogenous conditions on the postwar economy made it work.

In the course of the 1970s we entered a new era, dominated by the conviction that in the future the long-term rate of growth is going to be much lower—or that it should be lower or *must* be lower—a belief which in the nature of things carries a great deal of self-fulfillment within it. In consequence, underuse of resources already exists on a large scale. Thus the climate has changed twice: from the prewar depression to the postwar high-growth period of the 1950s and 1960s, and from that back again to the period of stunted growth in the 1970s. The two periods—high growth and stunted growth—require an explanation which links one to the other and reconciles them with the model of development before World War II which I used in *Maturity and Stagnation*. Before I try to do that in the second part of the paper, I want to deal with some aspects of my maturity theory which are related to well-known ideas in the contemporary literature. Perhaps some of my concepts will become easier to understand in this way, and in any event I shall have a formal apparatus to serve me in dealing with the difficult problems of the postwar scene.

First published by *Cambridge Journal of Economics* 3, no. 1 (March 1979). Copyright 1979 by Academic Press Inc. (London) Ltd.

The Maturity Theorem

Harrod's equation of 1939 implies a kind of maturity theorem, although he did not use this word. I shall write his equation in a slightly modified form, putting:

Y = gross product in real terms,
Y^* = capacity production in real terms,
I = gross investment in real terms,
S = gross savings in real terms,
u = utilization of capacity,
v = (marginal) capital-capacity ratio,
$d(r)$ = dropout rate of capital equipment as a ratio of gross capital,
d' = depreciation rate as a ratio of gross capital,
r = growth rate of capital equipment during the last n years,
n' = expected lifetime and
n = actual lifetime.

$$Y(t) = u(t)Y^*(t), \tag{1}$$
$$\Delta Y(t) \cong u(t)\Delta Y^*(t) + Y^*(t)\Delta u(t), \tag{1a}$$
$$I(t) = v\Delta Y^*(t) + d(r)vY^*(t). \tag{2}$$

From (1a) and (2):

$$I(t) \cong [v/u(t)]\Delta Y(t) - v[\Delta u(t)/u(t)]Y^*(t) + d(r)vY^*(t), \tag{2a}$$
$$S(t) = sY(t) + d'vY^*(t), \tag{3}$$
$$I(t) = S(t). \tag{3a}$$

From (2a) and (3):

$$\Delta Y(t) \cong \Delta u(t)Y^*(t) + (s/v)u(t)Y(t) + [d' - d(r)]u(t)Y^*(t),$$
$$\Delta Y(t)/Y(t) \cong \Delta u(t)/u(t) + (s/v)u(t) + d' - d(r). \tag{4}$$

From the definition of utilization, gross investment and gross saving (equations (1), (2) and (3) respectively), we derive the extended Harrod equation (4). It differs from Harrod's equation in so far as he used the capital-output ratio, which can be considered a product of the capital-capacity output ratio and the degree of utilization of capacity. I introduce these two factors separately, because the capital-capacity ratio is a technological element, whereas the degree of utilization reflects the state of effective demand.

Another difference is that I formulate the equation in terms of gross investment and saving. Harrod assumed that the dropout of equipment and the depreciation are always equal, and he therefore formulated the equation in terms of gross investment and saving. The last term in (4), therefore, does not appear in his formulation. In a later paper Harrod recognized that linear depreciation will be

greater than the dropout of equipment in a growing economy, and
A. Bhaduri has provided an elegant mathematical treatment of
these relationships.[2] For a uniform expected lifetime n' the depreciation ration d' is the reciprocal of this expected lifetime ($d' = 1/n'$)
and it is applied to gross capital $vY^*(t)$. (For heterogeneous equipment with different lifetimes d' will be reciprocal of the weighted
harmonious mean of the different lifetimes.) Dropout as a proportion of gross capital will depend on the actual lifetime n and also on
the rate of growth of capital r in the preceding n years. We therefore write the dropout ratio $d(r)$ as a function of the growth rate r.
For steady state growth $d(r)$ will be given by

$$d(r) = re^{-nr}/(1 - e^{-nr}),$$
$$d(r) < 1/n \text{ for } r > 0,$$
$$d(r) = 1/n \text{ for } r = 0.[3]$$

$d(r)$ is a decreasing function of r. Thus, the greater the accumulation during the preceding lifetime n of the equipment, the greater
will be the discrepancy between depreciation and dropout. The two
ratios will be equal only in the stationary state, provided that expected and actual (ex post) lifetimes are equal. In the context of
this paper interest centers on the premature or delayed withdrawal
of equipment which may prevail in different situations, in other
words, on (temporary) changes in actual lifetimes which take place
against a background of unchanged depreciation rates. For the
moment we shall disregard the question of dropout and depreciation altogether and return to it later.

In equilibrium utilization will be constant and the first term on
the right of (4) will vanish. Starting from this position, let us suppose that the rate of growth is reduced to a lower level by certain
exogenous influences; utilization will then decline until it reaches a
level at which equilibrium is again established. If the lower utilization, however, reacts unfavorably on investment, the left-hand side
of the equation (4) will again decline and a process of continuing
decline of growth will be set in motion. The reverse process will
take place if the growth rate is lifted from equilibrium to a higher
level, subject to the qualification that the ceiling of capacity production cannot be surpassed. Writing in the 1930s Harrod had in mind
the downward process. If the system had been adjusted, by its rigid
saving ratio, to a high rate of growth, and if at a later date—
whether for demographic reasons or because of a slowing of technical progress—a lower growth rate obtained, secular depression
would prevail.

Stepping now outside Harrod's text, we may say that the saving
ratio, of course, depends on the share of profits in the national

income, and its rigidity ultimately reflects the rigidity of the income distribution. How far does this rigidity hold and on what does it depend? The share of profits in the short run (in the course of the cycle) is strongly influenced by utilization. To separate this influence let me represent, for a closed system, the relation of wages and salaries (W), net profits (P), and income (Y) in a way strongly reminiscent of Kalecki:

$$W + P = Y - d'vY^*.$$
$$W = \lambda Y + \mu Y^*, Y \leq Y^*. \text{[4]} \tag{5}$$

The two terms on the right-hand side of (5) represent the contribution of direct labor and overhead labor; the latter is assumed to move in proportion to production capacity.

We are now going to express profits and savings as ratios of capacity production. It would be more in keeping with common usage to express them as ratios of the (net) capital stock, in other words, as profit rate and a corresponding "saving rate." However, in order to avoid introducing an additional variable with its own problems, it is preferable to work with the capacity production as a proxy for the capital stock.

We obtain then from (5) the net profit after depreciation

$$P = (1 - \lambda)Y - \mu Y^* - d'vY^*, (Y \leq Y^*), \tag{6}$$
$$P/Y^* = (1 - \lambda)u - \mu - d'v = p(u). \tag{7}$$

$p(u)$, an increasing function of utilization, will be called the profit function. This function plays an essential role in what follows. We need it to distinguish between those shifts to or from profits which are due to effective demand, and those which result from changed price-cost relations independent of demand. The neoclassical tradition now in vogue takes great delight in confusing these two cases of a shift in profit. In fact, neoclassicism does not admit of anything but full utilization in the long run, and even in the short run adopts the same assumption when considering practical problems. For the Keynesian tradition, on the other hand, the concept of utilization is of central importance.

Kalecki achieved the above-mentioned distinction by introducing the markup of prices on prime cost.[5] A shift to profits could occur through an increase either in markup or in demand. The above concept of the profit function is plainly aiming at a more general (less specific) formulation of the same idea.

We now derive gross saving, which consists of the gross savings of capitalists

$$S' = [s_1 p(u) + d'v] Y^*$$

and the savings of employees

$$S'' = s_2[u - p(u) - d'v]Y^*.$$
$$S = S' + S''.$$

Thus we get gross saving as a ratio of capacity output, which we call the savings function *s(u)*:

$$s(u) = S/Y^* = (s_1 - s_2)p(u) + d'v + s_2 (u - d'v) \qquad (8)$$

or, alternatively, inserting the expression (7) for *p(u)*:

$$s(u) = [s_1 - (s_1 - s_2)\lambda]u - (s_1 - s_2)\mu + (1 - s_1)d'v. \qquad (8a)$$

It can easily be seen that the savings function is an increasing function of $p(u)$, provided that $s_1 > s_2$; in other words, the ratio saved out of profits is larger than the ratio saved out of wages. It is also an increasing function of *u*, provided

$$(1 - \lambda)s_1 > \lambda s_2.$$

The savings function $s(u)$ might now be inserted in the modified Harrod equation (4) in place of the term $su(t)$ (the constant savings-income ratio). I shall, however, choose a different representation, which permits us to distinguish between exogenous and endogenous influences on the growth rate.

Let us simply put saving (equation (3)) equal to investment (equation (2)). Investment consists of a part which generates new capacity—call it $I'(t)$—and a part which merely replaces equipment which drops out. This replacement is equal to $I(t - n)$, where *n* is the lifetime. The lifetime is, however, not given beforehand, since obsolescence is not "technological," but varies according to the state of business. I prefer for this reason to denote the replacement demand, as before, by $vd(r) Y^*(t)$, that is, as a function of past accumulation *r* which may vary according to the scarcity or abundance of equipment in relation to demand.

We have, therefore, for the gross investment in terms of capacity output:

$$I(t)/Y^*(t) = I'(t)/Y^*(t) + vd(r). \qquad (9)$$

Let us now suppose that the capacity-generating investment is determined by investment decisions taken a certain time τ previously, and that these decisions depend inter alia on the degree of utilization, as well as on the internal saving of the enterprises S'. We thus write:

$$\varphi[u(t - \tau), S'(t - \tau)] = I'(t)/Y^*(t)$$

expressing the capacity-generating investment as an increasing function φ of past utilization and entrepreneurial saving. Inserting into (9) and putting investment equal to saving (8), we can write:

$$
\begin{aligned}
\varphi[u(t - \tau), S'(t - \tau)] \\
= (s_1 - s_2)p[u(t)] + s_2[u(t) - d'v] + d'v - d(r)v \\
= [s_1 - (s_1 - s_2)\lambda]u(t) - (s_1 - s_2)\mu + (1 - s_1)vd' - vd(r).
\end{aligned}
$$
(10)

We can now represent exogenous influences by shifts in the function φ. If there is, for example, a drying up of the sources of innovation or a general decline in confidence, then φ will shift downwards. The equation tells us, supposing that $(1 - \lambda)s_1 > \lambda s_2$, that this will lead to a decline in utilization, and this in turn will act on the investment decisions (left side of (10)), leading after a certain time to a further decline in investment and again to reduced utilization and so on. This downward movement may be braked by increased dropouts of equipment and, if government is introduced into the model, by automatically increasing budget deficits.

A digression on tax-financed spending

For the purposes of later arguments the effects of a budget expansion financed by increased taxation will now be discussed, before we return again to the main thread of the argument. Let us assume for this purpose that the budget is automatically balanced, the receipts of new or increased taxation being spent immediately.

If a uniform and proportionate tax θ is levied on profits and if profits are positive, the profits after tax will be (from (7))

$$
[(1 - \lambda) u(t) - (\mu + vd')] (1 - \theta);
$$

wages may be similarly taxed at a rate θ' and equation (10) will then be modified as follows:

$$
\begin{aligned}
\varphi[u(t - \tau), S'(t - \tau)] = s_1[(1 - \lambda)u(t) - (\mu + vd')](1 - \theta) \\
+ s_2[\lambda u(t) + \mu](1 - \theta') + vd' - vd(r).
\end{aligned}
$$
(11)

If a profit tax θ is newly introduced this would appear to reduce disposable income and saving. In view of the predetermined investment (left side of (10)), however, saving cannot decline. If, in the simplest case, workers' saving s_2 is zero, then the utilization will increase just enough to restore the profit after tax and the saving out of it to its former level. The profits tax will be paid out of the increase in profits before taxation due to the higher utilization.

If workers do save but are not taxed, their savings may increase with increased employment, and that means that profits after tax will not remain at their former level but will decrease. The effect is, however, doubtful because the increased employment may increase consumers' credit and spending on durables.

If wages, however, are taxed too, this counteracts the decline of profits after tax. In fact, if the tax on wages is sufficiently high, profits after tax may even increase. In practice, since the saving of employed people is very unequally distributed, the tax on wages will reduce it less than proportionately and will fall more on consumption, while the profit tax will fall largely on savings. A profits tax is therefore far more likely to stimulate demand and increase utilization than a tax on wages. (We assume always that tax receipts are spent simultaneously.)

Distribution and growth

While, in my interpretation of Harrod's world, income distribution is rigidly given and does not change, except to the extent to which it depends on u, we get a quite different picture from Kaldor's model of distribution.[6] Here the rate of growth of capital and of capacity (the left side of (10)) is somehow given exogenously, and the profit function is a variable which adjusts to it so as to produce just enough saving for the predetermined investment.

What is the mechanism underlying this idea? It will only apply, says Kaldor, if full employment is established. Here Kaldor refers explicitly to Keynes' "How to Pay for the War." The Kaldor distribution theory differs from Keynes' theory of the inflationary gap only in so far as the former presupposes that the workers (trade unions) put up with the shift in distribution so that no inflationary spiral arises. This is due to the long-run nature of this process, in which the distributional shift proceeds only slowly. Limits, both upwards and downwards, to the possible adjustment of the profit shares are recognized by Kaldor. His model today appears as a rather optimistic picture of the possible working of full employment, written at an early stage of the period of full employment (1955). (A surprising feature of the theory is that full employment—or overfull employment—is supposed to favor a shift to profits.)

In a somewhat formal way the idea of Kaldor's distribution theory runs parallel to the picture of distribution which I gave (in *Maturity and Stagnation*, chs. 5 and 9) for a competitive economy, which I suppose might have corresponded to historical reality in the United States before the emergence of oligopolistic structures. In such an economy there would be a great number of producers, many of them near the margin of existence. If any of them acquired differential advantages by means of new methods, they would expand quickly and gain room by pushing out high-cost producers. Any appearance of exceptional profits, a very likely concomitant of technical innovation, would soon lead to an expansion of capacity of the favored firms, and from there to an attempt to capture markets from the high-cost producers by cutting prices. In the long run this mechanism would at the same time reestablish a "normal" (desired) degree of utilization, and reduce the profit margins to a "normal" level. What is "normal" in this context depends, however, on the rate of growth of capital. Referring to equation (10) we can see that if utilization is to be kept at a certain level in the long run, then an increase (decrease) of the left side of the equation requires a shift upwards (downwards) of the profit function $p(u)$.

This argument is formally analogous to Kaldor's equation, but the mechanism behind it is quite different. I assume that a low growth rate, since it tends to lead to excess capacity, sets up an increase in competitive pressure. To reestablish a normal desired degree of utilization, high-cost producers have to be driven out, which requires a cut in the industry's average profit margins. A high growth rate of capital, on the contrary, will lead to high utilization and therefore a lessening of competitive pressure. There is less need to fight for markets by pushing out high-cost producers and the average profit margins will therefore increase.

In the process of adjustment to a change in the growth rate of capital, the variation in lifetime of equipment plays a role. High growth rate and high utilization will tend to retard withdrawal of equipment, thus lengthen actual lifetime and shift the dropout function $d(r)$ downwards, so that the difference $d' - d(r)$ will rise above its average long-term level. A low growth rate and utilization will lead to some premature withdrawal of equipment, and therefore to a decrease of $d' - d(r)$ below its long-term average. Clearly these movements, in so far as they are operative, serve to accommodate the increased or decreased growth rate. The change in the difference $d' - d(r)$ acts, however, only as long as the transition to a new equilibrium proceeds. This equilibrium will be established by a shift of the profit function $p(u)$, and the consequent shift in the saving function $s(u)$, such as to permit the reestablishment of a normal degree of utilization at the given growth rate. This is a long-run process. In the course of the trade cycle, the adjustment of utilization prevails.

The adjustment of the profit function to the growth rate must be seen against the background of a dynamic economy in which there is always a balance of two opposing forces. Owing to innovations, etc., there emerge again and again exceptional profits, which tend to push the profit function upward. At the same time, owing to the aggressiveness of expanding firms and the diffusion of previous innovations, there is a pressure which at the same time drives out high-cost producers and lowers the profit function. According to whether growth is fast or slow, one or the other of the two tendencies will be strengthened, and the balance will shift in one or the other direction.

It should be noted that, while Kaldor is really interested mainly in the case of an upward pressure of growth rates, which maintains full employment, my own treatment of distribution only considers the effects of a declining growth rate, simply because this was the problem posed by the mature economy of prewar times.

Although I devoted much effort to the description of distribution in a competitive economy, my chief point was really that this mechanism no longer works very well when an economy with many producers is superseded by an oligopolistic economy. Here aggressive price strategies become very risky, because the few main producers all have substantial margins, and to drive out one of them would require a ruinous price war. If the growth rate declines, the oligopolists are therefore more prepared in most cases to accept low long-term rates of utilization than to engage in cutthroat competition. That means that the profit function becomes fairly rigid, and the weight of adjustment is thrown on utilization, with adverse effects on investment and further growth. We are back to Harrod's model. We might define maturity as the state in which the economy and its profit function are adjusted to the high growth rates of earlier stages of capitalist development, while those high growth rates no longer obtain.

But why did the growth rate ever start to decline? What is the reason for the initial decline (which, as we can see from equation (10), will initiate a cumulative further decline)? I also tried to answer this more difficult question, although I cannot find parallels or support for this answer in contemporary literature. I assumed that with the transition to an oligopolistic structure the big firms must have increased their profit margins (markup); in other words, the profit function must have shifted upwards. This could not increase the profits for the economy as a whole, since they are determined by investments, which in turn are governed by past decisions (see equation (10)). Therefore the oligopolists' attempt to increase profits could (apart from a redistribution of profits between different sectors of business) lead only to a decline in utilization. This, on my assumptions, will have an adverse effect on investment decisions, because the firms will be fearful of increasing excess capacity, even if their total profits have not declined. Consequently, investment will decrease in the following period. The primary setback to the growth rate will have occurred.

An alternative explanation is based on the idea of a "technological wave" engendered by a particularly fertile innovation, like the railway, which is followed by a string of after-effects (building of new towns, opening up the West) and further innovations, effects which, however, weaken and exhaust themselves after a time.[7] When I wrote *Maturity and Stagnation,* I wanted to deny all influence of innovations on the accumulation of capital. I think now that this was foolish and I subscribe to Kalecki's view that innovations are capable of generating a trend. A stream of innovations would be expressed as a shift of the function φ in equation (10).

On the other hand, this does not mean that I am convinced that the technological wave explanation is an adequate substitute for my own explanation. The timing of the exhaustion of this wave remains rather indeterminate: could it not have lasted longer? It seems that the timing must be strongly influenced by effective demand, so that in default of other explanations there is still room for my own theory.

Two Phases in the Development of Postwar History

The contrast between the postwar full employment era and the prewar stagnation must be viewed against the background of great institutional changes. The postwar economy has been transformed by the unprecedented role which government, public policy, and politics have played. Governments have become more conscious of their role in the economy and of their responsibilities, and to this extent the influence of Keynesian economics on postwar history is undeniable ("full employment as an innovation").

In view of the large role of governments, the dominant attitudes and beliefs of public men are of some importance for the trend of events. The full employment period was dominated by growth optimism and by a certain recognition of government responsibility for full employment. The subsequent period of stunted growth has been dominated by a readiness to accept high unemployment and low growth rates. I shall argue that, to a very large extent, the driving force underlying the growth period was the contribution of two very distinct elements. First, there was a conscious political and moral reaction against prewar conditions, particularly in certain European countries. Second, there was the tension between the superpowers which led to large armament spending and technological competition, as well as to the economic cooperation of the

Western industrial countries under the leadership of the United States.

In Europe a strong impulse was created by the import of American technology, which acted like a stream of innovations drawn from the available stock of accumulated know-how in the United States. To the extent to which this was helped by the Marshall Plan and technical assistance, it also comes under the heading of international cooperation.

In the subsequent period of stunted growth, the driving forces of expansion weakened with the relaxation of tension between the superpowers. This is at any rate evident in the field of international cooperation, currency, and trade. At the same time the sustained growth of the previous period had itself produced a reaction which undermined it. The long period of accumulation had created a large gap between ordinary replacement of equipment and depreciation.[8] The increased standard of living and extension of social insurance produced a growth of personal savings, with adverse effects on the rate of profit. The opportunities for introducing new technology in Europe from a ready stock of accumulated know-how in the United States began to dwindle. The traumatic entry of the environmental and energy problems onto the scene threw an embarrassing burden on industry and government.

Finally, full employment and social-reform policies led to a growing resentment of workers' claims and trade-union power. It also led to complaints about work discipline and to the emergence of stiffer opposition to economic intervention.

In fact, the business opposition to full employment policies, which Kalecki had so vividly described in his analysis of the "political business cycle" gathered more and more strength toward the end of the growth period. It seems to have now, however, a more persistent and lasting character than in Kalecki's political cycle, so that we might rather speak of a "political trend."[9] This policy of stagnation is likely to continue, since governments are preoccupied with inflation and the public debt. Budget deficits can only disappear if private investment soars again. This is unlikely in view of excess capacity, which would only disappear if there were fiscal expansion.

The full employment era

The arguments will now be spelt out in detail, first for the growth period.

First, there was an increase in government spending, financed in part by taxation on profits. As shown above, this spending increases

Table 1
Taxation, Government Spending and Capacity Utilization in the United States
(% of private gross national product at factor cost)

	1929-38	1951-57	1958-68	1969-73	1974-77
Corporate tax liability	1.4	6.6	5.5	4.7	4.6
Personal taxation, nonwage	1.7	3.6	3.3	3.3	—
Profit taxes	3.2	10.2	8.8	8.0	—
Government dissaving	2.1	0.2	0.7	0.5	2.4
Foreign balance	0.5	0.9	0.4	−0.3	0.5
Gross private domestic investment	11.0	19.3	18.4	18.7	18.2
Government spending on goods and services	15.5	24.5	26.3	27.5	27.0
of which: federal government	4.4	15.4	13.6	11.5	9.9
of which: military	—	13.4	10.7	8.5	6.6
Personal saving	3.0	5.4	5.2	6.2	5.5
Corporate profit before tax	4.4	14.0	12.4	10.5	11.2
Corporate profit after tax	3.0	7.3	6.9	5.8	6.6
Corporate tax as % of profits before tax	33	48	44	45	41
Utilization of capacity in manufacturing, %	—	90	84	80	—
Ditto, new series	—	—	—	83	80
Increase in labor force, %	1.2	1.3	1.3	2.4	2.3

Sources: U.S. Department of Commerce, Survey of Current Business, National Income Supplement; Federal Reserve Bulletin.

capacity utilization and thus stimulates private investment, as is evident from equation (11). Adverse effects of taxation were avoided by tax allowances for investing firms.

The case of the United States may be taken as an illustration (see Table 1). Profit taxes as a percentage of national product were much higher after the war, especially in the 1950s, than before. Budget deficits were lower than before the war, but not so much as to compensate for the increased taxation of profits. On balance, therefore, the budget was expansionist and increased utilization in industry. This, I maintain, has contributed to the high postwar investment activity.

The bulk of the additional spending in the 1950s was for military purposes. This, in fact, was a political precondition for the imposition of high profits taxes. Later, military spending declined while civilian spending by states and local governments increased. Taxation on profits also declined somewhat (see table).

In Europe, in the early stages of postwar growth civilian expenditure, especially public investment, already played a much larger role in the expansion of government spending. In fact, military spending in some countries usually overstrained their already fully employed economies, instead of serving, as it had in the United States, to prop up full employment.

Second, tension between the superpowers led to an intensive technological competition between East and West, having its strongest effects in the decade 1957-68 which opened with Sputnik and ended with student unrest. The so-called competition of systems was responsible for a great acceleration in spending on research and development in the West. Moreover, it set in motion a major educational effort in both the United States and Western Europe. Although the R & D expenditure (of which half to two-thirds was financed by governments in the United States, Britain, and France) was to a great extent for military and space research, its indirect effects on the pace of technological progress in general, and therefore on private investment activity, were considerable. The aftermath of wartime innovation itself provided a great stimulus to industry in the postwar period. This was possible only because of the nature of modern war and the attitude of today's military men. There is hardly an activity in our society which is as thoroughly based on science as warfare.

Third, the *postwar* tension brought about a close cooperation between the Western countries under the leadership of the United States. This meant freer trade and a workable international currency arrangement. Although Bretton Woods (which was a symbol of American dominance) did not really provide that (as Balogh argued, it had already virtually broken down by 1947), the Marshall Plan and American lending made the postwar currency arrangements work up to a point.[10]

Successful international cooperation under the Marshall Plan and the OEEC, later the OECD, resulted in a vast increase in international trade. It can hardly be stressed enough that this cooperation was a necessary condition for the establishment of high levels of employment in Europe.

Fourth, in Europe a special growth factor was at work, which was only indirectly linked to the development of international cooperation. After the war many European countries were behind the United States in technology. In catching up they were drawing on a readymade stock of know-how, which explains why technological progress and productivity growth were so rapid, much more so than they ever could have been if the skills had had to be developed from current expenditure on R & D. The process of importing technology was much furthered by the Marshall Plan and by technical assistance, but even more by the general intensification of trade and communications.

The spurt of what for Europe were innovations, but in America was common practice, involved a strong stimulus to investment. This stimulus shifted the function φ in equation (10) upwards. The gradual drying up of opportunities for imitation, in other words, the exhaustion of the stock of old skills, meant that the function φ was bound to shift gradually downwards again.

Stunted growth

In the course of the growth period the tension between the superpowers declined. At the same time there has been a certain shift of economic weight and power away from the United States to other industrial countries and from the industrial to the third world. As a result, economic cooperation declined. As long as the Western countries were dominated by the fear of a common danger, they were prepared to overlook their differences and rally round a common leader. With the decline of this fear the centrifugal forces in the West gained strength. The leading position of the United States was impaired by the challenge from Europe and Japan to its technological supremacy, and by its increasing dependence on foreign energy and materials. A symptom of the decay of U.S. leadership was the formal dismantling of Bretton Woods and the suspension of dollar convertibility.

The old world order has really come to an end with the breakdown of unquestioned confidence in the dollar. Yet there is nothing else taking its place. One is reminded of the situation at the start of the world depression in the 1930s when, as Kindleberger notes, Britain ceased to play its role as stabilizer of the economic world system, and nobody else took its place.[11] The stabilizing function, according to Kindleberger, was exercised by countercyclical long-term lending, by discounting in times of crisis, and by keeping an open market for distress goods.

We are really back in the period before Bretton Woods, when Keynes, Kalecki, and Schumacher formulated their international currency plans for a system which would not favor one-sidedly the surplus countries and would not have a deflationary bias.[12] The problems are all there and the solutions have been suggested. The surpluses of the OPEC countries and others ought to be channeled into investment in the poor developing countries by an international bank.[13] The same institution ought to be equipped and prepared to step in whenever trouble develops in the eurodollar market. Stabilization by buffer stocks ought to be undertaken in commodity markets, in order to eliminate an important source of instability.[14] The fact that no serious steps are taken in these direc-

tions reflects the absence of any adequate international cooperation. The present situation directly and indirectly produces a
restrictive climate. The deficit countries are forced into drastic restrictions and unemployment, while the surplus countries refuse to
expand. Protectionism develops quietly but irresistibly. The existence of hundreds of billions of dollars of "speculative" funds in
the world carries with it the danger of snowballing financial collapse. It is too much to expect business confidence to thrive on this
ground. I now turn to various negative feedbacks produced by
growth over a fairly long period:

(1) There is the factor treated by Harrod and Bhaduri—the difference between ordinary replacement demand (dropout of equipment) and depreciation. This difference has increased over the
growth period. It means that a lot of new production capacity can
be created by investing depreciation funds alone. The paradox,
observed in Germany, of low net investment in the 1970s and considerable excess capacity might be explained in this way. Inflation
serves to counteract this tendency in so far as it increases the current value of the replacement demand. The balance of the two
factors is different in different countries.

(2) Many countries show an increasing trend of personal savings
as a proportion of disposable income. One hesitates to touch this
subject on account of the uncertainties of the data. How much of
personal saving is really saving of business? Can one trust the data,
given that saving is a residual? Also consumers' debt is included in
savings as a negative term. Yet the impression is that there is really
an increase in genuine household saving, and that it results from
growing prosperity. If so, then it should depress the profit rate and
undistributed profits (via a reduction in utilization), as can be seen
immediately from equation (10), if we assume the growth rate of
capital as given. Since it is unlikely that business will increase its
indebtedness very much, the increased personal saving would have
to be borrowed by the government if restrictive effects were to be
avoided.

(3) Since the prosperity of Europe was probably to quite a large
extent based on catching up technologically with the United States,
the gradual dwindling of opportunities to draw on this ready-made
stock of proven and common skills is bound to have strong effects.
The rate of growth of output per head cannot remain at its former
level in many European countries. Equally the stimulus for investment emanating from this relatively easy and convenient method
of technical progress, which is open only to those who are back-
ward, is bound to decline. In abstract terms we may say that the
function φ of equation (10) has shifted downward.

(4) Environmental and energy problems entered into the consciousness of government, businessmen, and public very abruptly in the late 1960s. One would think that a serious effort to tackle them would require large investment and therefore stimulate growth of capital, though not of productivity or capacity. It may also be surmised that the obligation to find solutions for certain environmental problems in the long run will have a beneficial effect on technical progress, and "spin-off" also here, as in military research. What happens directly, however, is that business, especially in some industries (paper, steel, motorcars), is faced with increasing burdens, although in many cases these can be passed on to the consumer.

The question of the effects of environment and energy on investment and effective demand is highly ambiguous. Whether they will be stimulating or restrictive really depends on the wider context of the situation. If a number of other elements favor pessimism and shaken confidence, then so will these factors. Restriction of growth will appear as a method of stemming the tide of increasing energy requirements, and of ever-increasing environmental difficulties. This is how some governments see it, but since the argument has gained wide currency it may have contributed its share to the erosion of business confidence.

(5) The most striking feature of the new economic climate is no doubt the changed attitude of governments towards full employment and growth. The United States and Germany were the first to display this change, but it has gradually spread to other countries as well. The argument of these governments, or their economists, is that the objective circumstances have changed, and that they were constrained to give up policies which do not work in the new circumstances. What are these objective changes? In economists' terms they can be easily described as a shift in the Phillips curve, but what this means in fact is not exactly easy to understand, since the Phillips relation is primarily a statistical relationship which broke down with the "wage explosion" of 1969-71. The explanation given for this breakdown, or shift, is that trade unions and workers have become more conscious of price changes and more inclined to anticipate them, and that workers as a result of increased social benefits are less willing to work; consequently voluntary unemployment has increased. (A curious footnote to this phenomenon is that the supply of female and juvenile labor has increased strongly. Unemployment is concentrated in these groups, where the new entrants into the labor market do not qualify for assistance.) Thus, it is concluded that higher unemployment is necessary to contain the rise in wages within reasonable limits.

There are those—like myself—who cannot agree with these arguments. They find that the wage "explosion" is more plausibly explained by the increasing burden of income tax and other deductions from wages.[15] They are under the impression that it is not so much objective circumstances which have changed as political attitudes. This can be explained as a reaction against the long period of full employment and growth which has strengthened the economic position of workers and the power of the trade unions, and has led to demands for workers' participation. It has also led to mass migration (of blacks in the United States, of foreign workers in Europe), which has caused turmoil or apprehension of it (in the United States the race riots of the middle 1960s, in Europe political resentment and a fear of introducing a new proletariat). This migration has contributed to urban hypertrophy and the crisis of the cities.

The political reaction against growth (for which the Club of Rome and Professor Forrester have written the bible) has not been confined to sections of big business, and the banks in particular, but also finds support among large strata of the middle classes (professional people, managers, etc.). This explains why Gerald Ford nearly won the 1976 election and why Helmut Schmidt has considerable support for his phlegmatic attitude toward unemployment.

The attitudes and policies of governments in turn react on business, including those sections of it which are not happy with the current trend. Formerly there was a general conviction in most countries that the government would intervene to prevent a prolonged depression; this reduced uncertainty and therefore made for higher and more stable private investment. This confidence has been shattered. Here is another reason why the function δ has shifted downward.

If the reasons 1 to 5 are correct, we must expect low growth for some time to come. Can the economic system adjust itself to a low growth rate? The upshot of my arguments in the first part of this essay is that it would require a downward shift of the profit function, in other words a long-term change in distribution, to get a smooth adjustment to a lower growth rate. But my observations on the oligopolistic structure of our economy still hold. Apart from short periods, companies do not engage in cutthroat competition, and they protect their high mark-ups. It is therefore likely that the profit function will not shift downward and that the weight of the adjustment will be thrown on the degree of utilization. This will tend to create stagnation.

Some observers, such as the European Economic Commission,

see the outlook in quite a different light. They anticipate increasing capital coefficients and low profit margins. The reasons for the expected increase in capital coefficients are environmental protection, energy conservation, development of new energy sources, and increases in service outputs where high capital coefficients prevail. The arguments are correct, but they do not carry much weight if governments are slow in acting on the energy question and if, because of a reluctance to incur debt or to tax profits, they refrain from building as many hospitals, schools, etc., as they should.

The argument about profits is based on a downward trend of the share of profits before tax in many countries since the 1960s. It has been shown for England and other countries that this downward trend does not apply to profits after tax.[16]

Of course, profits have been low since the onset of the recession on account of excess capacity. There is another long-run influence, namely the increase in nonenterprise savings, which must tend to depress profits and the degree of utilization. This can be remedied only by government deficits, unless there is some institutional reform by which the outside savings are channeled into the enterprises as "risk-capital." As long as such institutions are not created and as long as governments are scared of the increase in public debt, the increase in outside savings does provide a reason for falling profits. But this is not a question of a downward shift of the profit function which would ease the situation. In fact, it only reinforces the tendencies for a decline in utilization which flow from the low growth rate and therefore does not contradict my own description.

Notes

1. R. H. Harrod, "An Essay in Dynamic Theory," *Economic Journal* 49 (March 1939): 14-33, and *Towards a Dynamic Economics* (London: Macmillan, 1948); Josef Steindl, *Maturity and Stagnation in American Capitalism* (New York: Monthly Review Press, 1976).
2. R. F. Harrod, "Replacements, Net Investment, Amortisation Funds," *Economic Journal* 80 (March 1970): 24-31; A. Bhaduri, "Unwanted Amortisation Funds," *Economic Journal* 82 (June 1972): 674-77.
3. Bhaduri, "Unwanted Amortisation Funds."
4. Michal Kalecki, *Theory of Economic Dynamics* (London: Allen and Unwin, 1954), p. 40.
5. Ibid., ch. 1.
6. Nicholas Kaldor, "Alternative Theories of Distribution," *Review of Economic Studies* 23 (February 1956): 83-100.

7. Paul A. Baran and Paul M. Sweezy, *Monopoly Capital* (New York: Monthly Review Press, 1966), ch. 8.

8. See Harrod, "Replacements, Net Investment, Amortisation Funds"; Bhaduri, "Unwanted Amortisation Funds."

9. Michal Kalecki, *Selected Essays on the Dynamics of the Capitalist Economy* (Cambridge: Cambridge University Press, 1971), pp. 138–45.

10. T. Balogh, *Fact and Fancy in International Relations* (London: Pergamon Press, 1973).

11. Charles P. Kindleberger, *The World in Depression, 1929-1939* (London: Allen Lane, 1973).

12. Michal Kalecki and E. F. Schumacher, "International Clearing and Long-term Lending," *Bulletin of the Oxford Institute of Statistics* 5, supplement (August 1943): 29-33.

13. Balogh, *Fact and Fancy.*

14. Nicholas Kaldor, "Inflation and Recession in the World Economy," *Economic Journal* 86 (December 1976): 703-14.

15. See H. A. Turner, D. Jackson, and F. Wilkinson, *Do Trade Unions Cause Inflation?* (Cambridge: Cambridge University Press, 1972); M. A. King, "The UK Profits Crisis," *Economic Journal* 85 (March 1975): 33-54.

16. Turner et. al., *Do Trade Unions Cause Inflation?* and King, "The UK Profits Crisis."

John Bellamy Foster

THE LIMITS OF U.S. CAPITALISM: SURPLUS CAPACITY AND CAPACITY SURPLUS

For anyone interested in understanding the confused state of contemporary economics, it is significant that John Maynard Keynes couched the modern theory of national output primarily in terms of the employment of labor. In this, as in other important respects, his approach differed markedly from that of the neo-Marxian economist Michal Kalecki, who discovered all the essentials of "the Keynesian revolution" some years before Keynes. Kalecki always went straight to the heart of the modern employment problem: the degree to which *existing capital stock* is gainfully employed (and the effect of this on new investment). Unemployed labor does not, in itself, pose a problem for capital (which bases its rule on the existence of a sizeable industrial reserve army), but unemployed plant and equipment is quite a different matter. In general, we can say that capitalism, taken in its entirety, is concerned with the full utilization of employed labor power and *existing material capital;* the full employment of labor as a whole is inimical to its nature and purpose.

To be sure, the concept of "full employment" can be used to suggest either "as near full employment [of labor] as is reasonable" (in Joan Robinson's words), or full utilization of practically attainable productive capacity. And if the economy were to be seen only in static terms, there would be no perfectly obvious reason to choose one point of view over the other. But in the real world economy of capitalist dynamics, the beginning and end-all is capital accumulation. Marx's own theory of labor employment ("the general law of accumulation") was deduced from the motion of capital itself. A political economy of growth conceived primarily in terms of the employment of workers, however much this may conform to humanity's real interests, only serves to obscure the broad outline of history.

Considered in this way, it is clear that the object of Keynesian economics in its heyday (now past) was to promote full capacity production, according to "ideal" capitalist standards (complete realization of potential surplus product), and not full employment of labor in any real sense. Thus the Keynesian miscarriage should not be viewed as the inability of capitalism to abolish unemployment (which was always self-evident and never seriously contemplated), but in terms of its outright failure even to get as far as the elimination of undesired excess capacity.[1]

Small wonder that the expression "full-employment capitalism," commonly used to characterize economic conditions (and policy) during the first quarter-century after World War II, is of dubious value. Without question, some concrete way of distinguishing the previous period of relative prosperity from the current era of stagflation is needed. But mythologizing the past will not help. "Full-employment capitalism," even if understood in the limited sense of full capacity output *with involuntary unemployment,* was never realized. And in this lies the chief clue to the present economic impasse.

A realistic way of dealing with the facts would focus on the existence of "equilibrium excess capacity" (the inability of the system, *even during its prosperity phase,* to close the gap between actual and potential capitalist output), in spite of the prodigious amount of waste which has gone into propping up the productive core of the economy. In this way we could begin to understand why socialism as a mere objective necessity is long overdue.

A plausible theory of contemporary economic stagnation in its making would have to take account of the fact (brilliantly foreseen by Rosa Luxemburg) that capital is unable to centralize markets at a rate equivalent to the ongoing centralization of production and appropriation. As accumulation expands in both relative and absolute terms, a proportionately larger amount of demand needs to be accounted for out of profits (rather than wages) in the form of further productive investment. But such investment, besides providing profits for capital, has the additional property of being useful. And its ultimate use is the production of goods for final consumption. With a high rate of accumulation, however, the share of consumption itself is depressed. Hence, in practice, an investment boom soon reaches the point where further investment in plant and equipment is no longer warranted, given existing profit margins.

This contradiction, though inherent to accumulation itself, only emerged as a serious impasse for capitalism once it had passed from its competitive to its monopoly stage. The modifications in the nature of pricing, output, and investment introduced by giant corporations have limited, to a very large extent, the system's room to maneuver. To understand why this is so, it is necessary to turn to the theory of monopoly capital, as exemplified by the neo-Marxian tradition of Michal Kalecki, Josef Steindl, Paul Baran, Paul Sweezy, and Harry Braverman.

Although the neoclassical myth of "perfect competition" never actually pertained, it is nonetheless true that the small firm capitalism of the nineteenth century was, in certain very important ways, more competitive than the mature capitalism of our day. At this point in our argument, we can differentiate between early and late capitalism by listing three distinguishing characteristics of the former (though, as we shall see later, this is by no means exhaustive): (1) price competition (prices rose *and fell* in response to changes in supply and demand), (2) full capacity production under equilibrium (noncrisis) conditions, and (3) virtually automatic accumulation (allocation of capital for expanded reproduction of investment goods and wage goods) of the vast portion of surplus value created. It is worth noting that all of these conditions were generally assumed by Marx himself in his theory of a "purely capitalist society," modeled after the economic reality of his day.

It has long been understood by economic theorists, though as a rule only radicals have been willing to face up to the fact squarely, that the modern economy is dominated by a handful of giant firms that do not engage in traditional price competition. To the extent that they enjoy some degree of monopoly over their markets, these corporate leviathans can raise prices to increase their profit margins (and the rate of surplus value), provided that they exercise careful control over their output (supply). In concerete terms, this usually takes the form of restricting output to a level consistent with prevailing or planned monopolistic profit margins.

Naturally, no corporation will ever be able to control output and impose price increases at will. A number of constraints, such as the threat of ultimately generating new competition, will enter the picture to a greater or lesser extent. More important, prices and profits are always limited by what the market will bear. Within these limits, however, the giant firm often has considerable latitude to raise its rate of surplus value by imposing an excessive price markup (by competitive standards) on prime production costs, at the expense of real wage growth and the profits of smaller, more competitive capital. The fact that most major industries are dominated by a very few (oligopolistic) firms rather than by a single "pure monopoly" in no way alters the essential nature of the case, since these firms, by a process of indirect collusion (following the price leader), tend to price much as a pure monopoly would.[2] Thus, since the turn of the century (with the noted exception of the Great

Depression) the overall price level has gone only one way—up—a fact which clearly marks U.S. monopoly capitalism off from the small-firm American economy of the nineteenth century, when falling prices were the rule.

Output can only be "rationally" controlled by planning some degree of utilization of existing capital stock, and through the careful expansion of plant and equipment in accordance with some intended operating rate. Notwithstanding popular myth and economic parables, it is a well-known fact among economists that the modern large firm seldom utilizes its productive capacity to its full potential but instead maintains some level of planned excess capacity. The reasons for this are fairly straightforward. Idle capacity is kept in reserve to enable a firm to take advantage of sudden increases in demand or to drive out potential competitors. Corporations also engage in the practice of "building ahead of demand" during a boom. It can therefore be assumed that the level of planned surplus capacity will always (even during a peak in the business cycle) tend to be somewhat higher than zero.

The very notion of planned surplus capacity suggests that it is possible to have either "undesired excess capacity" or insufficient reserve capacity (both in relation to the individual firm and, by aggregation, to the economy as a whole).[3] If the utilization of plant and equipment falls below the planned level, we can safely assume that business has far less incentive to invest in additional productive capacity. Conversely, if the operating rate of industry rises to the extent that the amount of idle capacity is less than the planned level, business will readily invest in additional means of production.

If asked to account for undesired excess capacity, a mainstream economist would answer that this is the result of "disequilibrium" (crisis) conditions. Yet, as we shall demonstrate later on, there is ample evidence to suggest that considerable amounts of undesired excess capacity have consistently *prevailed* in peacetime (we are clearly deviating from the usual practice of established economics here, which claims that the early 1950s and mid-1960s were times of "peace"). And with undesired excess capacity as a fairly persistent condition, productive investment itself is seriously dampened over the long-run.

It is essential to understand that this undesired excess capacity is nonetheless deliberately held by the giant corporations. In the face of a downward shift in demand, monopoly capital maintains its high profit margins (and excessive rate of surplus value) by adjusting its rate of output—which in the short run means its operating rate, and in the long run its rate of productive investment or capital formation—rather than lowering prices. But what causes the downward shift in demand in the first place? The main answer is obvious: growth of monopolistic profit margins.

Capital has always faced a double barrier to accumulation posed by accumulation itself. On the one hand, it maximizes its potential profits by raising the rate of exploitation of labor power. To do this, capital engages in an incessant battle for infinite control over the labor process. Its main weapons are its capacity to revolutionize the means of production (including the further subdivision of tasks within the workplace), and its ability to discharge workers. On the other hand, as the rate of exploitation rises within production, capital finds it increasingly difficult (though not necessarily in the same proportion) to realize its potential profits by selling the goods which could at present be produced. By keeping down the relative value of real wage income, capital at the same time restricts the demand for wage goods (leaving out the effect of credit, and assuming quite reasonably that workers don't save) to exactly that amount.[4] Hence, surplus value produced can only be realized to the extent that a corresponding demand for capital goods (means of production) and capitalist luxury consumption (which must be withdrawn from surplus value) is found. The latter is restricted by the tendency for even the most ostentacious consumption to reach its natural limits quickly, and by the inner necessity of the capitalist (and particularly the corporation) to accumulate. Investment in capital goods, as mentioned previously, is limited by the fact that such investment is useful. This is because fixed capital is also productive capacity, the value of which is lost if not used. But if used to capacity, a rapid expansion of investment ensues, up to the point where a sufficient portion of output cannot be sold. Sooner or later (and under modern conditions usually sooner), the market for means of production is temporarily undermined by the limited market for final consumption. This is the social disproportionality problem between productive capacity and consumption potential which was at the core of Lenin's theory.

Of course capital can always overcome this problem of realization or "underconsumption" to a limited extent, and especially during certain favorable historical periods. Capitalism, as the Russian economist Tugan-Baranovski long ago emphasized, is not a harmonious system but an antagonistic one.[5] The production of exchange value, which is the sole concern of capital, has its own absurd necessity, somewhat independent of the fulfillment of real social needs. Means of production, after all, can be produced for the purpose of creating more means of production and so on. However, one does not have to be fresh out of a course in logic to see that such a process (much to capital's horror) is limited. Capital is never completely able to escape the fact that a commodity, in order to be marketable, has to have both an exchange value *and a use value,* and in the last instance the purpose of all plant and equipment is to serve final consumption.

The foregoing leads us to the conclusion that for capital the rate of surplus value is always, in certain respects, both too high and too low; and particularly so in times of economic crisis. It is too low for the simple reason that potential surplus value is enlarged in direct proportion to any reduction in the value of real wages as a percentage of total social product. It is too high since the market for wage goods, upon which any sustained growth in output depends, is limited to the level of real wages. Confronted with this double-horned dilemma, capital has a tendency to impale itself on the second while staring fixedly at the first.

The monopoly rents charged by the modern giants of capital, and the output and investment strategies upon which these rents are predicated, intensify this general tendency toward overaccumulation (implicit overproduction), which is embedded in the very nature of the capitalist system. On the one hand, the monopolistic corporation is enormously successful at accumulation (partly as a result of its management of labor power which it directly controls, and partly due to its power to appropriate the benefits of growth which would otherwise accrue to workers and small-scale capital). On the other hand, it only accomplishes this by carefully controlling both current output and the growth of potential output. Hence, big business demonstrates an enormous fear of overinvestment, and of spoiling its entrapped market. Its conservative investment strategy is exemplified by its tendency to sandbag innumerable innovations which threaten existing capital values and market power. Thus the *modus operandi* of monopoly capital pretty much guarantees that insufficient productive investment will be forthcoming to compensate for the enormously centralized pattern of accumulation. Consequently, a bottleneck of surplus capital appears in the monopoly sector(s), with a concomitant tendency toward secular stagnation—defined by Paul Sweezy as "a combination of sluggish growth, rising unemployment, and a chronically low level of utilization of productive capacity."[6]

When U.S. monopoly capitalism operates at a rate anywhere near its full capacity level it throws off a massive quantity of profits or actual economic surplus.[7] We may use the term "capacity surplus" to refer to that level of surplus which is realized when all surplus capacity has been fully eliminated. This, in fact, means that the total surplus value potentially produced in the labor process is now actually produced and realized. Under U.S. monopoly capitalism thus far this point has only been reached during World War II; and has only come within sight, in any case, with the help of enormous quantities of wasteful consumption by industry itself. In practice, the actual surplus accruing to capital—it would only confuse matters to speak of total surplus value in amounts not determined by the actual rate of exploitation of labor power *with full capacity production*—is almost always much lower than capacity surplus, in direct proportion to the level of surplus capacity that exists within the economy. Hence, monopoly capitalism systematically deviates from the "ideal" standards of capital itself, which require that potential surplus product be entirely realized.

Hindered by their inability to utilize capital equipment that they already have at their disposal, the giant corporations refuse to invest at a high rate, but consume revenue in numerous socially unreproductive ways. Only the government is able to artificially induce these firms to expand their output and investment more fully. But the very conditions upon which such state intervention is predicated make this reliance on socially unreproductive external markets dynamic and inflationary. Having induced industry to expand faster than is warranted by the underlying economic conditions, the state must give it an even larger injection in the next budget, and so on. Thus a huge inflationary overhang, and a massive debt structure, appears cumulatively on top of an economy which at its roots demonstrates an almost permanent tendency toward stagnation. The modern term for this general condition is of course "stagflation."

It is surely of more than passing interest that our approach here finds strong support in the historical evidence itself. In 1960 Donald Streever constructed a famous index of capacity output of U.S. manufacturing and mining for the years 1920-55. A slightly more refined version of the Streever data was shortly afterwards developed by V. Lewis Bassie, then Director of the Bureau of Economic and Business Research at the University of Illinois. Following a method employed by Baran and Sweezy, who used Streever's data (*Monopoly Capital*, pp. 237-43), we can derive a rough indication of the operating rate of U.S. industry by dividing the Streever-Bassie capacity index into the Federal Reserve Board's series for industrial production.[8] The resulting index of capacity utilization (up to 1947) is shown in columns 1 and 3 of Table 1. Alongside this series, in columns 2 and 4, is placed U.S. government data on gross plant and equipment expenditures over the same period.

These figures give us a reasonably accurate representation of the basic changes that occurred in the U.S. economy during this critical

Table 1
Capacity Utilization in Manufacturing and Mining and Gross Plant and
Equipment Expenditures in Manufacturing, 1920-47

	(1)	*(2)*		*(3)*	*(4)*
	Capacity utilization	Gross manufacturing plant and equipment expenditures in billions of 1958 dollars		Capacity utilization	Gross manufacturing plant and equipment expenditures in billions of 1958 dollars
1920	95	5.4	1934	58	2.3
1921	69	3.9	1935	63	2.6
1922	74	4.2	1936	74	3.7
1923	91	4.9	1937	83	4.7
1924	86	4.2	1938	62	2.9
1925	87	4.8	1939	68	3.5
1926	88	6.0	1940	79	4.7
1927	84	5.7	1941	93	6.0
1928	80	6.3	1942	108	3.3
1929	85	7.3	1943	131	2.5
1930	72	4.8	1944	137	3.2
1931	57	2.8	1945	126	5.5
1932	45	1.4	1946	96	9.5
1933	48	2.2	1947	94	10.6

Sources: V. Lewis Bassie, *Economic Forecasting* (New York: McGraw-Hill, 1958), p. 688; *Historical Statistics of the United States: Colonial Times to 1970* (Washington D.C.: Department of Commerce, 1975), Part II, pp. 682-83.

period, which included the Great Depression and World War II and ended with the unrivaled hegemony of U.S. monopoly capitalism within the world order. Looking first at the capacity-utilization index, it is immediately clear that an overabundance of capacity has been a persistent problem for U.S. capitalism. The notorious boom of "the roaring twenties" was based on an overexpansion of investment (capital goods production rose at an average annual rate of 6.4 percent) in relation to consumption (consumer durables and nondurables grew at rates of 5.9 and 2.8 percent, respectively).[9] Hence, we see a gradual enlargement of excess capacity during the twenties. When the bubble finally burst in 1929 this already sizeable amount of surplus capacity grew to vast proportions. In 1932 at least 55 percent of all plant and equipment in the United States was lying unused. Moreover, the depression continued to drag on with no sign of internally generated recovery. In the 1938 downturn the output of U.S. manufacturing and mining was 38 percent short of its potential.

However, in 1939, with the beginning of World War II in

Europe, conditions changed. Over the next five years, fueled by the tremendous demand for war goods, the operating rate of American industry skyrocketed, and in 1944 *exceeded* "capacity output" by well over 30 percent. After World War II there was a sudden drop in the utilization of capacity, which by 1947 was already forty-one points lower than its wartime peak.

Perhaps even more significant is the relationship between the rate of capacity utilization (columns 1 and 3) and gross fixed capital investment in manufacturing (columns 2 and 4). A mere glance at the figures shows that there is a direct correspondence between upward and downward movements in capacity utilization, on the one hand, and the rise and fall in investment activity, on the other.[10] In 1928, however, we see a rise in investment at the very moment that capacity utilization was experiencing a serious drop. Undoubtedly, this is an indication of the infamous speculative boom of the period, which further contributed to the building up of overcapacity, and brought the expansion of the twenties to an abrupt end. During World War II there also appears to be a discrepancy between movements in capacity utilization and investment. Yet, in this case, the exception to the general rule is more apparent than real. During its World War II years the U.S. economy was, in a very real sense, operating at an overheated level by capitalist standards. The massive outpouring of government subsidized unproductive war expenditures was by then occurring at the direct expense of capital goods and wage goods. The immense profits available for the production of each additional tank and airplane had siphoned capital away from social reproduction in the usual sense (the expansion of the capacity to produce and consume) and geared it to the creation of sheer waste on an unprecedented scale. Under these circumstances, net investment tended to stagnate, in direct proportion to the expansion of output *beyond* normal capitalist capacity.[11] Consequently, in the immediate post-World War II years, industrial investment soared, even as the operating rate of industry moved below its wartime level. Corporations hurriedly attempted to once more enlarge their plant and equipment; spurred on by the vast amount of unrealized (and liquid) consumer demand which had built up during the war years, and by the new hegemonic role of North American capitalism within the global system.

Our case here receives further support if the economic record for the period of undisputed U.S. hegemony is consulted. Since 1948 the Federal Reserve Board has maintained its own index of capacity utilization. This new series, together with data on gross nonresidential fixed investment, is provided up to the year 1975 in Table 2 (which, it should be noted, cannot be directly compared to

Table 2
Capacity Utilization in Manufacturing and Gross Nonresidential
Fixed Investment Expenditures, 1948-75[a]

	(1) Capacity utilization	(2) Gross nonresidential fixed investment in billions of 1972 dollars		(3) Capacity utilization	(4) Gross nonresidential fixed investment in billions of 1972 dollars
1948	82.5	$51.1	1962	81.6	$ 72.0
1949	74.2	46.0	1963	83.5	75.1
1950	82.8	50.0	1964	85.6	82.7
1951	85.8	52.9	1965	89.6	97.4
1952	85.4	52.1	1966	91.1	108.0
1953	89.2	56.3	1967	86.9	105.6
1954	80.3	55.4	1968	87.1	109.5
1955	87.1	61.3	1969	86.2	116.8
1956	86.4	65.4	1970	79.3	113.8
1957	83.7	66.2	1971	78.4	112.2
1958	75.2	59.3	1972	83.5	121.0
1959	81.9	63.6	1973	87.6	138.1
1960	80.2	66.9	1974	83.8	135.7
1961	77.4	66.7	1975	72.9	119.3

[a] Not directly comparable to Table 1.

Sources: The Economic Report of the President, 1981, p. 281; *The National Income and Product Accounts of the United States, 1929-76*, Supplement to the *Survey of Current Business*, September 1981, pp. 202-3.

Table 1).[12] Once again we find that there is a strong positive correlation between movements in capacity utilization and industrial investment. Capacity utilization and investment declined hand in hand as the United States continued to wind down from World War II. But with the onslaught of the Korean war, utilization again rose rapidly (with investment close behind) to a level (in 1953) which was not passed until the United States invaded Vietnam. After the Korean war there is an immediate nine-point drop in the operating rate of U.S. factories, with a corresponding sag in investment.

Between 1955 and 1957 a discrepancy in the movements of utilization and investment is indicated, with investment rising by $5 billion at the same time that utilization has dropped over three points. Since real investment in plant and equipment was occurring at a time when business was already cutting back on the operating rate of its existing factories, it is scarcely surprising that during 1957-58 there was a massive increase in surplus productive capacity, with utilization dropping seven points in a single year. Over the same year, gross capital formation, reflecting this development, dropped by over 10 percent. A similar if less apparent dynamic followed the other years (1959-60 and 1968-69) when investment rose while utilization fell. In 1961 investment stagnated and then bounced back, along with capacity utilization, during the following year. This resilience is undoubtably a reflection of the enormous boost in military spending which occurred from the outset of the Kennedy administration, based initially on the infamous "missile gap" hoax. In 1968-69, as the rate of expenditure for the war in Indochina was beginning to weaken (in the face of impending Viet-namese victory), investment again rose while utilization was on the decline. This unwarranted growth of capital formation clearly set the stage for the well-known crisis of the U.S. economy (and the dollar) in 1970-71, as the contradiction between actual and poten-tial output widened.

At any rate, the index of capacity utilization provided by the Federal Reserve Board clearly demonstrates that the post-World War II U.S. economy has always been in greater danger of stalling than overheating, despite an inflation of rhetoric to the contrary. At no time in the years covered here, except during the Korean and Vietnamese wars, did the U.S. economy achieve anything even distantly resembling full capacity output. And of course things have only gotten worse as the general crisis of U.S. capitalism has deepened. In 1975 capacity utilization dropped to 72.9 percent. In the years immediately afterwards it rose slowly, but by 1979 had not yet reached its 1970 level.[13] Naturally, with the appearance of the new phenomenon of "back-to-back recessions" in 1980, 1981, and 1982, utilization of productive capacity once again plummeted, with the average shortfall of actual output from capacity output in 1982 rising to 30 percent. Millions of workers are unemployed because capital is unable, given existing profit margins, to realize its capacity surplus, and this in direct proportion to the surplus capac-ity which has appeared in the economy.

Of course it is conceivable that one might interpret the above evidence in another way altogether. It is obvious that utilization of capital stock and investment are always, to some extent, mutually determining. A tendency for investment to stagnate could there-fore be seen as producing the excess capacity rather than the other way around (in which the latter assumes the role of a servomechan-ism or shut-off valve for the former). However, it would then be necessary to explain why investment (capital formation) follows a pattern which can be described as fluctuation around a trend-line of zero net investment, in conjunction with a constant and widen-ing gap between potential and actual capitalist output.

One of the most common ways of explaining the ups and downs

in capital formation, particularly within the more traditional Marxist circles, is to turn to the rate of profit itself. Business expands production when it is profitable to do so and refrains when it is not. Undoubtedly, as V. Lewis Bassie pointed out in the work referred to above, "This line of thinking is incontrovertible if one does not look beyond profits to the underlying conditions on which they depend" (p. 361).

Thus, one might argue that investment rises when the average rate of profit rises and falls when it falls. But then one has to explain why profits rise and fall. And, moreover, why the gross profit *margins* of the largest corporations have tended to widen over time. Within traditionalist Marxian literature it is often suggested that there is a secular tendency toward a falling rate of profit due to the growing capital intensity (in value terms) of industry, relative to the rate of exploitation. Yet, the empirical basis for such a theory is extremely weak. For good reason, there are no serious historical studies which indicate that this tendential law has any direct and *consistent* bearing on the evolution of the capitalist mode of production over the last fifty years or so. It therefore requires a rather large leap of faith to assume that it can be utilized to explain either the relative slow growth of capital formation under modern U.S. capitalism (by historical standards) or the year-by-year fluctuations in investment and operating rate.

In any case, what is determinant for new investment is not so much current earnings as expected earnings on new productive capacity. An approach that centers on capitalized use values has the advantage of emphasizing the root factor determining long-term profit expectations, and hence the willingness to invest. An overcapacity to produce in relation to existing markets will generally dampen new investment *even if* profit rates were previously rising.

At least as far as the long run is concerned, economists generally look on investment as being exogenously determined. The chief element in this regard is of course innovation (or revolutionization of the means of production). Far from controverting our thesis, however, this factor can be brought into play in order to elucidate, on a more fundamental level, the problem of maturity and stagnation. Monopoly capital theorists, particularly Baran and Sweezy, have generally argued that the transition of capitalism from an economy of small firms to one dominated by giant corporations with considerable discretion in their actions has drastically altered the role of innovation as well. In the first place, there has been a general shift in the focus of accumulation. Under the early industrial period of competitive capitalism there was a rapid expansion of department 1 (producing means of production), allowing capitalism to sustain an accelerated rate of growth. As capitalism "matured" in certain states, however, the possibilities for revolutionizing the means of production tended to diminish relative to the scale of the economy as a whole. It was no longer a matter of simply replacing precapitalist relations of production with the form and content of modern industry, but of replacing already existing capital with marginally more efficient capital, and at a time, moreover, when the capacity to produce was already near the ceiling warranted by existing and prospective markets. In addition, monopoly capital has had the effect (as Joseph Schumpeter understood) of staving off certain investment opportunities. Of course certain epoch-making innovations like the steam engine, the railroad, and the automobile (which contributed substantially to the most recent wave of prosperity in the U.S. economy) might feed a new period of growth. But innovations of such quantitative and qualitative signficance are few and far between.

In fact, if monopoly capitalism were no more than what we have emphasized thus far it would be difficult to see how such a system could survive at all. At this point, it is useful to recall Tugan-Baranovski's notion that capitalism is an antagonistic system. It survives beyond its comparatively rational and historically necessary competitive stage only by intensifying its antagonistic and irrational characteristics. In a nutshell, the prevalence of surplus capacity makes waste (i.e., the production of luxury goods such as military hardware, and unproductive outlays on circulation, like advertising) enormously profitable. Indeed, expenditures on war have the peculiar use value (for capital alone) of expending rather than augmenting productive capacity, while neither depending on nor seriously cutting into wage-based demand. Capital therefore loses much of its traditional indifference to particular use values, having discovered that it is able to promote certain commodities which have the special property of being useless from the standpoint of social reproduction; and which therefore provide seemingly inexhaustible markets for the absorption of economic surplus (though over the long run this simply produces stagflation).[14]

Marx believed that capitalism *as a comparatively rational and socially necessary* stage in historical evolution would in his lifetime fall prey to its own internal contradictions. He was correct. By the final quarter of the nineteenth century monopoly capitalism had emerged: a society which was increasingly irrational even by capitalist standards, and which sustained itself (and this is where Marx may have underestimated capital) by its very irrationality. In fact, the massive contradictions of the contemporary socioeconomy in the advanced industrial states (and the increasingly deranged forms of dependent capital that have been forced upon the third world) are due almost entirely to the fact that socialism as a mere objective necessity is long overdue.

Notes

1. The real slack in the labor market should never be confused with official unemployment statistics, which are based on a straightjacket survey that counts as unemployed only those who are immediately available for work and who have actively sought employment during the last four weeks—thereby systematically excluding discouraged job-seekers, the underemployed, and those who would be more than willing to join the labor pool if adequate opportunities for productive employment were available. On top of this, much of existing employment is devoted to the production of sheer waste, from the standpoint of social reproduction. As a general rule, we can say that the sum of actual unemployment, underemployment, and socially unproductive (or unreproductive) employment is always much higher than the amount of potential labor power that the system can absorb, on a productive basis, at full capacity output. Thus social liberal economists sometimes use the term "Marxian unemployment" to refer to the level of real unemployment which exists at Keynesian "full employment equilibrium" (or full capacity capitalist output). See Adrian Wood, *A Theory of Profits* (Cambridge: Cambridge University Press, 1975), pp. 124-28. All of this merely indicates that the growth rate of capitalism is inherently depressed, in relation to the planned growth in output of a rationally organized socialist society.
2. Contrary to widespread impression, there is no determinate theory of monopoly price. Mainstream textbooks still present the notion (useful as a first approximation) that the price and output of the "pure monopoly" will be determined by the point at which marginal revenue and marginal cost for an additional unit of output are equated. Business, however, has no concept of marginal revenue (as Joan Robinson, Josef Steindl, and Paolo Sylos-Labini have emphasized). The most that can be said with any certainty is that the markup will be determined by the "degree of monopoly" and what the market will bear.

   It is worth adding that the neoclassical practice of equating monopoly with "pure monopoly," and then claiming that the real situation in concentrated markets is one of "imperfect competition," which can be generalized as "perfect competition," is both erroneous and deliberately misleading. One might get closer to the truth by saying that the determining element within the modern economy is one of *impure monopoly,* in which the nature of competition is transformed.
3. The argument in this and the following paragraph is based on Josef Steindl, *Maturity and Stagnation in American Capitalism* (New York: Monthly Review Press, 1976), pp. xiv, 9-14.

4. Aside from the fact that workers are by necessity long-term dis-savers, the assumption that they refrain from saving is more than reasonable in this context, since any savings out of wages would only make the realization problem, based in the wage goods sector, more serious, while not otherwise altering the general case.

   The overall theory of distribution employed here is fundamental to both Marx and Kalecki.

5. See Michal Kalecki, "The Problem of Effective Demand with Tugan-Baranovski and Rosa Luxemburg," in this volume.

6. Paul M. Sweezy, *Four Lectures on Marxism* (New York: Monthly Review Press, 1981), p. 43.

7. Leo Huberman and Paul M. Sweezy, "U.S. Capitalism at an Impasse," *Monthly Review* 14, no. 5 (September 1962): 225-35.

8. See also An Economic Observer, "Idle Machines," *Monthly Review* 14, no. 2 (June 1962): 84-95.

9. John Kenneth Galbraith, *The Great Crash, 1929* (New York: Avon Books, 1979), p. 155.

10. Anyone acquainted with Keynesian theory would no doubt expect such a correspondence, since higher investment *(ceteris paribus)* induces higher utilization in the short run. But it should be kept in mind that the other components of aggregate demand in a closed economy—consumption and particularly government—do not always follow a course that parallels that of capital formation. All that can be said with certainty then is that high utilization tends to spark investment and low utilization shuts it off. The operating rate therefore plays the role of a "thermostatic device."

11. Proof of this can be found in graph form on page 349 of Bassie's study, referenced in Table I above. The same chart reveals an almost exact positive correlation between *calculated* new investment (with the capacity and production indexes as the independent variables and capital formation as the dependent variable) and *actual* new investment. In fact, the coefficient of determination, r^2 (percent of total variance in one set of data which can be accounted for by its linear relationship to another), was .97.

12. Two issues demand brief consideration here. First, the Streever-Bassie index, while employing extremely sophisticated techniques for the year-by-year calculation of real capital formation and its effect on capacity, has as its benchmark the famous estimation of capacity utilization for 1929, provided by Edwin G. Nourse and associates in *America's Capacity to Produce* (Washington, D.C.: The Brookings Institution, 1934), and like most studies relying heavily on a single benchmark could be expected to produce a larger margin of error over time. It is therefore best to switch over to the more credible Federal Reserve Index once that series begins in 1948. Nonetheless, it is worthwhile to point out that as the Streever-Bassie estimates of utilization are, on the average, slightly above those of the Federal Reserve during the years (1948-54) when the two indexes overlap, it would be logical to infer that the latter series, if employed earlier, might well have indicated even larger amounts of excess capacity than are shown in Table I.

Second, for recent years there are four major indexes of U. S. manufacturing capacity (including that of the Federal Reserve) which can be expected to differ slightly as to the absolute amount of excess capacity at any given point in time (though the cyclical swings are always very similar). For the textbookish economist, optimal capacity is defined as the minimum point on a short-run average cost curve (where it is tangent to the long-run average cost curve), which means that utilization of capacity is determined without reference to the expected price of output. What survey-based capacity utilization indexes (provided by the Federal Reserve, McGraw-Hill, and the Bureau of Economic Analysis) actually measure, however, is an estimation by business itself of its excess capacity, which (for large firms at least) takes account of both cost and price. Generally, we can assume that business specifies its present undesired excess capacity, and not its reserve or its "engineering" (real) excess capacity. This presumption is reinforced by the fact that all plants that are completely idle are excluded from the capacity estimates. Thus all such estimates are notoriously conservative in real terms, as the data for World War II indicate. But since much of our interest here is in understanding the relationship between the willingness of business to actually invest and its undesired excess capacity (judged by capitalist standards), it is the normal perception of business itself which is of chief importance. The Federal Reserve's composite index is probably superior to the pure survey approach (McGraw-Hill and BEA) since it merges survey information with data on capital formation. For a useful discussion see John E. Cremeans, "Capacity Utilization Rates—What Do They Mean?" *Business Economics* 13, no. 3 (May 1978): 41-46.

13. This is true for Japan as well, which by 1979 had only regained 90 percent of its 1970 level, and where underutilization of capacity has now become a serious problem (accompanied by slower growth of capital formation). See Takafusa Nakamura, *The Postwar Japanese Economy* (Tokyo: University of Tokyo Press, 1981), pp. 231-33, 247.

14. Edward N. Wolff has provided a pathbreaking statistical study of waste in the U. S. economy, using the national income and product tables, which has verified Baran and Sweezy's hypothesis of "the tendency for the surplus to rise." See his "Unproductive Labor and the Rate of Surplus Value in the United States, 1947-1967," *Research in Political Economy* 1 (1977): 87-115.

Part IV

MONOPOLY PROFITS AND ECONOMIC SURPLUS

The essays in Part IV are concerned with monopolistic profit margins and the utilization of potential surplus product in advanced capitalism. Building on Joseph Gillman's classic study, *The Falling Rate of Profit,* Jacob Morris examines the general laws of monopolistic accumulation, focusing on the role of unproductive expenditures. Paul M. Sweezy offers a defense of Marxian value theory in which he discusses the significance of monopoly profits for value-based analysis, followed by a brief examination of contemporary conditions of financial instability. Ron Stanfield presents an alternative way of conceptualizing economic surplus from that provided in *The Political Economy of Growth* by Paul A. Baran and *Monopoly Capital* by Baran and Sweezy. Henryk Szlajfer, in the final essay in this part, attempts to demonstrate that the concept of economic surplus, as introduced by Baran and Sweezy, forms an absolutely necessary complement to "the traditional calculus of surplus value" under conditions of monopoly capitalism. The categories of potential and planned surplus are seen as elaborations of long neglected aspects of the "Marxian cognitive perspective," which provide the concrete basis for understanding the centrality of nonproductive labor (and nonproductive consumption) in modern capitalism.

Jacob Morris

PROFIT RATES AND CAPITAL FORMATION IN AMERICAN MONOPOLY CAPITALISM

Arthur Burns, former chairman of the board of governors of the Federal Reserve System, and the 1977 toast of the town among the head men of American capitalism, did a lot of speech-making that year to various business groups. His main theme was the low current rate of business spending for new plant and equipment, in other words, the low current rate of physical capital formation. Dr. Burns argued most persuasively that our country needs a very big increase in such job-creating capital formation in order to materially reduce unemployment and materially increase production. Since increasing production would also counteract the inflationary forces in the economy, Dr. Burns projected the vision of a big upsurge in physical or "real" capital formation as the only sound remedy for the unemployment and inflation sicknesses which plague our country.[1]

Dr. Burns attributed the abnormally low current rate of real capital formation to many factors—to uncertainty in the minds of business leaders about the economic and tax policies of the Carter administration, to the fears and confusions of an inflationary era, to the energy and oil crisis, and to everything else that's wrong with the world, but especially to what Dr. Burns considers to be an abnormally low rate of profit on invested capital in the United States in recent years. According to Dr. Burns, when the profit rates of American nonfinancial corporations are properly adjusted to a *real* basis by eliminating illusory, inflation-caused accounting profits (inflationary fluff, in Dr. Burns' words) the result is an after-tax rate of return on stockholders' equity which has averaged only about 3.25 percent per annum during the current decade, up to the end of 1977.

Contemplating this unusually low figure with appropriate horror, Dr. Burns advocated big cuts in corporate income taxes to

Reprinted from *Science & Society* 43, no. 4 (Winter 1979–80): 409–29.

restore a level of profitability which would revive business confidence. Thus business would acquire both the means and the courage to materially enlarge its spending for new plant and equipment. Of course this would tend to increase the federal government deficit sharply, and that would never do, so Dr. Burns also advocated big cuts in government spending for social welfare programs—but with no cuts in the sacrosanct military budgets, of course. With a good outlook for business profits, and better prospects for an eventual balancing of the federal budget, business confidence, according to Dr. Burns, would be restored and real capital formation would surge ahead, producing the host of beneficial consequences which he foresees.

We might remark, parenthetically, that the Carter administration, after replacing Dr. Burns as Federal Reserve Board chairman, adopted most of his economic policy recommendations, later in 1978. However, as part of their effort to appease the foreign-policy hawks and construct a new cold war political consensus, the administration actually went beyond Burns' economic recommendations and materially increased the military budget. The principle of deficit spending for military purposes seems to be more firmly entrenched than ever. Only the principle of deficit spending for social welfare purposes has been proscribed.

Returning to our main theme, the writer of this essay is an Old Believer when it comes to the question of the validity of the Marxian law of the falling tendency of the rate of profit, but he finds it hard to believe that the real rate of corporate profit has fallen quite as low as Dr. Burns makes out. As a matter of fact several business economists have spotted weaknesses in the methods used in computing profit rates such as Dr. Burns' 3.25 percent. It seems that what has been overlooked is that the dollar liabilities of corporations to bondholders and other creditors depreciate (in terms of dollars of constant purchasing power) at the rate of inflation (around 6 percent per annum before 1978) and that this depreciation of liabilities is a gain to the stockholders which has to be recognized in the kind of *real* profit-rate calculation that Dr. Burns is talking about. Our own rough calculations indicate that the correct figure for the real annual rate of profit on stockholders' equity between 1970 and 1977 has been in the neighborhood of 6 percent, rather than around 3 percent as Dr. Burns would have it. These low figures compare with conventional accounting profit rates (undeflated) of about 13 percent per annum.[2]

Whatever the correct real profit rate is for the decade of the seventies, we have no doubt that it is lower than the corresponding rates for the decades of the 1950s and 1960s. Nor do we doubt that it is less than half of the comparable rate for a hundred years ago. What we do doubt is that the current weakness in real capital formation has very much to do with the current low profit rate figures produced by the application of deflating techniques. One reason we say this is that the capitalist decision-makers don't know much about Dr. Burns' deflated profit rate, can't figure out what it means if they do know about it, and don't much care in either case. To them a dollar is a dollar—*pecunia non olet*—and it matters not at all whether the profit dollar arises from production, from inflation, from speculation, or from some form of business or financial manipulation. We agree with the business economists who attribute the low current rate of real capital formation not primarily to low profits, but mainly to the need of corporations to add to money capital reserves because of the uncertainties and confusions of these inflationary times.

More generally, it is our argument that low profit rates are not the cause, in a simple immediate sense, of low capital formation. Rather the reverse is the case. We shall argue that monopoly capitalism exhibits, by reason of its essential nature, a declining propensity for real job-creating capital formation and an increasing propensity for spurious capital formation which creates no new jobs at all. We believe that these complementary propensities play an important causal role in many of the distinctive economic phenomena of the present time, such as the combination of inflation and unemployment which has come to be known as "stagflation." We refer also to the high apparent rates of profit *before* the inflationary hot air is squeezed out as well as the low real rates of profit *after* the inflationary hot air is squeezed out. There is also the other side of spurious capital formation, that is, the pathological and wasteful consumption (including military consumption) which justifies a characterization of latter-day American monopoly capitalism as a kind of perverted consumption society which is rapidly losing all its capacity for socially desirable capital formation and economic progress.

We shall concentrate here on the profit rate and develop our analysis of its relation to capital formation in three sections, as follows:

(1) Marx's theory of the falling tendency of the rate of profit;
(2) Gillman's modification of Marx's theory for the era of monopoly capitalism;
(3) modification of Gillman's theory to include spurious capital formation.

Marx's Theory of the Falling Tendency of the Rate of Profit

Marx's theory, simplified to its barest essentials, may be stated in three fairly short sentences. Because of the deep preference of the capitalists for labor-saving investment, each year's increment of productive capital tends to provide less new labor employment than the preceding year's increment. Therefore total labor employment tends to grow, with time, more slowly than the total accumulation of productive capital. Finally, since profits find their ultimate source in labor employment, total profits also tend to grow more slowly than invested capital, so that the rate of profit on invested capital tends to fall.

Let us examine this oversimplified argument a little more closely. If we let E stand for total employment and let C stand for the total accumulation of productive capital (defined as the total replacement cost of existing depreciated plant and equipment plus materials inventories, in dollars of constant purchasing power) then the argument is that E/C tends to decrease with time. This is the result of the striving of the capitalist masters of the system, essential to the survival of the system and their dominating class power, to hold down wage costs and create unemployed labor reserves (the industrial reserve army of the unemployed). The falling E/C ratio, brought about by investment in labor-saving plant and equipment and by the creation of technological unemployment, is an expression of the action of the main economic forces which keep the working class in an exploitable relationship to the capitalist class.

Now, according to the value theory of the Marxian system, the employment of labor is the source of the stream of surplus value. Surplus value (S) is the difference between national income ($S + V$) and wages of productive workers (V). Surplus value includes all forms of property income plus all forms of unproductive expenditure. Profit in Marxist usage includes only property income; therefore profit means surplus value less unproductive expenditure. If we assume provisionally that profit is proportional to surplus value and that surplus value is proportional to employment, then a falling E/C ratio implies a falling S/C ratio and hence a falling rate of profit. To get closer to the reality of the profit rate which motivates capitalist decision making, the denominator C should be enlarged to include accumulated money capital and the value of productive land. We do not make this refinement and simply assume that S/C, with C as previously defined, is a good surrogate for a more precise definition of the profit rate when the center of interest is the historical trend of the profit rate on invested capital, rather than the correct absolute size of the profit rate.

The main criticism that can be made of Marx's theory is that a falling E/C ratio does not necessarily imply a falling S/C ratio. The installation of labor-saving plant and equipment is made for the very purpose of extracting more profit out of each hour of employment so that it is logical to expect that the ratio S/E will rise as the ratio E/C falls. Now since S/C is the arithmetical product of S/E and E/C, a fall of E/C combined with a rise in S/E may produce an S/C which remains fairly constant, or even increases.

It is rather obvious, of course, that working-class resistance to exploitation may slow up the increase in S/E or even produce a flat trend in that ratio. This kind of trend would lead to the desired theoretical result of a falling rate of profit and it is possible that Marx had something of this sort in mind. However the theory, as he developed it formally, does not invoke the principle of working-class resistance to exploitation. The pure argument appears to be that no matter how much S/E increases, the fall in the E/C ratio will dominate the compounded result and produce a falling S/C ratio.

Now it can be shown by a bit of rather simple mathematical reasoning that S/C will indeed tend to fall, no matter how fast S/E increases, but only in the special case in which it is assumed that the total invested net capital C increases more rapidly than the national income.[3] This seems to be an unrealistic assumption when we are dealing with a fully developed capitalist economy such as that of the United States. Here the total value of accumulated physical capital is subject to continuous and large downward adjustments in value because of depreciation and obsolescence. (Most new gross capital formation in the United States, massive as it is, does little more than offset the depreciation and obsolescence of existing capital.) New gross capital formation would have to increase very rapidly as a proportion of national income to produce any sort of significant increase in the ratio of accumulated net capital value to national income. Thus the validity of Marx's theory for a mature capitalist economy appears to be linked to rather implausible assumptions about trends in new gross capital formation which, however, are reasonable enough for a capitalist economy in its period of youthful vigor.

Gillman's Modification of Marx's Theory for the Era of Monopoly Capitalism

The Marxist economist Joseph Gillman was very troubled by the weakness in the logic of Marx's development of his falling rate of profit law. He was also profoundly convinced that little of value would remain of Marx's economic thought if that law were shown to be invalid. Gillman appraised the essence of Marx's economic thought as a belief that the same complex of historically developing socioeconomic forces of capitalism which produced the growing misery of the working class in its multiple economic, social, cultural, occupational, and psychological aspects also produced in the falling rate of profit the source of profound tensions, conflicts, and splits in the ruling capitalist class itself.

Gillman summed up the significance of Marx's profit law in his book *The Falling Rate of Profit* as follows:

> Indeed it would seem that if there were no deep-seated, systemic tendency of the rate of profit to fall, with all the attendant consequences which Marx ascribed to it, it would be hard to envisage the development of such conflicts within the capitalist class and between it and the working class as would become a threat to the continued existence of the system. To be sure, like all living organisms, it would be beset with pains of growth and development. But these could be regarded as transitory hardships originating in remediable causes and as furnishing no basis for its ultimate breakdown and for the ultimate necessity of its replacement by another social system of production.[4]

As to the political significance of Marx's profit law, Gillman observed that

> in the Marxist view, no social class system can come to an end solely because of a rising discontent of its underlying, exploited population. Severe discontent and conflict must develop also within the ruling class. This opens up opportunities for alliances between certain of its segments and the discontented masses with respect to given short-term objectives. At critical moments these alliances are transformed into working class leadership which spearheads the revolutionary overthrow of the existing social system.

Finally, if it should turn out that the falling rate of profit is only a Marxist illusion, Gillman concluded that "capitalism, unlike all its predecessor class systems, can be assumed to be possessed of the elixir of perpetual life, and the advocates of a socialist' solution to the ills of capitalism become but Don Quixotes tilting at windmills."

After prolonged study of Marx, and also of the works of Ricardo, Keynes, Schumpeter, Veblen, and Mitchell, in his search for new theoretical insights into the problem of the falling rate of profit, Gillman decided that it was time to shift the emphasis of his studies, for a while, to empirical investigation. He pointed out that

Marx did not have the facts against which to test his law of the falling tendency of the rate of profit. They first had to emerge from generations of capitalist production. But we now have a considerable accumulation of such facts, and it seems high time that, with Francis Bacon, we counted the horse's teeth instead of continuing to speculate about their number.

Gillman then embarked on an intensive statistical study of capital formation and the rates of profit in U. S. manufacturing industries in the approximately century-long period 1849-1952. The results of this study and the theoretical speculations which it engendered were presented in the book referred to.

Gillman, following Marx in essentials, conceived of the rate of profit as the ratio of two other rates. The first of these is the rate of surplus value (or rate of exploitation) defined as S/V, where S is the surplus value emerging in a year and V is the wage bill for the year. The second rate is the so-called stock basis computation of the organic composition of capital C/V, where C, called constant capital, is the average value of the net depreciated stock of productive capital (plant, equipment, and materials inventories) employed in production during the year, V remaining as before. This involves essentially the same definition of C as was employed in the preceding section on Marx's theory of the profit law. When the S/V ratio is divided by the C/V ratio, we obtain S/C, the surrogate for the annual rate of profit. If C/V tends to increase, with the passage of time, more rapidly than S/V, as Marx contended, then the rate of profit must fall.

Marx himself had employed a flow basis conception of the organic composition of capital where, in the ratio C/V, C was the constant capital *consumed* in a cycle of production and V (variable capital) was the corresponding wage bill of the production cycle. This led to a rate of profit for a production cycle which had to be operated on in a rather complicated way by a set of turnover rates for the various capital components in order to arrive at the desired end result of the rate of profit on the *stock* of invested capital. Gillman eliminated the need for determining and employing capital turnover rates by directly using a stock basis concept of the organic composition of capital.

Gillman discovered that the factual evidence for U. S. manufacturing industries for a period of approximately forty years, 1880-1919, tended to confirm Marx's theory. (It was impossible to make the appropriate computations for earlier periods.) During the forty-year period in question, the organic composition of capital on the C/V stock basis appears to have increased steadily and materially while the surplus value or exploitation rate S/V increased more slowly. The result was that the S/C profit rate surrogate declined fairly steadily. Over the forty-year period the decline in the profit rate appeared to be in the neighborhood of 50 percent.[5]

By contrast, the factual evidence for the approximately thirty-year period 1920-52 told a quite different story. During this period the organic composition exhibited an essentially flat or moderately decreasing trend while the surplus value rate exhibited a somewhat increasing trend. In consequence the surrogate profit rate exhibited a mild upward trend. It seemed clear that the sharp downward trend in the rate of profit of the earlier period had been arrested in the later period, if not actually reversed.

Gillman regarded the 1880-1919 period as the period of transformation in the United States of competitive capitalism into monopoly capitalism and the subsequent period as the era of full-blown monopoly capitalism. During the earlier transition period the trends in organic composition, surplus value rates, and profit rates appeared to Gillman to have retained the character which Marx observed in Britain in the middle of the nineteenth century, when the British competitive capitalist system was in its heyday. But with the full emergence of monopoly capitalism in the first quarter of the twentieth century, quantitative changes occurred in the organic composition trend which Gillman believed to be associated with the deep qualitative and structural differences between competitive capitalism and monopoly capitalism.

Gillman concluded that monopoly capitalism does not exhibit a tendency to an increasing organic composition of capital and that the Marxist profit law in its original form is not applicable to monopoly capitalism. A good deal of Gillman's book is devoted to his explanation for the alleged cessation in the rise of the organic composition of capital in U. S. monopoly capitalism since World War I. In this paper we will confine ourselves to what we judge to be his single most important argument, although it is one which pertains to capital formation in general, and not merely to employment. This argument, which appears also in the writings of Hansen, Sweezy-Baran, Kalecki, and many others, holds that the circumstances which condition monopoly capitalism's drive for maximum profits generate barriers to the expansion of invested physical capital. By contrast, the profit maximization objectives of competitive capitalism operated in a framework which produced no such barriers to vigorous expansion of invested physical capital.

For our purpose here it is sufficient to fix attention on only one of the many qualitative differences between twentieth-century monopoly capitalism and nineteenth-century competitive capitalism. The modern monopoly capitalist firm may conclude that its profits will be maximized if it restricts production and investment in productive facilities (i.e., restricts production and real capital formation) and instead raises its prices. However, to make the new price schedule stick it may find it necessary to increase its budget for sales and advertising expense and to make arrangements for additional bank credit for its wholesale customers and for its wholesale customers' retail customers. The nineteenth-century capitalist firm operating under competitive conditions had no such option available to it. It had to accept market-determined prices and could not risk a price deviation which could be maintained only by incurring sales and advertising expense of unknown and unpredictable size. Nor was there in existence in the competitive capitalist system that dense network of financial connections among government, banking, and industry which is the basis for the modern monopoly capitalist system of business and consumer credit, with its potential for copious and almost instantaneous expansion.

The typical monopoly-capitalist process of restricting production and increasing prices tends to produce a double-barreled effect in widening the gap between the potential effective demand and the corresponding social aggregate of planned supply prices. On the one hand the effective demand potential is damaged by the trend toward lower real capital formation; on the other hand the gap between it and the supply price aggregate is widened by the trend toward monopolistic price increases. A Marxist would put it that monopoly capitalism tends to produce a double barrier in the path of surplus value realization. When bourgeois economics finally discovered the realization problem, which it called the effective demand gap, in the 1930s, this generated the Keynesian revolution which mistakenly attributed the gap to a mythical declining psychological propensity to consume rather than to the systemic propensities of monopoly capitalism for *attempting* to enlarge profits without simultaneously enlarging its investments in real physical capital.

According to Gillman's analysis, monopoly capitalism copes with its self-created effective demand gap by enormously increasing unproductive expenditures or consumption. He used the symbol U to represent the annual total of such expenditures. Such U expenditures occur in three principal forms:

(1) government expenditures financed by taxes and loans of federal, state, and municipal governments;
(2) individual consumption financed not out of current wages, but by the creation of consumer indebtedness, including home mortgage indebtedness;

(3) expenditures for salesmen, advertising, and similar selling activities.

Gillman regarded the social aggregate of U-type expenditures as a form of consumption of surplus product and of surplus value. He retained the Marxist symbol S to represent the gross amount of surplus value produced and he designated $(S - U)$ to represent the net amount of surplus value realized. To him U expenditure represented a mass of potential real job-creating capital formation which had been aborted and lost to society. Like any other component of the total effective demand, it provided markets for current output and employment and, under certain circumstances, the expansion of U expenditure could temporarily stimulate an expansion of production and employment. This was the side of U expenditure that the Keynesians saw and made so much of. The loss of *future* production and employment capacity involved in U expenditure escaped their attention, and to this day it still does. But to Gillman, as a Marxist, this loss of future productive capacity was the aspect that justified the characterization of "unproductive" which he attached to the forms of surplus-product consumption which entailed such a loss.

Gillman's empirical studies suggested to him that because of the inner nature of monopoly capitalism (which includes of course its imperialist war-making propensities), the unproductive consumption of surplus product, the U-type expenditure, constituted a high and more or less steadily increasing fraction of total S and of total national income. U-type expenditures also existed under the conditions of nineteenth-century competitive capitalism, but they were a small part of total S and total national income and played an insignificant role in the process of capital and profit formation. But with the massive quantitative growth of U expenditures in the era of monopoly capitalism, qualitative changes in this process occur.

To Marx, observing and analyzing British capitalism in the heyday of the competitive era, it seemed clear that the observed falling tendency in the rate of profit must be linked to the high and increasing rate of new capital formation. Now if one closed one's eyes to the massive growth of U-type expenditures in the twentieth century, and continued to use the S/C formula, one would have to conclude that under monopoly capitalism there was no evidence of a falling tendency in the rate of profit and that this was consistent with the related tendency for new real capital formation to slacken off. However, in Gillman's view, S/C could no longer serve as the surrogate formula for the rate of profit when such massive portions of S were consumed by taxes and other forms of unproductive expenditure. He suggested that a more accurate surrogate formula for the rate of profit in the era of monopoly capitalism is $(S - U)/C$ and that with the use of this formula one could assert that the law of the falling tendency of the rate of profit continued to operate in the era of monopoly capitalism. But whereas under conditions of competitive capitalism the falling tendency of the profit rate was rooted in a rising tendency in the rate of new capital formation, in the era of monopoly capitalism it was rooted in a rising tendency in the rate of unproductive consumption and a falling tendency in the rate of new capital formation.

If he were alive today, Gillman would say, I think, that Dr. Burns was standing things on their heads. It is not the falling tendency of the rate of profit which produces a falling tendency in the rate of real capital formation; it is (at the time of writing at any rate) rather the reverse. Or perhaps he would say that both tendencies are inherent in monopoly capitalism and that they feed on each other, that they are, to use Marxist language, dialectically related. Looking at the matter historically, the falling tendency of the rate of profit emerged in circumstances where there had been a rising tendency in the rate of real capital formation. This falling tendency was one part of a complex of causes which eventually produced the transformation of competitive capitalism into monopoly capitalism. Full-blown monopoly capitalism in time reversed the previous trend in real capital formation, providing along with this reversal of trend a new causal basis in unproductive expenditure for the falling tendency of the rate of profit.

Extension of Gillman's Theory to Include Spurious Capital Formation

Gillman was well aware of the fact that his $(S - U)/C$ formula, while closer to empirical reality than the simpler S/C formula, was still a long way from describing the kind of profit rates which emerged when one processed the accounting data in business and personal income statements and balance sheets. He pointed out one reason for this—the fact that a substantial portion of U expenditures are capitalized, that is, paid for by the creation of debt. Since one man's debt is another man's financial asset, the capitalization of U expenditure is a process whereby such expenditure simultaneously creates financial assets. Gillman called such capitalization *spurious capital formation*. A major form of spurious capital is government debt, that is, federal, state, and local government bonds, notes, certificates—financial assets generated by government, or government IOUs whose proceeds are used to pay for that portion of government U expenditure which is not paid out of tax proceeds. The financial mechanisms of monopoly capitalism function with especially great efficiency in the area of production of government IOUs.

The government IOUs, though we may call them spurious capital, are as good as cash to the government's creditors, and that part of government expenditures which is paid for by an increase in government IOUs does not have the effect (as does government expenditure paid for out of tax revenue) of diminishing the national aggregate of recorded accounting profits of business firms and individuals. Spurious capital formation originating with government is an alternative to taxation and thus tends, initially at least, to increase the rate of profit over what it would be without spurious capital formation.

A major feature of spurious capital is that it is a financial asset form which has no productive physical capital assets behind it; that is why Gillman called it "spurious." The expansion of spurious capital does not expand productive capacity and employment opportunities; it does not create new jobs. Not only is it a process of consumption without a production counterpart, not only does it gobble up current production without laying the basis of future production, but the moment after it is created and has put on its government uniform, it is ready to function as new money and credit and go forth into the world to gobble up future production as well. Thus the process of spurious capital formation is inherently inflationary even though its modern forms originated within the bowels of monopoly capitalism as an antideflationary process, as a process designed only to facilitate the realization of surplus value and the maintenance of effective demand. But any antideflationary process which is sufficiently enlarged automatically becomes an inflationary process. In the United States after World War II spurious capital formation rapidly crossed the invisible boundary line between antideflation and inflation. By the same token the reduction of spurious capital formation generates deflationary tendencies.

It goes beyond Gillman's concepts to assign consumers' debt, including home mortgages, to the category of spurious capital. Yet consumers' IOUs of all kinds are very similar to government IOUs. They originate in the unproductive consumption of part of the social surplus product. They are financial assets without employment-creating productive capital behind them. And like government IOUs they are easily produced and easily converted into cash under the system of financial mechanisms created by American monopoly capitalism. Thus one form of monetization of consumer debt is seen in the operations of savings banks and savings and loan associations. The assets of these institutions consist largely of home mortgages. But their depositors, who are the beneficial owners of these mortgages, think of their bank-deposit credits as cash and use them as cash. Accordingly we shall treat consumers' IOUs as forms of spurious capital.

As a matter of fact, a significant quantity of business IOUs (i.e., business loans from banks which are part of the banks' financial assets, and which can be discounted for cash at the Federal Reserve Bank) are also in the category of spurious capital. Spurious capital is formed here to the extent that the loan proceeds have been used for expenditures other than productive plant, equipment, materials, fuel, or wages, in other words, for the unproductive consumption of part of the social surplus product.

The reader will recall the crucial part played in the Marxian system by the notion that, with the passage of time, new increments of net real capital provide for smaller and smaller employment increments. This notion is crucial for both Marx's theory of the increasing misery of the working class and his theory of the falling tendency of the rate of profit. Using the symbols previously defined, the notion asserts that there is a declining tendency in the ratio E/C. Now let us redesignate C, the value of the accumulated net depreciated stock of physical capital, as C_r so that the subscript "r" will remind us that we are referring to real capital, and then let us introduce the symbol C_s to stand for the accumulated total of spurious capital of which the main forms are government and consumer debt. Then we can surely say that if E/C_r tends to decrease with time, $E/(C_r + C_s)$ will decrease even more rapidly since increments of C_s provide no new employment at all. We can also say that the more rapidly C_s increases relative to C_r, the more rapidly will the ratio of employment to total capital fall.

Superficially it would seem that Gillman's theory of the falling tendency of the rate of profit is just the opposite of Marx's theory. Marx said that the major causal factor is the *increasing* rate of real capital formation. But according to Gillman the major causal factor in the era of monopoly capitalism is the *decreasing* rate of real capital formation. However, with the introduction of the notion of spurious capital formation, Gillman's proposition can be converted into the statement that the major causal factor is the increasing rate of total capital formation (relative to employment) within which the spurious capital component increases more rapidly than total capital, while the real capital component rate actually decreases. We can also put it that Marx's theory of the profit rate holds for monopoly capitalism, but with the increasing substitution of spurious capital for real capital.

In order to deal with the influence of spurious capital formation on the formation (and deformation) of the rate of profit, we need to introduce one more symbol to represent the portion of the annual U expenditure which is capitalized. This portion, which we designate as U_c, represents the current year's increment in the accumulated total of spurious capital, that is, the current year's increase in the total of government and consumer debt. We can also think of U_c as the current year's increase in the kind of financial assets which have no real capital counterpart. The relation of C_s, the total of such financial assets, to U_c is that C_s is the sum of the U_c of the current year plus the U_c of all previous years.

The formula for the average rate of profit which is derived from the social or national aggregate of the balance sheets and income statements of all owners of real and spurious capital is evidently $(S - U + U_c)/(C_r + C_s)$. To explore how this five-term formula works, let us start at a time (e.g., the 1930s) when U_c is small relative to U and $S - U$, and C_s is very small relative to C_r, because large-scale spurious capital formation is a brand new phenomenon. Then the formula produces results very close to Gillman's formula $(S - U)/C_r$.

Let us now move into a period (e.g., 1946-55) when U_c first becomes large relative to U and $S - U$ but C_s is still small relative to C_r. Now the formula produces results close to $(S - U + U_c)/C_r$, that is, a rate of profit which is substantially higher than by Gillman's formula because of the addition of U_c to the numerator of the profit formula. Finally let us consider a period (e.g., the past twenty years) in which not only is U_c large relative to U and $S - U$, but in which C_s becomes significantly large, and with the passage of time, even larger, relative to C_r. Under these conditions all five terms in the expanded formula are significant and the rate of profit will obviously tend to fall relative to its level at the time when spurious capital formation first became important. From these considerations we would expect the overall social rate of profit, as calculated by conventional accounting methods, to be substantially higher in the decade 1946-55 than in the decade of the 1930s or in the decade of the 1970s.

Simple algebra will show that the profit rate based on the full five-term formula is a weighted average of two rates, the first $(S - U)/C_r$ and the second U_c/C_s, where the respective weights are $C_r/(C_r + C_s)$ and $C_s/(C_r + C_s)$. If C_s tends to become large relative to C_r, that is, if spurious capital becomes the dominating element in total capital formation, then the U_c/C_s ratio becomes the dominating factor in the profit rate. Under these conditions the conventional profit rate becomes largely a ratio of current spurious capital formation to past spurious capital formation.

The general structure of the full five-term formula for the rate of profit shows that the long-term trend of the rate must be downward if U absorbs more and more of S and if spurious capital formation increasingly replaces real capital formation. However, it also shows that there is likely to be significant instability in the year-to-year profit rate figures because of the pressure and variability of the U_c factor. If this factor becomes negative because of debt reduction, the average profit rate can plunge to zero, or below.

Up to this point our analysis has tacitly assumed a stable price level. However, it is now a commonplace among accountants and business economists that inflation artificially inflates profit rates computed from accounting figures which do not recognize price changes in the components of the stock of physical capital. The value of plant, equipment, and material inventories is almost invariably shown on business books at original (historical) cost less allowance for depreciation, also based on original cost. Now depreciation as a percentage of cost is usually greatly overstated so that the values assigned to C_r are too low for that reason. But even more important, depreciated capital goods cannot be replaced at original cost; they have to be replaced by capital goods priced at current levels. Thus C_r has to be adjusted upward for two reasons: to eliminate excessive percentage depreciation and to reflect the change from original costs to current replacement costs. Such an adjustment tends to reduce the profit rate because C_r occurs in the denominator of the profit formula.

Inflation also tends to overstate the S item in the profit formula numerator because of the understatement of capital consumption charges entering as an item of deduction into the computation of S. Such capital consumption charges, consisting of charges for depreciation of plant and equipment and charges for consumption of materials, are understated if, as is usual, the charges are based on original cost rather than on current replacement cost. The overstatement of S will be reduced, however, if the schedule of depreciation percentages is simultaneously corrected to an economically realistic level. Thus S has to be corrected upward to eliminate excessive percentage depreciation but downward to reflect the change from original costs to current replacement costs. The net of the two counteracting corrections is downward according to work done by government economists cited by Dr. Burns.

The effect of correcting S and C_r to eliminate the effects of inflation and of excessive depreciation percentages is to reduce S

and increase C_r and thus to reduce the rate of profit because the numerator of the profit fraction is reduced while the denominator is increased.

The correction of profit-rate calculations to eliminate the inflationary fluff is a very complicated technical matter. Things become even more complicated if it is desired to break down the overall social profit rate into a profit rate on entrepreneurial capital (e.g., the rate of profit on corporation net worth) and the profit rate on rentier capital. It should be noted that our five-term formula produces only an overall social or national average rate of profit for all owners of real and spurious capital. It should also be noted that rentier capital includes more than spurious capital; it also includes loans made via bonds, notes, mortgages, and bank credit which are used by the borrowing business firms to acquire real physical assets, in other words, plant, equipment, and materials. To that extent rentier capital includes a real capital component.

Let us suppose that the owners of the bonds of a corporation, the rentier capitalist sector of that corporation, so to speak, receive a 6 percent per annum interest rate on the bonds. Suppose further, for simplicity, that the rate of inflation is also 6 percent per annum. In that case the real rate of profit to the rentier capitalist is zero because the annual interest received just offsets the annual depreciation in the purchasing power of the bonds' fixed dollar value. (In fact the real rentier profit rate is less than zero if the rentier capitalist has to pay income tax on his interest income.)

Now all of the physical assets of the corporation, including that portion provided by the rentier capitalist sector, appreciates in terms of current dollar value by the rate of inflation. Thus, though the entrepreneurial capitalist (the stockholders) pay 6 percent on bonds to the rentier capitalist, this cost is offset by the 6 percent increase in the current dollar value of the physical capital acquired with the proceeds of the bonds. In real terms the entrepreneurial capitalist pays nothing at all to the rentier capitalist. (In fact the former makes a further profit out of rentier capital because of the income-tax deduction for interest paid.)

The upshot of this argument is that if you want to determine the real rate of profit on entrepreneurial capital you must not only correct it down by the elimination of inflationary fluff (the understatement in C_r and the overstatement in S), but you must also correct it upward for depreciation overstatement and to allow for the gain made at the expense of rentier capital. It is likely that during the 1950s and 1960s the gains made by entrepreneurial capital at the expense of rentier capital, plus the gains hidden by excessive depreciation percentages, offset the inflationary fluff components due to price understatement of C_r and price overstatement of S. If seems very likely that the apparent, or accountant's, rate of profit was not too far from the real or economic rate of profit in the 1950s and 1960s. However, it seems clear from the government studies cited by Dr. Burns that in the 1970s the apparent entrepreneurial rate of profit, because of the upsurge in inflation, began to deviate significantly from the real (deflated) economic rate of profit. This is the reason for the present growth of concern about the reliability of the rates of profit on entrepreneurial capital which emerge from conventional accounting data.

There seems to be little reason to doubt the validity of Gillman's thesis that there is and has been a falling tendency in the rate of profit in American monopoly capitalism which is associated with the tendency toward increasing unproductive expenditure and spurious capital formation. However, it is also the case that spurious capital formation, and the inflationary process of which it is a necessary condition, produce complicated smoke-screen phenomena which can conceal a downward tendency in the real (deflated) rate of profit. The recent work done by government and private economists, which Dr. Burns referred to in his 1977 speeches, and which seeks to get at the real trends behind the inflated conventional accounting data, seems to us to be producing real profit-rate estimates for recent decades which are pretty much in line with Gillman's $(S - U)/C$ approach for the preinflation prewar decades. Gillman's average annual profit rate for the 1919-39 period, for U.S. manufacturing industries, came out at about 9 percent.[6] Using the methods Dr. Burns approves of, the average deflated annual rate of return on stockholders' net worth for all U.S. nonfinancial corporations comes out at about 5 percent for the 1950-76 period. Adding something for the profits accruing to stockholders out of the practically free use of rentier capital (excluded in the 5 percent Burns result), we come out somewhere in the neighborhood of 7 percent for the recent period. The two figures, 9 percent and 7 percent, are in line, and the trend *appears* to be downward.

That the two figures are in line is not surprising because the process of eliminating the effects of inflation is pretty much the same thing as eliminating the effects of its essential financial condition, which is spurious capital formation. If you eliminate the effects of spurious capital formation and inflation, what you have left is Gillman's $(S - U)/C_r$ formula as it would work out under stable price conditions. As to the apparent downward trend just referred to, we must admit that both figures are much too rough for any firm conclusions about the trend without a great deal of more refined statistical analysis. Just to mention one defect in the figures, Gillman was unable to eliminate the effects of spurious capital formation in his calculations. Of course, in the period 1919-39 there wasn't much spurious capital formation to eliminate. Massive spurious capital formation started with World War II. There are also other technical reasons why Gillman's profit rates and Burns' deflated profit rates are not sufficiently comparable for firm conclusions to be drawn about trends.

What strikes one most about the current deflated profit figures is their low level and the strong impression they convey of a greatly weakened real capital accumulation process. If our analysis is sound, we must conclude that these low profit rates are much more effect than cause of the weakness in real capital formation. We view this weakness as a symptom of the pathology of aging monopoly capitalism. The effects of this capital formation weakness on profit rates have been covered up by deficit spending, spurious capital formation, and inflation. Now that the illusion of high profitability has been shattered as a result of the analysis of the worldwide inflationary crisis, the prestige of Keynesian stimulation policies has declined materially. Keynesian stimulation is now widely perceived as an essential factor in the generation of the inflationary crisis and its illusions.

Nevertheless, Keynesian stimulation will still be employed in the United States, even intensified, in the area of military and armament expenditure and production. It is only in the area of social welfare expenditure that Burnsian stimulation is to be substituted for Keynesian stimulation; only here is the U.S. administration willing to gamble that real capital formation will be generated in the private business system to replace the spurious capital formation associated with government deficit spending. If the gamble fails, the inflationary crisis may be converted into a deflationary crisis with the kind of massive unemployment that hasn't been seen in the United States since the 1930s.

Notes

1. Arthur F. Burns, Address at Gonzaga University, Spokane, Washington, October 26, 1977. All references to Burns are from this source.
2. Citibank, April issues of *Monthly Economic Letter;* 13 percent is the aver-

age of annual manufacturing industry profit rates for 1970-77 as given
in the April issues.

3. *Science & Society* 31, no. 3 (1967): 304.
4. Joseph M. Gillman, *The Falling Rate of Profit* (New York: Cameron Associates, 1958), pp. 8, 9.
5. Ibid., table E, p. 55.
6. Ibid., table H, p. 97.

Paul M. Sweezy

MARXIAN VALUE THEORY AND CRISES

There is, in my opinion, no direct connection between value theory and crises, nor between the kind of price theory some wish to substitute for value theory and crises. Crises (in the broad sense that Marxists ordinarily use the term) are enormously complicated phenomena, and they differ from one another so much that no general theory, and still less no simple theory, can hope to provide more than the beginning of a serious analysis of any given crisis situation. Nevertheless, I think it is true that crises cannot be understood properly unless they are envisaged as integral to an overall conception of the nature and functioning of the capitalist accumulation process, and I for one find the theory of value to be the only basis on which such a conception can be built.

Perhaps I should say that I find it the only basis presently available on which such a conception can be built. I am aware that those, like Ian Steedman, who want to throw out the theory of value altogether but who nevertheless concede that it provided the approach which enabled Marx to arrive at his understanding of the accumulation process still do not think that value theory is in any way essential to this achievement. You can, they say, substitute price theory à la Sraffa without precluding any further inquiries along Marxian lines you may care to undertake. To quote Steedman (the concluding sentence in his recent book *Marx After Sraffa*): "It can scarcely be overemphasized that the project of providing a materialist account of capitalist societies is dependent on Marx's value magnitude analysis *only* in the negative sense that continued adher-

First published in *Monthly Review* 31, no. 3 (July-August 1979): 1–17. This is a somewhat extended and edited version of a paper presented at a three-day colloquium on the general subject of "Value Theory and Contemporary Capitalism" which took place in London in November 1978 under the joint auspices of the *New Left Review,* the *Cambridge Journal of Economics,* and the Conference of Socialist Economists, which publishes the journal *Capital and Class.* At the center of many of the discussions were the ideas set forth in the recent book by Ian Steedman, *Marx After Sraffa* (London: New Left Books, 1978). Steedman was also one of the principal speakers and an active participant in the discussions at the colloquium.

ence to the latter is a major fetter on the development of the former."[1]

It has occurred to me that by speaking of Marx's "value *magnitude* analysis," Steedman may be implying that there is another kind of value analysis, a *qualitative* value analysis, concerned with social relations rather than economic magnitudes, which helps instead of hindering "the project of providing a materialist account of capitalist societies." If so, I entirely agree with him. Only I happen to believe that the marriage of the qualitative and quantitative analyses was one of Marx's greatest achievements and that separating them runs the danger, as in the case of separating Siamese twins, of killing them both.

In many years of writing and teaching (which also ought not be separated), I have found this a position difficult, and all too often impossible, to explain. Those brought up in capitalist society are as a rule totally accustomed to the increasingly elaborate division of labor which it fosters and which is reflected in a corresponding division of knowledge and the professional specializations which deal in knowledge. Against this background, it is only natural to take for granted that theoretical systems can be taken to pieces, with some parts being retained and others rejected, more or less as diners confronted with a smorgasbord take the dishes that appeal to them and bypass the others. Anyone who thinks in this way has little hesitation in disassembling Marx's analysis of capitalism and holding onto or discarding constituent components according to his or her particular tastes. It doesn't occur to such a person that the theoretical system may be more like a machine or an organism which needs all its parts to function.

But analogies can be no more than suggestive. Let me try to make my point more directly. Roughly the first two parts of the first volume of *Capital* plus most of the first three chapters of the third part (amounting in all to about one-quarter of the volume as a whole) are predominantly qualitative in the sense indicated, that is, they focus on identifying and clarifying the basic relations of commodity-producing societies in general and capitalism in particular. Thereafter—and this holds in the main for the second and third volumes as well—there is a heavier emphasis on quantifying these relationships or rather the economic variables and their interconnections which express these relationships. Throughout, reasoning is in terms of value theory, and there is no effort to make an explicit distinction between the qualitative and quantitative dimensions of value. For Marx the quantitative is saturated with the qualitative, and the qualitative is expressed through the quantitative.

The beauty of this approach, as I see it, is that it enables us to achieve a clear and coherent vision of capitalism *as a historical process.* The early history of capitalism is seen not (or not only) as a chaos of rapine and violence but as the process through which the distinctively capitalist mode of production came into the world, with the capital/labor relation replacing the lord/serf relation as the central relation of exploitation in a new form of class society. Every class society is characterized by the necessary/surplus labor dichotomy, hence by an implicit rate of exploitation; but only in capitalism does this take the value form, with the rate of exploitation expressing itself as a rate of surplus value. This, and *not* the rate of profit (as Steedman et al seem to believe), is the crucial variable which enables Marx to get a firm handle on the history of capitalism. By dividing surplus value into absolute surplus value and relative surplus value (neither of which would make sense without the concept of a *rate* of surplus value), Marx was able to lay bare the anatomy of the class struggles which were endemic to capitalism from its earliest beginnings. This task was carried through in the third and fourth parts of the first volume of *Capital,* and especially in the incomparable chapter 15 on "Machinery and Modern Industry."[2]

From there, using the results already achieved, Marx went on to analyze the accumulation process, showing among other things: (1) how the mechanism for adjusting the rate of wages to the value of labor power is radically different from that which adjusts the price of any other commodity to its value, with the reserve army of labor (or relative surplus population) playing the key role of "pivot upon which the law of demand and supply of labor works";[3] (2) how the normal outcome of capitalist accumulation must be a polarization between riches and poverty; (3) why the form of the accumulation process must be one of cyclical ups and downs rather than a linear progression; and (4) the manner in which competition of capitals must lead, via concentration and centralization, to its own transformation into monopoly.

Have I made my point now, that is, that it was through marrying qualitative with quantitative value theory that Marx was able to illuminate the history of capitalism in a way that no theorist before or after him has been able to hold a candle to? If not, perhaps it will help to quote Schumpeter, who was a severe critic of Marx but at the same time understood what Marx was trying to do better than most of those who consider themselves to be Marxists. The following passage from Schumpeter's *Capitalism, Socialism, and Democracy,* if I interpret it correctly, says about Marx's achievement pretty much what I have been trying to express but does so in very different language:

> There is . . . one thing of fundamental importance for the methodology of economics which he [Marx] actually achieved. Economists have always either themselves done work in economic history or else used the historical work of others. But the facts of economic history were assigned to a separate compartment. They entered theory, if at all, merely in the role of illustrations, or possibly of verifications of results. They mixed with it only mechanically. Now Marx's mixture is a chemical one; that is to say, he introduced them into the very argument that produces the results. He was the first economist of top rank to see and to teach systematically how economic theory may be turned into historical analysis and how the historical narrative may be turned into *histoire raisonnée*. (p. 44)

Schumpeter could hardly have been expected to agree that value theory was the key to Marx's success in this enterprise, but it is difficult to see how he or anyone else could deny that it guided Marx every step of the way. And it would be equally difficult to make out a case that any theorist since Marx, dispensing with the theory of value, has had a success comparable to his.[4] Nor do I think it at all likely that anyone following the advice of Ian Steedman, Joan Robinson, and others to chuck the theory of value in favor of a Sraffa-type theory of prices will make any significant contribution to the solution of Marx's "problematic."

Here we meet what I suppose would be the ultimate objection of these critics of value theory. Economic magnitudes in the real world, as Marx was of course well aware, are expressed in terms of prices of production, not values. From a Marxist standpoint this, in and of itself, is not a weakness or flaw in the theory, rather the contrary. Reality is made up of appearance *and* essence. Prices of production belong to the realm of appearance, values to the realm of essence. Unless we can move back and forth between them as needed, we can never achieve more than a quite superficial understanding of capitalism. *But,* say the critics, you *cannot* move back and forth between the two realms except under very special assumptions; and if these assumptions are dropped, seriously misleading distortions result.

This at any rate is the way I interpret Steedman's argument which is summed up in a diagram on page 48 of *Marx After Sraffa.* The diagram has a box on its left-hand side labeled "Physical production and wage data." From this an arrow (a) in the northeasterly direction connects to a box labeled "All value quantities," and another arrow (b) in the southeasterly direction to another box labeled "Profits and prices."[5] Between the value box and the price box there is a dotted and interrupted arrow (c). Steedman comments: "The dashed and 'blocked off' arrow (c) represents the fact that one cannot, in general, explain prices and profits from value quantities as set out in the general value schema. . . . We thus have to picture our theoretical structure as having a 'fork-like" character, with a value prong, arrow (a), and a 'profit-price' prong, arrow (b). *There is,* in general, *no way from one prong to the other."* (p. 49) This, unless I have misunderstood Steedman, is his entire reason for wanting to jettison what he calls value magnitude analysis.

My answer is essentially simple, though it could undoubtedly be elaborated at considerable length. Despite what Steedman says, there *are* general ways of getting from the value prong to the price-profit prong. This of course is what is known in the Marxist literature as the transformation problem. As is by now well known, the way proposed by Marx himself is faulty (Steedman spends more space on this than he needs to, in view of the large amount that has been written on the subject in recent years). But there are other ways which are logically impeccable. One is the Bortkiewicz solution of which there are a number of variants and refinements; and another is what may be called the iterative solution, presented most fully by Anwar Shaikh.[6] It is true that in general a logically satisfactory solution to the transformation problem yields results different in certain respects from those of Marx's faulty method. Total price does not equal total value, and the rate of profit in the price scheme is not equal to the rate of profit in the value scheme. But there is no reason to think that these differences have any special bearing on the structure and functioning of the capitalist economy, from which it follows that analyzing the accumulation process on the basis of values yields results which do not need to be altered in any significant way by shifting to prices.

Aha, you may say, if this is true, then why do we need the value analysis at all? Reality presents itself in terms of prices. If it can also be analyzed in terms of prices, why bother with those alleged value "essences" and the whole rigamarole of transforming them into prices? But wait a minute! I did *not* say that reality could be analyzed in terms of prices: I said that the results of the analysis would not be significantly altered by shifting to prices. I do not believe that the analysis could (or would) have been made in terms of prices. And the reason is that the key concept and variable in the analysis, the center of gravity which holds everything else in place, is the rate of surplus value, *and it is precisely the rate of surplus value which disappears, vanishes without a trace, from an analysis made in terms of prices.*[7]

I would like to stress here, though it is not possible to develop the point within the limits of this essay, that in comparison with the rate of surplus value the rate of profit is both a secondary concept and one which, taken by itself, tends strongly to foster fetishistic thinking. The notion that the rate of profit is somehow, and unlike the rate of surplus value, an "operational" concept in terms of which capitalists make decisions is without foundation. Capitalists do not know what the average rate of profit is, and each one makes decisions on the basis of his own rate of profit which is rarely, and then only by accident, equal to the average rate. (This is of course even more true when we abandon the competitive assumptions which make the average rate the norm around which individual rates tend to fluctuate.) And the fact that the rate of profit states a relationship between profit and total capital rather than between profit and variable capital all too easily—as shown by the entire history of bourgeois economic thought—gives rise to the theory of the productivity of capital, an example *par excellence* of fetishistic thought.

Crises must of course be analyzed within the framework of a theory of the accumulation process, and in this restricted sense value theory is essential to the analysis of crises. An understanding of the accumulation process tells us why crises are possible and even inevitable. But a great deal more is involved, and if we are to understand particular crises we have to take account of much that does not figure in value theory. Here I want to focus on two factors which I believe play a specially important role in the crises which characterize the present phase of capitalist development, including the one which the capitalist world is currently undergoing. These are (1) monopoly (using the term to include oligopoly), and (2) finance (money and debt). I shall limit myself to the briefest possible outline.

As pointed out above, the competition of capitals leads, via the twin phenomena of concentration and centralization (both inseparable aspects of the accumulation process), to the replacement of free competition by various forms of monopoly. This in turn means that the mechanism whereby an average rate of profit is formed ceases to operate in the assumed way, and without an average rate of profit there is no longer any reason to assume an orderly correspondence between values and prices of production. If we start from a situation (competitive capitalism) in which economic reality presents itself in terms of prices of production, we now have a situation (monopoly capitalism) in which this role is played by monopoly prices. These are transformed prices of production in exactly the same sense that prices of production are transformed values.[8] There is, however, this difference, that there are no general rules for relating monopoly prices to prices of production as there were for relating prices of production to values. About all we can say is that monopoly prices in various industries tend to be higher than prices of production in proportion to the difficulties new capitals have in entering those industries. And of course a corresponding hierarchy of profit rates will emerge, highest in the industries most difficult to enter, lowest in those where entry is free (as is assumed to be the case under competitive capitalism). An average rate of profit still exists in a mathematical sense, but it is not one which tends to impose itself on individual capitals and it does not govern the distribution of surplus value throughout the system as the average rate of profit does under competitive conditions.

I have long been arguing, beginning with *The Theory of Capitalist Development* and on various occasions since, that the transition from competitive capitalism to monopoly capitalism has a profound effect on the accumulation process.[9] The redistribution of surplus value in favor of large monopolistic units of capital and to the disadvantage of small competitive units greatly enhances the system's accumulation potential. At the same time, however, attractive outlets for capital investment are curtailed. To put it another way, the big monopolies tend to be very profitable and hence able to accumulate rapidly; but at the same time they are afraid of spoiling their own markets by overinvesting, so they go slow in expanding their productive capacity. To protect their monopolistic positions they erect what barriers they can against outsiders invading their markets (one of the most effective ways is to maintain a considerable margin of unused capacity which can be quickly activated in retaliation against unwanted newcomers). Such typical monopolistic behavior adds up to a recipe for much slower growth than the economy would be capable of, and slow growth relative to the economy's potential is another name for stagnation, precisely the situation in which the global capitalist system now finds itself.

The implication of this line of reasoning is that in a developed monopoly-capitalist economy (and especially one in which the process of monopolization is continuing or even accelerating as it has been in the United States and Western Europe throughout the present century), stagnation—slow growth, heavy unemployment, much idle productive capacity—must be regarded as the norm, not the exception. Hence what needs to be explained is *not* stagnation but extended periods of buoyancy and rapid expansion such as we in the West have been living through since World War II.

This is the problem which Paul Baran and I posed and attempted to explore in *Monopoly Capital*. Clearly it requires that attention be directed not only to the internal logic of the accumulation process—a logic which cannot help but be abstract in the sense of focusing on a small number of variables—but also to the overall historical environment within which the accumulation process unfolds. In interpreting the development of U. S. capitalism over the past century, Baran and I attributed decisive importance to "epoch-making innovations" (the railroad and the automobile) on the one hand and major wars and their aftermaths on the other. The great railroad boom of the second half of the nineteenth century, we argued, came to an abrupt end with the panic of 1907. Incipient stagnation characterized the period from then until 1914 when World War I took over, followed by its aftermath boom and the automobile-led prosperity of the 1920s. Stagnation, unmitigated by further shocks or stimuli, set in with the cyclical downswing of 1929-33 and lasted throughout the decade of the 1930s. This was interrupted by World War II, which was duly followed by a reconversion and reconstruction boom.

After that, however, and largely as a consequence of the vast changes in the structure and organization of world capitalism brought about by the war, the historical determinants of the course taken by the accumulation process were transformed in important respects. There was never any doubt that the internal logic of the monopoly-capitalist system was functioning in what had long since become the normal fashion, but the environment within which this logic worked its way was new and enormously complicated. Baran and I did not attempt to analyze this new pattern of interaction in any detail, and the few comments we devoted to it were unsystematic and impressionistic.[10]

It is of course not my intention to try to repair this omission here. I want only to mention what we can now see in retrospect were some of the major factors, and to stress one, the huge growth of debt, which I think has been unduly neglected, and is just at this time precipitating what I have elsewhere called a "crisis within the crisis."[11] It needs to be integrated into the theory of the accumulation process in a way which, so far as I am aware, has not yet even been attempted.

By far the most important postwar development was the imposition of U.S. hegemony on the capitalist world: for the first time since the decline of British hegemony in the late nineteenth century, the international capitalist system came under the dominant leadership of a single great power. This had, among other things, the following consequences: (1) the establishment of a new international monetary system based on the gold-linked dollar which now served as standard of value, reserve currency, and international means of payment; (2) the extensive dismantlement of old empires and of the trading and currency blocs which had grown up in the interwar period, with a resultant vast growth of world markets, including the capital market and (to a lesser but still important extent) the market for labor power; (3) the build-up in the United States of a military machine of historically unprecedented proportions which had the dual function of policing the world capitalist system and facing up to the military power of the "socialist" bloc under the hegemony (until the Sino-Soviet split) of the USSR. In discharging its global responsibilities the United States was involved in fighting two major regional wars—in Korea and Vietnam—and many lesser armed confrontations.

In this new historical environment capitalism experienced a secular boom comparable to, and in many respects exceeding, anything in its earlier history. The accumulation of capital on a world scale was released from paralyzing restrictions which had grown up during and as a result of the Great Depression of the 1930s. The United States, benefiting from its hegemonic position and with its economy continuously stimulated by enormous military budgets, acted as a dynamo standing at the center of the system as a whole and driving it inexorably onward and upward. As always happens in such a period but now more than ever, capitalists became infected with a spirit of optimism which was reinforced and provided with a seemingly scientific foundation by various brands of "new economics" purporting to prove that panics and depressions were a thing of the past and that ahead lay endless expansion punctuated only by minor setbacks and recessions. In this heady atmosphere, there seemed to be few limits to the amount of capital investment which could be profitably undertaken, the only question being whether the payoff would begin next year or a few years later. Under these conditions the exigencies of competition dictated action now, and the combined action of all the competitors created mutual markets for their products which appeared to be self-sustaining, and hence to guarantee against the old disease of overproduction.

What was really happening of course was what had happened innumerable times in the past: behind the illusion of self-sustaining growth was the process of building up excess capacity. What brought the true situation to light was the cyclical downturn of 1974, coinciding with sharply increased oil prices following the Yom Kippur war of 1973. Suddenly the economic climate changed: excess capacity showed up in industry after industry—steel, automobiles, shipbuilding, textiles, heavy chemicals, and many more; capital accumulation faltered; unemployment grew beyond anything known in the postwar period; the rate of growth of industrial production fell below the postwar average and remained there even during the ensuing cyclical upswing. A new period of stagnation, reminiscent of the 1930s, had apparently arrived.

There was, however, one highly significant exception to this pattern—the United States itself. There the cyclical upswing began early in 1975. By the end of 1976 the growth rate of industrial production was back up to the postwar averge, and it has remained above the average ever since. At the same time the unemployment rate, which had reached 8.5 percent of the labor force in 1975, has steadily declined to 6 percent at the time of writing (November 1978).[12]

Why this exception? The answer is clear: the expansion of the U.S. economy has been fueled by a veritable explosion of public and private debt. To quote the most prestigious journal of American business and finance: "Since late 1975 the U.S. has created a new debt economy, a credit explosion so wild and so eccentric that it dwarfs even the borrowing binge of the early 1970s" (*Business Week*, October 16, 1978). The crux of this phenomenon has been the growth of consumer debt which both causes and reflects the leading role of consumption in the current recovery (contrary to the usual pattern of investment-led recovery). Also important has been the persistence of federal government deficits (almost $50 billion in 1978) into the fourth year of a cyclical recovery, a quite unprecedented occurrence.

But it is not only at the national level that the financial sector has played a crucial part in the recent behavior of the capitalist system. Thanks to its hegemonic role, the United States was able to supply the liquidity requirements of a rapidly expanding world capitalist economy through running a persistent deficit in its balance of payments. The dollars thus injected into the central banks and monetary systems of other countries served for more than a decade to lubricate the global mechanisms of trade and finance while conferring on the United States itself a seemingly limitless power to command the resources and control the destinies of the subordinate units in the world system. This continuing deficit in the U.S. balance of payments was also the main source of what came to be known as eurodollars, a form of transnational money not under the control of any central bank or governmental authority. Eurodollars in turn became the basis of a credit expansion which added many billions to the pool of dollars outside the United States. It is symptomatic of the uncontrolled (and unprecedented) nature of this phenomenon that no one knows how large this pool is, though it certainly runs into hundreds of billions and some estimates have been as high as $600 billion.

Borrowers from this vast pool of money have included not only corporations and financial institutions but also governments all over the world. To quote again the *Business Week* report cited above:

> It is that massive flow of funds from the international market that is enabling nations to keep rolling over old debt and taking on new debt nearly without limit. In just four years, the industrialized countries of the world have doubled their Euromarket debt, the less developed countries that do not export oil have tripled their Euromarket debt, and now even many of the OPEC nations themselves are borrowing on so vast a scale that they will owe nearly $10 billion by the end of this year, compared with a mere $990 million in 1974.

This enormous expansion of debt, on both the national and international levels, has of course had the effect of cushioning the impact of the sharp downturn of 1974: without it there can be little doubt that the end of the secular postwar boom would have been the beginning of a depression at least comparable to that of the early 1930s.

Stressing the role of debt expansion in the recovery from the recession of 1974-75 is necessary, but it could also be misleading if it were taken to imply that we are dealing here with a factor which has become important to the functioning of capitalism only in recent years. The truth is, as Marx himself observed many times and in many contexts, that debt (or credit which is the same thing looked at from the other side) has been crucial to capitalism since earliest times. The growth of long-distance trade is scarcely imaginable without a developed credit system; the public debt acted as a lever of primitive accumulation and has always been a keystone of every modern banking system; all the great speculative manias that have punctuated the history of capitalism, from the South Sea Bubble through the Crédit Mobilier to the great Wall Street stock market boom and crash of the 1920s, have been exercises in the use and misuse of credit; one can even argue, as Sàmir Amin has recently done, that the functioning of a fully developed, highly complicated capitalist production/circulation process—such as Marx sought to portray in the expanded reproduction schemes of volume 2 of *Capital*—would be impossible in the absence of credit.[13] And yet it would be hard to deny that something quantitatively and qualitatively new has been added in the latest period, beginning with the establishment of U. S. hegemony at the end of World War II and growing steadily in importance ever since.

This is obviously not the occasion to try to elucidate a subject which is as complex as it is important. I will only mention some of the main elements which would have to be taken into account and accorded their due weight: (1) the development, pioneered by the United States, and greatly facilitated by improved communications and information-processing technologies, of a comprehensive and flexible network of financial institutions geared to serving the needs of giant corporations and the governments which support and defend them; (2) the multinationalization of banking, following in the wake of the multinationalization of industrial and commercial capital; (3) the adoption by capitalist states, directly and through their central banks, of fiscal and monetary policies aimed at preventing the recurrence of serious depressions, such as that of the 1930s, which are perceived by all ruling bourgeoisies as a potentially mortal threat to the continued existence of capitalism. Fiscal and monetary policies of this kind began to be consciously formulated in the 1930s and became normal and accepted functions of the capitalist state after World War II. Originally conceived as anticyclical (e.g., government deficits in the down phase of the cycle would be matched by surpluses in the upswing), these policies were gradually extended to encompass antistagnationist goals, in other words, to exercise an uninterrupted expansionary pressure on overall demand for goods and services. In the United States, which has been the leader in developing these policies (just as it has been in fashioning the new financial institutions to implement them), government deficits had become perennial before the end of the 1960s; and the explosion of private debt, a major consequence of expansionary fiscal and monetary policies, likewise began long before the recession of 1974-75.

One might suppose, following the logic of Keynesian theory, that persistent expansionary fiscal and monetary policies of this kind could at least overcome the tendency to stagnation. But, paradoxical as it may seem, this has not been the case. The underlying reason is that the economies of the advanced capitalist countries, which constitute the core of the global capitalist system, are by now so dominated by giant monopolistic corporations able to control their price and output policies in the interest of maximizing profits that a very large part of the impact of expansionary fiscal and monetary policies takes the form of inflation rather than increases in real output. Furthermore, inflation, once it has reached a certain intensity in terms of magnitude and duration, tends to perpetuate itself through its effects on costs (including the cost of living which is a major determinant of wages) and on expectations.

None of this is to argue that the explosion of debt—which we can now see is but one manifestation of a very complex set of financial and political mechanisms—has no countercyclical and/or counter-stagnationist effects. Without it capitalism would probably long since have sunk into a state of near collapse. But sooner or later— and perhaps sooner rather than later—it may turn out that the cure creates problems no less serious than the disease. Already the chemical mixture of growing monopolization, exploding debt, and endemic inflation has given rise to a situation of great and growing instability and tension, reflected particularly in increasingly erratic movements in world financial and foreign-exchange markets. Only time will tell what the future holds in store, but even now it seems safe to say that the crisis of world capitalism is only in its early stages and that many shocks and surprises still await us.

Notes

1. I should add that I doubt that Sraffa would endorse this view. Steed-man himself points out that "Sraffa's *Production of Commodities by Means of Commodities* presents *no* criticisms of Marx": it was, in other words, what its subtitle proclaims, "A Prelude to a Critique of Economic Theory," economic theory of course meaning neoclassical orthodoxy. And Joan Robinson, who was as down on value theory as Steedman and put her own interpretation on Sraffa's work, warns against attributing her view to Sraffa: "Piero," she said, "has always stuck close to pure unadulterated Marx and regards my amendments with suspicion" ("The Labor Theory of Value," *Monthly Review* 29, no. 7 [December 1977], p. 56*n*).
2. How solidly Marx established the framework for his analysis is shown by the way Harry Braverman could use it without essential modification more than a hundred years later, in *Labor and Monopoly Capital*, to bring the story up to date.
3. This mechanism, not to mention its enormous implications for the functioning of capitalism, necessarily escapes the attention of those who, like Steedman, confine their attention to economies which are "fully developed, capitalist commodity economies, in which *all* [emphasis added] production activities are organized and controlled by capitalists (or their agents)" (*Marx After Sraffa*, p. 16). This just happens *not* to be true of capitalism in the real world where production of by far the most important single commodity, labor power, is *not* organized or controlled by capitalists. Much that is most distinctive and valuable in Marx's analysis of capitalism stems from the fact that he never for one moment lost sight of this crucial difference between labor power and other commodities. Let me add, though this is not the place to elaborate on the matter, that, if account is taken of this special characteristic of labor power, it involves a total misconception of

Marx's theory to write, as Steedman does: "Wages are treated in this work, as they were by Marx, as being exogenously determined . .·. in a given economy in a given period" (ibid., p. 20). It could be argued, to my mind unpersuasively, that Marx treated *the value of labor power* as exogenously determined, but never wages.

4. Schumpeter himself might be put forward as a candidate for the honor, and his own conception of the scope of his theoretical endeavor would at least give the nomination a certain plausibility. But, as I have argued elsewhere (*Modern Capitalism and Other Essays* [New York: Monthly Review Press, 1972], pp. 140-41), history has not dealt kindly with Schumpeter's theory of capitalist development in the more than half a century since it was first formulated; and of course as far as Marxists are concerned the absence of any theory of class antagonism or class struggle from Schumpeter's version of *histoire raisonée* renders it largely irrelevant. On this, see my note "Schumpeter's Theory of Innovation" in *The Present as History* (New York: Monthly Review Press, 1953), pp. 274-82.

5. By "prices" Steedman means what Marx called "prices of production"; neither is concerned with market prices.

6. "Marx's Theory of Value and the 'Transformation Problem,'" in Jesse Schwartz, ed., *The Subtle Anatomy of Capitalism* (Santa Monica, CA:: Goodyear Publishing, 1977). For the record I should like to state that an arithmetical version of the iterative solution was put forward in an unpublished manuscript many years ago by my late friend Harmon Alexander, who at the time was a screen writer and only later, in his fifties, acquired a formal training in economics.

7. I did not understand this when I was writing *The Theory of Capitalist Development* some four decades ago. As a result the fifth and sixth sections of the chapter on the transformation problem (entitled respectively "The Significance of Price Calculation" and "Why Not Start with Price Calculation?"), while not wrong, do not reach the heart of the matter, which is the crucial role of the rate of surplus value in the entire Marxian theory of capitalism.

8. It follows of course that monopoly prices are *also* transformed values. Hence analyzing monopoly prices does not imply repudiating the theory of value (as some critics of Paul Baran's and my *Monopoly Capital* have alleged). But, as argued in *Monopoly Capital* and also below, shifting from value to monopoly price does have important consequences for the accumulation process, which is not true of shifting from value to price of production.

9. See, e.g., *The Theory of Capitalist Development* (New York: Monthly Review Press, 1942), ch. 15; *Modern Capitalism and Other Essays*, pp. 39-42; "Some Problems in the Theory of Capital Accumulation," *Monthly Review* 26, no. 1 (May 1974): 40-42.

10. See pages 244-48. This brevity was at least partly because *Monopoly Capital* was conceived and largely written in the early stages of the postwar prosperity and, as noted, "it is still not possible to say when the whole movement will lose its momentum" (p. 245). In the event the

momentum was sustained for more than a decade after this was written.

11. *Monthly Review* 30, no. 7 (December 1978).
12. It should be obvious that this performance of the U. S. economy, so much stronger than that of the other advanced capitalist countries, has acted to keep the latter from faltering even more dramatically than has been the case. Without a relatively vigorous U. S. recovery, the world capitalist system would have been in considerably worse shape than it actually is.
13. Samir Amin, *The Law of Value and Historical Materialism* (New York: Monthly Review Press, 1978), p. 22.

Ron Stanfield

A REVISION OF THE ECONOMIC SURPLUS CONCEPT

It is the purpose of this paper to refine the economic surplus concept developed by Paul Baran and by Baran and Paul Sweezy.[1] The concept suggested here accords closely to Baran's "potential economic surplus" in that, on the one hand, it includes the gap between potential and actual output not included in his "actual economic surplus." On the other hand, the present paper makes no attempt to allow for the increased production that would occur were there rational socialist planning as in Baran's "planned economic surplus."

Although the intent is to improve the measurement of the economic surplus, the actual measurement is not attempted here.[2] Rather, space is devoted here to a description of the methodology suggested for such measurement. The procedure is to define the economic surplus, and then to suggest methods for its quantification.

Definition of the Economic Surplus

The economic surplus is the difference between what a society can produce, its *potential output,* and the necessary costs it must incur in producing this output, its *essential consumption.* This accords perfectly with Baran's definition of the potential economic surplus.

> Potential economic surplus is the difference between the output that *could* be produced in a given natural and technological environment with the help of employable productive resources, and what might be regarded as essential consumption. This . . . refers to a different

*The author gratefully acknowledges the assistance of Nelson Peach, Tom Curtis, and John Piercey of the University of Oklahoma, Norman, in the genesis of this article. This article was first published in the *Review of Radical Political Economics* 6, no. 3 (Fall 1974): 69–74. Copyright by the Union for Radical Political Economics, November 1974.

quantity of output than what would represent surplus value in Marx's sense. On the one hand, it *excludes* such elements of surplus value as ... *essential* outlays on government administration and the like; on the other hand, it comprises what is not covered by the concept of surplus value—the output lost in view of underemployment or misemployment of productive resources.[3]

If we unravel Baran's somewhat tedious working, we find two clear differences between the concept Baran had in mind as here quoted and the concept to be found in the later work done in collaboration with Paul Sweezy.[4] First, the entire public budget is construed as part of the surplus in the later work.[5] This is clearly at odds with the exclusion from the surplus of "*essential*" outlays on government administration.

Moreover, the earlier view of Baran seems to accord more closely with the definition of the surplus given in the later work. Baran and Sweezy give the surplus an introductory "briefest possible definition as the difference between what a society produces and the costs of producing it."[6] If this be the case, then a portion of government expenditures should be included in essential consumption, that is, excluded from the surplus. For example, a portion of educational expenditures is necessary to allow consumption at the socially judged minimal level and to reproduce workers, that is, their children, at the workers' level of skill. Similarly, a portion of the public budget for roads, transportation, and health services should also be considered essential consumption. And, to the extent that government provides elements of essential consumption, general administration of government must be judged essential.

It is curious that the Marxist literature, so convinced of the necessity of socialism, has traditionally neglected the necessity of social consumption. It appears that in driving home the point that the state is an instrument of class struggle, Marxist thought has largely ignored state functions which are necessary costs of production more or less independently of the class struggle. Independently, does not, of course, deny interaction of social consumption and the class struggle. For, albeit that the existence of class relations influences the quality and quantity of social essential consumption, the point is that, however variable, such consumption does exist. One must demand that, in a body of literature so enamored with necessary social costs of production and the economic surplus in excess thereof, attention be given to costs of production which arise in the public sector.

The second difference between Baran and Baran and Sweezy involves the "*essential* consumption of capitalists" referred to by Baran in his earlier work. In the later *Monopoly Capital*, all nonwage, nonsalary income is relegated to the economic surplus. Thus provision is not made for essential consumption of capitalists and rentiers. Nor also, with the inclusion of wages and salaries in surplus industries such as advertising in the surplus, is allowance made for essential consumption of "unproductive" workers.

There is reason for objection to this procedure beyond consistency with Baran's earlier formulation—indeed, consistency with the earlier formulation is desirable only if there is reason to believe that formulation to be superior. I contend that such superiority does exist due to the inoperability of the competitive law of value. As Sweezy has stated, the law of value is one historical means of coordination which is superceded with the advent of conscious planning. "It follows that insofar as the allocation of productive activity is brought under conscious control, the law of value loses its relevance and importance; its place is taken by the principle of planning."[7]

With the rise of monopoly corporatism and Keynesian statism,[8] such a supersession has occurred. The market is no longer an impersonal allocative and distributive device; rather it is an instrument of planning.

> Technically, but only technically, the market mechanism still allocates resources to uses. The underlying reality can be understood best by reference to an example of a planned economy—where the planning authority relies on the market mechanism to allocate resources, but where, also, it substitutes its own preferences for those of the consumer. . . . Suppose now that instead of a public planning authority we are dealing with a huge corporation in private hands that owns (directly or indirectly) all productive units in the economy. Such a super-monopolist has no less power than would the planning authority. . . .
>
> With this interpretation, Galbraith's argument—that in the modern industrial state planning is superseding the market—has an important and revealing meaning. . . .
>
> What is remarkable is that this valuable insight into the workings of contemporary capitalism is shared by so few.[9]

Baran and Sweezy partially recognize the eclipse of the law of value in their discussion of sales effort expenditures and other forms of institutionalized waste.[10] These elements are forms of the surplus which would be minimized in a competitive context. Otherwise, since they could not cut into the subsistence of the productive class, they would have to cut into the unearned incomes of the dominant class. Why then have these activities grown so in the era of monopoly capitalism? Precisely because the law of value is not operative. Wages are not equal to subsistence, nor do the prices of property commodities represent necessary supply prices.

Thus distributive income shares are no longer adequate guides to the economic surplus.[11] This defining away of the relative shares aspect of the surplus should not be interpreted as denying the importance of the surplus in either the analysis of class relations or the inequality of income distribution. The dominant class still appropriates the surplus to its own ends. That is, the surplus is still used in a manner that protects the vested positions of power and prestige in the status quo. Moreover, the distribution of income remains clearly relevant in this distribution of power and prestige. The current analysis simply separates these two important sets of questions rather than lumping them together as the surplus. On the one hand, the surplus measures the amount of output the use of which involves a large element of social choice. On the other hand, the question of the distribution of income and power concerns the manner in which this choice is made and the participants who dominate the process.

Quantification of the Economic Surplus

It is suggested here that the economic surplus be approached from the output rather than the income side. The economic surplus is defined as the difference between potential output and essential consumption. Potential output is the output attainable if productive resources are fully employed. Essential consumption is that consumption necessary to reproduce the extant productive capacity.

Potential output

The new economics of the post-World War II period offers a variety of full-employment output estimates. The author's own method uses the potential output estimate of the Brookings study in the early 1930s as a base.[12] To this base the author applies the growth rates of the potential output series provided by James W. Knowles.[13]

Essential consumption

Essential consumption includes personal essential consumption and social essential consumption. Personal essential consumption is that consumption necessary to provide the entire population with the socially judged minimally adequate consumption. The author

uses the "modest but adequate" budget of the Bureau of Labor
Statistics for minimally adequate consumption. There is ample evidence that this budget is intended to reflect a minimum budget in
terms of prevailing social judgment.

> The budget was designed to represent the estimated dollar cost
> required to maintain the specified family at a level of adequate liv-
> ing—to satisfy prevailing standards of what is necessary. . . .
> The budget represents the annual cost of a worker's family budget
> which includes the kinds and quantities of necessary goods and ser-
> vices, according to standards prevailing in the large cities of the U.S.
> The intention of the budget is to measure the cost of current prices
> in large cities of family living which meet American standards of what
> is required. The budget therefore should represent the necessary
> minimum with respect to items included and their quantities as deter-
> mined by prevailing standards of what is needed for health,
> efficiency, nurture of children, social participation and the mainte-
> nance of self-respect and the respect of others.
> Although the level of living represented by the budget cannot be
> briefly described by words having scientific precision yet, the concept
> of a necessary minimum is a reality. Judgment is constantly being
> expressed as to what is necessary. . . . When it is said that the budget
> recommended is intended to cover the common interpretation as
> including what will meet the conventional and social as well as biolog-
> ical needs. It represents what men commonly expect to enjoy, feel that
> they have lost status and are experiencing deprivation if they cannot
> enjoy, and what they insist upon having. Such a budget is not an
> absolute and unchanging thing. The prevailing judgment of the nec-
> essary will vary with the changing values of the community, with the
> advance of scientific knowledge of human needs, with the productive
> power of the community and therefore what people commonly enjoy
> and see others enjoy.[14]

Social essential consumption includes essential social overhead
consumption and essential capital consumption. The author estimates social overhead consumption by using actual government
expenditures and adjusting them for elements that are either investments or nonessential consumption. Expenditures for general
government, international affairs, civilian safety, sanitation, postal
services, and resource preservation are deemed to be purely essential social overhead expenditures.[15]
Of the remaining expenditures, only those for transportation
and utilities, education, and health and hospitals are considered to
involve elements of essential social overhead consumption. However, each group also includes elements of investment, and therefore not essential consumption. That is, some of the expenditures
are necessary to maintain the existing productive capacity; some

serve to increase this capacity. Hence, each must be adjusted according to the consumption/investment distinction.

This adjustment is made in different ways for each. For transportation and public utilities, changes in constant dollar GNP are used to make the adjustment. The rationale for this procedure is that of technical proportionality. Given some increase in physical production, it may be supposed that a roughly proportionate increase occurs in the facilities for transporting this produce. Since several means of transport are involved, there is some room for technical change and varying proportions in this procedure, for example, the shift from rail to air transport.

The application of this proportionality assumption is somewhat more dubious with respect to public utilities output. However, this is mitigated by the small volume of expenditures net of revenue for public utilities.

The adjustment of educational expenditures is made using changes in the level of educational attainment of labor-force participants. The reasoning involved is that the size and educational levels of the labor force at the beginning of a period are part of the productive plant and must be maintained. The labor force is used rather than the population as a whole because educational expenditures on those persons not entering the labor force are properly considered a part of the surplus.

The adjustment for expenditures on health and hospitals is a difficult one. Clearly expenditures increasing the level of health of the work force is investment whereas expenditures to maintain health are essential consumption. Due to the lack of a more appropriate indicator, the author uses changes in the volume of hospital admissions to make this adjustment.

For all these cases, the 1929-70 period is arbitrarily divided into two subperiods, 1929-50 and 1950-70. Ratios are then formed with the subperiod beginning and ending magnitudes of each of the indicators—constant dollar GNP, educational attainment and size of the labor force, and hospital admissions. Each ratio is then applied to the appropriate expenditures for the appropriate subperiod to separate essential consumption and investment elements.

Essential capital consumption is based upon physical obsolescence rather than technological or economic obsolescence.[16] Economic obsolescence involves instances in which a capital good is discarded not because it is worn out nor because an alternative is more efficient, but because demand shifts or demographic changes have led to a decline in the need for output. Economic obsolescence is thus due largely to the anarchic "competitive waste" of the capitalist system; such phenomena as capacity expansion in the fact of declining capacity utilization.[17] It is thus placed in the economic surplus.[18] Technological obsolescence is also placed in the economic surplus. It is so placed inasmuch as it is clearly a part of capacity-increasing investment.

The method used to estimate essential capital consumption concentrates largely upon avoiding the distortion caused by legal changes associated with taxation. The method and data provided by Allan H. Young are used.[19] Of various alternative methods provided by Young, the one used is that designated "historical cost, straight line, F service lives." Historical cost refers to original cost and straight line to one of several accounting methods for the treatment of depreciation. The term *F service lives* refers to the schedule of service lives of capital goods, as periodically published by the Internal Revenue Service.[20]

Young's data are for nonfinancial corporations, omitting other businesses and residential structures. Thus, to get figures relevant to the current study, his figures are divided by the Office of Business Economics nonfinancial corporate depreciation figures. Then, this ratio is applied to OBE's total depreciation figures to estimate the relevant depreciation magnitudes.

These three elements—essential personal consumption, essential social overhead consumption, and essential capital consumption—are then summed to form total essential consumption.

Surplus Elements Imbedded in Market Prices

Before subtracting essential consumption from potential output to form the economic surplus, it is necessary to adjust both the consumption and the output series. This adjustment is made necessary by the existence of surplus elements imbedded in market prices that are of such a nature as to be not amenable to direct exclusion in the simple manner of excluding payroll taxes, life insurance premiums, and governmental transfer payments. The later elements are simply deducted from the BLS's budget estimates.[21]

The imbedded surplus elements are of two types. Type one involves surplus income elements: profits, government revenues not previously omitted, rent, and interest. Type two involves the output of surplus industries (net of type one elements in these industries): advertising, finance, insurance, and real estate. These two types are summed and their ratio to GNP for a given year is used to delete them from the essential consumption figure for that year.

Table 1
The Economic Surplus, Annually, 1929-70 (in billions of 1958 dollars)

Year	Potential GNP	Actual GNP	Essential consumption	Economic surplus[a]
1929	$147.0	$123.4	90.1	56.9
1930	155.0	110.1	89.9	65.1
1931	160.3	103.8	92.4	67.9
1932	158.7	87.5	91.0	67.7
1933	161.0	86.7	89.8	71.2
1934	162.3	94.3	87.9	74.4
1935	165.1	103.1	88.7	76.4
1936	171.6	119.3	93.7	77.9
1937	175.5	125.0	96.0	79.5
1938	179.2	117.5	97.3	81.9
1939	185.7	128.4	102.5	83.2
1940	187.6	136.8	100.2	87.4
1941	194.1	159.3	97.5	96.6
1942	208.9	185.8	105.1	103.8
1943	227.9	219.8	106.3	121.6
1944	246.2	243.2	108.8	137.4
1945	257.2	242.2	108.9	148.3
1946	253.7	208.5	104.3	149.4
1947	253.4	203.0	107.1	146.3
1948	252.9	206.8	108.9	144.0
1949	265.2	208.4	114.7	150.5
1950	266.8	221.7	117.7	149.1
1951	282.2	243.5	125.1	157.1
1952	297.6	254.0	135.4	162.2
1953	311.9	267.1	143.9	168.0
1954	320.8	260.1	149.1	171.7
1955	329.0	274.6	153.1	175.9
1956	346.6	280.2	158.6	188.0
1957	362.7	284.2	162.7	200.0
1958	376.1	281.8	168.9	207.2
1959	385.2	294.6	171.8	213.4
1960	396.4	301.9	178.8	217.6
1961	409.0	306.3	184.9	224.1
1962	418.7	322.6	189.3	229.4
1963	430.3	333.4	195.0	235.3
1964	441.4	348.0	200.3	241.1
1965	456.5	368.6	206.0	250.5
1966	474.7	394.9	212.1	262.6
1967	500.3	410.5	217.4	282.9
1968	519.4	428.9	226.0	293.4
1969	547.3	445.7	233.4	313.9
1970	573.8	446.4	273.2	336.6

[a] The economic surplus is calculated using potential GNP and essential consumption.

Source: Ron Stanfield, *The Economic Surplus and Neo-Marxism* (Lexington, MA: Heath Books, 1973), tables 5-15, 7-5, and 7-6.

The adjustment of potential output follows the same procedure except that only type-one elements are deleted. This follows from an important distinction between type-one and type-two elements. Type-two elements represent resources which could be used to produce output other than the sales effort and other middling activities. On the other hand, the type-one elements are solely of income distributive interest. They represent income transfers, not productive resources. Hence, only type-one elements need be deleted from potential output whereas both types need to be deleted from essential consumption.

Table 1 gives the author's estimates of potential GNP, essential consumption, and the economic surplus. In addition, for purposes of comparison, an actual GNP series is included. The actual GNP series has been adjusted for type-one imbedded surplus elements in order that it be consistent with the author's series.

Notes

1. Paul A. Baran, *The Political Economy of Growth* (New York: Monthly Review Press, 1957), ch. 2; Paul A. Baran and Paul M. Sweezy, *Monopoly Capital* (New York: Monthly Review Press, 1966).
2. The sole exception is the appended table giving the author's estimates of the economic surplus for the period 1929-70. This table and the specific details of its derivation can be found in my book, *The Economic Surplus and Neo-Marxism* (Lexington, MA.: Heath Books, 1973).
3. Baran, *Political Economy of Growth,* pp. 23 and 23n (italics in original).
4. Baran and Sweezy, *Monopoly Capital.* The differences are even more clear given the statistical appendix to *Monopoly Capital* provided by Joseph Phillips.
5. Ibid., ch. 6 and p. 370.
6. Ibid., p. 9.
7. Paul M. Sweezy, *The Theory of Capitalist Development* (New York: Monthly Review Press, 1968), pp. 52-53.
8. A good description of the contours of this developing system is John Kenneth Galbraith, *The New Industrial State* (Boston: Houghton Mifflin, 1967).
9. Andreas G. Papandreou, *Paternalistic Capitalism* (Minneapolis: University of Minnesota Press, 1972), pp. 78-80.
10. Baran and Sweezy, *Monopoly Capital,* pp. 113-14.
11. Further ramifications of the inoperability of the law of value for neo-Marxist analysis are developed in the author's "Limited Capitalism and neo-Marxism" (unpublished).
12. Edwin G. Nourse and Associates, *America's Capacity to Produce* (Washington, D.C.: The Brookings Institution, 1934), pp. 416-22.
13. U.S. Congress, Joint Economic Committee, *The Potential Economic Growth in the United States,* by James W. Knowles, Joint Committee Print, Study Paper 20 (Washington, D.C.: GPO, 1960), p. 40.
14. U.S. Department of Labor, Bureau of Labor Statistics, *Workers' Budgets in the U.S.: City Families and Single Persons, 1946 and 1947,* bulletin 927 (Washington, D.C.: GPO, 1948), pp. 3-7.
15. The expenditures for resource preservation are included to approximate natural resource depletion.
16. Cf. Royall Brandis, "Obsolescence and Investment," *Journal of Economic Issues* 1 (September 1967): 169-72.
17. Cf. J. Steindl, *Maturity and Stagnation in American Capitalism* (New York: Monthly Review Press, 1952), pp. 4-14.
18. This is perhaps inconsistent with the decision not to deal with Baran's "planned economic surplus."
19. Allan H. Young, "Alternative Estimates of Corporate Depreciation and Profits: Parts I and II," *Survey of Current Business* 43 (April 1968): 17-28, and (May 1968): 16-28.
20. The schedule used is the one found in U.S. Treasury Department, Internal Revenue Service, bulletin F (revised January 1942), *Income*

Tax Depreciation and Obsolescence, Estimated Useful Lives and Depreciation Rates (Washington, D.C.: GPO, 1942).

21. These elements are omitted because they are provided under essential social overhead consumption. It would be double counting to include them in the personal figures as well.

Henryk Szlajfer

ECONOMIC SURPLUS AND SURPLUS VALUE UNDER MONOPOLY CAPITALISM

> . . . the production of relative surplus
> value, i.e., production of surplus value
> based on the increase and develop-
> ment of the productive forces . . . re-
> quires that the consuming circle within
> circulation expands . . .
> —Karl Marx, *Grundrisse* (New York:
> Vintage, 1973), p. 408.

1. Introduction

When Paul A. Baran introduced the concept of "economic surplus" in *The Political Economy of Growth,* the majority of Marxist
economists accepted his use of the term. Their willing acceptance
was due to the difficulties which had been associated with the use of
the category "surplus value" in analyzing the growth of underdeveloped capitalist economies and precapitalist modes of production.[1]

The category of economic surplus as presented jointly by Baran
and Paul Sweezy in *Monopoly Capital* was received quite differently.
The book was criticized principally because it "departed" from
Marxist tradition by introducing the new analytical category instead of the usual concept of surplus value.[2]

The widespread disapproval of the economic surplus concept,
introduced by Baran and Sweezy might be attributed to certain

This is a revised and extended version of an article that appeared in the
Review of Radical Political Economics 15, no. 1 (Spring 1983). Copyright by
the Union for Radical Political Economics, Winter 1982. It is based on an
earlier manuscript by the author: *Economic Surplus and Surplus Value: An
Attempt at Comparison* (University of Dar es Salaam, Economic Research
Bureau, Occasional Paper 78.3, August 1979).

differences in construction, when compared with Baran's original concept. It seems, however, that this cannot fully explain the enormous contrast in the reactions of Marxists in the two cases, especially in view of the secondary character of the differences in formulation. The fundamental methodological premises from which the two versions of economic surplus stemmed were identical. Thus we can only presume that the almost simultaneous reception of the concept of economic surplus as "innovation" and "heresy" resulted from a basic misunderstanding with respect to the underlying meaning of this category.

To be sure, the peculiar manner in which the economic surplus category was received does not relieve its authors of responsibility for at least some of the confusion provoked. It is true that the notion of economic surplus was neither precisely nor clearly presented in either *Monopoly Capital* or *The Political Economy of Growth.* Moreover, this category raises many doubts and objections from the point of view of Marx's labor theory of value and its leading category, surplus value. And it seems that Baran and Sweezy had not fully perceived all of the theoretical implications. It goes without saying that the salient aspects of the concept of economic surplus should be subjected to critical analysis.

Thus the main subject of this essay is the relationship between economic surplus and surplus value in the context of the actual functioning of modern monopoly capitalism. In my opinion, this approach can help clarify certain theoretical problems in relation to both Marx's theory of value and the laws of motion of monopoly capitalism. This would include such problems as the distinction between productive and nonproductive labor under monopoly capitalism; the role of nonproductive labor in the accumulation of capital; and the appropriate methodology for a critique of the capitalist mode of production.

However, the analysis of the relation between economic surplus and surplus value should not be limited merely to pointing out the basic differences. It seems necessary to go beyond pure "comparative analysis" in order to delineate certain significant determinants of the dynamics of accumulation under monopoly capitalism. Only in such a dynamic context is it possible to appreciate the importance of the category of economic surplus and to understand its place *within* the Marxian theory of capitalist development. That is why I have included in my essay a discussion of the relationship between capital accumulation (and the level of the rate of profit) and nonproductive labor. I think that unless this question is answered, any consideration of the category of economic surplus will lead to further confusion and misunderstandings. The same applies to the discussion on some basic assumptions of the Marxian "cognitive perspective" (paradigm). However, I have refrained from discussing here the problem of productive and nonproductive labor under monopoly capitalism, since I have dealt with this in detail elsewhere.[3]

2. *Baran's Contribution: Economic Surplus and New Questions*

The introduction by Baran of the categories of "actual," "potential," and "planned" economic surpluses was, first of all, an attempt to create instruments for the practical analysis of the problem of growth, both in developed and underdeveloped capitalist countries. Baran's main aim was to show that the rate of growth achieved was but a fraction of the capacities created by the current level of development of productive forces. As he put it in a letter to Sweezy, "in addition to what imperialism does, one should consider and indeed emphasize what its role is in *prevention* of what needs to be done."[4] The consequence of this kind of approach was not only the creation of new categories, but also the formulation of new questions addressed to Marx's economic theory.

Let us begin by quoting Baran's basic definitions. (1) "Actual economic surplus" is "the difference between society's *actual* current output and its *actual* current consumption." (2) "Potential economic surplus" is "the difference between the output that *could* be produced in a given natural and technological environment with the help of employable productive resources, and what might be regarded as essential consumption." (3) "Planned economic surplus" is "the difference between society's 'optimum' output attainable in a historically given natural and technological environment under conditions of planned 'optimal' utilization of all available productive resources, and some chosen 'optimal' volume of consumption."[5]

Taking into account Baran's indications, it is possible to define actual, potential, and optimal production as the actual, potential, and optimal national income (net production), which in Marxian terminology is described as $V + M$.[6] The actual, necessary, and optimal consumption consists of two components: the consumption of productive workers (V) and the consumption of capitalists, government, nonproductive workers, and so on financed from M. Thus the general scheme for the calculation of different types of economic surplus is presented in Figure 1.

Applying Marxian notation, we can describe the transition from

Figure 1. *Calculation of Economic Surplus*

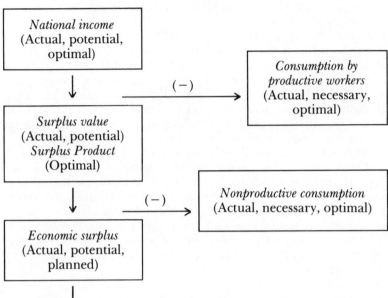

net production to economic surplus as follows: $(V + M) - V = M$; $M - Mo = Mc + Mv$. Thus the actual, potential, and planned economic surplus corresponds to the actual, potential, and planned accumulation fund.

This formal scheme can be enriched by accepting Bettelheim's realistic assumption that, from the point of view of the practical experience of economic growth, actual surplus should be treated as merely "available." The reason is that the surplus that can be used for development is not necessarily used for this purpose.[7] It is thus possible that a posteriori the difference $M - Mo$ is expressed by $Mcy + Mvy + Moy$, where Moy can be described as those losses in the actual economic surplus which result from the fact that a part of the surplus is transformed not into additional productive capital

---

*In this and subsequent parts of the essay I will follow the accepted Marxian notation: C = constant capital; V = variable capital; M = surplus value; Mc = accumulation of means of production; Mv = accumulation of means of consumption; Mo = nonproductive consumption of surplus value.

but rather into nonproductive forms of national wealth (e.g., surplus transformed into a gold hoard). Thus we obtain the concept of "actual surplus used for development": $M - Mo = Mcy + Mvy + Moy$, and therefore $(Mcy + Mvy) < (Mc + Mv)$.

So much for the basic definitions. Their interpretation and critical analysis should begin with a recognition of the fact that Baran discusses the various forms of surplus "in terms of comparative statics," that is, he does not consider the mechanism which causes the transition from actual to either potential or planned surplus or vice versa.[8] Such a procedure enables him to make more precise the conceptual range of these categories, and thus the definition of their elements.

The concepts of actual and planned surpluses do not cause any serious problems of interpretation, especially as far as their different structures are concerned.[9] The first category covers the sum of profits after the payment of dividends and taxes and corresponds to savings which can be transformed into productive investment. The second category describes the net investment in the economy where the immediate goal is use value in general, and where economic activity is planned on a macroscale.

The category of potential surplus, however, does cause serious problems of interpretation, especially as far as its relation to planned surplus is concerned. According to Baran, the potential surplus is larger than the actual one if the following elements are taken into consideration: (1) the possibility of limiting ruling class consumption in capitalist society, as well as that of the "middle class" therein, and thus a limit to nonproductive individual consumption Mo; (2) conceivable limitations on the number of nonproductive workers, and transfer of part of them to productive activities, so that here again national income $(V + M)$ grows; (3) the possibility of additional production through liquidation of losses connected with the wasteful organization of the actual production apparatus (growth of M); and the potential creation of additional production through elimination of unemployment (growth of $V + M$).[10]

Thus the transition from actual to potential surplus means simultaneously an enlargement of the accumulation fund and a change of the product mix. This corresponds to Baran's definition of productive and nonproductive labor, which mixes, to some extent, the point of view of global capital and that of socialist rationality. First, he states that if the result of labor is a good actually transformed into a physical element of the accumulation fund, the labor is productive. Second, he also states that if a given good is produced merely because the existing socioeconomic system so requires, the labor spent is of an unproductive character.[11] It is clear that to identify the greater part of the elements of potential surplus mentioned above requires a combined application of criteria of both productive and nonproductive labor.

However, this approach practically eliminates the qualitative distinction between potential and planned surplus. To make this point clear, let us take a closer look at the logic of Baran's argument.

During a "state of emergency" (e.g., war), the problem of economic surplus appears as a need to transform a maximum part of M into $Mc + Mv$, and therefore as a necessity to minimize the losses in $V + M$ resulting from the anarchy of production and from Mo. The market mechanism and interests of individual capitalists are subordinated to that of the class of capitalists as a whole. Thus during the "state of emergency," a negative correlation also occurs: as Mo approaches its maximum limit, $Mc + Mv$ tends to its minimum and vice versa.

How are things during peace time? At this point, Baran emphasizes that the estimation of losses within $V + M$ and $Mc + Mv$ must be made from the point of view of socialist rationality, which "tolerates" as necessary—because we are analyzing the capitalist economy—the incomes of capitalists. Why, however, does he not say that we should analyze these losses from the point of view of the reproduction of global capital? This latter point of view contains, as implied by Marx's theory of productive and nonproductive labor (applied to competitive capitalism), the possibility of capital's "self-criticism." This states, among other things, that when the problem of discrepancy between the accumulation of individual and global capital appears, then the above-mentioned negative correlation is one of the most fundamental criteria by which productive and nonproductive labor may be distinguished.[12]

Baran does not discuss this problem: he just points out that under monopoly capitalism the negative correlation between nonproductive labor and production of surplus value is not the only significant one. He assumes that within certain limits, when Mo approaches its maximum, $Mc + Mv$ also tends to its maximum. In this situation, the definition of productive and nonproductive labor from the standpoint of global capital becomes more complicated, as well as insufficient.

Of course, Baran is right in indicating that under monopoly capital the correlation between nonproductive labor and the growth of surplus value can be positive within certain limits (I discuss this below), and this is not the object of my doubts at the moment. The problem lies in his presentation of potential surplus which, if applied to normal conditions of the operation of capitalism, differs both in quantity and structure ("quality") from actual surplus. The quantitative difference consists in pointing out the discrepancy between $V + M$ that can be and is actually produced. The qualitative difference follows from contrasting the physical structure of $V + M$ in societies that seek to maximize either the use-effect or profit.

This way, the basic logic of the category of planned surplus inheres in the category of potential surplus, and thus the difference between these categories becomes obscure and difficult to grasp. I do not think one can build two different categories based on one and the same criterion (socialist rationality). To be sure, Baran stresses "the economic surplus under socialism may be smaller or larger than the actual economic surplus under capitalism, or may even be equal to zero if society should choose to refrain from net investment."[13] But this at best introduces the quantitative difference between planned and potential economic surplus.

What is the way out of this situation? I think it necessitates a reinterpretation of the category of potential surplus. This category should be transformed into an instrument for the critique of capitalist society from the point of view of capital. This will allow us, on the one hand, to grasp the principal differences between planned surplus and its other forms, and, on the other hand, to understand not only the logic of accumulation of monopoly capital from the point of view of its own criteria but also the social and political consequences of this logic. Baran's statement that "the exercise of self-criticism is just as onerous to a ruling class as it is to a single individual" should not be made absolute. A certain kind of "constructive self-criticism" is always acceptable to both the ruling class and the individual because its object is the greater effectiveness of one's own activities, in terms of both domination and less dubious criteria. The critique of capital from its own point of view is an example of this type of "self-criticism." This means that the point of reference for calculating potential surplus now becomes potential surplus value, and not the surplus product of a future socialist economy with the product mix specific thereof. The only reflection of this potentiality is the discrepancy that exists between the national income achieved while fully utilizing the stock of productive capital and the available humanpower, on the one hand, and the national income really achieved, on the other. We do not formulate any a priori postulates concerning this income's physical structure.

Transformation of the category of potential surplus in this direction opens up the possibility of analyzing waste (nonproductive labor) from the point of view of capital and the process of its accumulation. At the same time, this transformation creates the necessary element for the development of a more general critique of monopoly capitalism that is based on the category of planned surplus and socialist rationality.[14] In a later part of this essay, I shall try to demonstrate that the explicit introduction of this second-level critique is necessary under conditions of monopoly capitalism, in view of the considerable impairment of the critical outlook inherent in global capital's own limited point of view. Under competitive capitalism, this point of view played the role of a sui generis external point of reference. It is in this sense also that Baran's insight, that the analysis of new forms of waste requires a new definition of productive and nonproductive labor, proves correct.

3. Economic Surplus and Surplus Value: An Introduction

In *The Political Economy of Growth* the category of economic surplus was identical with the concept of the accumulation fund. In Baran and Sweezy's *Monopoly Capital,* the point of reference of the category of economic surplus is surplus value directly. What is more, Baran and Sweezy explicitly declare that their notion of economic surplus is by no means a revision of Marx's category but merely a change of a terminological nature, dictated by, one may presume, didactic motives.[15]

This statement of Baran and Sweezy's threw Marxists into confusion—and not without reason. As a matter of fact, the authors of *Monopoly Capital,* with the help of Baran's definition of productive and nonproductive labor, showed *practically* the limitations of the traditional calculus of surplus value under capitalism. They also reminded their readers—once again practically, and not in a theoretical discourse—of the need to return to the most elementary rules on which Marx's critique of capitalism had been constructed. Still a decade ahead of the currently fashionable "back to Marx" trend, they did it in a manner shocking to present-day "purists," without falling to their knees before any comma or full stop that Marx had put in *Das Kapital.* I shall try to show that despite what Baran and Sweezy claim, their concept of economic surplus is in fact something more than a mere change of terminology, as well as to indicate the theoretical implications of their approach, and its usefulness.

Michele Salvati points out that the category of economic surplus is defined in *Monopoly Capital* in various ways; at the same time he states that the "multiplicity . . . of definitions is a result of objective obstacles of that analytical category: there is no simple definition."[16] No doubt, this is a correct remark. Still, it should be completed by the observation that the multiplicity of definitions does not necessitate "a mess," as Otto Nathan seems to suggest; Baran and Sweezy attempted to present a "final" version of the economic surplus.[17]

It is possible, I believe, not only to reconstruct the logical arrangement of particular definitions as they appear in *Monopoly Capital* but also to indicate the "final" definition. Let us point out that in the first two chapters of their book, the authors use the simplest form of surplus, that is, the concept of profits as indicated by national income statistics. In chapters 3 and 4 they remark that the surplus also includes ground rent, interest, and a part of over-extended depreciation funds. The specific form of the surplus is also embodied in unemployed labor and underutilized productive capital. In chapter 5 they present two further components of surplus: expenditures of the nonproductive sphere and "selling costs." And in the last chapter they include in the surplus state expenditures covered by corporate taxes. Thus the multiplicity of definitions does not mean a lack of logic, but results from the authors' method of handling the problem. They start from the simplest forms and pass on to more complicated ones. The final definition of the economic surplus is given in the statistical appendix, worked out by J. D. Phillips.

The fact that the category of economic surplus from *Monopoly Capital* refers directly to that of surplus value and to all its components is the result of Baran and Sweezy's conception of the main subject of research. They formulate it as the "generation and absorption of the surplus under conditions of monopoly capitalism." They then add:

> We believe that this is the most useful and enlightening way to analyze the purely economic functioning of the system. But, no less important, we also believe that the modes of utilization of surplus constitute the indispensable mechanism linking the economic foundation of society with what Marxists call its political, cultural and ideological superstructure. In some societies this mechanism is relatively simple and its effects easily accessible to analysis. . . . In other societies the connecting mechanism between economic and noneconomic phenomena is vastly most complicated and may come to play an important role in the functioning of both the foundation and the superstructure. We believe that monopoly capitalism is a society of the latter type and that any attempt to understand it which omits or slights the modes of utilization of surplus is bound to fail.[18]

In this perspective, of crucial importance to the reproduction of the system as a whole is not only the accumulation fund ($Mc + Mv$) but also the size and structure of nonproductive labor (Mo). On the other hand, however, it should be noted that Baran and Sweezy paid much greater attention to the analysis of the process of utiliz-

ing the economic surplus than to that of its production.[19] The production of surplus has been shifted onto a more distant plane. In
consequence Baran and Sweezy did not notice that their category
necessitates a reinterpretation of the concept of surplus value. The
concept of economic surplus includes elements that are uncovered
by even the most broadly interpreted category of produced and
realized surplus value. Thus the authors of *Monopoly Capital* did not
explicitly formulate the need to reinterpret the theory of productive and nonproductive labor, or the necessity of precisely rede-
fining the methodological aspect in studies of modern capitalism.

However, before we analyze the category of economic surplus as
formulated in *Monopoly Capital*, it seems necessary to return to
certain questions that arose from the analysis of Baran's category of
potential surplus. The main issue is the problem of the new role of
nonproductive labor in the process of capital accumulation.

The opinion that under monopoly capitalism the role of nonproductive labor is qualitatively different from the role it fulfilled
in competitive capitalism is a subject of heated discussions among
Marxists. Some authors firmly deny any need to change the standpoint saying, among other things, that as far as value relations and
profit determinants are concerned, the problem of nonproductive
labor is identical in both forms of capitalism. Others claim that a
theoretical analysis of the growth of monopoly capitalism is inconceivable without consideration of the new role of nonproductive
labor. Here I would like to present briefly some theses concerning
the relationship between nonproductive labor and the volume and
rate of profit in two models of capitalism. I believe that a consideration of this question will enable us to understand why the
introduction of the category of economic surplus has become necessary. The new role of nonproductive labor as well as its new
forms are the direct result of the way in which monopoly capital
overcomes the barriers of accumulation—the barriers it has raised
itself. In this sense, the category of surplus can be justified inasmuch as monopoly capital does indeed modify the conditions of
extended reproduction of capital.

4. Nonproductive Labor and the Rate of Profit in Two Models of Capitalism

Three theses can be formulated concerning the role of nonproductive labor in the Marxian theory of relative prices and accumulation (the "quantitative aspect" of the labor theory of value).
They can be stated as follows: (1) nonproductive labor is an alterna-

tive to expenditures on productive labor; (2) nonproductive labor plays a passive role when determining the level of production and profits; and (3) the level of the rate of profit is mainly determined by conditions of production for those goods which are consumed by productive workers.

In the conditions described by these theses one observes a direct relationship between Marx's theory of value (and abstract labor) and the theory of relative prices (prices of production). As Soviet economist A. A. Konius points out, the "laws of the labor theory of value are realized not automatically but only when in the national economy surplus value reaches its maximum and when each particular enterprise also tends to achieve the highest profit, and the rate of profit in all enterprises is identical."[20] Alfredo Medio, in turn, defines the assumptions under which this relationship holds (the so-called transformation problem) as follows:[21] (1) the technical conditions of production are given; (2) only "basic products" affect the level of the rate of profit and relative prices;[22] (3) it is possible to construct an "average commodity" whose price of production is equal to its value, and the organic composition of capital necessary for producing this commodity is average; and (4) the average rate of profit (π) is calculated as a relation $\tau/w + 1$, where τ = the rate of surplus value produced by global capital and w = the organic composition of capital in the economy as a whole.[23]

The above assumptions are useful not only for devising a solution to the "transformation problem." They also make it possible to indicate with greater precision the role of nonproductive labor in the process of capital accumulation, and to define the level of the rate of profit in a model of competitive capitalism.

A conclusion of many solutions of the "transformation problem" is that in both Marxian and Ricardian (or neo-Ricardian) theory nonproductive labor plays a purely passive role. For example, in the famous von Bortkiewicz equation, describing the factors affecting the level of the rate of profit, the output of the sector producing luxury goods ("nonbasic products" in Sraffa's terminology) does not exert any influence on the determination of the level of that rate.[24] Medio also comes to the same conclusion:

> Equilibrium in the production of non-basic commodities will be reached through an adjustment of their prices with respect to the prices of other commodities. An obvious consequence . . . is that the organic composition of non-basic commodities does not play a part in determining the "average" organic composition of capital.[25]

Thus, in the model of competitive capitalism, where the propensity to transform surplus value into productive investment is extremely high (there is a tendency to achieve the maximum level of production), the level of the rate of profit is determined by the wage level of productive workers (the technical conditions of production being given). In other words, assuming given capital intensity (and productivity of labor) and a tendency toward full capacity utilization, the rate of profit is a function of the rate of surplus value. Sraffa writes it down as a linear function: $r = R(1 - w)$; where r = the rate of profit in the economy as a whole, R = the maximum rate of profit (when wages = 0), and w = the share of wages in the product.[26]

This function not only points to the negative correlation between the rate of profit and wages but it is at the same time a record of a definite theory of distribution. The theory postulates that if the level of wages as well as the technical conditions are given, then the level and rate of profit and relative prices that set the distribution of global surplus value among capitals of various size are also given.

It is clear that in this theory, nonproductive labor, as well as playing a passive role, is also an alternative to productive labor. Marx stated it explicitly: "My power to employ *productive laborers* by no means grows in the same proportion as I employ *unproductive laborers,* but on the contrary diminishes in the same proportion."[27] Hence, under conditions where both the share of global surplus value in the product and its volume are determined by the capacity of the system to transform the maximum part of profits into additional *productive capital,* the tendency to minimize nonproductive labor is a structural feature of production as a whole.

Under conditions of monopoly capital the theses concerning the role of nonproductive labor can be formulated as follows: (1) nonproductive labor is a *complementary* way of using up surplus value; and (2) nonproductive labor performs an active role in defining the general level of production, and, more specifically, the level of the rate of profit is determined by both the conditions of producing goods consumed by productive workers, and by the general dimensions of effective demand.

At the same time let us stress that none of Medio's assumptions are fulfilled. We are unable to present the technical conditions as data since under monopoly capital the choice of technology depends directly on corporate policy. Moreover, the concept of the "average rate of profit" becomes obscure because of the permanent and considerable differentiation of rates of profit. And last but not least, we are unable to give the notion of "average commodity" (that plays the important role of numeraire in the "transformation problem") any essential meaning. As a result, it seems that the Marxian theory of relative prices ceases to have any cognitive value.[28]

Should we thus totally reject the Marxian labor theory of value, including its "qualitative aspect" as well? I do not think so.

More than thirty years ago Joan Robinson wrote: "It is necessary . . . to supply a theory of the rate of profit based on the principle of effective demand."[29] She was not quite correct. In light of conclusions from the discussion of Sraffa's book, and of neoclassical theories of capital and distribution, it seems necessary to construct a theory of profit and relative prices based on both the theory of effective demand and Marx's theory of exploitation. If the model of monopoly capitalism, showing an equilibrium with simultaneous unemployment and underutilization of constant capital, destroys the neoclassical theory of relative prices and distribution, that is, destroys, in effect, "economic theory" as a whole, then within the Marxian labor theory of value the main result of this model is the loss of the timeliness of the "quantitative aspect" of the labor theory of value.[30] The "qualitative aspect" of this theory, pointing to the sources of profit and surplus value, remains valid.[31] It also constitutes a necessary element of a possible new "quantitative" theory of profit and prices that would fulfill the conditions of monopoly capitalism.

Yet, why should we bring in the principle of effective demand at all? (If the Marxist "purists" are shocked by the term "effective demand," let us reformulate this problem in the following way: the question is to consider the fact that it is only in the dubious context of "Say's Law" and the competitive model that the difference between surplus value produced and surplus value realized is equal to zero.)

As has been demonstrated by Michal Kalecki, Josef Steindl, and Paolo Sylos-Labini, under monopoly conditions where profit margins tend to be rigid, there is a tendency to shift income not from wages onto profits but from potential workers' income onto excess capacity. Thus the shift finds its expression in the growth of unemployment and in underutilization of productive resources.[32] In this situation, with the "degree of monopoly" given, the volume and rate of profit are determined by both the rate of exploitation and the conditions of realization of production, that is, by effective demand. Accordingly, with a given theoretical distribution of the national income between wages and profits (the theoretical rate of profit), the actual rate of profit can even be negative. Nobuo Okishio hits the nail on the head, writing:

> A positive rate of exploitation is merely a necessary condition of the existence of positive profits. Because the positiveness of the rate of exploitation only assures the production of surplus, it does not imply its conversion into monetary form. For this, the existence of sufficient

demand is required. A positive rate of exploitation is the necessary condition on the production side.[33]

That is why it seems obvious that in a system where both the volume and the level of the rate of profit are regulated *ceteris paribus* by two variables, the thesis that they are determined only by conditions of production of wage goods is insufficient. It allows us merely to understand and calculate the theoretical rate of profit while it leaves the actual rate of profit still undetermined.

In this new structural context, the role played by nonproductive labor starts to be more complicated. In a model of capitalism characterized by chronic underutilization of the productive capital and by inability to induce the production of economic surplus by means of classical instruments (capitalists' consumption and their productive investment together with the consumption of productive workers), the role of nonproductive labor has to be radically different from its role in the competitive model. What is more, nonproductive labor can no longer be treated as a sort of residual. It should be put, just like monopoly, in the very center of economic analysis. The "nonbasic products" enter the model of monopoly capitalism with the same rights as "basic products" do, determining both the general level of production and the volume and rate of profit.[34]

Marx neither considered nor could foretell such a role for nonproductive labor in his magnum opus. But what really matters today is not so much a "pure" critique of Marx's approach to the problem, but a positive overcoming of its limitations. Thus, to what degree have Marxist economists considered this important change in the role of nonproductive labor in the functioning of modern capitalism?

The answer is brief: to a barely perceptible degree. As a matter of fact, if we do not count works by Rosa Luxemburg, Kalecki, and Baran and Sweezy, only Joseph Gillman has attempted to point to the role of nonproductive labor in determining the rate of profit in monopoly capitalism.[35] Yet Gillman's attempt was a limited one for two reasons: (1) he did not present a satisfactory explanation of the principles governing the economic mechanism which would make it necessary to consider nonproductive labor in calculating the rate of profit; and (2) he did not consider the necessity of taking into account, in the theory of monopoly profit, the existence of nonproductive labor as a factor positively influencing the rate of profit.[36]

According to Gillman, the rate of profit in the economy as a whole can be calculated as $P = S - U/(C + V + U)$; where $S =$

surplus value (flow), C = constant capital (stock), V = variable capital (stock), and U = nonproductive expenditures (stock).

Such a formulation is made ex post, where the maximum volume of surplus value is given and where there appears only the problem of its distribution into productive labor, nonproductive labor, and profits. Gillman's equation explicitly assumes a negative correlation between the rate of profit in the economy as a whole and the sum total of nonproductive expenditures. This kind of correlation is valid, however, only in circumstances where the productive potential is fully utilized. Then, indeed, every increase of U causes a decrease of P, both absolutely and relatively. But Gillman's equation does not show how under monopoly capitalism the global surplus value is determined by nonproductive labor, or how this labor, through the multiplier mechanism, makes possible a transformation of the theoretical rate of profit into an actual one.

However, in the above equation, there is an implicit observation that under monopoly capitalism nonproductive labor can no longer be excluded from our considerations when calculating the level of the rate of profit—at least for purely quantitative reasons. This simultaneously contradicts the conclusion that was formulated in relation to the model of competitive capitalism.

In a dynamic formulation, when we assume a variable degree of utilization of capital stock, the rate of profit is positively correlated with the level of U, up to the moment of achieving equilibrium between potential and actual degrees of utilization of capital stock. In other words, the volume of surplus value and the actual rate of profit are to a certain extent so correlated that when U approaches its maximum value, P also is at its maximum. Within these limits, to be sure, an increase of U results in a relative decrease of P (in relation to the rate of profit that could be hypothetically achieved with no nonproductive labor), but at the same time it causes its absolute growth.

Using Sraffa's equation in a modified form, we can write $P = \lambda\,[R(1 - w)]$; where λ = the output/capital ratio.

This equation indicates that the level of the actual rate of profit depends *ceteris paribus* on the rate of surplus value (here the most important role is played by the "degree of monopoly") and the degree of utilization of capital stock. However, the factors that affect λ and allow its maximization are usually at variance with the tendency to increase $(1 - w)$. This variance appears as an absence of effective demand ("markets"). Within monopoly capitalism, a growth of nonproductive labor as the method to maximize λ becomes the solution.[37]

These substantial changes in the theoretical approach to the role played by nonproductive labor, where monopoly capitalism is concerned, have been the focus of sharp criticism by Ernest Mandel. Therefore it seems essential to provide a brief consideration of his critique.

The following contains the essence of Mandel's critical remarks:

> The labor theory of value implies that . . . the total mass of surplus value to be distributed every year is a *given quantity*. It depends on the value of the variable capital and on the rate of surplus value. . . . Once this simple basic truth is grasped, one understands that the displacement of free competition by monopolies does not basically alter the problem *in value terms*.[38]

This quotation testifies, I believe, to Mandel's ambiguity as far as the assumption of full utilization of the system's productive capacities is concerned. For if we treat the quantity of surplus value as merely "given," we must at the same time claim that the only significant effect of monopoly is the redistribution of this surplus value. In his remarks Mandel does not make any allowance for the fact that, apart from the redistribution effect of monopoly, the same monopoly simultaneously diminishes the actual surplus value, and thus exerts a definite influence on the conditions of production. In a situation like this Marx would probably say "there is a devil of a difference" whether the surplus value that could be distributed among capitalists was smaller or greater. Mandel's "simple basic truth" is thus based on an allegation that under monopoly, just like in competitive capitalism, the question of investment incentives is automatically solved on behalf of expansion and accumulation, no matter what the conditions of realization are. Also, his remarks unceasingly reflect the vision of the nineteenth-century kind of crisis, with graphic pictures of a "commodity glut" caused by an unlimited expansion of investment. Notwithstanding Mandel's claim that modern capitalism is characterized by "twin problems of surplus value realization and surplus capital investment," the main constraint of monopoly capitalism is the monstrous growth of a "capital glut." The problem of realization *sensu stricto* has become almost totally absorbed by the problem of utilization of the capital stock and the increase of nonproductive labor.

Using the concepts of theoretical and actual rates of profit it is possible to show that Mandel analyzes only those factors that explain the theoretical distribution of value between wages and profits, that is, the relation $R(1 - w)$. But despite the fact, already indicated above, that this relation is of principal importance to the Marxian labor theory of value in its "qualitative aspect," it was a satisfactory condition for the elaboration of the "quantitative aspect" only in the freely competitive stage of capitalism.

5. *Economic Surplus and Surplus Value: A Continuation*

The above considerations on the role of nonproductive labor have been based on the generally accepted assumption, both in Marxist and non-Marxist literature, that under monopoly capitalism there is to be found a strong tendency to expand nonproductive expenditures. This general type of expenditure may be treated as a particular case of the so-called external market or, as Arun Bose writes, as "a strictly *non*-neoimperialistic method of solving the demand-supply disproportions problem or declining aggregate consumption-rate problem of the capitalist economy."[39]

The appearance of this tendency does not mean, however, that all the problems connected with the utilization of productive capital, and with "vanishing" investment opportunities, have been resolved. Despite state interventionism and other forms of regulating the economy, and despite also the expansion of nonproductive expenditures, crises are by no means "songs of the past."[40] Without going deeper into these problems, I would only like to point out that the expansion of nonproductive expenditures is fully subordinated to the criteria of capitalist rationality. Since an individual capitalist calculates in categories of profit and outlays, and not in those of surplus value or economic surplus, an extravagant expansion of nonproductive expenditures is curtailed by the fact that these expenditures are an element of constant capital in this calculation—and as such have to be rationalized.[41] Thus capitalist rationalization of nonproductive labor weakens the anticrisis impact of those expenditures.

This should be borne in mind, because in the analysis above I considered the role of nonproductive labor from the point of view of global and not individual capital. But that point of view permits only some forms of nonproductive labor to be found in modern capitalism. An analysis of the category of economic surplus should permit, I believe, a discovery of new forms of nonproductive labor. At the same time, this category should clearly indicate the need of going beyond the point of view of global capital in the discussion of the consequences of capitalist accumulation.

In this context, let us begin by quoting the basic definitions of economic surplus employed in *Monopoly Capital.*

(1) At the outset, the authors define economic surplus as "the difference between what a society produces and the costs of producing it," treating it as a "first approximation to a fully developed concept of the economic surplus."[42] Thus defined, economic surplus is the sum of profits as shown by national income statistics.

(2) From the costs of production the authors deduct interest, ground rent, excessive depreciation, selling costs and wages of non-

productive workers employed in services, and so on. Thus they arrive at the following definition: economic surplus is "the difference between total social output and the socially necessary costs of producing it."[43]

(3) The third definition of economic surplus is included in the statistical appendix by J. D. Phillips. When estimating the volume of economic surplus, Phillips writes:

> The totals of . . . three major categories of economic surplus—property income, waste in the business process, and government expenditure—were . . . added together to obtain our grand totals. It should be noted, however, that these totals still do not include all elements of surplus. . . . One of these elements is the penetration of the productive process by the sales effort. . . . Another element which might reasonably be incorporated in the surplus, but is omitted here, is the output foregone owing to the existence of unemployment.[44]

A comparison of this last definition of economic surplus with the category of surplus value shows that these two are by no means synonymous.

Let us analyze the first part of definition (3): *"property income, waste in the business process, and government expenditure."* (a) Property income covers net profits after deducting the economic depreciation, rent, and interest. (b) Waste in the business process has to do with the outlays on sales. Depending on the type of enterprise and on the organization of advertising and finances, these outlays emerge either in the enterprise itself or in a special service sector. From the point of view of global capital the application of the term "waste" suggests the nonproductive character of these expenditures. (c) Government expenditures are financed from taxes which are levied on the incomes of enterprises and consumers, including productive workers. As far as taxes are imposed on the latter, they are a form of redistribution of a part of the variable capital on behalf of the state; at the same time this redistribution—just like taxes from profits—is of a nonproductive character (the authors implicitly assumed that the state does not fulfill the role of capitalist).

The sum total of elements (a), (b), and (c) corresponds to the notion of *produced and realized surplus value* and is equal to the second definition quoted above.

Let us now analyze the second part of definition (3). To make the task easier I shall consider separately its two elements: (d) "Output foregone owing to the existence of unemployment." The inclusion of lost production in the economic surplus (production lost because of the underutilization of productive resources) causes only quantitative changes in the surplus value actually produced and realized. Thus instead of writing about the actual surplus (actually

produced and realized surplus value), the authors write about the
potential surplus (potential surplus value). (e) "The penetration of
the productive process by the sales effort." This element of economic surplus is represented by costs caused by "planned obsolescence" of production and a change of the model (generally, as a
result of stimulating effective demand) "when no fundamental
change in quality or usefulness is involved."[45] Baran and Sweezy
cite studies indicating for example that

> the real cost of production of a 1949 automobile built with the tech-
> nology of 1956-1960 would have been less than $700. If we assume
> further that a rationally designed car could have been turned out at a
> cost of, say, $200 less than the 1949 model, and assume further the
> existence of an economical and efficient distribution system, we
> would have to conclude that the final price to consumers of an auto-
> mobile would not need to exceed something like $700 or $800. The
> total saving of resources would then be well above $11 billion a year.
> On this calculation, automobile model changes in the late 1950's were
> costing the country about 2.5 percent of its Gross National Product![46]

They state the general principle as follows:

> On a social scale the identification of that part of the social product
> which represents sales costs, and should therefore be included in
> surplus, necessarily involves a comparison of the hypothetical costs of
> a hypothetical product mix with the actual costs of the actual product
> mix.[47]

Note that definition (3), which I consider to be a fully developed
concept of economic surplus, does not actively use definition (1),
but definition (1) actually represents the view of individual capital
(in *Monopoly Capital,* that of the "big corporation"). Economic surplus, as expressed in this definition, is the operative, quantified
goal of the corporation. In turn, definitions (2) and (3) refer to the
economic process as a whole. They are categories of theoretical
analysis and they do not occur in the capitalist firm's economic
practice.

Let us leave unanswered such questions as how to define the
"costs socially necessary" under monopoly capitalism, and whether
or not all government expenditures should be included in the economic surplus. Instead let us concentrate on the differences between definitions (3) and (2) and their significance.

It seems that these differences raise the issue of a broader interpretation of the concept of "waste in the business process." In that
broader approach, waste includes two basic, qualitatively different
elements.

The first element is symbolized by advertising, the costs of which are calculated as part of the global costs the firm has to bear to function. This element more or less corresponds to Marx's concepts of circulation and of commercial capital, as being deductions from the global surplus value. From the point of view of global capital, expenditures on advertising and other types of sales services are of course nonproductive.

The second element describes the production of goods consumed by both productive and nonproductive workers, that is, the production of commodities that to a great extent compose the elements of reproduction of variable capital. From the point of view of both individual and global capital, work spent to produce these commodities is productive. Thus it would be absurd to include these goods in the surplus, within the framework of the traditional calculus of surplus value.

Let us formulate this contradiction between the surplus value calculus and the calculus of economic surplus in another way.

From the point of view of the reproduction of capital, commodities included in the second element of "waste in the business process" can be described, following Marx, as the nonproductive spending of labor time only when they are consumed as income or when the natural form makes their inclusion in the reproduction process impossible. And vice versa, the time spent to produce them shall be called productive when these commodities become components of the reproduction of variable and/or constant capital.

If the commodities which Baran and Sweezy include in the category of sales efforts are thus also included in the consumption of productive workers (thereby becoming an element of variable capital), then from the point of view of the surplus value calculus there are no substantial reasons not to recognize the labor spent on the change of model as value-creating and as productive labor. The inputs of time necessary to produce an "obsolete" commodity ($C + V$) will find their place in the rubric of "costs socially necessary," and the surplus value (M) included in those commodities will find its place in the rubric of "global surplus value." It is unacceptable in the traditional calculus to try to determine the *value* of those commodities ($C + V + M$) as an element of surplus value, and also as an expression of nonproductive labor. The argument that those commodities, just as armaments, are produced merely to increase effective demand (the U factor in Gillman's equation) cannot be maintained in the calculus of surplus value. The commodity resulting from "planned obsolescence" is potentially (and actually, in general practice) an element of the reproduction of variable capital. Of course, the same cannot be said about armaments. The nature of military expenditures makes it impossible to use weapons as constant or variable capital.

Thus the problem appears clear: while still remaining on the ground of the traditional calculus of surplus value certain characteristics specific to monopoly capitalist forms of nonproductive labor and surplus labor time are lost (with surplus product treated, consequently, as merely an "antagonistic form" of the surplus labor time). Element (e) of the fully developed notion of economic surplus not only defines the basic difference between the category of surplus value and that of economic surplus, but also is an attempt to open the way to the analysis of new forms of nonproductive labor.

Moreover, it is not a difference that can be neutralized by means of an automatic broadening of the surplus value category. Indeed, this difference signals the need to reconsider the "cognitive perspective" of the Marxist analysis of capitalism. The change should be an active utilization of the category of planned surplus as qualitatively different from those of actual and potential surpluses. As a matter of fact, definition (3) is simply an implementation of the critical potential included in the notion of planned economic surplus. However, as I earlier observed, Baran and Sweezy were not aware of this fact.[48]

The basis of the proposed change is the substantial transformation in the functioning of capitalism expressed by the new role of nonproductive labor, which I have already mentioned in the previous section. While enlarging upon the conclusions formulated in that section, at this point I would like to emphasize that the evolution of capitalism, which ended in the formation of monopoly capitalism, contributed, among other things, to a negative overcoming of contradictions between exchange value and use value in general. As a result, use values (and in general, material wealth) are included in the sphere of the direct determination of the accumulation of capital. Use values and social needs have lost their external, "transcendental" character and have transformed themselves into a function of capital. Next, Marx's original designation of use value in general as a precondition of a commodity can now be juxtaposed to the designation of the commodity as a precondition of use value. As Salvati notes, if nineteenth-century capitalism transformed use values into commodities, then modern capitalism transformed commodities into use values.[49]

Developing this thesis, one can say that in the conditions of competitive capitalism (and the domination of absolute surplus value), labor time was a measure of the exchange value of a commodity;

but in conditions of monopoly capitalism (and the domination of relative surplus value), it becomes a measure of specifically capitalist use values as well. It should further be stressed that the mechanism which adjusts disproportions between producing "anything" and producing "useful things" has also been weakened. As a consequence the tendency to produce "anything" is increased. Material wealth thus becomes an economic category and not merely an element of natural process.

A theoretical analysis of these changes requires the application of categories that would permit us to grasp all the basic trends and consequences of accumulation under monopoly capitalism. The category of planned economic surplus meets, I believe, this criterion and at the same time allows for the development (and not the negation) of Marx's original "cognitive perspective." In the last part of my essay I hope to present arguments supporting this hypothesis.

6. Elements of the Marxian Paradigm: Economic Surplus as a Complement to Surplus Value

According to István Mészáros, Marx wanted "to unveil not the 'weak' points of the capitalist system (which were anyway quite obvious, because of their striking human repercussions, to many moralist critics well before Marx), but its 'strong' ones."[50] In the Marxian theoretical system, the "strong point" of the capitalist mode of production is the relation between this mode and the development of the productive forces. This thesis appears throughout the *Grundrisse* and *Das Kapital,* not to mention *The Communist Manifesto.* And it is characteristic that Marx considered one of the major achievements of classical political economy to be Ricardo's perception of this "strong point" of capitalism.[51]

Still, this "apology" for capitalism appeared in a specific context in works by Marx. On the one hand, Marx underlined the fact that under capitalism the productive forces developed with a speed unprecedented in any other mode of production. On the other hand, he pointed out that the long-term development of the productive forces was restricted by conditions of capitalist reproduction. In other words, the practical application of capitalist rationality was seen as contributing to the establishment of the necessary material link in the transition to a classless society, while imposition of the very same rationality appeared to be increasingly counterproductive from the historical standpoint of the development of the productive forces.

I believe it is easy to notice in this approach an epistemological procedure that referred to an external criterion of assessment of the system as a whole. As a matter of fact, Marx's critique of capitalism, derived from the analysis of relations between this system and productive forces, implied the existence of this kind of criterion: this was the point of view of a socialist economy. Of course, this approach did not mean the substitution of analysis of the inner laws of the capitalist economy with an analysis of the laws governing a socialist mode of production. Instead, it meant an extension of the critical analysis by setting aside the limits imposed by the rationality prevailing in the system studied. Marx claimed that one could not understand the origins or the entirety of the effects provoked by the anarchy of capitalist production without referring to the vision of a planned economy; one could not understand the concept of surplus value without referring to the concept of surplus product that expresses a joint expenditure of labor by "associated producers." Just as the "bourgeois economy supplies the key to the ancient," so the vision of a socialist economy forms a natural point of departure in the comprehensive critique of capitalist society.[52]

This approach was metaphorically described by Baran and Sweezy as a "confrontation between reality and reason."[53] Earlier Baran had written that "it is only the standpoint which is intellectually outside the prevailing social order . . . that permits critical insight into that social order's contradictions and hidden potentialities."[54] Various definitions of the category of economic surplus introduced by Baran and Sweezy reflect the dual character of the critique of capitalism contained in the Marxian paradigm: the critique from the point of view of its own criteria of development and rationality (reflected in the concept of potential economic surplus as synonymous with the category of potential surplus value), and from the point of view of the prospects of development of productive forces and socialist criteria of rationality (reflected in the concept of planned economic surplus).

Analyzing the relationship between capitalism and productive forces, Marx emphasized, above all, the problem of *historical functions* of capitalist accumulation. He said that from the point of view of the future socialist society, and at the same time from the standpoint of productive forces, the "historical mission" of capital was fulfilled the moment a social need for surplus labor time was created, as well as the achievement of such a level of development of the productive forces that their further growth would require not so much a longer social-labor time as a shorter one. In the following fragment of the *Grundrisse* these criteria of historical valuation of capitalism were explicitly formulated:

> The great historic quality of capital is to *create* this *surplus labor,* superfluous labor from the standpoint of . . . mere subsistence; and its historic destiny (Bestimmung) is fulfilled as soon as, on one side, there has been such a development of needs that surplus labor above and beyond necessity has itself become a general need arising out of individual needs themselves . . . and . . . when the development of the productive powers of labor . . . have flourished to the stage where the possession and preservation of general wealth require a lesser labor time of society as a whole, and where the laboring society relates scientifically to the process of its progressive reproduction.[55]

And there immediately followed the conclusion that "*capital is productive, i.e. an essential relation for the development of the social productive forces.* It ceases to exist as such only where the development of these productive forces themselves encounters its barrier in capital itself."[56]

Still, there arises a question: With the help of what criteria is investigation on the level of the development of productive forces possible?

In Marx's works at least two mutually conditioned criteria can be distinguished. First, the relation between surplus and necessary labor times; second, the relation between constant capital and variable capital. Thus the criteria are the *rate of surplus value* and the *organic composition of capital.* In Marx's opinion, production of value, based on the extension of constant capital and on the reduction of necessary labor time, is a characteristic feature of mature capitalism; at the same time it is an indicator of the level of development of capital. So we can say that the growth of the rate of surplus value, as far as it is conditioned by the growth of the organic composition of capital, is an appropriate criterion for assessing the level of development of the productive forces.

However, this development takes place within the framework of contradictions specific to capitalism. Though an increase in the rate of surplus value represents *ceteris paribus* an augmentation of surplus labor time, at the same time its growth represents a reduction in labor's relative "purchasing power." And this contradiction, to all intents and purposes, expresses the existence of four limitations to the process of capital accumulation:

(1) *necessary labor* as limit on the exchange value of living labor capacity or of the wages of the industrial population;

(2) *surplus value* as limit on surplus labor time; and, in regard to

relative surplus labor time, as barrier to the development of the forces of production;

(3) what is the same, the *transformation into money,* exchange value as such, as limit of production . . .

(4) [this is] again the same as *restriction of the production of use values by exchange value;* or that real wealth has to take on a *specific* form distinct from itself; a form not absolutely identical with it, in order to become an object of production at all.[57]

The consequence of these limits is that a greater and greater part of the productive potential is being shifted to the nonproductive sphere of circulation, permitting the transformation of potential surplus value into actual surplus value. What is more, the limits (2) and (4) appear as a symbiotic link between the spheres of circulation and production, the result of which is the transformation of "real wealth" into a specific capitalist category.

And so there arises the next question: Does the traditionally calculated rate of surplus value make it possible to show the real relationship between the surplus and necessary labor?

Still, the answer to this question depends not so much on the precision of the calculus applied as on the aim of our analysis. When Marx was writing about the tendency toward the reduction of necessary labor time, he stressed that "capital here—quite unintentionally—reduces human labor . . . to a minimum. This will redound to the benefit of emancipated labor, and is the condition of its emancipation."[58] This way, the rate of surplus value appeared to Marx not only as a measure of exploitation but also as a measure of chances of the emancipation of the working class in the new society.[59]

If we look at the process of capital accumulation in modern monopoly capitalism from this standpoint, then the traditional calculus of necessary and surplus labor time on the all-society scale will prove insufficient. This is because the microeconomic tendency to reduce necessary labor time in the production process itself is accompanied by the macroeconomic tendency to increase nonproductive labor.[60] The growth of nonproductive labor involves both its traditional forms as well as new ones, which even from the point of view of global capital are treated as "necessary labor," that is, as productive. That is exactly why it seems necessary to introduce the category of planned surplus that would show the really existing chances of labor emancipation directly; thereby it also becomes necessary to introduce some supplementary criteria to define productive and nonproductive labor, which will make it possible to distinguish waste inherent in the category of "necessary labor" (calculated traditionally, i.e., from the point of view of global capital). The use of the category of economic surplus makes it possible to answer the question: "What are socially necessary costs when, in Veblen's words, the distinction between workmanship and salesmanship has been blurred?"[61]

Consequently, I would insist that the category of economic surplus introduced by Baran and Sweezy is an analytical category adjusted to conditions of modern capitalism. It is the category enabling an evaluation of the economic possibilities of labor emancipation, as well as an instrument for the critical analysis of the way these possibilities are taken advantage of within the framework of monopoly capitalism. In this sense, the category of economic surplus is not an alternative to the category of surplus value. On the contrary, it is a consistent and historically justified development of the surplus value category.

7. Conclusions

Let us sum up the above discussion on the relationship between economic surplus and surplus value.

(1) From the point of view of capital the problem of accumulation and its limits manifests itself as a quantitative difference between "what is" and "what is possible" within the framework of given and indisputable social conditions of production. But a real understanding of the limits of capitalist accumulation requires a treatment of capital as merely a historic stage of the development of productive forces. Thus it requires an undertaking of critical analysis, the first premise of which should be to question the universality of capitalism's rationality.

(2) It is impossible to formulate such a premise with no outside point of reference—without a vision of a socialist economy. In this perspective, the problem is properly distinguished, in its two aspects, that is, as a problem of waste from the point of view of capital and that of waste resulting from the very existence of capital as a social relation.

(3) In the category of economic surplus, this dialectical duality of the research problem is fully included. For as much as the category of potential surplus (in accordance with the interpretation presented in section 2) included a critique from the point of view of capital, the category of planned surplus expands upon this critique, so that it encompasses the wider realm of two rationalities:

(a) based on private capitalist appropriation of labor time, and (b) resulting from both the social ownership of means of production and the principle of planning.

(4) The traditional calculus of surplus value makes it theoretically impossible to consider the additional labor time included in the concept of "waste" as it occurs in the spheres of production (the problem of average organic composition of capital and choice of technology under monopoly) and of consumption (the problem of the structure of demand). From the point of view of planned economic surplus the theoretical and practical analysis of nonproductive labor time included in those spheres is possible.

(5) From the methodological standpoint, as Salvati points out, construction of the category of planned surplus is based on two premises: (a) the precise definition of the set of consumer goods which are socially necessary, and (b) determination of the optimal technologies used in the production of these goods.[62] If the premises are given, the calculation of necessary and surplus labor time should not be an insurmountable technical obstacle.

(6) First tentative estimates of economic surplus show clearly the ever-faster growing difference between the volume of surplus value and that of economic surplus. The data quoted by Baran and Sweezy indicate that whereas in 1929 the relation between economic surplus and the total of "classical" elements of surplus value amounted to about 1.75:1, by 1963 it was 3.12:1. And that is not all. Ron Stanfield, using the category of planned economic surplus, estimated that in 1970 economic surplus, measured as the difference between "potential GNP" and "essential consumption" (a sum of essential personal consumption, essential social overhead consumption, and essential capital consumption), had been $336 billion.[63] In the same year, GNP actually produced was estimated as a bare $446.4 billion.

(7) These tentative estimates indicate that both from the point of view of its own criteria of rationality, as well as from that of the development of the productive forces, capitalism is to an ever greater degree a destructive system. At the same time, these estimates reveal how great is the potential to liberate labor that lies at humanity's hand today. One can only hope that this potential will be more rationally and humanely utilized than is the case for today's so-called actually existing socialism in Eastern Europe.

Translated from the Polish by Maria Chmielewska-Szlaifer

Notes

1. An excellent example of applying the category of economic surplus to studies of East European feudalism can be found in the pioneer book by the Polish historian Witold Kula, *Théorie économique du système féodal* (Paris: Mouton, 1970). In the context of the theory of underdevelopment, Andre Gunder Frank interestingly applied this category in *Capitalism and Underdevelopment in Latin America* (New York: Monthly Review Press, 1969).

2. The list of critics is very long; thus let us restrict ourselves to a few examples: Ernest Mandel, "The Labor Theory of Value and 'Monopoly Capital,'" *International Socialist Review* (July-August 1967); Ph. Herzog, *Politique, économique et planification en régime capitaliste* (Paris: Éditions Sociales, 1971); A. Pavlenko, "Po povodu odnoii modeli monopolistitsheskovo kapitalizma," *Nauchnyie Doklady Vysshey Shkoly—Ekonomitsheskiie Nauki*, no. 8 (1969); V. N. Bader, H. Ganssmann, W. Goldschmidt, and B. Hoffmann, "Zur Kritik an Baran und Sweezys Theories des Monopolkapitalismus," in *Monopolkapital: Thesen zu dem Buch von Paul A. Baran and Paul M. Sweezy* (Frankfurt a/Main: EVA, 1969).

3. "Waste, Marxian Theory and Monopoly Capital: Towards a New Synthesis," in this volume.

4. Quoted in Paul M. Sweezy, "Obstacles to Economic Development," in C. H. Feinstein, ed., *Socialism, Capitalism and Economic Growth: Essays Presented to Maurice Dobb* (Cambridge: Cambridge University Press, 1967), p. 191. Elsewhere, I presented a critique of the manner in which this methodological guideline is used by so-called "economics of development." See "Estado no capitalismo dependente: Brasil, uma tentativa de analise teorica," *Estudios Latinoamericanos* 4 (1978). At this point, I would like to emphasize that inasmuch as the rule of two levels of critique is observed, this guideline fulfills a useful role.

5. Paul A. Baran, *The Political Economy of Growth* (New York: Monthly Review Press, 1957), pp. 22-23, 41-42.

6. Ibid., 22*n*.

7. Charles Bettelheim, "Le surplus économique facteur de base d'une politique de développement," in *Planification et croissance accélérée* (Paris: Maspéro, 1973), p. 70.

8. Baran, *The Political Economy of Growth*, p. 22.

9. Writing this I have in mind only the basic differences in the *criteria* according to which these categories are constructed. The structure of planned surplus is of course one of the most controversial topics in the economies of socialism.

10. Baran, *The Political Economy of Growth*, pp. 23-41.

11. Ibid., p. 32.

12. See Szlajfer, "Waste," in this volume.

13. Baran, *The Political Economy of Growth*, p. 43.

14. This thesis is consistent, I believe, with Marx's methodological sugges-

tion that "one can understand tribute, tithe, etc., if one is acquainted with ground rent. But one must not identify them." Karl Marx, *Grundrisse* (Harmondsworth: Penguin in association with *New Left Review*, 1973), p. 105.

15. Paul A. Baran and Paul M. Sweezy, *Monopoly Capital* (New York: Monthly Review Press, 1966), p. 10.
16. Michele Salvati, "Monopolkapitalismus," in Bader et al., *Monopolkapital*, p. 113.
17. Otto Nathan, "Marxism and Monopoly Capital: A Symposium," *Science & Society* 30 (Winter 1966): 487-96. See also Megnad Desai, *Marxian Economic Theory* (London: Grays-Mills, 1974), p. 115.
18. Baran and Sweezy, *Monopoly Capital* p. 8.
19. In a personal letter to me, dated June 4, 1972, Paul Sweezy agreed with this opinion.
20. A. A. Konius, "Teoria wartosci oparta na pracy a ekonometria" (Labor Theory of Value and Econometrics), in *Problemy ekonomii planowania i ekonometrii* (Problems of Economics, Planning and Econometrics) (Warszawa: PWN, 1967), p. 150.
21. Alfredo Medio, "Profits and Surplus Value: Appearance and Reality in Capitalist Production," in E. K. Hunt and Jesse G. Schwartz, eds., *A Critique of Economic Theory* (Harmondsworth: Penguin, 1972), pp. 330-41.
22. "Basic products" are defined by Sraffa as those commodities which are directly or indirectly used for production of all others (including commodity-labor power). "Nonbasic products," in turn, are defined as those commodities which "are not used, whether as instruments of production or as articles of subsistence, in the production of others." Piero Sraffa, *Production of Commodities by Means of Commodities: Prelude to a Critique of Economic Theory* (Cambridge: Cambridge University Press, 1963), p. 7.
23. This relation is calculated with an implicit assumption of a full utilization of constant capital.
24. Quoted in Paul M. Sweezy, *The Theory of Capitalist Development: Principles of Marxian Political Economy* (New York: Monthly Review Press, 1968), pp. 123ff.
25. Medio, "Profits and Surplus Value," p. 341.
26. Sraffa, *Production of Commodities by Means of Commodities*.
27. Karl Marx, *Theories of Surplus Value*, Part I (Moscow: Progress Publishers, 1969), p. 406.
28. See Paul M. Sweezy, "On the Theory of Monopoly Capitalism," in *Modern Capitalism and Other Essays* (New York: Monthly Review Press, 1972) and Joan Robinson, *Economic Heresies: Some Old-Fashioned Questions in Economic Theory* (New York: Basic Books, 1971), pp. 135-40. It should be stressed here that under monopoly the corporation's control over prices and technical progress makes it impossible to answer the question of which technology is most efficient both from the point of view of profit maximization and from that of minimization of the joint labor time. See Salvati, "Monopolkapitalismus."

29. Joan Robinson, *An Essay on Marxian Economics* (London: Macmillan, 1967), p. 50.
30. John R. Hicks emphasizes this point in *Value and Capital: An Inquiry into Some Fundamental Principles of Economic Theory* (London: Oxford University Press, 1946), p. 83.
31. Dobb points out that "the classical Marxian explanation for the emergence of surplus value continues to apply to modern capitalism, as to its earlier stage. . . ." See Maurice Dobb, "A Note on Distribution and the Price Markup," in this volume.
32. Michal Kalecki, *Selected Essays on the Dynamics of the Capitalist Economy, 1930-1970* (Cambridge: Cambridge University Press, 1971); Josef Steindl, *Maturity and Stagnation in American Capitalism* (New York: Monthly Review Press, 1956); Paolo Sylos-Labini, *Oligopoly and Technical Progress* (Cambridge, MA: Harvard University Press, 1962). One of the latest contributions to this subject is Hukukane Nikaido's *Monopolistic Competition and Effective Demand* (Princeton, N.J.: Princeton University Press, 1975). However, the author's assumption of static equilibrium, and lack of consideration of factors determining the choice of the level of profit margins leading to the transformation of Pareto's optimum into a monopoly optimum (tolerating the coexistence of excess capacity and unemployment), means that his critique never gets beyond the point of logical possibility. In comparison with the Kalecki-Steindl-Labini approach it is by no means a sensational conclusion.
33. Nobuo Okishio, "A Mathematical Note on Marxian Theorems," *Weltwirtschaftliches Archiv* 91 (1963).
34. This is the very idea of Arun Bose's concept of a "mature capitalist economy with a partially decomposable physical structure." Arun Bose, *Marxian and Post-Marxian Political Economy: An Introduction* (Harmondsworth: Penguin, 1975), chs. 9 and 10.
35. Joseph Gillman, *The Falling Rate of Profit* (New York: Cameron Associates, 1958).
36. James F. Becker, "Social Imbalance and the Marxian System," in David Horowitz, ed., *Marx and Modern Economics* (New York: Monthly Review Press, 1968), pp. 270-90.
37. As Kalecki pointed out, the thesis could be extended by considering the relationship among profits, wages, and excess capacity. According to him, "a wage rise showing an increase in the trade-union power leads—contrary to the precepts of classical economics—to an increase in employment. . . . the class struggle as reflected in trade union bargaining may affect the distribution of national income but in more sophisticated fashion than expressed by the crude doctrine: when wages are raised, profits fall *pro tanto*." Michal Kalecki, "Class Struggle and the Distribution of National Income," in this volume.
38. Mandel, "The Labor Theory of Value and 'Monopoly Capital.'" A few years later, Mandel accepted the thesis of the positive correlation between volume and rate of profit and the expansion of nonproductive labor—without blinking an eye. See his "Introduction" to Karl Marx,

Capital, vol. 2 (New York: Vintage, 1978).

39. Bose, *Marxian and Post-Marxian Political Economy*, p. 171.

40. See Michal Kalecki, "The Marxian Equations of Reproduction and Modern Economics," in this volume. For a different point of view see K. K. Kurihara, *Essays in Macrodynamic Economics* (London: Allen and Unwin, 1972), ch. 4.

41. See P. J. Dhrymes, "A Comparison of Productivity Behavior in Manufacturing and Service Industries," *The Review of Economics and Statistics* 45, no. 1 (1963), and *The New Technology* (London: Counter Information Services Report, n.d.).

42. Baran and Sweezy, *Monopoly Capital*, pp. 9, 72.

43. Ibid., p. 112.

44. Ibid., p. 370.

45. Ibid., p. 381.

46. Ibid., p. 137.

47. Ibid., p. 134.

48. In a personal letter to me, dated November 25, 1971, Sweezy indicated that initially he considered the concept of economic surplus as merely an extension of the category of surplus value. However, he later realized that this was not quite correct. In some fragments of *Monopoly Capital* there appeared, according to Sweezy, elements of potential surplus and probably also an element of planned surplus. But this is not the greatest paradox of the situation. None of the Marxist critics attacking Baran and Sweezy for their "schism" from the Marxian category was at the same time able to prove what (except terminology) that "schism" was. Salvati was the only one who at least got close to the conclusions proposed here. Still, Salvati claims that the "schism" was fully justified and necessary. Apart from Salvati, only a conservative critic of the New Left, Assar Lindbeck, properly understood some elements of the crucial distinction between economic surplus and surplus value. See Assar Lindbeck, *The Political Economy of the New Left: An Outsider's View* (New York: Harper & Row, 1971), pp. 73ff.

49. Salvati, "Monopolkapitalismus," p. 107.

50. István Mészáros, "Conceptual Structure of Marx's Theory of Alienation," in E. K. Hunt and Jesse G. Schwartz, eds., *A Critique of Economic Theory*, p. 145.

51. Marx, *Grundrisse*, pp. 410ff.

52. Ibid., p. 105.

53. Baran and Sweezy, *Monopoly Capital*, p. 138.

54. Baran, *The Political Economy of Growth*, p. 26.

55. Marx, *Grundrisse*, p. 325.

56. Ibid.

57. Ibid., p. 415ff.

58. Ibid., p. 701; see also p. 159.

59. Salvati, "Monopolkapitalismus," pp. 106ff.

60. Paul A. Baran and Paul M. Sweezy, "Economics of Two Worlds," in David Horowitz ed., *Marx and Modern Economics*, pp. 291-311.

61. Baran and Sweezy, *Monopoly Capital*, p. 133.

62. Salvati, "Monopolkapitalismus."
63. Ron Stanfield, "A Revision of the Economic Surplus Concept," in this volume. See also his *Economic Surplus and Neo-Marxism* (Lexington, MA.: Heath Books 1973); and Michael Kidron, "Waste: U.S. 1970," in *Capitalism and Theory* (London: Pluto Press, 1974).

Part V

PRODUCTIVE AND NONPRODUCTIVE LABOR

In his contribution to this part Henryk Szlajfer attempts a major methodological and historical reevaluation of the Marxian "cognitive perspective," concentrating on the changing role of productive and nonproductive labor. He examines the question from the three standpoints of individual capital, global capital, and society as a whole, and emphasizes the transformation in the use-value basis of the capitalist economy that accompanies the transition from freely competitive to monopolistically competitive stages of development.

Henryk Szlajfer

WASTE, MARXIAN THEORY, AND MONOPOLY CAPITAL: TOWARD A NEW SYNTHESIS

1. Introduction

Today the distinction between productive and nonproductive labor is a domain unique to Marxian political economy, although it was not Marx who originally introduced this problem into the economic discussion. Because of the lack of any other point of reference, I will here concentrate exclusively on *Das Kapital* and the Marxist literature.[1] I wish to stress, however, that my aim is a systematic analysis of the *problem,* which is why I restrict critical remarks concerning its history to the necessary minimum.

The problem of productive and nonproductive labor, seen from the perspective of modern capitalism, manifests itself concretely in three forms: (1) the rapid expansion of employment in the service sector; (2) the commercialization and "capitalization" of this sector together with the labor relations prevalent therein; and (3) the production of commodities (e.g., armaments) that we do not want to recognize as expressions of socially productive activity.[2] In other words, the problem of productive and nonproductive labor is described empirically as *a tendency toward growing waste.*

The theoretical analysis of the empirical phenomena connected with this problem requires that we attempt once again to determine which criteria will allow us to distinguish productive from nonproductive labor; that these criteria be used to analyze the actual conditions of monopoly capitalism; and that we arrive at some conclusion on the extent to which Marx's own cognitive perspective provides us with tools for an exhaustive inquiry into the causation and forms of expanding economic waste.

This essay is a considerably expanded and revised version of the annex to my monograph *Economic Surplus and Surplus Value: An Attempt at Comparison* (University of Dar es Salaam, Economic Research Bureau, Occasional Paper 78.3, August 1979).

2. Historical Heritage

The controversy about the criteria of productive and non-productive labor has been, above all, a controversy about the place of the use-value category in the Marxian labor theory of value and theory of accumulation. Recently, there have also appeared sociological and political interpretations of this problem, where the issue of productive and nonproductive labor is analyzed within the context of functional or disfunctional roles, from the point of view of capitalism as a sociopolitical system.[3] In my considerations, I omit this kind of interpretation.

Historically, Marxists were prone to remove the category of use value beyond the problematics of political economy. This is best exemplified by the polemic of Rudolf Hilferding against Böhm-Bawerk. Hilferding wrote that "the natural aspect of the commodity, its use-value, lies outside the domain of political economy."[4] Similar statements can also be found in a textbook by Paul Sweezy.[5] The backing for this kind of interpretation was usually found in the following quotations from *Theories of Surplus Value:*

> Productive labour, in its meaning for capitalist production, is wage-labour which, exchanged against the variable part of capital . . . reproduces not only this part of capital . . . but in addition produces surplus-value for the capitalist.[6]
>
> . . . the designation of labour as *productive labour* has absolutely nothing to do with the *determinate content* of the labour . . . the particular use-value in which it manifests itself.[7]

On the basis of these quotes, it was generally concluded that the notion of use value did not play any role in Marxian economic theory, insofar as its analysis of capitalist society was concerned, because this concept referred only to the relation between humanity and nature, making use value primarily the ahistorical domain of bourgeois economics.

Reaction against this kind of formulation of the problem of use value appeared relatively late. But criticism of the traditional formulation of productive and nonproductive labor, on a significant scale, started in the 1950s.

We can schematically distinguish two trends in the reevaluation of the historic interpretations. The first, most amply represented by Roman Rosdolsky, aimed, above all, to show that the category of use value occupied an important place *within* Marxian economic theory.[8] Rosdolsky convincingly pointed to a number of aspects of Marxian theory, where this category played an active role (the problems of money, labor force, schemes of reproduction, fixed and circulating capital). However, he did not distinguish clearly between use value in general and the specifically capitalist use value, which I discuss below. The basic works of Ernest Mandel, written in the 1960s and 1970s, remain in the same critical current.[9]

Jacob Morris' discussion of Joseph Gillman's book *The Falling Rate of Profit*, at the end of the 1950s, started the other current of critical analysis.[10] Concurrently, there appeared Paul Baran's definition, in *The Political Economy of Growth*, which presented a new point of view on the entire problem. In contrast to Morris, who tended to show that the criteria of productive and nonproductive labor should be derived from the schemes of reproduction and the technical conditions of capital accumulation, Baran clearly transgressed the procedure of a "simple exegesis" of Marx's texts. After accepting the point of view of the accumulation of capital, Baran made the first step toward a new definition of productive and nonproductive labor. Let us recall his definition: nonproductive labor "consists of all labor resulting in the output of goods and services the demand for which is attributable to the specific conditions and relationships of the capitalist system, and which would be absent in a rationally ordered society."[11]

One can say at once that this definition refers to a different cognitive perspective than the one characteristic of the traditional interpretations. Paradoxically, this is an orthodox Marxist perspective in the sense that its point of departure is the *historicity* of the capitalist mode of production. However, it overlooks all of the secondary criteria applied so far (material and nonmaterial goods, technical conditions of production and distribution of use value, manual and mental labor, etc.). This is an innovative perspective and, at the same time, an orthodox Marxian one, because *it allows us to ask not only about waste from the point of view of capital, but also about waste due to the very existence of capital as a social relation.* This way of posing the question makes it possible to undertake a theoretical analysis of new forms of productive and nonproductive labor under monopoly capitalism.

In principle, none of the later discussions went beyond an elaboration of the critical trend based on the insights of either Rosdolsky or Morris. Moreover, a majority of Marxists condemned Baran's, and then Baran and Sweezy's, conception, as they had in relation to the category of economic surplus (which Baran and Sweezy had derived largely from their understanding of productive and nonproductive labor).[12]

In my considerations, I adopt Baran's point of view to the extent that it demands that we apply the principle of historicism. This, however, does not relieve us from answering the question as to what degree the original statements of Marx allow for a "painless" adoption of Baran's point of view. As a result of our analysis, it could turn out that Marx's theses are also subject to the principle of historicism, and thus will have to be reformulated. The Marxian method of analysis will not suffer from that. But some Marxists inevitably will.[13]

3. Marxian Theory: Two Levels of Analysis

In Marxian economic theory both the use-value problem and those of productive and nonproductive labor are conceived in terms of two distinct levels of analysis. On the first level, Marx distinguishes the notions of *general* and *specifically capitalist use values* (productive labor). On the second level, these notions are related to the *conditions of reproduction of individual and global capital.*[14]

Therefore a reconstruction of the Marxian theory of productive and nonproductive labor requires a consideration of both levels of analysis. For a concentration on one of them leads, alternatively, either to a mechanical repetition of the first or of the second of Adam Smith's definitions. In this way the originality of the Marxian approach is reduced to a single choice between the "right" or "wrong" Smith.[15]

Let us then consider both levels of analysis, opening with that of use value and productive labor: "Only bourgeois narrow-mindedness," wrote Marx, "which regards the capitalist forms of production as absolute forms . . . can confuse the question of what is *productive labour* from the standpoint of capital with the question of what labour is productive in general, or what is productive labour in general."[16]

In this quotation there is a clear distinction between two types of productivity: productivity from the point of view of capital and productivity in general. A similar distinction is to be found in Marx's analysis of use value:

> Labour which is to produce commodities must be useful labour; it must produce a *use-value;* it must manifest itself in a *use-value.* And consequently only labour which manifests itself in *commodities,* that is, in *use-values,* is labour for which capital is exchanged. This is a self-evident premise. But it is not this concrete character of labour . . . which forms its specific use-value for capital and consequently stamps it as *productive labour* in the system of capitalist production.[17]

This provides a clear distinction between use value in general and specifically capitalist use value. As a result we obtain the following sets:

(1) Productive labor in general   = Σ Use value in general
(2) Productive labor from the   = Σ Specifically capitalist
     capitalist standpoint   use value

In addition, it is clear that set (1) constitutes a premise of set (2). This can be interpreted in such a way that the relation between the sets (1) and (2) can be put down in the following way:

$$\Sigma(1) \leq \Sigma(2)$$

In what conditions do we have inequality and in which conditions do we find equality? The answer to this question requires an analysis of the second level, that is, the conditions of reproduction of individual and global capital.

The text of *Capital* suggests that Marx's main goal was to stress those aspects of use value and productive labor which were specific to capital. This resulted from his work's general purpose: presentation of a critical analysis of those concepts and categories which in bourgeois thought had been designated as "natural," in other words, eternal. Moreover, showing the specifically capitalist form of those concepts and categories as well as the phenomenon of fetishism did not mean losing sight of the general characteristics included, for example, in the notions of surplus value or labor. At any rate, one can certainly interpret the Marxian guideline in such a way that surplus value is merely a capitalist form of surplus labor time, and capitalism an antagonistic form of social production.

Thus there must exist a mechanism of *mediation* between the two above-distinguished sets. *The contradiction between individual and global capital is this mechanism.* The following thesis can be formulated: if in the analysis having individual capital as its point of departure the organic unity of the two aspects of productive labor and use value becomes torn, on the macroeconomic level, when we study the reproduction of global capital, we get this unity again. This unity results from the fact that if the chief goal of an abstract labor is multiplication of its value, it can be realized mainly through the growth of material wealth (a sum of use values in general). It is worth stressing that this thesis reflects precisely the methodology used by Marx when he solved other problems as well. Let us recall, at least, the problem of discrepancy between *labor time* and *socially necessary labor time*, which determines the value of the commodity.

In this case also, we have to do with the mechanism of mediation between the micro- and macro- level of analysis.[18]

From the point of view of the individual, abstract labor, the definition of productive labor as generating surplus value for the owner of capital, does not raise any doubts. Since for an individual capitalist, the concrete, material shape of the commodities produced in his enterprise is really of no significance, he multiplies his capital both in the material and nonmaterial spheres. According to Marx, "one sphere of production is, in fact, just as good or bad as another."[19]

However, the above definition of productive labor is not sufficient "in the study of the total social capital and of the value of its products."[20] This results from the consideration that "the conditions of social reproduction are discernible precisely from the fact that it must be shown what becomes of every portion of value . . . of total product."[21]

In a comprehensive and extensive explanation Marx discusses explicitly the role which use value plays in his theoretical system. This explanation develops further the above conclusions:

> So long as we looked upon the production of value and the value of the product of capital individually, the bodily form of the commodities produced was wholly immaterial for the analysis. . . . So far as the reproduction of capital was concerned, it was sufficient to assume that that portion of the product in commodities which represents capital-value finds an opportunity in the sphere of circulation to reconvert itself into its elements of production and thus into its form of productive capital; just as it sufficed to assume that both labourer and the capitalist find in the market those commodities on which they spend their wages and the surplus-value. This merely formal manner of presentation is no longer adequate in the study of the total social capital and of the value of its products. The reconversion of one portion of the value of the product into capital and the passing of another portion into the individual consumption of the capitalist as well as the working class form a movement within the value of the product itself in which the result of the aggregate capital finds expression; and this movement is not only a replacement of value, but also a replacement in material and is therefore as much bound up with the relative proportions of the value-components of the total social product as with their use-value, their material shape.[22]

Thus during the process of reproducing global capital it can turn out that labor, which from the point of view of an individual capitalist would be defined as productive, shall in fact be included in the nonproductive labor.[23] A very obvious example is production of gold (in the form of money). According to Marx, the surplus labor embodied in gold "is *pro tanto* a diminution of the volume of social production," it is labor drawn out from the accumulation of capital with no chance of restoring it.[24] As Marx wrote, "to accumulate it is necessary to convert a portion of the surplus-product into capital. But we cannot, except by a miracle, convert into capital anything but such articles as can be employed in the labour process (i.e., means of production), and such further articles as are suitable for the sustenance of the labourer (i.e., means of subsistence)."[25]

Gold (in the form of money) is not a use value in general, that is, it is not an element of real wealth; it is however a specifically capitalist use value.[26] The question of gold is, as Marx stressed, a problem of the commodity deprived of one of its basic characteristics, namely, of use value in general. It is a commodity which becomes such as a result of becoming a use value (though only a *formal* one) in the very process of capitalist production. In other words, *it is a commodity transformed into a formal use value.*

We can add here that the notion of productive labor is to a certain extent defined already in the notion of a commodity as a unity of abstract labor (value) and concrete labor (use value). The labor that does not create use value in general is not productive from the standpoint of the reproduction of global capital. In other words, *from the standpoint of global capital, production of the means of production and consumption is the first step leading toward the production of surplus value; it is the fundamental condition limiting the sample of use values that can potentially appear as capital.* But this negative assumption is still not sufficient to fully define productive labor. That is why Marx introduces another criterion, amply discussed in the literature—a functional one. He labels as productive that labor which is expended while producing use values, which in the process of reproduction will function in turn as capital, since when exchanging money for nonproductive labor "money and labour exchange with each other *only* as commodities. So that instead of this exchange forming capital, it is expenditure of revenue."[27]

It must be emphasized, however, that the functional criterion does not introduce particularly drastic changes to the above-presented analysis. For this is a restrictive criterion in that it excludes from the set of productive labor (from the point of view of capital) that type of labor which is transformed into an element of consumption, financed from surplus value. This functional criterion is meant to formulate the question from a standpoint applicable to both individual and global capital.

From the analysis made so far, two conclusions result. First, according to Marx, capitalism is only an antagonistic form of produc-

Table I

Standpoint	Goal of production	Sphere of production	Result of labor
Individual (abstract) capital	Surplus value as a "strategic" goal	Material and nonmaterial production	Exchange values (= use values for others) and then capital
Global capital	Surplus product as a "strategic" goal	Material production	Use values in general transformed into exchange values and next into capital
Society	Surplus product as a "tactical" goal	Material production	Use values in general

tion; second, capital is only a specific form of labor and surplus product and hence only a historical form of use value in general. Table 1 summarizes the discussion so far.

4. Some Other Criteria

Before I proceed to the critical analysis of Table 1, I would like to mention other criteria used to distinguish productive from nonproductive labor.

The most common criterion is the one based on the distinction between manual and mental labor. The critics of Marx's theory are also more than willing to stress this criterion. For instance, Leszek Kolakowski writes:

> In general we gather from Marx that productive labour is physical labor applied to material objects; but from *occasional* remarks it appears that he was prepared to count as producers those who did not work directly on the material themselves but enabled others to do so—for example, engineers or designers in factories. In this case, however, the distinction is highly obscure and has given rise in the socialist countries to practical as well as theoretical dilemmas. (Emphasis added.)[28]

Well, in Marxian theory, the criterion mentioned by Kolakowski has a clearly defined status. First, this criterion does not refer to the distinction between productive and nonproductive labor specific either to capitalism or socialism, but to historical forms of the *tech-*

nical division of labor. Secondly, since Marx treated the technical division of labor as an integral element of the development of productive forces (and these cannot be described in categories of "stagnation" or the "ultimate state"), the notion of the productive worker who produces the use value in general cannot be defined once and forever. This notion has a historical dimension and each time it is conditioned by the current level of the development of the productive forces.[29]

From Marx's works one can also deduce another criterion of productive activity, which has been constantly overlooked by traditional interpretations, and relates to the notion of the *productive role of capital.* This criterion goes beyond the traditional framework of the analysis of the problem, while *its point of reference is the historical function of capital.*

One of the aspects of the historical function of capital, stressed by Marx in the *Grundrisse* in particular, is the production of new needs, and along with them, of the need of surplus labor time. To the extent to which capital produces such needs, and, in this way, transforms the pressure of surplus labor time into the routinized activity internalized by workers, it can be determined as one that fulfills productive functions. Looking at the problem from the point of view of production, this is tantamount to the statement that capital favors the development of productive forces, in a definite way. At this moment Marx did not hesitate at emphasis, writing, for instance, of "the great civilizing influence of capital."[30] Also, he points to three basic ways in which capital affects needs (i.e., produces use values in general): "Firstly, quantitative expansion of existing consumption; secondly: creation of new needs by propagating existing ones in a wide circle; *thirdly:* production of *new* needs and discovery and creation of new use-values."[31]

As I have already stressed, the criterion of productivity so defined does not relate to the distinction between productive and nonproductive labor directly. But it suggests several directions to be followed in the further discussion of the problem. The first direction leads to a deepened analysis of the category of use value, while the second consists of the development of the category of specifically capitalist and formal use value within the context of monopoly capital.

5. More on Use Value in General

There is no doubt that wherever Marx wrote of use value, he associated this notion with that of a useful thing, useful to the consumer in general. A given sphere of production, he wrote, "would be useless if the commodities it produced did not satisfy some social need."[32] Also the above-specified third form of capital's impact on consumption, through the "production of *new* needs," was identified by Marx with the positive activity to which "a constantly expanding and constantly enriched system of needs corresponds."[33]

This means that according to the theory presented in *Capital,* goods produced in the sphere of material production, in the sphere that creates social wealth, were, ipso facto, useful goods. Their utility did not result from the very process of capital accumulation but appeared within the process as an independent factor. According to Marx, use values "constitute the substance of all wealth whatever may be the social form of that wealth."[34] And in another place: "So far . . . as labour is a creator of use-value, is useful labour, it is a necessary condition, independent of all forms of society."[35] Therefore the fundamental conclusion formulated by Marx in relation to use value reads as follows: "The utility of a thing makes it a use value. . . . *This property of a commodity is independent of the amount of labour required to appropriate its useful qualities*" (emphasis added).[36]

From the above quotations one can conclude, I believe, that in Marxian theory use value is an element of the natural process, whereas the enlargement of the "basket" of use values constitutes a social process. Thereby utility of goods does not require the expenditure of labor—it is given externally. The expenditure of labor is required when this utility is appropriated. Gough hits the nail on the head writing: "For Marx . . . a use-value is anything which is demanded. Thus a historical perspective . . . is not extended to question the nature of the goods produced themselves."[37]

6. Monopoly Capital and Waste

If we assume that the interpretation of the Marxian theory of use value is correct, then it seems to be at variance with the practical experience of monopoly capitalism. For the unidirectional dependence—use value in general → exchange value → capital—does not fully reflect the complex process of socialization of use value, that is, of its transformation into an element of social existence. Also, it means that this category has both lost the attribute of "externality," and is ill-suited to comprehend the necessity of expending labor not only during the act of appropriation, but during the *production of the utility of a commodity* as well.

These suggestions require a return to the questions Marx posed in the *Grundrisse*. When discussing the status of the category of use value there, Marx by no means considered this question as settled (as in the first chapter of *Das Kapital* or in *Zur Kritik der politschen Okonomie*). On the contrary, he assumed that one should explain "to what extent use value exists not only as a presupposed matter, outside economics and its forms, but to what extent it enters into it."[38] The above-presented analysis gives rise also to other questions concerning the notions of specifically capitalist and formal use values.

However, are there any particular reasons to refer these questions to the problems of monopoly capital? I think so. The realities of monopoly capital turned out to be a very forceful stimulus inducing economists to bother to analyze both the problem of waste and the structure of social output—in short, to recognize use value as a legitimate object of economics. It is precisely under monopoly capital that the traditional forms of nonproductive labor became intensified, and that new forms of waste appeared. The impact of old and new forms of nonproductive labor on the structure of production and consumption, as well as on the rate of accumulation of capital, became so considerable that one could no longer simply ignore it, or treat it as a mere addition to the "proper" interests of the political economy of capitalism.

Next, in line with the Marxian method, one should look for the causes of the rise to economic preeminence of nonproductive labor in the process of capital accumulation itself, in the manner in which the barriers restricting accumulation under monopoly have been partially transcended. Elsewhere I write more amply on the qualitatively different role of nonproductive labor in the process of monopoly accumulation, in comparison to free competition.[39] At this point it is enough to observe that nonproductive labor plays an active role (unforeseen by Marx) in determining the volume of profits and surplus value as well as the rate of profit. Under conditions of chronic underutilization of productive capacities (a structural feature of the monopolistic economy), it serves to lessen the disparity between potential surplus value and surplus value actually produced.[40] Michal Kalecki encapsulated this "paradox," inherent in the economic role of waste, with the curt remark that it "permits profits to increase above the level determined by private investment and capitalists' consumption."[41]

It is in this sense that the analysis of the problem of "growing waste" appears as a new line of economic analysis—complementary to the analysis of producing surplus value.[42] Yet this complementariness should not be understood in a simplistic manner, as a mere mechanical extension of the field of analysis. If we claim that accumulation of capital becomes unfeasible without a growth of nonproductive labor, this means that nonproductive labor becomes one of the main conditions of the production and realization of surplus value.

However, to point to the positive correlation that occurs between capital accumulation and augmentation of nonproductive labor is just the first step toward the analysis of the forms of waste characteristic of monopoly capital. The hypothesis of the existence of a dependence relation of—capital → exchange value → "produced use value"—can be proven only by the analysis of new, specific forms of nonproductive labor and use values, the utility of which is unequivocally related to the functioning of capitalism, and not with the growing circle of "wants" (in the Marxian sense). To some extent this is tantamount to the analysis of the so-called dependence effect, defined by Galbraith as "the way wants depend on the process by which they are satisfied."[43] However, I write "to some extent," because I do not mean the implied distinction between the "essential needs" and the higher, "contrived wants" created by the development of productive forces, but use values whose only function is to produce surplus value and to accelerate the rate of capital accumulation. Thus I mean use values, the existence of which has a historical dimension that is limited by the horizon of capital accumulation.[44]

It is easy to notice that this way of grasping the problem is very close to Baran's already quoted definition of nonproductive labor. Indeed, I cannot imagine how one could discuss the problem of nonproductive labor under monopoly without the use of this definition. I will try to show that it constitutes the necessary modification of the Marxian concept, adjusted to the realities of monopoly capital.

7. Military Production: The Case of Formal Use Value

Baran's definition of nonproductive labor refers to the concept of a rationally organized socialist economy. That is why the range of nonproductive labor delimited by this definition does not coincide with Marx's concept. This is obvious since Baran adopts the criterion of use value in general. However, the definition supplied by Baran—even if we agree that it does not reflect the specificity of capitalism—allows us to identify new forms of nonproductive labor from the point of view of global capital. But this is not all. At the same time, this definition shows clearly the limitations of the critical potential of this point of view under monopoly conditions. In the nineteenth century, the adoption of the point of view of global capital involved a danger of formulating pessimistic opinions on the future of capitalism (Ricardo). However, since the beginning of the Great Depression in 1929, this point of view has been the basis for practical operations to save capitalism (various forms of state interventionism and planning). This is because certain ways of wasting the productive forces, closely related with the functioning of the monopolistic economy, can be discovered only through the critique of global capital.

Let us consider the case of military production. A lot has been written on its significance for the accumulation of monopoly capital. At this point it is enough to point out that conservative estimates concerning the years 1947-72 presented the following fundamental relationship between armaments and accumulation in the U. S. economy: "Through the multiplier effect roughly 25 percent of the GNP in any given postwar year has been (directly or indirectly) generated by the military expenditures. The partial creation of postwar 'prosperity' through the generation of roughly $2 trillion of military waste is certainly one of the most glaring postwar capitalist contradictions."[45]

Military production (which we can treat as a specific case of the production of "luxury goods") is a form of nonproductive labor from the point of global capital. At the same time, it is an obvious example of productive labor from the point of view of individual capital employed in the production of "luxury goods." This way, in military production we find the pure essence (and contradictions) of specifically capitalist use value and productive labor, the fundamental feature of which is to increase surplus value.

However, inasmuch as this production constitutes an "ideal" example of the specifically capitalist productive labor, it is also a tremendous waste of productive forces. Yet one must not content oneself with merely stating this fact. First, under monopoly capital, as already indicated, this waste is the elixir of life that brings in accumulation of global capital. Second, military production is an obvious case of the *commodity transformed into use value*, the utility of which is produced by the entire socioeconomic system of capitalism.

Discussing the problem of this production in the context of the Marxian theory of productive and nonproductive labor, it must be stressed that armament—just like gold (in the form of money)—is a commodity that lacks use value in general. It cannot, even potentially, appear as a means of production or a consumer good, and labor spent to produce it is unreproducible. Consequently, we must admit that in the case of armaments we are concerned with a peculiar commodity that represents but a *formal use value.* This formal use value, as Marx stresses in his analysis of money, refers exclusively to its "specific social function." In a word, the utility of the military production is produced by the system of capitalist production itself. In this way we have at our disposal a clear example of goods and services the demand for which is, according to Baran, "attributable to the specific conditions and relationships of the capitalist system. . . ."

At the same time, the example of military production indicates that the functioning of monopoly capital introduces a qualitative change in the relationship between the distinguished sets (1) and (2). In the conditions of premonopoly capital, acute economic crises that resulted directly from the anarchy in production used to restore the equilibrium which had been shaken by the excessive expansion of specifically capitalist use value—Σ (2). That is why I noted that use value in general is less than or equal to specifically capitalist use value, or Σ (1) $\leq \Sigma$ (2). Under monopoly capital this relation transforms into: Σ (1) $< \Sigma$ (2). This means among other things that expansion of waste and formal use values, combined with planning in the interest of capital, provides the basic method to curb the "simple" manifestations of the anarchy of production under monopoly capital. It is the "capitalist solution" to the contradiction between use value in general and exchange value.

However, military production, although it shows the emergence, in the shape of formal use value, of new types of nonproductive labor, can still be treated as an illustration of Marxian theory, one which can be easily explained within the conception of two levels of analysis for the interpretation of productive and nonproductive labor. Much more complicated to explain, within the original Marxian conception, are other forms of waste that occurred in connection with the functioning of monopoly capital. I shall try to sketch a possible solution in the final part of this essay.

8. *The Structure of Social Product and the Waste of Productive Forces*

In his schemes of reproduction Marx distinguished the department producing luxury goods demanded by the capitalist. At the same time, he pointed to its production as an example of non-productive labor from the point of view of global capital. In line with the Marxian theory of value, to include luxury goods in the working class' "consumer's basket" means to transform these goods into an element of the so-called historically determined minimum of consumption necessary to reproduce labor power. In this way, they automatically pass over to the department producing the means of the workers' subsistence. Labor so expended is productive from the point of view of both individual and global capital.

This short summary of the Marxian approach to the problem of changing physical composition of workers' consumption shows that the search for elements of waste in the structure of consumer demand seems to be—within this approach—a (theoretically) "suspicious" endeavor. Also, it becomes impossible to classify any good included in so-called mass consumption as waste.[46]

It is not difficult to guess the reasons why such conclusions are inevitable. In line with Marxian theory, all the goods included in mass consumption represent not only exchange value but use value in general as well. The commodity form of these goods does not change the fact that their utility is above all determined by the consumption requirements of the workers, and not by the needs of capitalist reproduction and commodity relations. In this way, however, Marx's limited historical interpretation of the problem of use value, the "essence" of material wealth, obstructs any concrete understanding of the changes that monopoly capital brings about in this field.

To overcome this limitation it is necessary to break with the still prevailing nonevolutionary interpretation; or, put differently, it is necessary to apply the historical approach to the analysis of the category of use value in general.

Fortunately, we also have at our disposal a theoretical category which makes it possible to begin to carry out such a change in "cognitive perspective." I believe there is no obstacle to our seeing in some elements of consumer demand not mere use values in general, but also a combination of use values in general and formal use values, or, in extreme cases, only the latter. In other words, the category of formal use value allows an identification of the goods and services whose utility is oriented exclusively (and above all) toward satisfaction of the requirements of capital accumulation.

However, from the point of view of global capital, those formal use values included in the workers' "consumer's basket" represent a specifically capitalist form of productive labor. Therefore this is sharply distinguished from Marx's example of gold in the form of money or the case of military expenditures. *These formal use values can be determined only in a new structural context, which is the critique of capital as such.*

It follows that under monopoly capital one can no longer maintain that the only difference between the points of view of global capital and "society" is the social form in which use value in general is produced and realized (see Table 1). By fully subjecting to itself the process of generating needs and thus the utility of goods, monopoly capital ensures that the difference between these points of view encompasses the structure of social product (including consumption) as well. Aliksander Ochocki correctly emphasizes that "eliminating capital, we cannot simply 'eliminate' the layer of exchange value but we must also transform the layer of use value."[47]

To be sure, to precisely delimit the borderline between goods representing, above all, formal use values and goods representing formal use value *along with* use value in general, is an extremely difficult task, one which depends on the level of development of productive forces in a given society. Nevertheless, for theoretical analysis it is enough at the moment to say that such a borderline does exist. (However, it should be strongly emphasized that to identify the primitive standard of consumption with "true needs," therefore looking for waste in the mere fact of enriched workers' consumption, leads to a blind alley.)

It is worth noting at this point that in other theoretical systems the problem of the structure of mass consumption, and of the functions of its particular elements, stopped being the "forbidden fruit" of theoretical reflection long ago. Unless I am mistaken, Thorstein Veblen was the first to question the nonevolutionary approach to this problem in his concept of "conspicuous consumption." At the same time, he observed that "nothing should be included under the head of conspicuous waste but such expenditure as is incurred *on the ground of an invidious pecuniary comparison*" (emphasis added).[48] Robert K. Merton, in turn generalizing Veblen's observation on the notion of "latent function" of consumption, stresses that "if the latent functions of status-enhancement or status-reaffirmation were removed from the patterns of conspicuous consumption, these patterns would undergo severe changes of a sort which the 'conventional' economist could not foresee."[49]

I think that in Baran's definition of nonproductive labor, and in Baran and Sweezy's conception of economic surplus, we find a distinct echo of Veblen's theory.[50] One can also contend that the Marxian category of formal use value is close to Merton's concept of "latent function." However, even if we agree that the concept of waste in consumption, referring to the basic Marxian reproduction framework, is indeed identical with the problematics covered by the concepts of Veblen and Merton, this does not yet exhaust the object of our analysis.

The literature so far stresses the problem of new forms of non-productive labor mainly from the point of view of the structure of effective demand (the "realization problem"). This standard approach seems to me inadequate as far as formal use value is concerned. Let us consider here the now-classic example of "produced use value," the car, described with some exaggeration by Mishan as "one of the great disasters to have befallen the human race."[51]

Today the car is treated as a "natural" element of mass consumption; at the same time, through the procedure of product differentiation and frequent model changes, its "latent functions" are kept up and its formal use value is continuously reproduced. *The socioeconomic history of the car* clearly shows the mutual penetration of use value in general and formal use value; it also points to the causality of production and consumption of formal use value on the one hand, and new forms of competition and unequal income distribution on the other. Joan Robinson draws the following conclusions from the history of the car: "By taking away demand from public transport, raising its costs, and finally making it unable to exist, the motor-car industry increases its own market, until everyone who is not destitute is obliged to run a car, and those who are destitute have to stay at home."[52] Even Tibor Scitovsky, who perceives in monopolistic competition only a method to "stimulate" and to "satisfy" the consumer, has to admit that the car "is a good illustration of the consumer's impotence once the producer has taken over decision-making."[53]

The above example illustrates, I believe, that *under monopoly capital the notion of nonproductive labor not only applies to definite methods of using the produced surplus value, but also embraces those labor inputs to the production of commodities having the trait of formal use value "produced" by the system.* In this way, we can treat advertising, costs of consumer credit systems and other financial institutions, as well as other forms of the general "sales effort," as sui generis "inputs" necessary to produce the commodities' utility and to transform them into "produced use values." From a short-run standpoint, "output" frequently appears as swift model changes, product differentiation, lowered quality standards, and so on. In the long run the same process is reflected in important changes in the structure of effective demand and production, forcibly conditioned by monopolistic competition and unequal income distribution.

However, at this point it should be stressed once again that formal use values, discussed against the example of the "latent function" of the car, are not able to perform a role similar to that performed, for example, by military expenditures. From the point of view of global capital, these use values are an example of productive labor; they fulfill the function of nonproductive consumption only indirectly, inasmuch as the production of their utility requires starting a mechanism of nonproductive consumption of capital (advertising, etc.). Thus in the monopoly stage, the global-capital standpoint justifies the continuous reproduction of waste; the critical potential of this point of view therefore becomes drastically limited.

In the historical context of "producing" utility of goods (as formal use values), the problem of model changes, product differentiation, or accelerated "turnover" of durable and semidurable goods appears as an inevitable consequence of this history, its logical supplement, and not as a "degeneration" or a misguided form of competition. Today this conclusion seems obvious, although—as illustrated even by the present essay which is concerned in part with "suspicions" about Baran's definition—its incorporation into the theory is still an open question. The example of the car points also to the appearance of a new dimension to the problem of productive and nonproductive labor, whose existence we did not even suspect until lately. Namely, whether and to what extent waste, connected with the large-scale appearance of formal use values and monopolistic competition, enters the sphere of productive forces.

However, a full conceptualization of the subject, which involves the relationship between the categories of productive and nonproductive labor on the one hand, and the assessment of the "productivity of capital" as a definite method of developing productive forces on the other, requires a separate study. Therefore I shall limit myself to indicating two possible ways of dealing with the above question, treating them as tentative proposals.

A narrow approach would point to the underutilization of productive capacities and labor or to arms production. These forms of waste are an obvious check upon the development of productive forces. However, this is a check upon the "quantitative" development only, that is, such that it contributes to a growing disparity between potential and actual production. Thus, from the point of view of global capital, this waste is a nonproductive utilization ("consumption") of productive forces. No doubt Baran's category of "potential surplus" is the theoretical category enabling an analysis of this kind of relationship between waste and productive forces.

We can also study monopoly capital's "qualitative" impact on productive forces. The distinguished new forms of nonproductive labor, analyzed from the point of view of the production process and in the context of the opposition between labor and capital, as well as in relation to monopolistic competition, imply a possible type of subordination of productive forces to monopoly capital which threatens their degradation and, in the longer run, regression. For example, there is no doubt that the procedure of product differentiation, closely connected with the production of formal use values, corresponds to the differentiation of the technological process itself, which restricts standardization, etc.[54] The effect of the present model of the development of productive forces on the natural environment and raw-material resources is equally obvious. And finally, the gravest example of the waste of productive forces is the degradation of both labor and technological progress, in the manner masterfully described by Braverman:

> . . . in addition to its technical function of increasing the productivity of labor—which would be a mark of machinery under any social system—machinery also has in the capitalist system the function of divesting the mass of the workers of their control over their own labor. It is ironic that this feat is accomplished by taking advantage of that great human advance represented by the technical and scientific developments that increase human control over the labor process.[55]

> . . . there is no question that from a practical standpoint there is nothing to prevent the machining process under numerical control from remaining the province of the total craftsman. That this almost never happens is due, of course, to the opportunities that the process offers for the destruction of craft and the cheapening of the resulting pieces of labor into which it is broken. . . . The design which will enable the operation to be broken down among cheaper operators is the design which is sought by management and engineers who have so internalized this value that it appears to them to have the force of natural law or scientific necessity.[56]

This approach would considerably widen the concept of nonproductive labor. It would embrace the production process itself as well as the method of its organization, and not only the way the existing capacities are utilized. And this outlook would question not only the productive nature of the making of formal use values, but also the productive character of the scientific management of labor under monopoly capitalism.

Needless to say, these approaches are not alternatives. On the contrary, the future of the problem of productive and nonproductive labor, as a question of overriding social importance, depends on treating them in conjunction, within the framework of one theoretical whole. Today, Marxists are faced with the task of working out a theory that would be a synthesis of Baran's approach to formal use values, and Braverman's analysis of the process of degradation of both labor and technological progress under monopoly capital. Perhaps the following observation by Marx, reflecting it seems to me the *methodological foundation* of the critique of capitalism included in *Capital,* can be the point of departure for this new synthesis:

> As soon as labour in the direct form has ceased to be the great well-spring of wealth, labour time ceases and must cease to be its measure, and hence exchange value [must cease to be a measure] of use value. *The surplus labour of the mass* has ceased to be the condition for the development of general wealth, just as the *non-labour of the few,* for the development of the general powers of the human head. . . . The free development of individualities, and hence not the reduction of necessary labour time so as to posit surplus labour, but rather the general reduction of the necessary labour of society to a minimum . . ."[57]

Translated from the Polish by Maria Chmielewska-Szlaifer

Notes

1. In the excellent textbook by Joan Robinson and John Eatwell, *An Introduction to Modern Economics* (London: McGraw-Hill, 1973), the reader will not find a word on the problem of productive and non-productive labor (not even in the chapter devoted to Marx).
2. Harry Braverman centers on the second problem in *Labor and Monopoly Capital: The Degradation of Work in the Twentieth Century* (New York: Monthly Review Press, 1974), ch. 19. However, his attempt at definition finished with the formulation of a tautology: "Labor may . . . be unproductive simply because . . . it is used by the capitalist . . . for unproductive rather than productive functions" (p. 415).
3. "Productive labor," writes James O'Connor, "is the labor of workers who accept the relationships which the boss forced on them, who compete with one another on the job, who guard the boss' privileges from one another, etc. Unproductive labor is the activity of workers who cooperate with one another to end competition, etc., or to create new production relations within which new productive forces can be produced." "Productive and Unproductive Labor," *Politics and Society* 5, no. 3 (1975): 322.
4. Rudolf Hilferding, "Böhm-Bawerks Marx-Kritik," *Marx Studien: Blätter zur Theorie und Politik des wissenschaftlichen Sozialismus* (Vienna, 1904). Quoted after Roman Rosdolsky, *The Making of Marx's Capital* (London: Pluto Press, 1977), pp. 73ff. However, Tadeusz Kowalik in his preface to the Polish edition of Hilferding's work observes that in *Finanzkapital* Hilferding discarded his earlier point of view. See: "Przedomowa" (Introduction) in *Böhm-Bawerk o markosowskie teorii war-*

tosci (Böhm-Bawerk on the Marxian Theory of Value) (Warszawa: PWN, 1962), pp. 7-9.

5. Paul M. Sweezy, *The Theory of Capitalist Development* (New York: Monthly Review Press, 1968). See also Howard Sherman, *Radical Political Economy: Capitalism and Socialism from a Marxist-Humanist Perspective* (New York: Basic Books, 1972).

6. Karl Marx, *Theories of Surplus Value,* Part I (Moscow: Progress Publishers, 1969), p. 152.

7. Ibid., p. 401.

8. Rosdolsky, *The Making of Marx's* Capital, pp. 73-95.

9. Ernest Mandel, *Marxist Economic Theory,* vol. I (New York: Monthly Review Press, 1970), p. 191, and *Late Capitalism* (London: Verso, 1978), pp. 403ff.

10. Jacob Morris, "Unemployment and Unproductive Employment," *Science & Society* 22, no. 2 (1958).

11. Paul A. Baran, *The Political Economy of Growth* (New York: Monthly Review Press, 1957), p. 32.

12. The only exception is Ian Gough's "Marx's Theory of Productive and Unproductive Labour," *New Left Review,* no. 76 (1972). I wish to stress my debt to Gough. After I had read his essay, I was convinced that we were proceeding in the same direction. At the same time, a number of theses made in Gough's essay allowed me to make precise my earlier attempts at an analysis of the problem of productive and nonproductive labor.

13. I fully share György Lukács' opinion in this respect: "Orthodox Marxism . . . does not imply the uncritical acceptance of the results of Marx's investigations. . . . On the contrary, orthodoxy refers exclusively to *method*." G. Lukács, *History and Class Consciousness: Studies in Marxist Dialectics* (London: Merlin, 1971), p. 1.

14. According to Maurice Godelier, the analysis presented in the first volume of *Capital* is of a microeconomic nature. On the other hand, Nagels claims that "from the first to the last letter of his economic writings Marx is a macroeconomist." J. Nagels, *Genèse, contenu et prolongements de la notion de reproduction du capital selon Karl Marx, Boisguillebert, Quesnay, Leontiev* (Bruxelles: Ed. de l'Institut de Sociologie de l' 'Université' Libre de Bruxelles, 1970), p. 115. (Godelier's thesis is quoted by Nagels on p. 114.) Nagel's statement seems to be exaggerated. His criticism of Godelier's thesis is justifiable only insofar as in Marxian theory the individual capital is treated as an embodiment of capital in general, as abstract capital. On the other hand, in his considerations on the schemes of reproduction, Marx presents the individual capital as in opposition to the global capital. In this sense Godelier's thesis should not be totally rejected.

15. In one of his recent publications Ernest Mandel has revised his earlier point of view which had identified the Marxian theory of productive and nonproductive labor with the so-called second Smithian definition. Presently, Mandel notices the difference between "the point of

view of the individual capitalist(s)" and "the point of view of the capitalist mode of production in its totality." The real difficulty here lies in the fact that Mandel does not relate those points of view to the analysis of various concepts of use value. See E. Mandel, "Introduction" to Marx, *Capital*, vol. 2 (New York: Vintage, 1978).

16. Marx, *Theories of Surplus Value*, Part I, p. 393.
17. Ibid., p. 400.
18. See Rosdolsky, *The Making of Marx's* Capital.
19. Marx, *Capital*, vol. 3 (Book III) (Moscow: Progress Publishers, 1974), p. 195.
20. Marx, *Capital*, vol. 2 (Moscow: Foreign Languages Publishing House, 1961), p. 394.
21. Ibid., p. 393.
22. Ibid., p. 394.
23. The absence of discrimination between the above-presented levels of analysis seems to explain the persistence of scholastic discussions on the *point* where the line dividing productive and nonproductive labor should be drawn. The stubborn blurring of the differences between individual and global capital, as well as between use value in general and specifically capitalist use value, has given an artificial birth to new "schools" of Marxism, which fight one another. If, for example, Morris (*Unemployment and Unproductive Employment*) claims firmly that the department producing luxury goods personifies, along with the costs of circulation, nonproductive labor (an example of a mechanical reduction of individual capital to global capital) the "fundamentalist" orientation carries out a "minor revolution," in the name of the "abstract-labor interpretation" of Marxism, recognizing both luxury goods and costs of circulation as examples of productive labor. According to the "fundamentalists," "the criterion for the distinction between productive and unproductive labour is exclusively the social form in which labor is undertaken, regardless of the content of the activity or of the nature of the product" (an example of a mechanical reduction of global capital to individual capital). See M. de Vroey, "On the Obsolescence of the Marxian Theory of Value: A Critical Review," *Capital and Class* 17 (Summer 1982): 55. Both "schools" negate the possibility of considering the problem of mediation between the two levels of analysis, opting for reductionism, i.e., a discovery of purely formal theoretical coherence where, in reality, we have to deal with the contradiction caused by the real movement of capital accumulation.
24. Marx, *Capital*, vol. 2, (1961), p. 357.
25. Marx, *Capital*, vol. 1 (Moscow: Progress Publishers, 1974), p. 544.
26. "The use value of the money commodity becomes two-fold. In addition to its special use value as a commodity (gold, for instance, serving to stop teeth, to form the raw material of articles of luxury, etc.), *it acquires a formal use value, originating in its specific social function.*" (My emphasis—H.Sz.) Marx, *Capital*, vol. 1, (1974), p. 93.
27. Marx, *Theories of Surplus Value*, Part I, p. 407.

roductive and Nonproductive Labor* *319*

28. Leszek Kolakowski, *Main Currents of Marxism: Its Rise, Growth and Dissolution*, vol. I (Oxford: Oxford University Press, 1978), p. 331.
29. "As the cooperative character of the labor process becomes more and more marked, so, as a necessary consequence, does our notion of productive labor, and of its agent, the productive laborer, become extended. In order to labor productively, it is no longer necessary for you to do manual work yourself; enough, if you are an organ of the collective laborer, and perform one of its subordinate functions. . . ." Marx, *Capital*, vol. 1, (1974), pp. 476ff.
30. Karl Marx, *Grundrisse: Foundations of the Critique of Political Economy* (Harmondsworth: Penguin in association with *New Left Review*, 1973), p. 409.
31. Ibid., p. 408.
32. Marx, *Capital*, vol. 3 (Book III) (1974), p. 195.
33. Marx, *Grundrisse*, p. 409.
34. Marx, *Capital*, vol. 1 (1974), p. 44.
35. Ibid., p. 50.
36. Ibid., p. 44.
37. Gough, "Marx's Theory of Productive and Unproductive Labour," p. 60.
38. Marx, *Grundrisse*, p. 268.
39. See "Economic Surplus and Surplus Value Under Monopoly Capitalism" in this volume.
40. For statistical series and interpretation see John B. Foster's "The Limits of U.S. Capitalism: Surplus Capacity and Capacity Surplus," in this volume.
41. Michal Kalecki, *Theory of Economic Dynamics* (London: Allen and Unwin, 1969), p. 51.
42. See Paul A. Baran and Paul M. Sweezy, *Monopoly Capital: An Essay on the American Economic and Social Order* (New York: Monthly Review Press, 1966).
43. John Kenneth Galbraith, *The Affluent Society* (Boston: Houghton Mifflin, 1969), ch. 11.
44. By combining the "dependence effect" with the general division between "essential needs" and higher, "contrived wants," Galbraith facilitated the attack by Hayek who considers any attempt to question the consumer's choices and the dogma of "consumer's sovereignty" a manifestation of totalitarianism. See F. A. Hayek, "The Non Sequitur of the 'Dependence Effect,'" *Southern Economic Journal* (April 1961).
45. James Cypher, "Capitalist Planning and Military Expenditures," *The Review of Radical Political Economics* 6, no. 3 (Fall 1974): 14. One frequently encounters the opinion that the growth of military expenditures has more to do with politics than economics. In line with this opinion, the growing waste that is necessary to reproduce the global capital can assume other forms, useful to society. In this way, the relation between monopoly capital and military production is incidental, and not causal. The point is, however, that the history of U.S.

monopoly capital clearly indicates that armaments have been a necessary form of waste because of purely economic reasons, and not only because of a confrontation with the Soviet Union. In Cypher's essay we find six arguments for this hypothesis: (1) "no private capitalist markets are encroached upon"; (2) "military expenditures are at least 'neutral' with respect to the distribution of socioeconomic power"; (3) "there is no increase in productive capacity which will add to conventional domestic market supply"; (4) "by increasing the government sector and working through the 'balanced budget multiplier effect' Keynes' anticipation of stagnation is forestalled"; (5) "military expenditures can be used as a countercyclical device"; and (6) "military expenditures have been significant in creating investment demands because the composition of final demands has been changed so often." Ibid., pp. 7-8, 11. See also M. Reich and D. Finkelhor, "Capitalism and the 'Military-Industrial Complex': The Obstacle to 'Conversion',", in David Mermelstein, ed., *Economics: Mainstream Readings and Radical Critiques* (New York: Random House, 1973), and Michael Kidron, *Western Capitalism Since the War* (Harmondsworth: Penguin, 1970), ch. 3.

46. I put aside the still existing, although economically less significant, production of luxury goods par excellence.

47. A. Ochocki, *Dialektyka i historia* (Dialectics and History) (Warszawa: KiW, 1980), p. 295.

48. Thorstein Veblen, *The Theory of the Leisure Class* (New York: Vanguard Press, 1928), p. 99. Quoted after R. K. Merton, *Social Theory and Social Structure* (Glencoe, Ill.: The Free Press, 1957), p. 70.

49. R. K. Merton, *Social Theory*, p. 70.

50. See David Horowitz, "The Case for a Neo-Marxist Theory," *International Socialist Review* (July-August 1967).

51. E. J. Mishan, *The Costs of Economic Growth* (New York: Praeger, 1967), p. 175.

52. Joan Robinson, "The Age of Growth," in *Collected Economic Papers*, vol. 5 (Cambridge, MA: MIT Press, 1980), p. 128. Bradford Shell's study informs that "since 1925 General Motors bought out electric mass transit systems in over 100 cities and converted them to motorized bus systems. GM accounts for 75% of American bus production. Moreover, the demise of efficient and updated electrical mass transit systems has also spurred automobile sales. GM is the world's largest automaker. . . . therefore once converting transit systems to buses, GM's best interest was served by converting the bus systems to automobiles as much as possible. . . . bus sales have fallen by about 60% since 1952. This was the year that General Motors achieved monopoly control of bus production." Quoted after S. Gowan et al., *Moving Toward a New Society* (Philadelphia: New Society Press, 1976), p. 140. (Snell's study was submitted to the U.S. Senate Subcommittee on Antitrust and Monopoly.)

53. T. Scitovsky, *The Joyless Economy: An Inquiry into Human Satisfaction and Consumer Dissatisfaction* (New York: Oxford University Press, 1976), p. 275.

54. See, for example, R. W. Crandall, "Vertical Integration and the Market for Repair Parts in the United States Automobile Industry," *The Journal of Industrial Economics* 16, no. 3 (July 1968).
55. Braverman, *Labor and Monopoly Capital*, p. 193.
56. Ibid., p. 199-200. See Stephen A. Marglin, "What do Bosses do?: The Origins and Functions of Hierarchy in Capitalist Production," *The Review of Radical Political Economics* 6, no. 2 (Summer 1974). For an excellent continuation of this line of analysis see Richard Edwards, *Contested Terrain: The Transformation of the Workplace in the Twentieth Century* (New York: Basic Books, 1979), ch. 7.
57. Marx, *Grundrisse*, pp. 705-6.

Part VI

THE STATE AND CRISIS

In this part John Bellamy Foster argues that each of the four approaches to Marxian crisis theory—falling rate of profit analysis, the profit squeeze model, disproportionality theory, and "underconsumptionism"—carries implications with respect to the role of the state in modern capitalist society, in general, and in the current historical conjuncture, in particular. An extended comparison of the political implications of each model ends with a detailed discussion of the role that state-promoted unproductive expenditures play in the neo-Marxian overaccumulation/underconsumption view.

John Bellamy Foster

MARXIAN ECONOMICS AND THE STATE

Studies by socialists in recent years have enormously enhanced our general understanding of the capitalist state. But surprisingly little insight has been gained into the link between the modern state and accumulation. To my mind, the chief reason for this blind spot is a basic uncertainty within the left itself about the revolutionary political status of certain forms of radical economics. In this essay I propose to do two things: detail the political implications of the major schools of Marxian crisis theory, and outline some of the distinguishing features of the state's role in accumulation under monopoly capitalism.

How can we account for the somewhat paradoxical fact that certain socialist models of the capitalist economy are often thought to be prone to political degeneration? In essence, there are four divisions among Marxists on the subject of crisis: (1) the falling rate of profit school, (2) disproportionality theory, (3) underconsumptionism, and (4) profit-squeeze analysis. All but the first of these have been classified, at one time or another, as vulnerable to reformist contamination. This ceases to be puzzling once one discovers that each of the last three approaches has some resemblance to a distinct strand within establishment economics.

The capitalist state is presumably powerless to break the famous "Law of the Tendency of the Rate of Profit to Fall," according to which any increases in the rate of exploitation of labor power, as accumulation proceeds, will be overshadowed by a rising organic composition of capital (capital-labor ratio), thereby decreasing labor's production of new value (and hence profits) per unit of constant (material) capital. Yet pure falling rate of profit theorists often find themselves in comparatively difficult straits when it comes to demonstrating either the reality of declining profits based on rapidly expanding organic composition, or the way in which the state in the Keynesian era could have managed to temporarily promote accumulation if such conditions had actually existed—a subject to which I will return later. Of course the mere fact that Marx

This is a slightly amended version of an article that appeared in *Science & Society* 46, no. 3 (Fall 1982): 257–83.

himself emphasized this law in the third volume of *Capital* is a strong inducement for the more fundamentalist Marxian economists to see it as the last word in crisis theory, irrespective of concrete historical analysis.[1]

Hilferding, Lenin, and many others, even to some extent down to the present day, have adhered to the disproportionality type of crisis theory.[2] In the most general terms, this broad approach is grounded on the lack of appropriate value proportions between individual branches and departments of production, which are nonetheless necessary for the *smooth* transformation of the capitalist system from one reproductive phase to the next. To put the matter differently, there is no immediate guarantee under capitalist conditions that the goods produced in each sector will be just the right amount so as to "clear the market," that is, without certain commodities being sold above or below their value. The very nature of the production and realization of profit under capitalism ensures that the economic system will deviate from any conceivable path of balanced growth, and will only be brought "back into line" by means of the ensuing economic disruptions. Thus the cyclical trials and and tribulations of capital as a whole are traced almost exclusively to the anarchic (planless) character of the market and the law of uneven development. Theorists operating along these lines normally utilize Marx's famous reproductive schemes in the second volume of *Capital* as a conceptual basis for their analysis of disequilibrium tendencies.

It is widely contended on the left that disproportionality theory is especially vulnerable (if not inherently so) to the myth of a potential state-led organized capitalism, in which social and economic harmony would prevail. Hilferding, along with other theorists at the head of German Social Democracy and Austro-Marxism, translated the notion of disproportionality under conditions of capitalist anarchy into a theory of proportionality in the case of state-directed production. Hence, "socialization" was thought to be synonymous with statism, or political elimination of competitive anarchy. The object then was simply to capture the capitalist state, in order to build a new society by enlarging upon the already existing administrative apparatus in the "public" realm (and through the now familiar policy of nationalization of the commanding heights of the economy).

Yet, whatever confidence these theorists had in the possibility of harmony between the economy and the existing state was based on a very weak form of disproportionality analysis, which merely stressed the chaotic relationship between various sectors of production. Insofar as this perspective failed consistently to locate the

source of capitalist contradictions in class struggles over the com-
moditization of labor power, it missed what was most essential to
Marx's economics (and political theory).

A more sophisticated approach, emphasizing deep-seated "disproportionalities in social production" (between production-goods
and consumption-goods departments), was to be found in the
works of Lenin and Bukharin (and obtained its most complete
expression much later in the work of Sydney Coontz). Lenin and
Bukharin argued that the fundamental contradiction of capitalism
is the tendency for the means of production to expand faster than
the consumption capabilities of the system; a reality which has its
basis in the social limitations imposed on the consumption of the
masses by capitalist exploitation. This underlying trend toward disequilibrium in social production was believed to be tied in turn to
the disproportionalities among branches of industry, resulting
from competition between individual capitals.

In my view, the "social disproportionality theory" advanced by
Lenin and Bukharin situated crisis tendencies in the very core of
the capitalist mode of production (i.e., the contradictions of the
exploitation of labor power). Theories of this type are not compatible with reformism. And this is true despite Bukharin's naive belief that a form of "state capitalism" could conceivably plan away all
crisis tendencies, including those which resulted from the limited
consumption of the direct producers.

Next to the falling-rate-of-profit school, the most influential
stream of radical economics since World War II has been "underconsumptionism." The mature version of this theory (to be found,
most notably, in the writings of Michal Kalecki, Josef Steindl, Paul
Baran, and Paul Sweezy) is a very complex conceptual apparatus
which brings together many of the most important insights of
Marx, Luxemburg, Lenin, and Bukharin.[3] This form of "neo-
Marxian" crisis theory, which is grounded on the theory of monopoly capital, can be reduced to eight closely connected observations:
(1) the tendency toward "social disproportionality" between productive capacity and consumption potential, with the former constantly threatening to outpace the latter; (2) a rate of surplus
extraction in the monopoly sector(s) which is so high that it represents the relative overexploitation of labor power, with realization
(or effective demand) difficulties replacing the falling-rate-of-
profit tendency as the main historical constraint on expanded reproduction; (3) the transformation of capitalist competition in the
monopoly stage, with price competition playing a much smaller
role; (4) replacement of the price mechanism by the relationship
between productive capacity and its utilization as the prime deter-

minant of investment decisions among monopolistic firms—resulting in a strong tendency toward underinvestment; (5) the appearance of secular stagnation, or an underlying trend toward relatively low growth over the long run, as a distinguishing characteristic of the mature economy; (6) growth of both conglomeration and multinational corporate imperialism as the giant firms attempt to escape the limitations of their markets; (7) an alteration in the role played by unproductive expenditures, which can no longer be seen as mere deductions from the social accumulation fund available to capital; and (8) the inability of the capitalist state to surmount the problems of overaccumulation, and the contradictory (stagflationary) consequences of its efforts to do so.

Evaluation of Marxian underconsumption theory has always been complicated by the existence of a fairly well-defined underworld of "social liberal" economists (e.g., John Hobson) who have argued that the main source of economic difficulties is the low wages of the masses. After the so-called Keynesian revolution of the 1930s this type of analysis became for a short time more "reputable," insofar as it focused on the problem of effective demand. Yet it is improbable that more than a handful of liberal economists themselves were ever so absolutely devoid of business common sense as to take seriously the idea that wage inflation (or even full employment in any real sense) could be an acceptable way for capital to solve its economic troubles—regardless of what the more utopian reformists, and an army of apologists with their introductory textbooks, may have sometimes claimed to the contrary. Radicals for their part had been forewarned by both Marx and Lenin against the adoption of such naive views—naive, that is, from the standpoint of class analysis.

It should of course surprise no one that radical critics of Marxian underconsumptionism have generally confused it with the crude non-Marxian underconsumptionism advanced by Hobson, or with the related social liberalism of left-Keynesians (such as Joan Robinson, and perhaps even Keynes himself). Yet such interpretations are totally misconceived. While social-liberal and Keynesian economists (of any variety) attribute the demand difficulties of capitalism to maldistribution of income, "imperfect competition," psychological errors, and wrongheaded fiscal and monetary policies, all of which presumably can be repaired through appropriate forms of state intervention, Marxian economists trace the problem to the dynamics of accumulation itself, and argue that intervention by the capitalist state, over the long run, only promotes even more explosive contradictions, accelerating the crisis of the world capitalist system. In fact, one of the strong points of modern Marxian underconsumption (or overaccumulation) theory, from the very beginning, has been its critique of the Keynesian notion of "capitalist state planning."

Profit-squeeze analysis presents us with an entirely different problem, and one that is worth considering in some detail. Inspired, in large part, by the so-called neo-Ricardian revival of classical economics, a considerable number of radical theorists—mainly in Britain, but also in the United States and Canada—have begun to focus once again on the wage-profit ratio as the primary explanation of crises.[4] The empirical component of these studies purports to show that the cyclical decline in profit rates can be attributed largely to increases in wage rates near the peak of each trade cycle. In the British context, it is frequently argued that the wage share of income has been steadily increasing over the last decade, with damaging consequences for profits. Moreover, it is presumed that this is the normal pattern of capitalist accumulation. Class struggle over wage rates and working conditions therefore becomes the immediate source of cyclical economic crises and secular decline of profitability under capitalism. It is characteristic of theorists in this tradition to place heavy emphasis on the power of trade unions to push up wage rates, while implicitly denying to monopolistic corporations even that modicum of control over prices accorded to them by the Galbraithian "countervailing power" thesis.

There is of course nothing particularly new about this approach which, along with its mainstream counterpart (differing substantially only in terms of political conclusions), is as old as capitalism itself. No one would deny that it captures an important part of the truth, though, in my view, its useful application *by itself* is quite limited.[5] Indeed, the notion that high wages almost alone can restrict the profitability of capital—with very little (if any) first order consideration of monopolistic pricing, productivity growth, the rate of exploitation and international competition—tends to present a case which is ideologically stacked against labor (though this clearly isn't the intention). The logical corollary is to be found in the idea that wage increases are, for the most part, responsible for inflation.

The enormous popularity that this mode of analysis has won during the last few years can no doubt be attributed to the fact that it reduces everything to a question of immediate political struggle along class lines. Capitalist profitability is believed, by most of those who adhere to this tradition, to be inconsistent with further improvements in wages and working conditions. Class resistance, initiated by the workers for the purpose of raising their living standards, will simply cause the whole capitalist machine to slowly grind to a halt. Once enough people become conscious of this it will be possible to use the mechanism of wage inflation as a *political* weapon in the revolutionary transition to socialism.

Notwithstanding the radical character of such pronouncements, the actual content of this theory (divorced from its nonessential political conclusions) remains pretty much what liberalism has been saying all along. Moreover, it requires a breathtaking leap in pure imagination to assume that bourgeois economics is so ill-adapted to the needs of bourgeois politics. In fact, if wage inflation is the only real obstacle to the smooth growth of capitalism, it is difficult to see why it would not indeed be "rational," as the vested interests argue, for workers in such cases to adopt a form of negative economism (controls on wages), so as to promote a new "take-off" in accumulation and some "reasonable" level of general prosperity (however small the "trickle down" effect might be).

It would be injudicious to imply that all theories which emphasize a wage squeeze on profits are open to the foregoing objections. Marx himself formulated a theory of crisis somewhat along these lines (although he visualized economic dislocations of this sort as extreme cases, and atypical of capitalist development overall). The more sophisticated variant of this general type of theory sees wage pressures on profitability almost exclusively in relation to the business cycle, rather than as an underlying secular tendency.[6] Moreover, the ultimate source of wage inflation, according to this type of analysis, is not growing trade-union power so much as accumulation itself, and the lumpiness of fixed capital investment. A phase of rapid industrialization brings about an excess of capital in relation to the quantity of cost-efficient labor power and material inputs available, thereby raising the level of wages and other costs until profits are squeezed and a business downturn occurs. Thus it is the exhaustion of the industrial reserve army rather than the political economy of trade unionism (as stressed in the more common version) which is primarily responsible for the profit squeeze—though the distinction is largely a matter of emphasis since the two factors are closely interrelated.

There is very little wrong with this more refined explanation of the profit squeeze, as far as it goes. Yet, as Sweezy pointed out in his classic 1942 study, *The Theory of Capitalist Development* (p. 155), such a conception of periodic crises in accumulation, associated almost entirely with high wages at the peak of each cycle, provides no basis for the notion of a secular tendency toward an imperiled economy, but simply conceives each crisis as a temporary restorative mechanism for capital, *and nothing more.* This is why so many theorists who highlight the wage squeeze on profits are inclined to try to translate it into a qualitatively different theory of accumulation over the long run. Stretched out into a long-run theory, however, profit-squeeze analysis is invariably pulled apart in one place or another. If, as seems certain, the rate of exploitation of labor power tends to rise with increasing productivity, it is the relative deprivation of labor power which is the most characteristic feature of advanced accumulation, and the ultimate source of crises. While the pressure of wages on profits always represents a Maginot Line for capital in any particular phase of accumulation, the most important way in which capital historically deals with this infringement on its *lebensraum* is to go around it, by increasing productivity, exploitation, and the displacement of labor power. Hence the notion of a wage squeeze on profits, while essential for a proper understanding of capitalist crises, tells us relatively little about the deepening of the "general crisis" of capitalist production, which stems from the tendency for the rate of exploitation to rise, rather than to fall, as accumulation develops.[7]

The very expansion of the state presence in the advanced economy is in large part due to the need to stabilize an economic order which constantly demonstrates a powerful tendency toward stagnation. The more refined (and carefully limited) version of profit-squeeze analysis does not enable us to analyze the state in this context properly since it generally underestimates the depth and duration of class-based contradictions, by tracing them almost entirely to periodic "wage-push" constraints on capital growth. Nevertheless, this type of politicoeconomic theory remains sufficiently Marxist in character to be consistent with revolutionary praxis.

Once it is understood that despite important differences in vision there is no definite causal link between any of the major schools of Marxian crisis theory and reformist politics, two obvious areas of inquiry remain. First, each of these streams of thought can be judged in relation to logical coherence and degree of compatibility with the totality of Marx's vision of capitalist transformation. This has been tried many times in the past and is (except for a few hints made throughout) beyond the scope of this essay. Second, it is possible to examine these theories, broadly conceived, in terms of their usefulness in accounting for discrete phenomena present in history. In my view, a great deal can be learned from the relative virtues of these theories by seeing them through the spectrum of the state. Moreover, I am prepared to suggest that only modern Marxian underconsumption theory (based on the overaccumulation tendencies of monopoly capital), which will be discussed in the third part of this essay, has been able to tell us much of value about the political moment in the advanced capitalist economy.

Let me digress for a moment to emphasize that nothing like a complete theory of the capitalist state can be derived a priori from any general theory of accumulation crisis. This statement also has its basis in two points. First, a general theory of crisis, in the sense of each of the models discussed above, is only the very beginning in understanding the historic specificity of any particular crisis. Which is to say that the phenomenon of economic crisis within capitalist society is enormously complex (not least of all because of the permutations of money and credit) and cannot be fully accounted for by a general theory, which may in fact miss much of what is most crucial to the present conjuncture.

Second, the state cannot be entirely subsumed under its accumulation function. It has become increasingly common for Marxists to divide the functions of the state into two categories: accumulation and legitimation. While the importance of the latter has frequently been overemphasized, it unquestionably plays a substantial (albeit secondary) role in determining the configurations of centralized political relations. Moreover, the state is not simply an executive committee of the capitalist class; it is also an object of class struggle in itself. Thus genuine populist elements have occasionally secured temporary beachheads on this predominantly foreign soil. While certain theorists (particularly of the structuralist variety) constantly refer to "the relative autonomy of the state" from the economy and the capitalist class, and even the abstract possibility of capturing the state (or enclaves therein) with the object of socialist transformation, it is assumed here that the actual room for political maneuver *within capitalist boundaries* is at all times seriously constrained by the imperative of accumulation (the need to reproduce existing class relations in ever more concentrated form).

To return to our main theme, it seems worthwhile to take a look at how the different models of economic crisis are used to explain the nexus between accumulation and the state. Pure falling-rate-of-profit theorists (in contrast to economists like Maurice Dobb and Ernest Mandel, with their multicausal models) place little direct emphasis on the realization crisis, which they classify as a secondary manifestation of the long-run decline in profitability.[8] Since the main problem for falling-profit-rate theory is a relative dearth of surplus value (caused by a decline in the ratio of capacity output to total capital stock), the "solution" (which is always temporary for capital) must place additional surplus value in the hands of capitalists in the most advanced sector. There are four main ways (excluding foreign markets) in which this can occur: introduction of innovations which economize on capital inputs; an increase in the rate of surplus value; an increase in its mass; and a wholesale redistribution of surplus revenue in favor of concentrated industry. Since the tendential law of the falling rate of profit itself is predicated on the assumption that the first three of these remain simply "countervailing factors," economists within this current tend to place must greater stress on the last variable.

What all such theorists have in common, therefore, is the concept of a massive rechanneling of surplus value already produced, for the purpose of subsidizing the imperiled capital-intensive sectors of the economy. But this very "rescue operation," promoted separately by monopoly capital and the state, has the paradoxical consequence of narrowing the scope of modern industry. Theorists in this general tradition often refer to the "devalorization" (or unproductive consumption) effects of this dual process of monopolistic and state expansion, both of which occur at the expense of competitive capital and workers (or, by means of inflationary financing, fall unevenly on society as a whole). Large parts of the economy then operate at a depressed rate of profit, with some industries in the "public" sector even operating at zero or negative profitability, in order to keep the monopoly sector afloat. This is what the French state monopoly capital theorists, in particular, see as "the crisis in devalorization."[9]

Advocates of the falling-rate-of-profit theory in English-speaking countries put far less emphasis on the role of *monopoly* capital in all of this, due largely to the enormous counterinfluence of the *Monthly Review* tradition, which has made the surplus profits of monopoly capital the linchpin in a theory of "the tendency for the surplus to rise" (Baran and Sweezy). Yet the general notion of devalorization, if in somewhat more obscure terms, remains the basis for the theory of the "hypertrophy" of the state. More fundamentalist theorists, such as David Yaffe, see the state economic sector as little more than a cancer for the capitalist order, since they adhere, in ahistorical fashion, to the traditional Marxian notion that state expenditure eats away at the total surplus value already created, without in any way expanding the social accumulation fund available to the system. The catch-22, according to all such theorists, is that the more the economy as a whole is devalorized, with the help of the state, in order to promote valorization in the capital-intensive sector, the greater the overall problem of social valorization (creation of new value) becomes.

Perhaps the most ironical facet of this theory is the way in which it relates, in a roundabout manner, to the current political division within mainstream macroeconomics. The more fundamentalist Marxists, as I have noted several times, generally think of the realization problem as simply an epiphenomenal form of the falling-rate-of-profit tendency. Moreover, they generally assume that surplus value is automatically accumulated (i.e., immediately reinvested in productive capacity). Thus there is a susceptibility to enter into something resembling Say's Law of markets (supply, if forthcoming, creates its own demand) by the back door. The necessary strategy for capital (and its state), according to this line of thought, is precisely what the fashionable "supply-side economics" is trying to put into practice: the shoveling of gold or its paper substitute into the coffers of big capital. Both radical falling-rate-of-profit theorists and the currently fashionable supply-siders (on the basis of visions of the social universe which are diametrically opposed) believe that the social accumulation fund available to concentrated industry is too small, given the costs which must be borne in production. Obviously, one should be extremely careful not to read too much into this partial and surface similarity, but it does help us to understand that there is a kind of supply-side/demand-side division within radical economics itself, with endangered profitability theories on one side and realization crisis theories on the other.

Be that as it may, the theory of the declining rate of profit in its pure form postulates an accumulation crisis in advanced industry which is of increasing tempo, while suggesting at the same time that state intervention designed to counter this is, for similar reasons, ultimately even more dangerous for the system. Economists operating within this frame of reference seldom consider capitalist-imposed limitations on the degree of state expansion, assuming that the state will simply absorb an ever greater portion of industry as a whole, and thus bring capitalism closer to its final resting place in socioeconomic catastrophe (revolution). Ironically, the entire conceptual framework associated with the tendential law of the falling rate of profit appears to systematically underestimate the importance which the capitalist state has actually assumed in temporarily propping up a stagnating economic system.

Profit-squeeze theory is more straightforward in what it has to tell us about the state and accumulation. Since the tendency toward economic standstill is attributed primarily to the squeeze of high wages on profits, the stabilization strategy of the state must be to promote unemployment, redistribute income from the bottom of the social hierarchy to the top, establish wage controls (if possible), etc. Since profits are presumed to be sparse, the state is forced to use every means at its disposal to subsidize capital itself. Moreover, this means a contraction of state spending as a whole (and particularly the "welfare" component thereof), since it is thought to be largely paid out of direct taxes on capital, thereby further reducing the share of profits in total income (a belief which, all things considered, is somewhat difficult to account for).[10] In a nutshell, this theory equates capitalist politicoeconomic necessity (which radicals must oppose from start to finish) with the actual programs of Thatcherism and Reaganomics (the supply side). Undoubtedly, such policies have always carried considerable weight within the ruling class. Yet there is much to suggest, both from the standpoint of theory and of capitalist practice, that political action of this sort will *not even temporarily* solve the problem of an investment strike, in cases where the root problem is not high wages, or "falling" profits, but a lack of markets in which to dispose the social output which could potentially be produced. Since profit-squeeze theory generally adopts the same one-dimensional economic perspective as bourgeois ideology, it is not surprising that the popular form of this theory (in spite of its obvious revolutionary credentials) has yet to prove itself to be anything more than an indifferent guide to practice.

The economic role of the state also enters into this theory through its critique of Keynesianism. It seems to be the general wisdom in this school that the growth of state expenditures in itself (and aside from the question of taxation) does little to avert crisis, but on the contrary may actually heighten such tendencies by reducing the size of the industrial reserve army. In sharp contrast to most other Marxian economic models, the augmentation of state spending (apart from the nationalization of certain industries) is seldom treated as a natural outgrowth of capital accumulation and crisis. Rather, the main determinants of such expenditures are generally thought to be political, and hence exogenous to the normal economic process: World War II, antisocialist adventurism, the politics of popular legitimation, a growth of "laborism," the illusions of Keynesianism, the political business cycle, "reflation," and so on. Once introduced, such expenditures tend to induce a chronic inflationary profit squeeze, and are subsequently cut back. Nor is it merely fortuitous that things develop in this fashion. The growth of state expenditures, in the final analysis, is accounted for by this school in much the same way as economic crisis itself is: in this case the *political* power of a relatively affluent laboring population. The advent of a slump undermines both the economic power of the workers, and the political power which is largely derived from it, thereby allowing the capitalist class to "dismantle" the "welfare state" (or reduce the so-called "social wage") with relative ease.

Disproportionality theory has added little to our understanding of the advanced capitalist state. The one exception is Sydney Coontz' magnum opus, *Productive Labor and Effective Demand* (1965). Following the essential form of Lenin's theory, Coontz analyzes the distributional effects of the division of production into a department for capital goods on the one hand, and consumption goods on the other. On this basis, he constructs a theory of accumulation and realization crisis, tests it for historical validity, and utilizes it to criticize post-Keynesian growth theories. A large part of his investigation was devoted to a devastating rebuttal of profit-squeeze interpretations of capitalist dynamics. Perhaps his most important contribution, however, was an attempt to reconceptualize Marx's theory of productive and unproductive labor (and productive and unproductive consumption) on historical grounds. This was founded on the belief that a theory of accumulation must account for the net social product and its utilization, in contradistinction to the gross revenue form of national income accounting adopted by establishment economics.

In fact, Coontz represents the bridge between the two major versions of realization crisis. While his close adherence to Lenin's method certainly must classify him as a disproportionality theorist, his results are coterminous with the most sophisticated version of underconsumption theory (the overaccumulation analysis of Josef Steindl). Coontz concludes that the very nature of advanced capitalist development generates a tendency toward overexpansion and overproduction in the consumer goods department, given the limits of effective wage-based demand; a reality which manifests itself in the form of capital saturation and excess capacity in the capital-goods department. Like Sherman, he never lets the reader forget that there are two sides to the "profit-consumption dilemma" facing capital. The relative overexploitation of labor power ensures that the realization problem will obstruct accumulation, while the imperative of lowering costs and raising the rate of exploitation (necessary in order for individual capitals to even maintain existing profit margins) makes it impossible for capital to escape the effective-demand gap by altering relations of appropriation and distribution on the supply (cost) side. He clearly believes that capital can obtain some degree of temporary relief through the proliferation of unproductive expenditures (particularly the militarization of monopoly capital), but this is a very limited and short-term answer. Sooner or later the piper has to be paid.

Many of the questions that Coontz raised have been worked out in greater detail by the monopoly-capital theorists of modern Marxian underconsumptionism. In the following section I will try to indicate briefly some of the more promising lines of inquiry which have been opened up by this tradition with respect to the state and economy. In doing so, I shall be presenting a sketch of how, in my view, one can best understand the state's role in accumulation, at the level of general principle.

The starting point is the "neo-Marxian" theory of monopoly capitalism. This paradigm, already discussed in some detail above, dates back to at least the early 1950s with the appearance, within a five-year span, of Steindl's *Maturity and Stagnation in American Capitalism* (1952), Kalecki's *Theory of Economic Dynamics* (1954), and Baran's *The Political Economy of Growth* (1957). In addition, it was during this same period that Baran and Sweezy began their work on *Monopoly Capital* (not published until 1966). Of course many of the initial breakthroughs had been made one or two decades before. The essential elements of Kalecki's theory were in place and published by the early 1930s (before Keynes wrote *The General Theory*), while Sweezy had forged some of the main components of present-day monopoly capital theory by 1942 in *The Theory of Capitalist Development* (though he had not yet satisfactorily worked out the connection between underconsumption and underinvestment). Together these works have shown beyond a shadow of a doubt that the giant firm has significantly modified the laws of motion of capitalism. To be more specific, monopolistic pricing has substantially altered the forms of appropriation, distribution, and utilization of surplus value in the modern capitalist economy. The tendency for the potential economic surplus to increase in size, with overaccumulation in the monopoly sector(s) due to the power of such firms to impose price mark-ups on value, has made "the profit-consumption dilemma" (as Coontz neatly puts it) the chief hole in capital's pot of gold.[11] Hence, the monopolistic structure of the modern economy produces a powerful disposition toward stagnation, coupled with an apparently endless inflationary spiral.

Baran and Sweezy point out in *Monopoly Capital* that the potential economic surplus leaves its "statistical trace not in the figures of profits and investment but rather in the figures of unemployment and unutilized productive capacity" (p. 218). Moreover, it is precisely the existence of *excess capacity* (most heavily based in concentrated industry) which discourages investment in further capital goods by monopolistic firms; and this of course underpins the entire tendency toward low growth in the advanced economy. To quote a recent issue of the most prestigious of American business publications: "Studies have shown that capital spending plans accelerate when operating [capacity utilization] rates move significantly above the 80 percent level and decelerate when they dip below it" (*Business Week,* August 3, 1981, p. 12). Gabriel Kolko explains much more:

> One index to the emerging contradictions in the capitalist economy after 1970 was the lower utilization of the productive capacity of manufacturing and major materials industries. Despite the business threats of that period of insufficient capital and profits to combat obsolescence, which were designed primarily to shock Congress into allocating yet more favorable tax provisions, the industrial plant far exceeded the domestic capacity to absorb its output. Industry, if anything, had overcapitalized during the postwar era. Five different indices all showed that 1970-1975 had the highest amount of unused capacity since World War II, with late 1974 and 1975 marking the nadir. Taking the Federal Reserve Board's index, the manufacturing utilization rate was 77.2 percent during 1970-1975 compared to 91.9 percent in the postwar high period of 1950-1954. In brief, the capitalist economy's traditional nemesis of inadequate demand and overexpansion had reappeared in almost classic form despite all the vast means that had been employed to counteract them. And for that reason the dilemma was all the more dangerous, as the efficacy of the postwar economic measures proved all too finite—and no better ones remained to be employed.[12]

And it is no wonder that the business community, as Kolko suggests, is worried. While capacity utilization over the entire period from the end of World War II to the present has remained on the average roughly around 80 percent (with little incentive to invest in additional plant and equipment, as the *Business Week* statement indicates), since 1974 it has shown a strong tendency to "dip below" the 80 percent level, according to official government underestimates (*Economic Report of the President,* 1981, p. 281).

The existence of mountains of idle productive capacity is a concrete sign of impending hard times; but we would be making a serious mistake, and a fundamentally un-Marxist one, if we were to stop here. Equally significant is the existence of enormous reserves of unemployed, underemployed, and socially unreproductive labor, which is sufficient to put all of this productive capacity and a good deal more into operation. This is a difficult problem to tackle since official statistics of unemployment overlook most of the actual reserve army. Perhaps the best treatment of this problem is to be found in an article written by Magdoff and Sweezy over ten years ago.[13] When official estimates for unemployment were logged at 6.2 percent (December 1970), Magdoff and Sweezy convincingly demonstrated that 9.4 percent would be a more accurate figure, given the underemployment of certain workers, and the exclusion from official unemployment data of all those discouraged job-seekers who have not actively sought employment during the last four weeks (at the time of the government survey). Moreover, by adding in extremely moderate estimates of the direct impact of the defense sector on employment, they persuasively showed that the level of unemployed, underemployed, and *unreproductive* labor was at least 25.1 percent (greater than unemployment during the Great Depression). It goes without saying that if similar estimates were to be made today, they would substantiate the fact that only military spending has kept the United States out of the deepest depression in its history.

Military spending is only the tip of the iceberg in terms of the proliferation of labor which, from the social standpoint, serves no useful purpose. The elimination of price competition as a major factor within the dominant sectors of the economy led to the emergence of numerous increasingly wasteful forms of "monopolistic competition": advertising campaigns, vast marketing empires, "product differentiation," expensive lobbying efforts, planned obsolescence, sumptuous packaging—the list is endless.[14] And there can be no doubt about the fact that the state (quite apart from so-called defense spending) is involved in the promotion of unproductive and socially useless expenditures, both within its own sphere and in the economy as a whole.

Given these conditions, it should be obvious to everyone that the problem of unproductive (and unreproductive) expenditures must be placed at the very center of our analysis. But, as all Marxists know, this is no easy task. Marx brilliantly distinguished, in relation to his own historical era, between productive labor, which enhances surplus value, and unproductive labor, which is exchanged against surplus value (in the form of mere revenue) already produced. He apparently thought that unproductive labor, which he generally associated with circulation under the domination of merchant (as opposed to industrial) capital, and with the luxury consumption of the landlord class, would tend to diminish (though not entirely disappear) as time went by. To make matters more complex, he seems to have believed that full utilization of productive capacity was the norm for capitalism, when not in an actual state of economic crisis. Hence, any unproductive expenditures were conceived as absolute deductions from potential surplus product. Marx, quite naturally, was generalizing upon the laws of motion of capitalism during his own time, and believed that competitive industrial capitalism was the last phase of the bourgeois order. Though he provided the analysis of concentration and centralization of capital upon which the later theory of monopoly capitalism was constructed, he generally thought this to be a sign of the coming socialist order, and not simply a transition from one stage of capitalism to another. In any case, he provided very little analysis of the problem which most concerns radicals engaged in the political struggle against monopoly capitalism: the utilization of potential surplus.[15]

Obviously, I have no intention of trying to provide a definitive answer to this massive problem here. But it should be equally obvious that no understanding of the economic presence of the capitalist state can be developed without crossing this Rubicon (however rash that may prove to be). The key, as I see it, is to be able to break down "the circular flow" of income and expenditures in the modern economy. Since it is well known that the theoretical basis for the most advanced forms of national income accounting were anticipated (and in part inspired) by Marx's reproduction schemes, this is not as difficult as it might appear at first glance. Following Kalecki, we can picture Marx's *tableau economique* for simple reproduction in terms of an input-output table of the double entry kind used by Wassily Leontief (the latter having derived his technique indirectly from Marx by way of Soviet planning).[16]

This is done in Table I. In accordance with Marx's model of simple reproduction all surplus value is consumed by capitalists and none is accumulated (an abstraction for theoretical purposes and in no way a real possibility for capitalism). In addition, as in all Marxian models of capitalist production, workers do not save but consume their entire income (an assumption which more or less conforms to reality). M is used as the symbol of Marx's constant capital (fixed plus circulating capital). V represents Marx's variable capital (wages), and S his surplus value (in this case, profits net of depreciation). C, I, and Y stand for the normal Keynesian aggregates of consumption, investment, and income (respectively). Production is divided into three departments (indicated by the vertical columns with the appropriate numerals above). The value of the output in each department consists of $M + V + S$ (with the subscripts indicating which department each component of value derives from). The output of department 1 equals total productive investment, I (which in this case merely replaces depreciated capital). The output of department 2 equals total productive consumption of wage goods, C_v (the subscript indicating consumption by variable capital). Department 3 equals the total unreproductive consumption of luxury goods by capitalists out of surplus value, C_s (which in simple reproduction is equal to total surplus value, as indicated by subscript s). If one then looks horizontally down the rows it is possible to see the demand which corresponds to the

Marx's "Tableau"	Table I		Simple Reproduction	
		Outputs (value produced)		
Inputs		Departments		
(Outlays)	1	2	3	*Totals*
Material (constant) capital	M_1	M_2	M_3	M
Wages (variable capital)	V_1	V_2	V_3	V
Surplus value (profits net of depreciation)	S_1	S_2	S_3	S
Totals	I	C_v	C_s	Y

$M = I; V = C_v; S = C_s; M_2 + S_2 = V_1 + V_3; V_3 + M_3 = S_1 + S_2; V_1 + S_1 = M_2 + M_3$.

output of each department. Hence, M (the total of $M_1 + M_2 + M_3$) equals I, $V = C_v$ and $S = C_s$.

Take a look at the vertical column representing department 2. The gross profits ($S_2 + M_2$) of this department (i.e., surplus value produced plus constant capital carried over into the value of the output) exceeds the value of the wage goods actually consumed by workers located in that department, which is equivalent to V_2. These gross profits must be equal to a corresponding set of wage goods that can be sold to wage earners in other departments. Hence we arrive at the result that $M_2 + S_2 = V_1 + V_3$. Using similar logic, we can see that $V_3 + M_3 = S_1 + S_2$. Finally, the demand of workers and capitalists that emerges in the capital goods sector (department 1) represents demand for the output of the other two departments, while $M_2 + M_3$ constitute outlays for department 1. Thus $V_1 + S_1 = M_2 + M_3$. All three equations must hold under a simple reproduction schema with three departments. Nor do the fundamental relationships change if one refines the model to incorporate the reality of accumulation and expanded reproduction. It is only by means of such exchanges that the output in the three departments (columns 1, 2, and 3) finds its natural demand (in the top three rows, respectively).

We are not fundamentally interested here in the conditions of equilibrium established by the preceding equations, so much as in the utilization of economic surplus. It is essential to understand that department 1 and 2 enter into social reproduction as productive investment in capital goods, and productive consumption of wage goods, while department 3 comprises the unreproductive consumption of luxury commodities. Thus department 3 equals the value of those commodities which do not enter into the socially necessary reproductive costs of the two primary departments, and which (to a greater or lesser extent, depending on historic conditions) represent a drain on potential economic surplus.

As I have noted, Marx leaned toward the view that unproductive expenditures would become increasingly less important under capitalism, and that social production as a whole would generally be confined to departments 1 and 2. Capitalists would tend to automatically invest the vast proportions of their income in productive capacity, except under conditions of crisis. They would therefore waste relatively little in luxury consumption. Whatever remained of department 3 would be a total loss for the system.[17] Hence Marx believed that whatever was productive for capital would tend to correspond to that which was socially reproductive for commodity society as a whole.

In our time things are a good deal more complicated. For example, expenditure on armaments is an enormous part of the advanced capitalist economy. This represents industrial activity which is clearly *productive* of surplus value, while at the same time constituting a form of unreproductive luxury consumption. Certain other forms of expenditure (both public and private) are unproductive in Marx's original sense (i.e., do not increase the total surplus value within the system), but are economically viable since they absorb a considerable portion of potential surplus product, thereby promoting the expansion of reproduction in spite of the chronic problem of markets.[18]

Of course the basic conditions of the present stage of accumulation are clear. Excess capacity on a massive scale has become a perpetual feature of mature capitalism. To use the language of mainstream economics, advanced capitalism always operates at a level well within its "production possibilities curve." Under such condtions, there is no clear trade-off between the production of one set of commodities and another. In fact, the production of luxury goods has its short-term advantages. Expenditure on armaments can enhance total surplus value and GNP by promoting the realization of profits, without at the same time expanding the effective demand gap by enlarging on productive capacity.

This is where the state comes in. Once it is recognized that the system does not naturally equilibrate itself at the full employment level (as Say's Law of Markets had postulated), it is fairly obvious that the gap can be filled by one component of demand or another, without necessarily taking away from income derived elsewhere. This is particularly relevant to the subject of government spending. For a long time it had been held by mainstream economists that government spending could not help out even under conditions of deep depression (the possibility of which was itself often denied), since (according to Say's Law) government expenditure would merely replace spending of a more efficient nature that would normally occur within the market. It was of course Keynes' great virtue to realize that Say's Law was largely dogma, and his great fortune (at least as far as his place in establishment economics is concerned) to have packaged his insights in such a way that they demanded no outright rejection of Say's Law of Markets, but rather provided seemingly infallible techniques for arriving at full employment equilibrium, with a little help from the friendly state.[19] In other words, Keynes legitimated from an establishment economic perspective what Schumpeter had called "the doctrine of spending" (first successfully practiced in Hitler's Germany). By way of the famous "multiplier" government spending could add to the total demand within the economy, and thus increase the wealth of the entire society. A counterpart to all of this was the idea that deficit financing in the short period could be utilized to increase government expenditure, without necessarily increasing tax burdens or raising the government debt. The cost (or a large portion of it) would be paid through an increase in government tax revenue as incomes went up. The fiscal power of the state, together with monetary "fine tuning," was thought by such leading lights as Paul Samuelson to guarantee endless economic prosperity.

So much for theory and dogma. Reality has been far more prosaic. The role of the state in the economy has steadily increased, but it has not, and could not, produce the galloping full employment equilibrium that the Keynesians ostensibly sought. There were two major reasons for this failure of Keynesian economics. First, establishment economics (but not the class structure of society) was predicated on a formal indifference to the way in which total social capital was to be utilized. Second, the monopolistic structure of the modern economy produced tendencies toward stagnation and inflation that went far beyond the very limited power of the capitalist state to tinker with the economy.

Keynesian economics (or "the neoclassical synthesis") was never built upon the kind of analysis of social reproduction in class terms illustrated by the input-output table above. While Marx thought of goods according to whether they were destined for productive consumption by workers, or for productive investment and unproductive consumption by capitalists, mainstream economists still think primarily in terms of "households," "consumers," and "entrepreneurs." Status quo economists make no distinction between productive/unproductive labor and consumption, relying almost entirely on a gross revenue form of national income accounting, which is largely indifferent to the use value structure of the economy.[20] This explains much of the current bewilderment about the decline in the official rate of productivity growth (which, to the extent that it has any real meaning at all, reflects the enormous growth of unproductive or "certified" consumption, and of waste in general—and this simply because capitalism has been *too productive*).

A good example of the myopic nature of capitalist "planning" is the heavy reliance in the U.S. economy on "defense" spending. From the short-term perspective of giant capital this is the most acceptable form of government expenditure, since it creates demand in concentrated industries (and in the economy as a whole) and results in enormous profits, while neither expanding productive capacity nor competing with private markets. But from the longer view, the proliferation of such waste poses an enormous economic burden on society and holds down the potential trend-rate of growth. It is simply a question as to when the short-term economic benefits for capital will be offset by the restructuring of the economy toward unreproductive consumption.

The problem of unproductive (and unreproductive) expenditures relates closely to James O'Connor's brilliant analysis of *The Fiscal Crisis of the State*. O'Connor divides state spending into three main categories: "social investment," "social consumption," and "social expenses" (which are meant to correspond roughly to departments 1, 2, and 3, as envisioned by Marxian analysis), and then considers the consequences for the demand and supply of public finance. He argues that each category of state expenditure tends to rise very rapidly; and this is especially true of social expenses (which, according to O'Connor, are "not even indirectly productive").[21] Social expenses skyrocket because of the inability of monopoly capital to find sufficient market outlets to justify full utilization of capacity. At the same time, the existing distribution of power within the society seriously limits the capacity of the state to collect additional tax revenues. Hence a "structural gap" emerges between the expenditure requirements and revenue of the state.

In his major essay on "National Economic Planning" in 1952 and again in *The Political Economy of Growth* (1957) Paul Baran presented his case as to why the capitalist state could not effectively fulfill the Keynesian dream of full employment equilibrium.[22] His answer rested on two limitations: first, a sufficiently realistic theory of the capitalist state immediately suggested that there were a number of routes to planning, even as visualized (occasionally) by Keynesians, which had to be completely ruled out, since they conflicted with the hegemony of the capitalist class (e.g., substantial attempts to promote greater equality in income distribution). Second, outside of fascism, the remaining possibilities pointed to the building up of inflationary pressures, within the general context of a mature stagnationist economy, which would in themselves be intolerable to capital.

In fact, Baran briefly sketched out a full-fledged theory of what amounted to *stagflation* as the ultimate consequence of "the doctrine of spending," some twenty years before establishment economists (and most radical economists as well) were forced to admit that this was a reality. His argument relied mainly on two further points: (1) the induced investment effects of government deficits tended to encourage monopoly capital to overestimate the upward elasticity of demand, therefore expanding capacity when this was not warranted by the actual laws of production and the market; more fiscal demands would then be placed upon government to compensate; and (2) deficit financing, particularly on unproductive outlays, would produce an inflationary "overhang" extremely dangerous to the system.

No economist in recent memory has shown an equal degree of prescience. The following metaphor goes a long way toward explaining the present economic sickness:

> To be sure, systematic wastage of a sufficiently large proportion of the economic surplus on military purposes, on piling up redundant inventories, on multiplying unproductive workers, can provide the necessary "outward impulse" to the economy of monopoly capitalism, can serve as an immediate remedy against depressions, can "kill the pain" of rampant unemployment. But as with many other narcotics, the applicability of this shot in the arm is limited, and its effect is short lived. What is worse, it frequently aggravates the long-run condition of the patient.[23]

Anyone who takes any interest whatsoever in such matters is likely to be familiar with the triggering factors behind the present economic crisis: the decline of U. S. imperialist hegemony, the fall of the dollar, a rise in oil prices, government debt economies, changes in the structure of productivity, and so on. It is necessary for radicals to dig beneath such superficial explanations, in search of deeper causes. It is basic to the liberal view that we are now confronted by a large number of haphazard factors which have little to do with the basic structure of capitalism. Marxists, on the other hand, should seek out those general principles which allow the economy, the state, and the present crisis to be seen as one unified historical whole. I believe that the Marxian "mature economy thesis" does exactly that.

Notes

1. As is the case of David Yaffe, "The Marxian Theory of Crisis, Capital and the State," *Economy and Society* 2, no. 2 (1973): 186-232; and Paul Mattick, *Marx and Keynes* (Boston: Porter Sargent, 1969). In contrast, a number of important radical theorists, less given to pure "capital-logic," have argued that the law of the falling rate of profit was valid for Marx's day (early industrialization), but does not apply equally well to a mature capitalist economy. See Paul M. Sweezy, "Some Problems in the Theory of Capital Accumulation," *Monthly Review* 26, no. 1 (May 1974): 44-45.

2. See Rudolf Hilferding, *Finance Capital* (London: Routledge & Kegan Paul, 1981), pp. 257-66; V. I. Lenin, *The Development of Capitalism in Russia* (Moscow: Progress Publishers, 1964), pp. 51-58; Bukharin in Rosa Luxemburg, *The Accumulation of Capital: An Anti-Critique* (New York: Monthly Review Press, 1973) and Nikolai Bukharin, *Imperialism and the Accumulation of Capital* (New York: Monthly Review Press, 1972), pp. 203-37; and Sydney H. Coontz, *Productive Labor and Effective Demand* (London: Routledge & Kegan Paul, 1965).

3. Although rooted in the literature, "underconsumption" is an unfortunate designation since it implies a naive, one-sided perspective which is far from the actual case. The most important works in this tradition include: Michal Kalecki, *Selected Essays on the Dynamics of the Capitalist Economy* (Cambridge: Cambridge University Press, 1971) and *Theory of Economic Dynamics* (New York: August M. Kelley, 1969); Paul M. Sweezy, *The Theory of Capitalist Development* (New York: Monthly Review Press, 1970); Josef Steindl, *Maturity and Stagnation in American Capitalism* (New York: Monthly Review Press, 1976); Paul A. Baran, *The Political Economy of Growth* (New York: Monthly Review Press, 1957); and Paul A. Baran and Paul M. Sweezy, *Monopoly Capital* (New York: Monthly Review Press, 1966).

4. The most influential (and most characteristic) study in this tradition has been Andrew Glyn and Bob Sutcliffe, *Capitalism in Crisis* (New York: Pantheon, 1972), but Raford Boddy and James Crotty, Ian Gough, Bob Rowthorn and John Harrison have all made contributions to this general school of thought. Makoto Itoh has developed very similar ideas. However, his main source of inspiration has been the formidable work of Kozo Uno in Japan (still virtually unknown in the West).

5. The factual basis for this theory is increasingly being called into question. As Steindl has suggested, the supposed wage "explosion" can be explained in large part in terms of *deductions* built into workers' pay checks. Recent revisions of British government statistics for the period cited by Glyn and Sutcliffe (the 1960s and early 1970s) have apparently undermined much of the empirical basis for a theory of secular profit squeeze, with respect to Britain itself, by shifting the official profit series upwards. Thus it now seems evident that there was no decline in the post-tax profitability for the British economy as a whole

between the early 1960s and the appearance of the oil shock in 1974. This conclusion, now backed up by the newly revised statistics, had already been anticipated by a number of economists. See Steindl, "Stagnation Theory and Stagnation Policy," *Cambridge Journal of Economics* 3, no. 1 (March 1979): 12-13; and D. Currie and R. P. Smith, "Economic Trends and Crisis in the U.K. Economy," in David Currie and Ron Smith, eds., *Socialist Economic Review* (London: Merlin, 1981), pp. 7-8.

6. For a distinguished example see Makoto Itoh, *Value and Crisis* (New York: Monthly Review Press, 1980). Raford Boddy and James Crotty stand out within this pattern of thought since they focus on the actual business cycle rather than on the "Kontradieff" or long wave. See Boddy and Crotty, "Class Conflict, Keynesian Policies and the Business Cycle," *Monthly Review* 26, no. 5 (May 1974): 1-17.

7. It is worth noting that Kalecki developed an entirely consistent theory of both the business cycle and secular trends in accumulation which emphasized a rising rate of exploitation as the main constraint on expanded reproduction. Sherman has recently supplemented Kalecki's theory so as to account for the phenomenon of a rising share of wages at the peak of each cycle. While Kalecki saw the utilization of productive capacity as the main factor determining investment by giant firms, with large amounts of unused capacity creating investment shortfalls and a downturn in the business cycle, Sherman has added to this the notion that an overabundance of capacity at the cyclical peak leads to a temporary decline in the utilization of employed workers (since layoffs lag behind cutbacks in production), which decreases labor productivity (as conventionally measured) and increases the wage share of income. See Kalecki, *Selected Essays on the Dynamics of the Capitalist Economy*, pp. 26-34; and Howard Sherman, "Inflation, Unemployment and the Contemporary Business Cycle," *Socialist Review*, no. 44 (March-April 1979): 87. For a persuasive rendition of Marx's model of wage determination, taking into account the theory of accumulation over the long run, see Steindl, *Maturity and Stagnation*, pp. 230-34.

8. The theoretical objection to multicausal models is cogently expressed by Itoh, *Value and Crisis*, pp. 138-39.

9. For an excellent summary of this see John Fairley, "French Developments in the Theory of State Monopoly Capitalism," *Science & Society* 44, no. 3 (Fall 1980): 305-25; also Nicos Poulantzas, *State, Power, Socialism* (London: New Left Books, 1978), pp. 163-79.

10. Glyn and Sutcliffe, *Capitalism in Crisis*, pp. 157-88; Ian Gough, "State Expenditures in Advanced Capitalism," *New Left Review*, no. 92 (July-August 1975): 53-92, and *The Political Economy of the Welfare State* (London: Macmillan, 1979); and Bob Rowthorn, *Capitalism, Conflict and Inflation* (London: Lawrence and Wishart, 1980).

11. The concept of economic surplus is a necessary analytical device once the issue of utilization arises. Total surplus value is the measure both of the social accumulation fund potentially available to capital in the

current period and of the extent of the realization problem. Consequently, it can be taken to be roughly equal to Baran and Sweezy's "potential surplus" (the surplus with full utilization). The "actual" or "effective" surplus always falls short of this under conditions of monopoly capitalist production without war (and even then surplus absorption problems arise). The definitive treatment of this subject is to be found in a monograph by Henryk Szlajfer (Warsaw): "Economic Surplus and Surplus Value: An Attempt at Comparison" (University of Dar es Salaam, Economic Research Bureau, Occasional Paper 78.3, August 1979), p. 61.

12. Gabriel Kolko, *Main Currents in Modern American History* (New York: Harper & Row, 1976), p. 339.

13. "Economic Stagnation and Stagnation of Economics," *The Dynamics of U.S. Capitalism* (New York: Monthly Review Press, 1972), pp. 43-53.

14. American cigarette firms alone spent $1 billion in advertising in 1981 (*Business Week,* December 7, 1981, p. 65).

15. Paul M. Sweezy, "Competition and Monopoly," *Monthly Review* 33, no. 1 (May 1981): 15-16.

16. Michal Kalecki, "The Marxian Equations of Reproduction and Modern Economics," *Social Science Information* 7, no. 6 (December 1968): 73-74; Luigi L. Pasinetti, *Lectures on the Theory of Production* (New York: Columbia University Press, 1977), pp. 4-8, 19-20, 35-46; and Karl Marx, *Capital,* vol. 2 (New York: Vintage, 1978), pp. 435-36, 458-509.

17. It is indicative that while Marx had actually employed a three department schema in the *Grundrisse,* he restricted his analysis in *Capital* itself to the two primary departments, the second of which he divided into two sub-departments, reflecting the distinction between departments 2 and 3.

18. In brief, there are three predominant categories of waste: (1) certain unproductive expenditures ("the sales effort," lobbyists, finance, insurance, management, etc.); (2) unreproductive luxury goods production (Department 3); and (3) the actual excess capacity which still remains.

19. The vested interests were allergic to Keynes' own views on capitalist maturity, which emphasized secular stagnation.

20. The increased use of Leontief-type input-output models has given establishment economics a slightly improved basis of analysis, but Leontief and his followers have generally reduced this framework to the unrealistic (nonclass) terms of general equilibrium theory.

21. I have argued above that outlays on department 3 are *productive,* insofar as they enhance surplus value (i.e., if capacity in departments 1 and 2 is not fully utilized), yet can never be *reproductive,* since they do not enter into the value of either capital goods or wage goods. To be sure, there are expenditures which are "not even indirectly productive," in that they do not even enter into the value of luxury goods, and hence fall outside of the reproductive schemes altogether. Unfortunately, O'Connor seems to lump all of this together in one rather confusing category. See *The Fiscal Crisis of the State* (New York: St.

Martin's Press, 1973); Gough, *The Political Economy of the Welfare State,* pp. 158-61.

22. See Paul Baran, *The Longer View* (New York: Monthly Review Press, 1969), pp. 115-38, *The Political Economy of Growth,* pp. 120-29; Sweezy, "Baran and the Danger of Inflation," *Monthly Review* 26, no. 7 (December 1974): 11-14.

23. Baran, The Political Economy of Growth, p. 121.

INDEX

Absentee Ownership and Business Enterprise in Recent Times (Veblen), 13

The Accumulation of Capital (Luxemburg), 12

Accumulation fund, 18, 60, 265–66, 270, 328, 334

AFL–CIO, 114

Amin, Samir, 246

Armco, 36

Austro-Marxism, 326

Balogh, T., 191

Baran, Paul, 17–19, 25–26, 41, 67–69, 92, 200, 204, 209, 224, 243, 251–53, 262–71, 275, 280–81, 284, 287–88, 299, 308, 310, 312, 314–15, 327, 333, 337, 334–45

Bassie, V. Lewis, 204, 209

Bettelheim, Charles, 265

Bhaduri, A., 181, 193

Boddy, Raford, 94, 102, 104, 106

Böhm-Bawerk, Eugen von, 42, 298

Bortkiewicz, Ladislaus von, 240, 272

Bose, Arun, 278

Braverman, Harry, 18–19, 66, 200, 315

Bretton Woods, 122, 191–92

Brookings Institution, 254

Bukharin, Nikolai, 15, 327

Bureau of Economic and Business Research, 204

Bureau of Labor Statistics, 68, 255, 257

Burns, Arthur F., 217–19, 231, 233–34

Business cycle, 98–111, 127–33, 164, 238, 329–31

Business Week, 245–46, 337–38

Capacity utilization, 8, 14, 16–17, 67, 88, 92, 100–1, 104, 127–28, 130–31, 144, 147–48, 152–53, 155, 162–65, 169, 173, 177, 180–84, 186–87, 189–90, 193, 195–96, 198–201, 203–9, 242, 244, 257, 274, 276–77, 307, 314, 327–28, 336–39, 342, 345

Capital (Marx), 12, 14, 26–30, 34–36, 42, 45–46, 165, 237–38, 247, 269, 283, 297, 307, 316, 326

Capital adjustment mechanism, 16, 144, 176

Capital-output ratio, 98, 105–6, 147, 163, 276

Capitalism, Socialism and Democracy (Schumpeter), 238

Carnegie, Andrew, 66

Carter, Jimmy, 114, 217–18

Chandler, Alfred, 66

Civil War (U.S.), 32–33, 120

Class Struggle, 12, 19, 34, 82, 102, 122, 220–22, 238, 252

Classical economics, 10, 27–28, 45–46

Club of Rome, 195

Cogoy, Mario, 41–42, 47, 49, 50–51

Commodity prices, 119, 192

The Communist Manifesto (Marx and Engels), 283

Competition
in banking, 137
free, 11, 27–29, 38, 57, 61, 120, 128–29, 134, 141, 224, 226–27, 271–73, 276–77, 307, 339
imperfect, 79–81, 328
low cost position and, 33–34
monopoly and, 30–36
perfect, 28, 80, 138, 200
price and, 32–33, 134, 200, 225, 327, 339

Competitive firms, 35, 37, 43, 109–
10, 129, 134–35, 142, 146, 148,
174–75, 200
Concentration and centralization,
12, 14–15, 19, 29, 32–33, 42, 44,
65–66, 111, 119, 199, 238, 339
Conglomeration, 328
Consumption
accumulation and, 7–8, 50, 52–
53, 92, 97, 140, 152, 199, 203,
205, 327
capitalist, 12, 77–83, 156, 159–
63, 202, 210, 272, 307, 309–
10, 340–43
durable goods and, 170–71, 173
essential, 251–259, 264
optimal, 264
perverted, 53, 219
propensity to, 104, 143, 167,
170–171
social, 252, 255–56
wage goods and, 12, 77–83, 156,
159–62, 202, 311–12, 340–43
*Contribution to the Critique of Political
Economy* (Marx), 307
Coontz, Sydney, 327, 336–37
Costs of circulation, 37–38, 281
Credit
cyclical character of, 58, 62–63,
108, 171
debt-equity ratio, 16
expansion of, 19, 121, 171, 225,
227–29, 243–48
Crédit Mobilier, 246
Crotty, James, 94, 102, 104, 106

Demand, effective, 12, 14, 58, 61–
62, 97–98, 103–5, 107–8, 129,
134–37, 140–48, 151, 153, 155,
162–164, 166, 180, 182, 201,
225, 228, 327, 342
class structure of, 12, 343
Democratic Party, 114
Depreciation funds, 193, 231, 270
Disproportionality, 20, 151–53,
202, 325–27, 336–37
Dmitriev, W. K., 85
Dobb, Maurice, 332

Domar, Evsey, 9, 163
Duesenberry, James, 170

*Economic Report of the President,
1981*, 338
Economic surplus, 16–18, 85, 87,
203–4, 210, 251–59, 262–71,
278–288, 345
dialectical duality of, 287–88
utilization of, 37–38, 270–71,
278, 337, 340–41
Economies of scale, 67, 174–75
Employment
full, 7, 9, 179, 185, 187–89, 191,
194, 198, 343–44
level of, 57, 67, 129, 136, 140,
169, 228–29
Engels, Frederick, 14–15, 30
Eurodollars, 245–46
European Economic Commission,
195

Falling Rate of Profit, 44–53, 94–
98, 105–6, 209, 218–34, 325–27,
332–34
The Falling Rate of Profit (Gillman),
222, 299
Fascism, 345
Federal Reserve Board, 112, 204,
206, 208, 217–18, 229
Finance Capital (Hilferding), 15, 31
The Fiscal Crisis of the State (O'Con-
nor), 344
Ford, Gerald, 110, 195
Forrester, Jay, 195

Galbraith, John Kenneth, 114,
253, 308, 329
General law of accumulation, 198
*The General Theory of Employment,
Interest and Money* (Keynes), 7,
12, 16, 63, 337
German Social Democracy, 326
Gillman, Joseph, 47, 219, 221–30,
233–34, 275–76, 281, 299
Global capitalist perspective, 266–
68, 281, 286, 288–89, 300, 303–
4, 309, 311, 314

Gordon, Robert, 9
Gough, Ian, 306
Gramm, Warren, 92
The Great Depression, 7–9, 11, 19, 33, 47, 57, 62, 65, 70, 95, 108–9, 120, 200–1, 205, 244, 309, 339
Grundrisse (Marx), 27, 262, 283, 305, 307

Haavelmo, T., 167
Hansen, Alvin, 8–9, 17–18, 20, 64, 67, 224
Harrod, Roy, 9, 163, 179–81, 183, 185, 187, 193
Hegemony (U.S.), 112–13, 191–92, 205–6, 244, 246, 345
Higgins, Benjamin, 9
Hilferding, Rudolf, 15, 17, 31, 38, 298, 326
Hitler, Adolf, 343
Hobson, John, 328
"How to Pay for the War" (Keynes), 185

Imperialism, 15, 38, 68, 119, 121, 328
Imperialism, the Highest Stage of Capitalism (Lenin), 15, 31
Imperialism and World Economy (Bukharin), 15
Income distribution, 167, 182, 185, 254
    accumulation and, 7–8, 159–62
    monopoly and, 37, 77–83, 86
    wages and, 77–83, 85–89, 103–4, 107–11, 154
Individual capitalist perspective, 280–81, 300, 302, 304, 311
Industrial reserve army, 198, 238, 330, 335, 338
Industrial revolution, 46, 61
Inflation, 17, 19, 68, 107–14, 178, 185, 204, 217–19, 228, 231–34, 247, 329–330, 343, 345
    income distribution and, 118
    monopoly and, 108–10, 119–23
Innovations, 8, 18, 64, 129, 140, 148, 154–55, 167, 172, 175–77, 186, 188–89, 191–93, 210, 243
Input-output table, 340–43
Interest, 62, 88, 107, 133, 137–38
    investment and, 138–39, 141
Internal Revenue Service, 257
Investment
    competition and, 11, 104, 134–35, 174–75, 224–25, 242
    composition of, 138
    demand and, 10, 57, 62–63, 65, 67, 77–84, 129–32, 134, 136, 139, 140, 152–55, 160–61, 162–63, 167, 180, 183–85, 187, 190, 198–99, 201–9, 244, 278, 328
    financing of, 129, 134, 142–48
    historical evolution of, 57, 61–65
    induced, 345
    labor saving, 141
    long-run, 164, 172, 209–10
    portfolio, 143, 146–47
    risk and, 173–75
    social control of, 141
    stagnation and, 8, 16, 19, 176, 307, 337–38
    surplus and, 18
    tragedy of, 16

Kahn, Alfred, 136
Kaldor, Nicholas, 147, 185–87
Kalecki, Michal, 11–12, 15–18, 67, 172–73, 176–77, 179, 182, 188, 192, 198, 200, 224, 274–75, 307, 327, 337, 340
Kennedy, John F., 208
Keynes, John Maynard, 7–8, 10–11, 16, 59, 63, 89, 107, 136–38, 141, 146–47, 167, 179, 185, 192, 198, 222, 328, 337, 343
Keynesian economics, 7–11, 16–17, 63, 67–68, 103, 107–8, 137, 141, 182, 188, 198–99, 225, 234, 253, 325, 328–29, 335, 340, 343–44
Kindleberger, Charles, 192
Knowles, James, 254

Kolakowski, Leszek, 304
Kolko, Gabriel, 338
Konius, A. A., 272
Korean war, 64, 100, 108, 207–8, 244
Kurihara, Kenneth, 9

Labor and Monopoly Capital (Braverman), 18
Labor process, 18, 34, 303, 314–15
Labor unions, 82–83, 93, 109, 194–95, 329–30
Lenin, V. I., 15, 17, 31, 38, 202, 326–28, 336
Leontief, Wassily, 340
Luxemburg, Rosa, 12, 38, 151–53, 155–58, 165, 199, 275, 327

Magdoff, Harry, 19, 57, 338
Malthus, Thomas, 11, 48
Mandel, Ernest, 277, 299, 332
Marginal efficiency of capital, 7, 138, 195, 210
Marris, Robbin, 143–44
Marshall, Alfred, 62
Marshall Plan, 189, 191
Marx, Karl, 10–11, 13–15, 18, 27–31, 34–38, 41–52, 57–60, 65, 67, 87–88, 92–94, 103, 159–60, 164, 198, 200, 210, 219–24, 226, 229, 236–40, 246, 262–63, 269, 272, 274–75, 281–85, 297, 299–307, 310–11, 316, 325–28, 330–31, 339–43
Marx After Sraffa (Steedman), 236, 239
Mattick, Paul, 50
Maturity, industrial, 7, 9, 64–65, 167, 173, 180, 187, 210, 221, 345
Maturity and Stagnation in American Capitalism (Steindl), 16–17, 167, 179, 185, 188, 337
Medio, Alfredo, 272–73
Merton, Robert, 312–13
Mészáros, István, 283
Military spending, 9–10, 17, 92, 112, 151, 156–57, 165, 188,

190–91, 206, 210, 219, 244, 282, 297, 309–11, 314, 339, 342, 344
Mill, John Stuart, 27, 48, 58, 62
Mills, Frederick, 105–6
Mishan, E. J., 313
Mitchell, Wesley, 222
Modigliani, Franco, 170
Monopoly, 8, 30–33, 108–12, 128–29, 200–1, 203–4, 336
  degree of, 12, 15, 80–82, 86, 274, 276
  value theory and, 18, 25–26, 33, 36–37, 41–44, 238, 341–42, 273, 276–77
Monopoly Capital (Baran and Sweezy), 17–18, 25–26, 41, 67, 204, 243, 252, 262–63, 269, 270–71, 278, 280, 337
Monopoly capitalism
  stage of, 11, 13–19, 30–31, 34–38, 53, 118–23, 204–5, 210, 219, 224–28, 233–34, 242–43, 253, 263–64, 274, 278, 282–83, 307–9, 313–14
  theory of, 13–19, 25–26, 29–38, 67, 209, 224–25, 242, 267–73, 327–28, 337, 339–40, 345
  transition to, 13, 65–67, 111, 119, 209, 224, 241–42, 282
Monthly Review, 19–20, 333
Morgan, J. P., 13
Morris, Jacob, 299
Multinationals, 247, 328
Murad, Anatol, 9
Nathan, Otto, 270

"National Economic Planning" (Baran), 344
Neoclassical economics, 9–10, 57, 138, 182, 343
Neo-Marxian economics, 11, 198, 200, 327
New Deal, 112
Nixon, Richard, 100, 110

Ochocki, Aliksander, 312
O'Connor, James, 344
Office of Business Economics, 257

Okishio, Nobuo, 274–75
Oligopoly, 17, 83, 108, 135, 138–42, 173–74, 185, 187, 195
Oligopoly and Technical Progress (Sylos-Labini), 17
Organic composition of capital, 42–43, 45–51, 95–97, 105–6, 220–24, 229–30, 272, 285, 288, 325
Organization for Economic Cooperation and Development (OECD), 191
Organization of Petroleum Exporting Countries (OPEC), 192, 246
Output
  class composition of, 10–11, 15–16, 60–61, 67, 340–42
  level of, 11, 15, 57, 60, 68–69, 98, 102–5, 130, 198–99, 200–4
Overaccumulation, 12, 16, 57, 61, 203, 328–29, 331, 336
Overinvestment, 107, 203
Overproduction, 11, 16, 49–50, 58, 61, 154, 203, 244, 277, 336
Oversavings, 17, 63

Papandreou, Andreas, 253
Phillips Curve, 194
Phillips, J. D., 270, 279
Pigou, A. C., 62
Political business cycle, 189, 335
The Political Economy of Growth (Baran), 17, 262–63, 269, 299, 337, 344
Porter, Michael, 33–34
Post-Keynesian economics, 11, 336
Price mark-ups, 80–82, 85–86, 182, 195, 200, 337
Prices of production, 26, 42–43, 239–42, 272–73
Principles of Economics (Marshall), 62
Principles of Political Economy (Mill), 27
Production in general, 300–1, 304

Productive Labor and Effective Demand (Coontz), 336
Productivity statistics, 68–69
Profit
  level of, 33, 77–79, 81–82, 135, 142, 152–54, 187, 196, 206
  share of, 87–88, 95, 99, 101–3, 159–62, 181–82
  theory of, 87
Profit margin, 12, 14–15, 17–18, 67, 69, 80, 85–86, 108, 186–187, 196, 199, 200–1, 336
Profit rate, 18, 87–88, 95, 97, 129, 144–48, 152–54, 193, 209, 217–24, 272
  business cycle and, 97–107, 110
  fetishism of, 241
  investment and, 98, 102, 128, 176
  monopoly and, 35–37, 42–43, 69, 174–75
  theoretical rate of, 272–77
  unproductive labor and, 225–34, 263, 271–76
Profit squeeze theory, 68–69, 93–94, 98–99, 102–4, 325, 329–31, 334–36

Qualitative value analysis, 237–38, 268, 274, 277

Raw material costs, 105–6
Reaganomics, 335
Realization, 17, 49, 52, 59–60, 67, 87, 94, 97, 103, 106, 165, 199, 225, 228, 274, 277, 279–80, 327, 334, 336
Recession of 1937, 9, 62, 108, 205
Rent, 48, 95
Rentier, 232–33
Reproduction schemes, 11–12, 15, 60–61, 65, 77–79, 81–82, 87, 152, 154, 159–64, 209, 298–99, 310, 340–44
  credit and, 246
Republican Party, 114
Ricardian economics, 11, 58, 272, 329

Ricardo, David, 48–49, 57–58, 142, 222, 283, 309
Rockefeller, John D., 67
Robinson, Joan, 11, 41, 50, 147, 198, 239, 274, 313, 328
Rosdolsky, Roman, 298–99

Sales effort, 37–38, 121, 143–44, 225, 253, 339
Salvati, Michele, 269, 282
Samuelson, Paul, 9, 107, 343
Saving, 61–65, 136–37, 140, 146, 172–73, 176–77, 180–85, 193
   durable goods and, 171
   hoarding and, 141
   propensity to, 140, 179
   surplus and, 266
Say's Law, 7, 9, 11, 57–59, 61–63, 70, 77–79, 274, 334, 342–43
Schmidt, Helmut, 195
Schumacher, E. F., 192
Schumpeter, Joseph, 8–9, 20, 64, 67, 210, 222, 238–39, 343
Scitovsky, Tibor, 313
Service sector, 19, 297
Shaikh, Anwar, 240
Sherman, Howard, 336
Simple commodity production, 57–58
Smith, Adam, 10
Socialism, 222, 330, 340
   "actual existing," 244, 288
   objective necessity of, 199, 211, 252
Socialist rationality, 266–68, 284, 286–88, 299, 304, 316
South Sea Bubble, 246
Speculation, 70
Spurious capital formation, 219, 227–34
Sraffa, Piero, 85, 87–88, 239, 272–74, 276
Stagflation, 68, 112, 199, 204, 210, 219, 328, 337, 345
Stagnation, 7–10, 14, 18–20, 53, 64, 68, 119, 121–22, 134, 181, 195, 203, 242–43, 245, 248, 328, 343, 345

Stanfield, Ron, 288
State
   crisis and, 325–45
   deficits and, 10, 132, 196, 218, 235, 245, 345
   fiscal crisis and, 344–45
   monopoly and, 333
   reform and, 326, 328–30, 333–35
   spending of, 10, 17, 63, 68, 112, 141–42, 156, 167–69, 189–90, 218, 225, 227–29, 332–35, 342–45
   stagflation and, 68, 204, 328, 345
   theory of, 331–32
Steedman, Ian, 236–40
Steindl, Josef, 16–17, 67, 200, 274, 327, 336–37
"The Stock Exchange" (Engels), 15
Stock market crash, 1929, 246
Streever, Donald, 204
Supply-side economics, 57, 70, 334–35
Surplus product, 19, 34, 57, 60, 67, 155–56, 228–29, 339
   surplus value and, 282, 284
Surplus value, 17, 25–26, 35–36, 42–47, 49–53, 69, 87, 92–94, 97, 118, 152, 200, 202–3, 220–21, 224–27, 230–33, 238, 240–42, 262–63, 265–67, 272–84, 302–3, 307, 309, 313, 325, 327, 329, 331, 337, 340–42
   antagonistic character of, 301–4
   domination of absolute form, 282
   historical specificity of, 284–87, 299–300
   planned surplus and, 282
   traditional calculus of, 281–82, 288
Sweezy, Alan, 9
Sweezy, Paul, 17–20, 25–26, 41, 57, 65, 67, 92, 200, 203–4, 209, 224, 243, 251–53, 262–64, 269–71, 275, 280–82, 284, 287–88,

298–99, 312, 327, 330, 333, 337–38

Sylos-Labini, Paolo, 17, 274

Taxation, 114, 141, 156–57, 167–69, 173, 184–85, 189–90, 217–18, 279, 343

Taylorism, 19, 34, 66–67, 315

Thatcherism, 335

Theories of Surplus Value (Marx), 298

The Theory of Business Enterprise (Veblen), 13, 31

Theory of Capitalist Development (Sweezy), 242, 330, 337

Theory of Capitalist Dynamics (Kalecki), 337

Transformation problem, 236–42, 272–73

Tugan-Baranovski, Michael, 15, 151–53, 155, 157–58, 202, 210

Underconsumption, 12, 14, 16, 49–50, 52, 60–61, 69, 91–93, 98–99, 106–8, 202, 325, 327–28, 331, 336–45

naive forms, 92–93, 328

Underdeveloped countries, 155–56, 165, 192, 211

Underinvestment, 17, 63, 328, 337

Unemployment, 9, 14, 62–63, 91–93, 100, 111–15, 127–29, 134–41, 169, 188, 194–95, 198–99, 217, 220, 242, 245, 266–67, 275, 279, 334, 338

Unemployment (Pigou), 62

United Alkali Trust, 30

Unproductive labor, 17, 38, 67, 69, 141, 145, 204, 206, 210, 219–20, 225–31, 253, 263–82, 286, 297–316, 328, 333, 336, 338–45

U.S. Steel, 13, 66, 111

Use value, 37–38, 43–44, 58–59, 203, 209–10, 266, 286, 298–311, 344

historical dimension of, 305–6, 308, 311, 316

monopoly capitalism and, 282–83, 306–8, 312–13

specifically capitalist, 210, 286, 299–301, 303–4, 307, 309–315

Veblen, Thorstein, 13–14, 18, 31, 38, 67, 222, 287, 312–13

The Vested Interests and the Common Man (Veblen), 13

Vietnam war, 69, 100, 207–8, 244

Wage and price controls, 95, 100, 107, 110–111, 114–15

Wages, 12, 36–37, 43–44, 48, 60–62, 85–89, 106, 127, 135, 159–64, 210, 238, 275, 334

effects of changes in, 77–83, 92–94, 127–29, 141, 335

share of, 68–79, 92–94, 98–105, 182, 194–95, 199, 202–3, 254, 274, 329, 340–2

taxes and, 195

Wall Street Journal, 94

Waste, 17–18, 38, 67, 69, 199, 204, 279–81, 286, 297, 299, 307–314, 339, 344

safety margin in, 38–39

Weisskopf, Thomas, 98, 100, 103, 105

"Why Stagnation?" (Sweezy), 20

Wicksell, Knut, 138, 141

World War I, 224, 243

World War II, 9, 16, 63, 108, 199, 204–6, 228, 242–43, 246, 254, 327, 335, 338

Yaffe, David, 44, 46–47, 333

Yom Kippur war, 244

Young, Allan, 257